WIRELESS NETWORKS AND MOBILE COMPUTING, VOLUME 4

WIRELESS LANS AND BLUETOOTH

WIRELESS NETWORKS AND MOBILE COMPUTING

Yi Pan
Series Editor

WIRELESS NETWORKS AND MOBILE COMPUTING, VOLUME 4

WIRELESS LANs AND BLUETOOTH

YANG XIAO AND YI PAN
EDITORS

Nova Science Publishers, Inc.
New York

Copyright © 2005 by Nova Science Publishers, Inc.

For permission to use material from this book please contact us:
Telephone 631-231-7269; Fax 631-231-8175
Web Site: http://www.novapublishers.com

NOTICE TO THE READER

The Publisher has taken reasonable care in the preparation of this book, but makes no expressed or implied warranty of any kind and assumes no responsibility for any errors or omissions. No liability is assumed for incidental or consequential damages in connection with or arising out of information contained in this book. The Publisher shall not be liable for any special, consequential, or exemplary damages resulting, in whole or in part, from the readers' use of, or reliance upon, this material.

This publication is designed to provide accurate and authoritative information with regard to the subject matter covered herein. It is sold with the clear understanding that the Publisher is not engaged in rendering legal or any other professional services. If legal or any other expert assistance is required, the services of a competent person should be sought. FROM A DECLARATION OF PARTICIPANTS JOINTLY ADOPTED BY A COMMITTEE OF THE AMERICAN BAR ASSOCIATION AND A COMMITTEE OF PUBLISHERS.

LIBRARY OF CONGRESS CATALOGING-IN-PUBLICATION DATA

Pan-Wireless LANs and Bluetooth / Yang Xiao and Yi Pan, editors.
        p. cm.
Includes index.
ISBN 1-59454-432-8 (hardcover)
1. Pan-Wireless LANs and Bluetooth. Yang Xiao and Yi Pan
QC173.7.T74   2005
530.14'072--dc22   2004024758

Published by Nova Science Publishers, Inc. ✦ New York

CONTENTS

PREFACE

Wireless Local area Network (LAN) and Bluetooth are two phenomenons in wireless networks. They become very successful in current market and are deployed in many different environments. However, there are still many issues such as Mobility Management support, Quality of Service (QoS) support, etc. The primary focus of this book is to present these two hot and rapidly evolving areas as well as issues and solutions. It is this realization that has motivated the editing of this book. The goal of the book is to serve as a reference for wireless LAN and Bluetooth. In this book, we review important developments and new strategies for these topics. Important features and limitations of methods and models are identified. Consequently, this book can serve as a useful reference for researchers, educators, graduate students, and practitioners in the field of wireless networks.

This book contains 13 invited chapters from prominent researchers working in this area around the world. The book is basically divided into two main parts. We believe all of these chapters not only provide novel ideas, new analytical models, simulation and experimental results and handful experience in this field, but also stimulate the future research activities in the areas of wireless LAN and Bluetooth.

The book is organized into two parts; a brief summary is listed as follows.

PART I: WIRELESS LAN

Chapter 1 considers the mobility support mechanisms of the IEEE 802.11 wireless LAN with multiple access points, and what mobility support is available today and what improvement in mobility support will be possible in the future are discussed. Chapter 2 describes research and standardization activities of QoS in wireless LAN, and discusses several adaptive mechanisms to enhance the performance of the upcoming 802.11e standard. Chapter 3 surveys the performance issues related to throughput and delay in 802.11 networks and describes proposals to overcome such shortcomings. Chapter 4 proposes an improved analytical model to derive some new performance metrics: frame-dropping probability, frame-dropping time, saturation limits, and number of retransmissions, as well as saturation throughput and saturation delay under more realistic assumptions. Chapter 5 considers the dynamic queue protocol and its steady-state performance analysis for wireless LAN with multipacket reception (MPR). Chapter 6 describes the concepts of busy tones and jamming signals and presents several MAC protocols that utilize the busy tones or/and jamming signals to prevent the hidden terminal problem, as well as some power control mechanisms and several priority MAC protocols that support QoS for multimedia applications via busy tones. Chapter 7 studies the current research and development advances in IEEE 802.11 wireless mesh networks (WMNs) including MAC, routing, network architecture, application scenarios, and implementation issues of IEEE 802.11 WMNs. Chapter 8 presents an analytical model of Enhanced Distributed Channel Access (EDCA) based on Markov Chain for average throughput achieved in the saturated situation.

PART II: BLUETOOTH

Chapter 9 studies piconet management and scatternet management in Bluetooth networks including dynamic role configuration protocols and power aware scheduling schemes. Chapter 10 models the performance of the piconet with TCP traffic, expressed through segment loss probability, round-trip time, and goodput, through both probabilistic analysis and discrete-event simulations. Chapter 11 introduces Bluetooth technology, and provides a survey and classification on scheduling algorithms in Bluetooth networks. Chapter 12 summarizes the criteria of scatternet design for Bluetooth network, reviews different scatternet formation algorithms for both single-hop and multi-hop networks, and surveys Bluetooth routing algorithms and review several scatternet topologies which have self-routing properties. Chapter 13 presents non-collaborative and collaborative methods to address the collision issue in high capacity Bluetooth access points (BAPs) design.

Of course, the represented topics are not an exaustive representation of the world of wireless LAN and Bluetooth. Nonetheless, they represent the rich and useful strategies and contents, that we have the pleasure of sharing with the readers.

This book has been made possible due to the efforts and contributions of many people. First and foremost, we would like to thank all the contributors for their tremendous effort in putting together excellent chapters that are comprehensive and very informative. We would also like to thank staff members at Nova Scientific Publishing, Inc. for getting this book together. Finally, we would like to dedicate this book to our families.

Yang Xiao
The University of Memphis, USA
Email: yangxiao@ieee.org
Yi Pan
Georgia State University, USA
Email: pan@cs.gsu.edu

ABOUT THE EDITORS

 **Yang Xiao** received his Ph.D. degree in computer science and engineering from Wright State University, Dayton, Ohio. He had been a software engineer, a senior software engineer, and a technical lead working in the computer industry for five years in early 1990s. He worked at Micro Linear as an MAC architect involving the IEEE 802.11 Wireless LAN standard enhancement work before he joined in The University of Memphis as an assistant professor of computer science in Aug. 2002.

Dr. Xiao is a Senior member of IEEE. He currently serves as an associate editor or on editorial boards for five refereed journals: EURASIP Journal on Wireless Communications and Networking, (Wiley) Wireless Communications and Mobile Computing (WCMC), International Journal of Wireless and Mobile Computing, International Journal of Signal Processing, and International Journal of Information Technology. He serves a (lead) guest editor for EURASIP Journal on Wireless Communications and Networking, Special Issue on "Wireless Network Security" in 2005, a (sole) guest editor for (Elsevier) Computer Communications journal, special Issue on "Energy-Efficient Scheduling and MAC for Sensor Networks, WPANs, WLANs, and WMANs" in 2005, a (lead) guest editor for (Wiley) Journal of Wireless Communications and Mobile Computing, special Issue on "Mobility, Paging and Quality of Service Management for Future Wireless Networks" in 2004-2005, a (lead) guest editor for International Journal of Wireless and Mobile Computing, special Issue on "Medium Access Control for WLANs, WPANs, Ad Hoc Networks, and Sensor Networks" in 2004-2005, and an associate guest editor for International Journal of High Performance Computing and Networking, special issue on "Parallel and Distributed Computing, Applications and Technologies" in 2003. He serves as co-editor for three edited books: Wireless LANs and Bluetooth (Nova Science Publishers, Hardbound, 2005), Ad Hoc and Sensor Networks (Nova Science Publishers, Hardbound, 2005), and Design and Analysis of Wireless Networks (Nova Science Publishers, ISBN:1-59454-186-8, Hardbound, 2004). He serves as a symposium co-chair for International Symposium on Wireless Local and Personal Area Networks in WirelessCom 2005. He serves as a symposium co-chair for Symposium on Data Base Management in Wireless Network Environments in IEEE VTC 2003. He serves as a TPC member for many conferences such as IEEE ICDCS, IEEE ICC, IEEE GLOBECOM, IEEE WCNC, IEEE ICCCN, IEEE PIMRC, ACM WMASH, etc. He serves as a referee/reviewer for many journals, conferences, and funding agencies such as Research

Grants Council (Hong Kong), Canada Foundation for Innovation, and Louisiana Board of Regents.

Dr. Xiao's research areas include Wireless LANs, Wireless PANs, and mobile cellular networks. He has published many papers in major journals and refereed conference proceedings related to these research areas, such as IEEE Transactions on Mobile Computing, IEEE Transactions on Wireless Communications, IEEE Transactions on Parallel and Distributed Systems, IEEE Transactions on Vehicular Technology, IEEE Communications Letters, IEEE Communications Magazine, IEEE Wireless Communications, ACM/Kluwer Mobile Networks and Applications (MONET), etc. His research interests are Security/ Reliable Communications, Medium Access Control, Mobility/ Location/ Paging Managements, Quality of Service, Energy Efficiency, and Routing in wireless networks and mobile computing including Wireless LANs, Wireless PANs, Wireless MANs, Wireless WANs (cellular networks), and Ad hoc & Sensor networks. (Email: yangxiao@ieee.org)

 **Yi Pan** received his B.Eng. and M.Eng. degrees in computer engineering from Tsinghua University, China, in 1982 and 1984, respectively, and his Ph.D. degree in computer science from the University of Pittsburgh, USA, in 1991. Currently, he is the chair and a Yamacraw professor in the Department of Computer Science at Georgia State University.

Dr. Pan's research interests include parallel and distributed computing, optical networks, wireless networks, and bioinformatics. Dr. Pan has published more than 80 journal papers with 28 papers published in various IEEE journals. In addition, he has published over 90 papers in refereed conferences (including IPDPS, ICPP, ICDCS, INFOCOM, and GLOBECOM). He has also co-edited 13 books (including proceedings) and contributed several book chapters. His pioneer work on computing using reconfigurable optical buses has inspired extensive subsequent work by many researchers, and his research results have been cited by more than 100 researchers worldwide in books, theses, journal and conference papers. He is a co-inventor of three U.S. patents (pending) and 5 provisional patents, and has received many awards from agencies such as NSF, AFOSR, JSPS, IISF and Mellon Foundation. His recent research has been supported by NSF, NIH, NSFC, AFOSR, AFRL, JSPS, IISF and the states of Georgia and Ohio. He has served as a reviewer/panelist for many research foundations/agencies such as the U.S. National Science Foundation, the Natural Sciences and Engineering Research Council of Canada, the Australian Research Council, and the Hong Kong Research Grants Council. Dr. Pan has served as an editor-in-chief or editorial board member for 8 journals including 3 IEEE Transactions and a guest editor for 7 special issues. He has organized several international conferences and workshops and has also served as a program committee member for several major international conferences such as INFOCOM, GLOBECOM, ICC, IPDPS, and ICPP.

Dr. Pan has delivered over 50 invited talks, including keynote speeches and colloquium talks, at conferences and universities worldwide. Dr. Pan is an IEEE Distinguished Speaker (2000-2002), a Yamacraw Distinguished Speaker (2002), a Shell Oil Colloquium Speaker (2002), and a senior member of IEEE. He is listed in Men of Achievement, Who's Who in Midwest, Who's Who in America, Who's Who in American Education, Who's Who in Computational Science and Engineering, and Who's Who of Asian Americans. (Email: pan@cs.gsu.edu)

PART I: WIRELESS LAN

In: Wireless LANs and Bluetooth
Editors: Yang Xiao and Yi Pan, pp. 1-21

ISBN: 1-59454-432-8
© 2005 Nova Science Publishers, Inc.

Chapter 1

MOBILITY SUPPORT IN IEEE 802.11 WLAN: ISSUES AND ENHANCEMENT

Sunghyun Choi[1] and Zhun Zhong[2]

Abstract

IEEE 802.11 Wireless LAN (WLAN) is rising as a popular means for the broadband access network. It is being deployed in many different environments including home, enterprise, and hot spot areas. In the enterprise networks as well as large hot spots, it is typical to have multiple access points (APs) to cover the geographical area in service. In such environments, smooth handoff is considered a very crucial service requirement to provide a seamless service to the users even during the movement. In this chapter, we consider the mobility support mechanisms of the IEEE 802.11 WLAN with multiple APs. We will discuss what mobility support is available today and what improvement in mobility support will be possible in the future.

Keywords: IEEE 802.11 WLAN, handoff, IEEE 802.11f Inter-Access Point Protocol (IAPP), mobile IP (MIP).

Introduction

Today, we are witnessing that IEEE 802.11 Wireless Local Area Network (WLAN) is rising as a popular means for the broadband wireless access network. It is being deployed in many different environments including home, enterprise, and hot spot areas. In the enterprise networks as well as large hot spots, it is typical to have multiple access points (APs) to cover the geographical area in service. In such environments, providing a seamless service to the users even during the movement via handoff, i.e., the switch from an AP to another as it

---

[1] Multimedia & Wireless Networking Laboratory (MWNL), School of Electrical Engineering, Seoul National University, Seoul, 151-744, Korea, (schoi@snu.ac.kr).
[2] Philips Research USA, Briarcliff Manor, New York 10510 USA, (zhun.zhong@philips.com).

moves around, is considered a very crucial service requirement. In this chapter, we consider the mobility support mechanisms of the IEEE 802.11 WLAN.

Background

We first describe the background information, which is needed in order to understand the mechanisms for the mobility support in the IEEE 802.11 WLAN.

802.11 MAC and PHYs

The IEEE 802.11 standard defines both the medium access control (MAC) and physical (PHY) layer specifications. The MAC layer can be divided into the MAC sublayer and MAC layer management entity (MLME) as shown in Fig. 2.1. The mobility support is related to the MLME functions, which we will consider further in detail in this chapter.

The MAC sublayer defines coordination functions, which determine when and how to transmit and receive frames in the shared wireless channel. The mandatory coordination function, called distributed coordination function (DCF), is based on carrier-sense multiple access with collision avoidance (CSMA/CA) protocol, in which a station basically transmits its pending frame only when no other stations transmit frames into the channel. This MAC is a distributed and contention-based protocol. This type of MAC can affect the handoff performance since the channel access time can be theoretically unbounded when the channel is heavily loaded. The 802.11 also defines an optional coordination function, called point coordination function (PCF), which is a centrally controlled contention-free protocol based on polling. However, since virtually none of the commercial 802.11 devices implement the PCF, we will focus our discussion on the mobility support in the DCF operation.

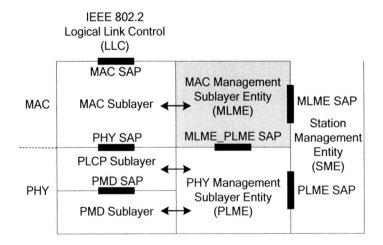

Fig. 2.1. IEEE 802.11 reference model.

The 802.11 defines multiple PHYs, namely, 802.11a [3], 802.11b [4], and recently standardized 802.11g [6]. Different PHYs operate in different frequency bands, and provides different transmission rates as summarized in Table 2.1. Currently, the 802.11b is the most widely deployed version of the 802.11. Different PHYs can utilize a set of frequency channels, which are dependent on a particular regulatory domain, e.g., a country. The number of available channels in the US is also found in Table 2.1. It should be noted that 12 channels of the 802.11a at 5 GHz are non-overlapping while 11 channels of the 802.11b/g at 2.4 GHz are overlapping. That is, two consecutive channels of the 802.11b/g are only 5 MHz apart while the bandwidth of each channel is 22 MHz. Accordingly, it is known that there are only three non-overlapping channels available at 2.4 GHz for the 802.11b/g. As will be discussed further, the number of channels can affect the handoff operation. For example, if there are more channels available, it could take more time to search for candidate APs to hand off to.

Table 2.1. Summary of different 802.11 PHYs.

	802.11a	802.11b	802.11g
Frequency bands	5 GHz	2.4 GHz	2.4 GHz
Number of available channels (in the US)	12 (of 20 MHz width)	11 (of 22 MHz width, overlapping)	
Supported transmission rates (Mbps)	6, 9, 12, 18, 24, 36, 48, 54	1, 2, 5.5, 11	1, 2, 5.5, 11, 6, 9, 12, 18, 24, 36, 48, 54

Multiple AP Environment

The very basic form of the IEEE 802.11 WLAN is called a basic service set (BSS). There are two forms of BSS: infrastructure BSS and independent BSS (IBSS). The infrastructure BSS is composed of an access point (AP), which works as the bridge between the (wireline) infrastructure and the wireless link, and a number of stations, which are associated with the AP. On the other hand, an IBSS is composed of a number of stations, which are communicating directly one another. This form of BSS is also referred to as an *ad-hoc* mode. However, this ad-hoc mode of IEEE 802.11 should be differentiated from the ad-hoc networking, for which the protocols are being defined by the Internet Engineering Task Force (IETF) Mobile Ad Hoc Networking (MANET) Working Group [33]. This is because the 802.11 ad hoc mode is limited to a one-hop wireless link, where multiple stations can communicate each other in a single hop while the IETF MANET is considering the ad hoc network without a wireline infrastructure, where the communications between two stations is supported via multiple wireless hops across other stations. It is straightforward that for the handoff discussion we are interested in the infrastructure BSS.

While a single AP may be enough to cover a small geographical area such as a home or a small hot spot, multiple APs are usually deployed to cover large hot spots or enterprise networks. In the latter case, the multiple APs are typically connected to each other via the wireline, e.g., the Ethernet link. A frequency channel planning can be an issue for multiple AP deployment in a given geographical area. To reduce co-channel interference, it is desired to use non-overlapping frequency channels for immediately neighboring APs. However, as mentioned earlier, there may not be enough non-overlapping channels available (e.g., only three for the 802.11b/g). Although one can avoid co-channel interference by allocating three non-overlapping channels to neighboring APs in a two-dimensional structure, it becomes problematic in the three-dimensional environments such as multiple-story buildings.

Therefore, it could be practically impossible to avoid the co-channel interference at least in the 802.11b/g WLANs. Fortunately, the 802.11 DCF MAC allows APs (or BSSs) in the same frequency channel to share the channel rather smoothly thanks to its carrier sense-based access mechanism.

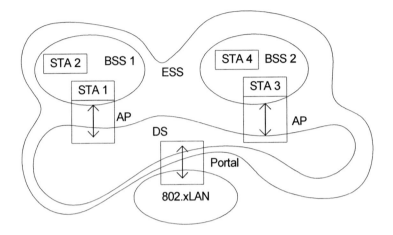

Fig. 2.2. Conceptual architecture of IEEE 802.11 WLAN.

APs can be connected via a network system called a distribution system (DS). A set of BSSs along with the DS form an extended service set (ESS) as shown in Fig. 2.2. An ESS is identified by a service set identification (SSID), which is often referred to as the "Network Name" in the commercial 802.11 WLAN devices. The APs periodically broadcast a management frame[3], called beacon frame, in which a field indicates the SSID so that the stations can identify the APs belonging to the same ESS. The beacon includes many other information fields crucial for the 802.11 WLAN operations, such as the time synchronization, power save support, etc. One may find that the concept in the infrastructure mode of WLAN in many ways resembles that of the wide-area cellular systems, where multiple base stations are connected via the wired links, and each base station serves an area called a *cell*.

The DS is typically based on the popular Ethernet. However, the 802.11 specification does not define how to establish the DS. Therefore, it is possible that the DS be constructed even using the 802.11 WLAN links. That is, the APs can communicate each other via the 802.11 WLAN. In the later part of this chapter, we will discuss how the APs communicate across the DS in order to support the mobility of the stations within the ESS.

(Re-)Association Procedures

In an infrastructure BSS, a station communicates via its AP only. That is, all the frames are either transmitted by an AP (i.e., downlink) or destined to an AP (i.e., uplink). Two stations associated with AP(s) cannot communicate each other directly even if they are within their frame transmission ranges. They can communicate indirectly either via their AP if both are in the same BSS, or via their APs and the DS if they are in different BSSs. We will not address

---

[3] A frame is referred to as the unit of a transfer or a packet in the layer-2 protocols.

this restriction in detail here, but it is due mainly to an easy support of the power saving of stations. On the other hand, the emerging IEEE 802.11e is expecting to support the direct communication between two stations in the same BSS in order to achieve a better link utilization [7].

In order to communicate via an AP, a station should associate with the AP first. However, before the association can be made, the following steps should be preceded. First, the station should know the existence of the AP in a specific channel. This can be done via a scanning process. Second, the station should be authenticated by the AP. We briefly explain the procedures needed until the association.

- **Scanning:** this is a process for a station to search surrounding APs. Note that the station should know the existence of the AP before trying to get associated with this AP. There are two different types of scanning: *passive* and *active*. With the passive scanning, the station detects the surrounding APs by receiving the beacon frames transmitted by these surrounding APs. This can be a slow process since the beacon transmission interval is typically about 100 ms (or 102.4 ms more exactly) even though it is configurable by the AP system administrator. The faster scanning process is the active scanning. With this type of scanning, the station broadcasts a probe request frame, then APs receiving this probe request responds with a probe response frame. If the searching station indicates a specific SSID in its probe request frame, only APs with a matching SSID responds. The probe response includes virtually the same information as the beacon frame, and hence the station receiving a probe response acquires all the necessary information to associate with the AP. When there are multiple APs found in the neighborhood, the station chooses one of them based on its implementation-dependent decision criteria. We will discuss this issue further later in the context of the handoff decision process.
- **Authentication:** this process is for the station to be authenticated with the AP by proving itself a valid station. There are two types of authentication as defined in the current 802.11 standard: open system and shared key. With the open system, the station sends an authentication request frame, and the requested AP responds with an authentication response frame. There is no specific security information conveyed in the authentication request frame in this case, but the AP can actually use the requesting station's MAC address to decide whether to authenticate the station or not. With the shared key method, a four-way handshake is used for the AP to check whether the requesting station has the same security key or not.
- **Association:** finally, the station can be associated with the AP by exchanging an association request and an association response frame. Through this exchange, the station is assigned an association identification, and the AP is informed some information required for the proper communication, e.g., the transmission rates supported by the newly-associated station.

Fig. 2.3 illustrates the association procedure assuming the active scanning and the open system authentication. Even though only a single AP is shown in the figure, there could be multiple APs, which receive the probe request, and respond with a probe response.

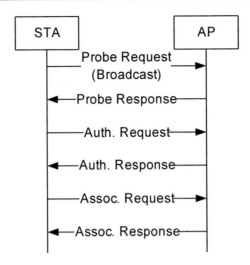

Fig. 2.3. IEEE 802.11 association procedure.

As will be further discussed later, basically the same procedure should be followed for the handoff of a station. However, in order for the AP accepting a station's association to differentiate between a new association and a handoff, the 802.11 defines two different frame types for the association request. The request for the handoff is called *reassociation* request, where the corresponding frame includes the MAC address of the old AP so that the new AP can communicate with the old AP to support the handoff process more efficiently.

It should be noted that a station can be associated with a single AP at a given time. It is natural since a simultaneous communication with multiple APs, i.e., soft handoff of code-division multiple access (CDMA) systems [35], is not supported in the 802.11 WLAN. Therefore, the 802.11 handoff is a *hard* handoff naturally. On the other hand, a station can be authenticated with multiple APs. Note that this can reduce the handoff time. However, this requires a station to search surrounding APs, and get authenticated in advance. This is often referred to as "pre-authentication."

Layer-2 vs. Layer-3 Mobility

Fig. 2.4 illustrates two different types of handoff events within a WLAN depending on whether the two APs involved in the handoff are in the same subnet or not. All the APs and stations in an ESS can be in the same subnet, i.e., all the APs are connected via IEEE 802.1d MAC bridges [10] (e.g., Ethernet switches), and the APs work in the bridge mode. When the two APs involved in a station handoff are in the same subnet, the handoff only involves a layer-2 mobility support without any intervention from the layer 3. See the handoff event labeled as "layer-2 handoff" in Fig. 2.4.

However, it may not be the case in other deployments. When the two APs are in different subnets (see the handoff event labeled as "layer-3 handoff" in Fig. 2.4), or the APs are in the router mode, a handoff involves layer-3 operations since the station cannot use the same IP address after reassociating with the new AP. This should be handled by mobile IP [21][22] as will be briefly discussed in Section 0.

After reassociating with a new AP, a broadcast frame (originating from the handing-off station) should be transmitted to the same subnet so that the layer-2 route tables in the MAC bridges including the APs can be updated. This operation basically completes the layer-2 handoff procedure thanks to the IEEE 802.1d's self-learning process of the routing table [10]. Issues in the layer-2 handoff will be further discussed in Section 0.

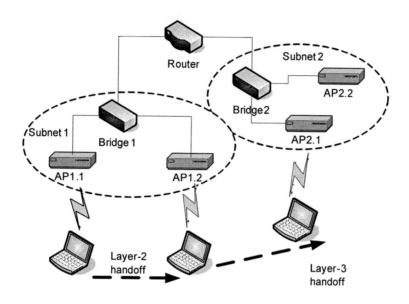

Fig. 2.4. Layer-2 vs. layer-3 handoffs.

Station's Handoff Procedure

In this section, we describe the operations performed by a handoff station. Note that in the IEEE 802.11 WLAN, the handoff decision, i.e., in terms of when to hand off and which AP to hand off to, is made by the station itself. Therefore, if the station does not perform the handoff procedure properly at the proper moment, the handoff may be very disruptive.

Scan of Surrounding APs

The first step in the handoff process is to find out the APs surrounding the station. Detecting the surrounding APs can be accomplished by utilizing the 802.11 scanning process as explained in Section 0. The same scanning process is used to search for APs in both the new association situation and the reassociation (or handoff) situation.

One major difference is that a handing-off station is currently associated with an AP so that the station cannot search for neighboring APs as freely as it could do for its initial association. In order to search surrounding APs, a station may have to go to the channels other than the one it currently operates on. Note that a station out of its operational channel may miss incoming frames from its associated AP. However, the 802.11 does not provide a means for a station to inform its AP that it would be out of its operational channel in order to search other neighboring APs.

Fortunately, a station can utilize the power saving mechanism, which works as follows. Under the 802.11 power save mechanism, a station can be either in the power save mode or in the active mode. When a station is in the power save mode, it can switch back and forth between the active and doze states periodically while a station in the active mode stays at the active state continually.[4] To serve a station in the power save mode, the AP buffers frames addressed to the station and indicates the existence of such buffered frames in the Traffic Indication Map (TIM) field of its beacon frames. Basically, a station in the power save mode awakes (i.e., goes to the active state) right before TBTTs to receive the beacon frames and check the TIM field. If the TIM field indicates no buffered frames, the station can go back to the doze state after receiving the beacon. Otherwise, the station should stay awake after the beacon reception and requests the transmission of the buffered frames by the AP. Therefore, a station known to be in the power save mode to its AP can actually go to other channels in order to search neighboring APs between two TBTTs without losing any incoming frame.

The scanning should be done in advance in order to reduce the handoff latency. It is known that the scanning consumes considerable amount of time in reality. A handoff algorithm that is not well designed may initiate the scanning process after losing the radio link with the currently-associated AP. This can result in a very poor performance in terms of the handoff latency. Moreover, a bad handoff algorithm can degrade the throughput of the WLAN. For example, consider the station moving from left to right in Fig. 3.1, it is possible that the station is still associated with AP1 at the specified location even if its communication link with AP1 allows only 1 Mbps transmission rate while its link with AP2 allows 11 Mbps rate. It is known that stations transmitting at low transmission rate can negatively affect the system performance, resulting in a low system throughput [13][34]. The station in the example should have reassociated with AP2 well before reaching the position indicated in the figure.

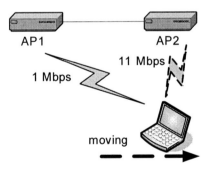

Fig. 3.1. Example of a bad handoff decision situation.

An advance periodic scanning may be desirable for a fast handoff. However, one should be aware that the usage of the power save mechanisms for scanning is not cost-free. For starters, using the power save mechanism when there are many incoming and outgoing frames

---

[4] In the active state, a station is ready to receive all the incoming frames while in the doze state, the station consumes a very low power such that it cannot receive incoming frames.

can degrade network performance, resulting in a low throughput. Another important algorithmic issue is when to scan and which channels to scan. In the case of the 802.11a, there are 12 channels available, and searching for the entire 12 channels could take considerable amount of time.

Handoff Decision Criteria

Having identified neighboring APs, the station needs to decide whether to stay with the current AP or to hand off to one of the neighboring APs found in the scanning process. Let's first consider how to choose the best candidate AP to hand off to. There can be multiple criteria to evaluate candidate APs:

- **Link quality:** Often represented as the signal-to-noise ratio (SNR), the link quality between the station and a candidate AP should be above a certain threshold in order to maintain a proper communication with the AP. The station can exclude neighboring APs with the link quality below the threshold from the candidate AP list.
- **Traffic load:** even if the link quality with a neighboring AP is excellent, the AP may not be a good candidate to hand off to if it is already serving many stations with heavy traffic load. Whenever possible, the station should choose an AP with a good link quality and moderate traffic load. This strategy is often referred to as "load balancing." Unfortunately, it is not possible to obtain such traffic load information in the current 802.11 WLAN. The emerging IEEE 802.11e MAC is expected to provide the traffic load information in the beacon frames transmitted by the APs [7].

To choose the best candidate AP, one can come up with a "handoff decision metric" by combining both the link quality and the traffic load. However, if a handoff decision is made as long as a candidate AP presents a higher metric than that of the current AP, it may cause the station to switch back and forth between APs due to time-varying channel and traffic load conditions, thus resulting in the system instability known as *ping-pong effect*. Note that both channel condition with a specific AP as well as the traffic load condition of the AP can vary over time even if a station does not move at all. Apparently, frequent handoff is not desired since (1) it consumes network resources in both wireless and wireline sides (as will be explained later) and (2) there may be some service disruption during the handoff. In order to avoid the ping-pong effect, some form of hysteresis should be employed. For example, another threshold can be used to make sure that a handoff decision is made only when the metric value of the new AP exceeds that of the current AP by at least the threshold [35]. The handoff decision criteria can be summarized as follows:

$$M_{candidate} > \alpha \text{ and } M_{candidate} - M_{current} > \beta,$$

where $M_{candidate}$ and $M_{current}$ represent the handoff decision metric values of the candidate and the currently-associated AP, respectively, and α and β represent the above-mentioned threshold values. How to determine the handoff decision metric as well as the threshold values should be a performance optimization issue.

Handoff Process

The actual handoff can be performed via an authentication and a reassociation with a new AP as explained in Section 0. The authentication could be done before the actual handoff moment, i.e., pre-authentication, in order to reduce the handoff latency. To complete the handoff procedure, the AP should interact with other APs as well as the DS for the proper reconfiguration (e.g., frame routing), as presented in the following section.

DS Support for Handoff – IEEE 802.11f IAPP

The handoff involves the communication between the APs, which relies on the DS. While the 802.11 defines the concept of the DS, it does not define how to implement the DS for the following reasons: (1) the DS involves the higher layer protocols above MAC hence is out of scope of the 802.11, which deals with the MAC and PHY only, and (2) it could be desirable to have the flexibility for the DS construction. Note that the DS can be constructed with any network link, e.g., even with the WLAN link, which is referred to as wireless distribution system (WDS). However, the lack of the standardized DS construction causes interoperability issues among APs from different vendors, especially, in the context of the handoff support. In the 802.11 WLAN (or more specifically, ESS), a station should have only a single association, i.e., the association with a single AP. However, the enforcement of this restriction is unlikely to be achieved due to the lack of the communication among the APs within the ESS.

The 802.11f [5] is a recommended practice for Inter-Access Point Protocol (IAPP), which specifies the information to be exchanged between APs amongst themselves and higher layer management entities to support the 802.11 DS functions. According to the IEEE standards terms, the recommended practice is defined as a document, in which procedures and positions preferred by the IEEE are presented. On the other hand, the standards like 802.11-1999 [1] are defined as documents with mandatory requirements.[5] It should be noted that the 802.11f does not define anything related to the station operation for the handoff. It is the 802.11 MAC management that defines the station scanning and reassociation procedures for the basic handoff support as discussed before.

Inter-AP Communication

The IAPP uses TCP/IP or UDP/IP to carry IAPP packets between APs, and also relies on Remote Authentication Dial In User Service (RADIUS) protocol [18] for APs to obtain information about one another. A proactive caching mechanism is also defined in order to provide faster roaming by sending the station context to neighboring APs before the actual handoff event.

Fig 4.1. shows the architecture of the AP with IAPP. Loaded with venders' proprietary features and algorithms, the AP management entity (APME) is a function external to the

---

[5] Within a standard specification document, both mandatory requirements and recommended practice can exist. Mandatory requirements are generally characterized by use of the verb "shall," whereas recommended practices normally use the word "should."

IAPP and is typically the main operational program of the AP. The 802.11-1999 [1] defines an entity called station management entity (SME), as shown in Fig. 2.1, and the APME of the AP incorporates the SME functions. As shown in the figure, the APME can manage/control the IAPP, 802.11 MAC, and 802.11 PHY via the IAPP Service Access Point (SAP), MAC Layer Management Entity (MLME) SAP, and PHY Layer Management Entity (PLME) SAP, respectively.

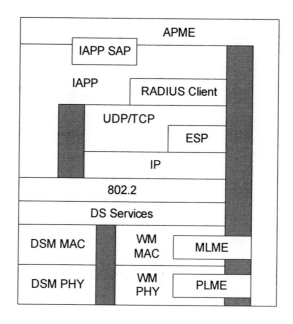

Fig. 4.1. IEEE 802.11 AP architecture with IAPP.

Some functions of the IAPP rely on the RADIUS protocol for the proper and secure operation. In particular, the IAPP entity, i.e., the AP, should be able to find and use a RADIUS server (1) to look up the IP addresses of other APs in the ESS when given the BSS Identifications (BSSIDs)[6] of those APs, and (2) to obtain security information to protect the content of certain IAPP packets. Actually, the RADIUS server must provide extensions for IAPP-specific operations, which are currently being defined by IETF [19].

The IAPP supports (1) DS services, (2) address mapping between AP's MAC and IP addresses, (3) formation of DS, (4) maintenance of DS, (5) enforcement of a single association of a station at a given time, and (6) transfer of station context information between APs.

IAPP Operations

There are three basic IAPP operations: (1) station ADD operation; (2) station MOVE operation; and (3) proactive caching. These operations are briefly explained below.

First, the station ADD operation is triggered when a station is newly associated with an AP. When a station is associated, the AP transmits two packets to the DS: layer-2 update

---

[6] The BSSID of a BSS is determined by the MAC address of the corresponding AP.

frame and IAPP ADD-notify packet. The layer-2 update frame is addressed at the broadcast address. Upon the reception of this frame, any layer-2 bridge devices, e.g., Ethernet switches connecting multiple APs within the ESS, update the routing table for the associating station according to the IEEE 802.1d bridge table self-learning procedure [10]. The IAPP ADD-notify packet is an IP packet with a destination IP address of the IAPP IP multicast address so that any receiving APs within the ESS remove a stale association with the associating station.

Second, the station MOVE operation is triggered by a station's reassociation when the station hands off from an AP to another AP. The station handing off from an AP transmits a reassociation request management frame to the new AP, where the reassocaition request frame includes the MAC address of the old AP. The new AP transmits two packets in this case as well: layer-2 update frame and IAPP MOVE-notify packet. The IAPP MOVE-notify packet is transmitted to the old AP, which in turn transmits an IAPP MOVE-response packet. The response packet carries the context block[7] for the station's association from the old AP to the new AP. Since the reassociation request frame from the station contains only the old AP's MAC address, the new AP needs to look up the IP address of the old AP with the help of a RADIUS server within the ESS. The purpose of the layer-2 update frame is the same as with the station ADD operation. One important fact is that the layer-2 update frame is broadcasted only after the IAPP MOVE-response packet is received from the old AP, as the final step of the hand-off procedure.

Third, the proactive caching is triggered when a station (re)associates with an AP or the context of the station changes. Basically, when the proactive caching is triggered by the APME of an AP, the AP (or the AP's IAPP entity more specifically) transmits the IAPP CACHE-notify packets to its neighboring APs. The notify packet includes the context of the corresponding station. This proactive caching can significant reduce the handoff delay by broadcasting the layer-2 update frame without waiting for the IAPP MOVE-response packet upon a reassociation, since the new AP has already received the context of the handing-off station from the old AP via the IAPP CACHE-notify packet earlier. One may question about how an AP gets to know its neighboring APs. For starters, the network administrator can manually pre-configure the neighboring AP list. Otherwise, this can be achieved via a dynamic learning process. That is, for each reassociation, the AP accepting the handoff station learns that the station's previously associated AP is one of its neighbors. The neighboring AP list can grow over time as more and more stations move around across the ESS.

IETF Mobile IP

As discussed in Section 0, a station cannot use the same IP address after a handoff if the new AP is in a different subnet from that of the old AP. The IETF Mobile IP can provide a seamless communication by using a single IP across multiple (sub)-networks [21][22].

Mobile IP provides mobility to mobile stations connected to the Internet. Fig. 5.1 illustrates an IP datagram flow under mobile IP. Node A (represented by a laptop computer in the figure) belongs to a network labeled as "home network," and has a permanent address.

---

[7] The 802.11f does not define what the context block could contain. The examples of the context include security and accounting information of the corresponding station.

When node A is away from its home network and located in a visited network, it registers an IP address called "care-of-address" with a node, called Home Agent, located inside its home network. When node B (labeled as "correspondent" in the figure), which is not aware of the current location of node A, sends an IP datagram at node A's permanent address, the datagram is intercepted by the home agent of node A. Then, the home agent forwards the datagram to the foreign agent (addressed at the care-of-address, which node A registered to the home agent), which in turn forwards the datagram to node A eventually. Whereas node A can send datagrams directly to node B, the corresponding datagrams from node B to node A need to be routed by the home agent and the foreign agent, resulting in an inefficient use of the network resources. This problem is known as triangular routing.

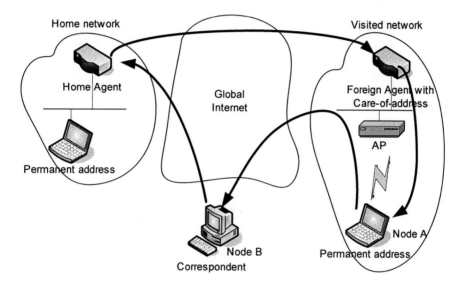

Fig. 5.1. Mobile IP datagram flow via triangular routing..

Mobile IP is basically composed of three operations: agent discovery, registration, and tunneling.

- **Agent discovery:** Mobility agents (in this case, the home agent or the foreign agent) advertise their availability on the subnet for which they would provide service. These advertisements are done via layer-2 broadcasts. The mobile station can solicit agent advertisements as well.
- **Registration:** When the mobile station moves away from its home network and enters a new visited network, it registers its care-of address with its home agent through its foreign agent.
- **Tunneling:** A datagram arriving at the home network is intercepted by the home agent, and is forwarded to the care-of-address via tunneling. For example, simple IP-within-IP encapsulation can be used for the tunneling.

For a layer-3 handoff, both agent discovery and registration processes should be performed. Unfortunately, both can be quite time-consuming. Moreover, the triangular routing can extend the end-to-end communication delay significantly depending on the geographical locations of the involved nodes. The standardization of mobile IP is still ongoing.

Mobility Scenarios

To illustrate what we have presented thus far, in this section we present mobility scenarios found in the real world WLAN deployments. Let's assume that we have deployed a WLAN in a building, where multiple APs are installed on each floor. Each floor constitutes an IP subnet. To provide a seamless mobility, we run both mobile IP and IEEE 802.11f IAPP. We consider two cases, namely, layer-2 and layer-3 handoffs, based on Fig. 2.4 in Section 0. Note that we do not have the home agent, foreign agent, and RADIUS server in the figure for simplicity.

Layer-2 Handoff

The station in consideration reassociates with AP1.2, which obtains the old AP (i.e., AP1.1)'s MAC address from the reassociation request frame. AP1.2 in turn gets the IP address of AP1.1 from a RADIUS server. With this IP address, AP1.2 sends an IAPP MOVE-notify packet to AP1.1. After receiving this packet, the old AP disassociates with the station and simultaneously responds with a MOVE-response packet including such information as the context block of the handoff station to AP1.2. If AP1.2 receives this packet in time, it confirms that the handoff is successful and completes the handoff process by sending a layer-2 update frame to the DS for a route table update.

Layer-3 Handoff

Now, the station hands off from AP1.2 to AP2.1, resulting in a change of the subnet. In the case of a subnet change, a layer-2 handoff should occur prior to a layer-3 handoff. That is, the station reassociates with AP2.1 first through the exactly same operations described above. When the layer-2 handoff is completed, the station listens to an agent advertisement from the foreign agent of mobile IP (or the station sends solicitation messages to the foreign agent to request an advertisement.) After getting an agent advertisement, the station becomes aware of that it is in a different subnet. It then sends a registration request to the foreign agent, where the request includes its permanent IP address, its home agent's IP address, care-of-address (in this case, the foreign agent's IP address), life time, and so on. Then, the foreign agent relays this packet to the home agent, and the home agent decides whether to accept this registration. If it decides to accept, the home agent updates its routing table and sends a registration reply to the foreign agent, which contains the station's permanent IP address, the home agent's IP address, lifetime, and so on. Upon reception of this packet, the foreign agent relays the packet to the mobile station, and then the layer-3 handoff is completed.

Related Standards

In this section, we discuss handoff related works in various task and study groups within the IEEE 802.11 standardization working group [1].[8] Note that, at the time of writing this book chapter, all of the task groups being discussed are still active. The following content reflects not only the current drafts but also proposals under discussion in the task groups. It should be understood that even the content in the current drafts may be changed in the final standard.

Task Group I (TGi) for Security Enhancement

IEEE 802.11 TGi provides an enhanced security specification, which defines a Robust Security Network Association (RSNA). An RSNA between a station and its AP can be made after the 802.11 authentication and (re)association are completed, where an open system authentication shall be used under the 802.11i specification. Establishing an RSNA consists of mainly two operations: (1) IEEE 802.1X-based authentication [11], and (2) temporal key establishment. Fig. 7.1 illustrates the 802.1X authentication, where a station (referred to as a supplicant in the 802.1X terms) and an authentication server authenticate each other, and the mutual authentication results in a pairwise master key (PMK) assignment to the station and its AP. Then, using the PMK, the station and AP perform a 4-way handshake in order to establish the pairwise transient key (PTK), which is used for the encryption of the frames upon an RSNA establishment. When the PTK is generated, an RSNA is established.

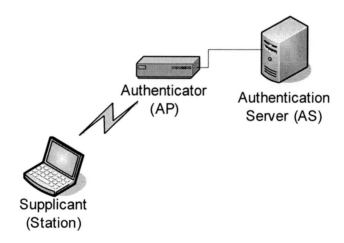

Fig. 7.1. IEEE 802.1X authentication.

The time-consuming four-way handshake has been a controversial topic in TGi discussion and finally triggered the spin-off of a new study group, which we will discuss in a later subsection. In the following, we will discuss the pre-authentication mechanism provided by TGi to facilitate fast handoff [23][8].

---

[8] For the standardization of a new protocol, a study group (SG) is formed first in order to determine the goal and scope of the new standard, then a task group (TG) is formed out of the study group. A new standard specification is generated by a task group, e.g., IEEE 802.11i is generated by Task Group I (TGi).

The 802.11i allows a supplicant station authenticated and associated with an AP to pre-authenticate (based on the 802.1X) with target APs via the current AP and the DS. To initiate the pre-authentication, the station transmits an IEEE 802.1X EAPOL-Start frame with the Destination Address (DA) being the BSSID of the target AP, and the Receiver Address (RA) being the BSSID of the current AP. The current AP receives the Start frame from its Wireless Medium (WM) port and forwards it to the DS via its DS port. The DS delivers the Start frame to the DS port of the target AP. Since the frame is destined to the target AP's BSSID, i.e., the MAC address of the AP's WM port, it is forwarded to the WM port, which then creates a logical WM port with an authenticator Port Access Entity (PAE). The Authenticator PAE responds by sending an EAP-Request destined to the MAC address of the supplicant station, encapsulated in an IEEE 802 frame using the pre-authentication EtherType. The frame is forwarded to the DS port, and the DS delivers it to the current AP, which finally forwards it to the station.

The conversation between the pre-authenticating supplicant station and the target AP continues via the current AP and the DS, until the EAP authentication succeeds or fails. A successful authentication results in Pairwise Master Key Security Association (PMKSA), which the station uses to complete the 4-way and group-key handshakes after a reassociation with the target AP.

To summarize, the 802.11i allows the station to pre-authenticate with the target AP during a normal operation on the current AP's current operating channel. The 802.11i does not specify how the station gets the identity of the target APs. The station may get the information via previous passive or active scanning. Otherwise, the information can be provided to the station by the current AP using the Site Report mechanism in 802.11k as explained in detail below.

Task Group K (TGk) for Radio Resource Measurements

IEEE 802.11 Task Group k defines mechanisms for radio resource measurement [9]. Some of the measurement results and measurement mechanisms can facilitate fast handoff.

Several independent empirical studies on 802.11 handoff showed that the most significant part of handoff latency goes to the scanning process [24][25]. To search for target APs, the station scan one channel at a time, using either passive or active scanning, and wait on that channel for a preset timeout before moving on to the next channel. Scanning all the 11 channels of 802.11b can take a couple of hundreds milliseconds using active scanning. If passive scanning is used, or if there are more channels to scan, the scanning process can take even longer. There can be basically two ways to shorten the scanning process: reducing the number of channels to scan and/or reducing the scanning time on each channel.

Limiting Scanning Channels

Under a normal deployment, there are only a handful of neighboring APs around. To avoid wasting time in scanning channels on which no neighboring AP operates, TGk provides the Site Report which contains pertinent information on a collection of neighboring APs known to the AP that sends it. An AP compiles its site reports and send it to the stations in its BSS upon request or autonomously whenever appropriate. The details of how AP compiles the Site Report are outside of the scope of this standard. An AP may get the information of neighboring APs from measurement reports received from the stations within the BSS, from management interface such as Simple Network Management Protocol (SNMP), or from DS via IAPP. The information provided in the Site Report includes each neighboring AP's operating channel, BSSID, capability, and supported PHY type, etc. This information therefore can be used by the station to limit the set of channels to scan for a possible handoff.

Fast Active Scanning

To scan for APs using active scanning as defined in the base line 802.11 specification [2], a station broadcasts a probe request on the channel of interest and waits for probe response(s) from the AP(s). The station moves on to another channel after a pre-set timeout timer expires.

Without prior knowledge about the identity of the neighboring APs, the probe request has to be sent to the broadcast address, which may result in simultaneous responses from multiple APs. To avoid collision, probe responses follows the same DCF rule to contend for accessing the medium as data frames from any other station do. As a result, the probe response from an AP could potentially be delayed by data frames from any station. Due to this reason, the timeout cannot be too short, as the station may otherwise miss a delayed probe response. Another reason to keep the timeout long is that the station has no prior knowledge on the number of probe responses to expect and may want to get as many probe responses back as possible. A typical timeout for active scanning is about 20ms.

The analysis above points out that it is the broadcast probe request that makes it difficult to shorten the active scanning timeout. Thanks to the Site Report, a station will have prior knowledge of the identities (i.e., BSSIDs) of the neighboring APs. The station may, therefore, choose to send a unicast probe request destined to a particular AP instead. Two benefits arise from using unicast probe request. First, there is no potential collision from multiple simultaneous probe responses. Second, there is no need to wait for more than one response.

To take advantage of these benefits, [26] proposed the following fast active scanning scheme. An AP may respond to a unicast probe request with a probe response at Short Interframe Space (SIFS)[9] time after receiving the request. Otherwise, if the probe response cannot be ready within SIFS time, the AP should send an acknowledgement (ACK) in response to the unicast probe request instead. When the probe response is ready, the AP can send it out as soon as the medium is idle for PCF Interframe Space (PIFS) time. This essentially gives the probe response frame higher priority to access the medium, as under the 802.11 DCF rule, any station needs to waits at least DCF Interframe Space (DIFS) time interval before transmitting any data frame, where DIFS is longer than PIFS. This proposal allows the station to know the existence of the AP in SIFS time and the probe response will not be delayed by more than one data frame transmission.

Fast Passive Scanning

Passive scanning is attractive since it causes no additional network traffic loads. Furthermore, in certain regulatory domains, active scanning is banned under certain conditions so that passive scanning may be the only choice. Despite its attractiveness, passive scanning usually takes longer than active scanning, as the scanning station needs to wait up to a beacon interval (typically 100 ms) to receive a beacon. It has been pointed out in [27] that passive scanning

---

[9] A SIFS is the shortest possible time interval between any two consecutive frame transmissions under the 802.11 specification.

can be very efficient if the station knows the Target Beacon Transmission Time (TBTT) of the neighbor APs. The proposal [28] therefore proposes to add the neighbor AP's TBTT information in the Site Report. Knowing when to expect a beacon from a particular AP on a particular channel, a station can switch to the channel right before the TBTT and switch back to the original channel right after receiving a beacon, or after a relatively short timeout should it miss the beacon.

Fast Roaming Study Group (FRSG)

As mentioned earlier, the enhanced security mechanism introduced in the 802.11i creates some challenges for fast handoff. The 802.11i uses the four-way handshake to setup the Pairwise Transient Key Security Association (PTKSA) upon a reassociation. There has been some concern that that the 4-way handshake process may be too slow to satisfy the needs of real-time low-delay applications such as Voice over IP (VoIP). In an empirical analysis [29], it is shown that even in the best case (i.e., no RF interference, fast Pentium 4 processor, and no RADIUS delay as in PMK caching), the 4-way handshake itself can take about 20ms to complete.

To address the fast roaming issues without jeopardizing the progress of the rest of TGi work, the group decided to spin off a separate new task group to provide solutions for fast roaming while TGi warps up its current draft. So far, the discussion in the new task group has pointed to two possible solutions to work on. The straightforward solution is to work on the 4-way handshake mechanism itself. The goal is to reduce the number of handshakes without compromising security.

An alternative solution approaches the problem from a different perspective. The current 802.11i draft requires that the negotiation and handshakes for security setup take place after the new AP notifies the DS about the new station-to-AP mapping. That is, the station breaks its connection to its current AP before engaged in the security negotiation and handshakes with the new AP, resulting in a data communication gap. Using the power save mechanism provided in the baseline standard, the station can carry on conversations with different APs on different channels in a time-sharing manner without losing packets. Instead of working on shortening the gap caused by negotiation and handshakes, an alternative solution aims for having these actions completed before breaking the association with the current AP. That is, the station negotiates and handshakes with the new AP while maintaining the association with the current AP. For example, [30] proposes an idea to break up the reassociation process, and create an interim state where the station can do all the actions needed to negotiate and handshake. Only after all the actions are done, the new AP announces the station-to-AP mapping.

Wireless Network Management Study Group (WNMSG)

The latest handoff-related development in IEEE 802.11 is the wireless network management study group, motivated by the need of service providers and enterprise network administrators to extend their management capability to the wireless network. Some potential topics that the group will deal with include remote client configuration/reset, interference mitigation, load balancing, client handoff, etc. [31]

As we presented in Section 0, the handoff as defined in the current 802.11 baseline standard is a station centered process. Unfortunately, this implies that the handoff performance (e.g., the handoff latency) can dramatically differ depending on the client side implementation. The new study group will likely to involve APs more in the handoff process. For example, a network-assisted approach might be proposed for client handoff.

There is no mechanism provided in the current 802.11 baseline standard to support load balancing, in that AP cannot direct a station to another AP. Furthermore, there is no mechanism for an AP to gracefully disassociate a station. According to the current standard, the AP can send a disassociation frame to a station, which results in an abrupt disconnect of the station from the AP. Without prior knowledge of the disconnection, the station cannot take advantage of mechanisms discussed above to start a handoff preparation before breaking the association with the current AP. One improvement may be to inform the station about the imminence of a disassociation as proposed in [32].

Summary

In this chapter, we have overviewed the mobility support mechanisms of the IEEE 802.11 WLAN. The functions defined in the current standard specifications as well as the related algorithmic issues, e.g., when to hand off, were discussed. The relationship between the emerging recommended practice IEEE 802.11f IAPP and mobile IP in the context of layer-2 and layer-3 handoffs was also considered. Finally, the current efforts within IEEE 802.11 standardization working group to make the 802.11 handoff faster and more reliable without sacrificing security were briefly summarized.

References

[1]   IEEE 802.11 Working Group, http://www.ieee802.org/11, on-line.

[2]   IEEE Std. 802.11-1999, *Part 11: Wireless LAN Medium Access Control (MAC) and Physical Layer (PHY) specifications*, Reference number ISO/IEC 8802-11:1999(E), IEEE Std 802.11, 1999 edition, 1999.

[3]   IEEE Std. 802.11a-1999, *Supplement to Part 11: Wireless LAN Medium Access Control (MAC) and Physical Layer (PHY) specifications: High-speed Physical Layer in the 5 GHZ Band*, 1999.

[4]   IEEE Std. 802.11b-1999, *Supplement to Part 11: Wireless LAN Medium Access Control (MAC) and Physical Layer (PHY) specifications: Higher-speed Physical Layer Extension in the 2.4 GHz Band*, 1999.

[5]   IEEE Std. 802.11f-2003, *Recommended Practice for Multi-Vendor Access Point Interoperability via an Inter-Access Point Protocol Across Distribution System Supporting IEEE 802.11 Operation*, June 2003.

[6]   IEEE Std. 802.11g-2003, *Supplement to Part 11: Wireless LAN Medium Access Control (MAC) and Physical Layer (PHY) specifications: Further Higher-Speed Physical Layer Extension in the 2.4 GHz Band*, June 2003.

[7]   IEEE 802.11e/D7.0, *Draft Supplement to Part 11: Wireless Medium Access Control (MAC) and physical layer (PHY) specifications: Medium Access Control (MAC) Enhancements for Quality of Service (QoS)*, January 2004.

[8]   IEEE 802.11i/D7.0, *Draft Supplement to Part 11: Wireless LAN Medium Access Control (MAC) and Physical Layer (PHY) specifications: Medium Access Control (MAC) Security Enhancements*, October 2003.

[9]   IEEE 802.11k/D0.12, *Draft Supplement to Part 11: Wireless LAN Medium Access Control (MAC) and Physical Layer (PHY) specifications: Specification for Radio Resource Measurement*, February 2004.

[10] IEEE Std. 802.1D-1998, *Part 3: Media Access Control (MAC) bridges*, ANSI/IEEE Std. 802.1D, IEEE 802.1d-1998, 1998 edition, 1998.

[11] IEEE Std. 802.1X-2001, *Standards for Local and Metropolitan Area Networks: Port-Based Network Access Control*, 2001.

[12] M. Portoles, Z. Zhong, S. Choi, and C.-T. Chou, *IEEE 802.11 Link-Layer Forwarding For Smooth Handoff*, Proc. IEEE PIMRC'03, Beijing, China, Sept. 7-10, 2003.

[13] M. Portoles, Z. Zhong, and S. Choi, *IEEE 802.11 Downlink Traffic Shaping Scheme For Multi-User Service Enhancement*, Proc. IEEE PIMRC'03, Beijing, China, Sept. 7-10, 2003.

[14] S. Pack and Y. Choi, *Pre-Authenticated Fast Handoff in a Public Wireless LAN based on IEEE 802.1x Model*, Proc. IFIP TC6 Personal Wireless Communications (PWC'2002), Singapore, October 2002.

[15] S. Pack and Y. Choi, *Fast Inter-AP Handoff using Predictive-Authentication Scheme in a Public Wireless LAN*, Proc. IEEE Networks'2002 (Jointly with ICN'2002 and ICWLHN'2002), Atlanta, USA, August 2002.

[16] RFC 2284, *PPP Extensible Authentication Protocol (EAP)*, March 1998.

[17] RFC 2716, *PPP EAP TLS Authentication Protocol*, October 1999.

[18] RFC 2865, *Remote Authentication Dial In User Service (RADIUS)*, June 2000.

[19] R. Moskowitz, *RADIUS Client Kickstart*, draft-moskowitz-radius-client-kickstart-00.txt.

[20] Kamerman and L. Monteban, *WaveLAN-II: A High-Performance Wireless LAN for the Unlicensed Band*, Bell Labs Technical Journal, Summer 1997, pp. 118-133.

[21] E. Perkins, *Mobile IP*, IEEE Communications Magazine, May 2002, pp. 66-82.

[22] RFC 3220, *IP mobility support for IPv4*, January 2002.

[23] Aboba, *Pre-authentication architecture*, IEEE 802.11-03-0647-00, July 2003.

[24] Z. Zhong, *RRM and roaming support*, IEEE 802.11-03/078r0, January 2003.

[25] Mishra *et al.*, *Fast handoffs using fixed channel probing*, IEEE 802.11-03-0540-00, July 2003.

[26] M. Ryong, F. Watannabe, T. Kawahara and Z. Zhong, *Fast active scan proposals*, IEEE 802.11-03-0623-00, July 2003.

[27] R. Wright, *A technique for fast passive scanning*, IEEE 802.11-03-0768-00, September 2003.

[28] M. Lefkowitz, *Neighbor TBTT offset*, IEEE 802.11-03-0860-01, November 2003.

[29] N. Petroni and W. A. Arbaugh, *An empirical analysis of the 4-way hand-shake*, IEEE 802.11-03-0563-00, July 2003.

[30] C. Chaplin, *Make before break*, IEEE 802.11-03-0770-00, September 2003.

[31] H. Worstell *et al.*, *The need for managed IEEE 802.11 devices*, IEEE 802.11-03-0950-01, November 2003.

[32] M. Lefkowitz and Z. Zhong, *Site report*, IEEE 802.11-03/174r2, May 2003.

[33] RFC 2501, *Mobile ad hoc networking (MANET): routing protocol performance issues and evaluation considerations*, January 1999.

[34] M. Heusse, F. Rousseu, G. Berger-Sabbatel, and A. Duda, *Performance anomaly of 802.11b*, Proc. of IEEE INFOCOM'03, 2003.

[35] T. S. Rappaport, *Wireless Communications: Principles and Practice*, Second Ed., Prentice Hall, 2002.

In: Wireless LANs and Bluetooth
Editors: Yang Xiao and Yi Pan, pp. 23-50

ISBN 1-59454-432-8
©2005 Nova Science Publishers, Inc.

Chapter 2

QoS Support for IEEE 802.11 Wireless LAN*

Qiang Ni[†] and Thierry Turletti[‡]
PLANETE Group, INRIA Sophia Antipolis

Abstract

In today's Internet, the emerging widespread use of real-time voice, audio, and video applications makes Quality of service (QoS) a key problem. Meanwhile, the Internet is getting heterogeneous due to the explosive evolution of wireless networks. QoS support in wireless networks is more challenging than in the wired networks since bandwidth is scarce, latency and bit error rate are high and characteristics of the wireless channel vary over time and space. The IEEE 802.11 standard is the most widely deployed wireless local area network (WLAN) infrastructure. However, it cannot provide QoS support for the increasing number of multimedia applications. Thus, a lot of research works have been carried out to enhance the QoS support in 802.11 networks. Recently, the IEEE working group has been working on a new QoS-enhanced standard, called IEEE 802.11e. This chapter describes all these research and standardization activities. We also show through simulations the performance of the upcoming 802.11e standard and discuss several adaptive mechanisms to enhance the performance of the upcoming 802.11e standard.

Keywords: Adaptive Enhanced Distributed Coordination Access (AEDCA), Fair Hybrid Coordination Function (FHCF), Hybrid Coordination Function (HCF), IEEE 802.11, IEEE 802.11e, Medium Access Control (MAC), Quality of Service (QoS), Service Differentiation.

AMS Subject Classification.

---

*This work was supported by the the French Ministry of Industry in the Context of the National Project RNRT-VTHD++, France.

[†]E-mail address: Qiang.Ni@sophia.inria.fr, PLANETE Group

[‡]E-mail address: Thierry.Turletti@sophia.inria.fr

1 Introduction

In the recent past, IEEE 802.11 wireless LAN (WLAN) has emerged as one prevailing wireless technology throughout the world and will also play an important role in the future fourth-generation wireless and mobile communication systems. The 802.11 technology provides a cheap and flexible wireless access capability, and it is very easy to deploy an 802.11 WLAN in offices, hospitals, campuses, airports, stock markets, etc. On the other hand, the number of multimedia applications have increased tremendously: people are willing to acquire voice, audio, and high-speed video services even when they are moving. However, multimedia applications require some quality of service (QoS) support such as guaranteed bandwidth, bounded delay and jitter. Providing such QoS support in 802.11 is challenging since the current 802.11 standard does not take QoS support into account [10, 20]: both the 802.11 medium access control (MAC) layer and the physical (PHY) layer are designed for best-effort data transmission. Considering that the MAC layer is essential for QoS support, a lot of research efforts have been carried out for the 802.11 MAC. This chapter will review these QoS enhancement research efforts and standardization activities. We also show through simulation results the performance of the upcoming QoS-enhanced IEEE standard named 802.11e. Moreover, several adaptive mechanisms to enhance the QoS performance of this upcoming standard are discussed.

The following section (§2) provides a brief overview of IEEE 802.11 WLAN. Section §3 illustrates the problems of QoS support in the original 802.11 MAC layer. The research efforts and standardization activities on QoS enhancements for 802.11 are addressed in Section §4. Section §5 presents simulation evaluations of the IEEE 802.11e and discusses several adaptive mechanisms to enhance QoS performance.

2 Overview of 802.11 Networks

2.1 The IEEE 802.11 Standard Family

The IEEE 802.11 WLAN standard covers both the MAC sub-layer and the PHY layer of the open system interconnection (OSI) network reference model [10]. The logical link control (LLC) sub-layer is specified in the IEEE 802.2 standard. This architecture provides a transparent interface to the higher layer users: stations may move, roam through an 802.11 WLAN and still appear as stationary to the 802.2 LLC sub-layer and above. This allows existing TCP/IP protocols to run over IEEE 802.11 WLAN just like wired Ethernet. Figure 1 shows a snapshot of IEEE standardization activities done for 802.11 PHY and MAC layers: In 1997, IEEE provided three kinds of options in the PHY layer, which are an infrared (IR) baseband PHY, a frequency hopping spread spectrum (FHSS) radio and a direct sequence spread spectrum (DSSS) radio. All these options support both 1 and 2Mbps PHY rates. In 1999, the IEEE has defined two high rate extensions: (1) 802.11b based on DSSS technology, with data rates up to 11Mbps in the 2.4GHz band, and (2) 802.11a, based on orthogonal frequency division multiplexing (OFDM) technology, with data rates up to 54Mbps in the 5GHz band. In 2003, the 802.11g standard that extends the 802.11b PHY layer to support data rates up to 54Mbps in the 2.4GHz band has been finalized. In parallel, several other 802.11 standardization activities are ongoing: 802.11h aims to enhance 802.11a with adding indoor and outdoor license regulations for the 5GHz band in Europe. The 802.11n is a new task group which proposes a high-throughput amendment to the 802.11 standard. The 802.11n will support at least 100Mbps throughput, as measured at the interface between MAC and higher layers. It is likely to choose multiple-input multiple-output (MIMO) antenna and adaptive OFDM as main PHY technologies. At the MAC layer, 802.11e will define extensions to enhance the QoS performance of 802.11 WLAN. The 802.11f will propose an Inter-Access Point protocol to allow stations roaming between multi-vendor access points. The 802.11i will propose enhanced security and authentication mechanisms for 802.11 MAC.

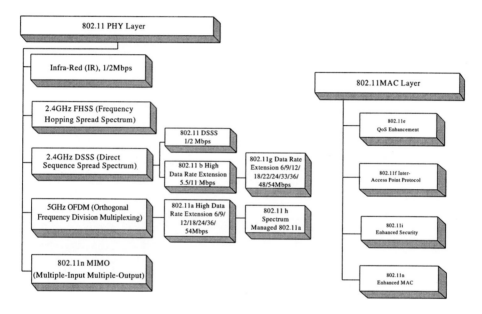

Figure 1: Snapshot of 802.11 PHY (left) and MAC (right) standardization activities

2.2   IEEE 802.11 MAC Layer

The 802.11 MAC layer aims to provide access control functions to the wireless medium such as access coordination, addressing or frame check sequence generation. Two different classes of wireless configuration have been defined for 802.11. An *Infrastructure Network*, where many stations can communicate with the wired backbone through an access point (AP), and the *Ad Hoc Network*, where any device can communicate directly with other devices, without any connectivity to the wired backbone. A group of stations coordinated by 802.11 MAC functions is called a basic service set (BSS) in *infrastructure mode* and independent BSS (IBSS) in *ad-hoc mode*, respectively. The area covered by the BSS is known as the basic service area (BSA), which is similar to a cell in a cellular mobile network.

The IEEE 802.11 MAC sub-layer defines two medium access coordination functions, the basic Distributed Coordination Function (DCF) and the optional Point Coordination Function (PCF) [10].

DCF: Distributed Coordination Function

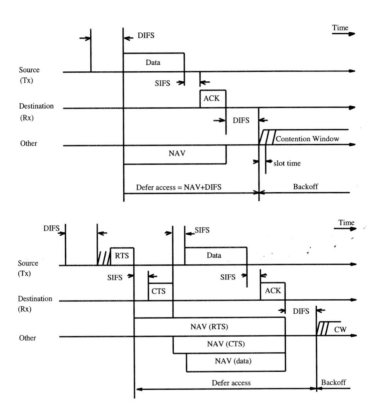

Figure 2: DCF access mechanism: CSMA/CA (up) and RTS/CTS scheme (down)

DCF is an asynchronous transmission mode based on Carrier Sense Multiple Access with Collision Avoidance scheme (CSMA/CA). Due to the significant difference between transmitted and received power levels, collision detection can not be implemented. Actually, two different carrier sensing mechanisms are used: PHY carrier sensing at the air interface and virtual carrier sensing at the MAC layer. PHY carrier sensing detects the presence of other STAs by analyzing all packets received from other STAs. Virtual carrier sensing is optionally used by a station to inform all other stations in the same BSS or IBSS how long the channel will be reserved for its frame transmission. To avoid collisions, the sender can set a duration field in the MAC header of data frames, or in the RequestToSend

(RTS) and ClearToSend (CTS) control frames. Then, other stations will update their local timers of network allocation vectors (NAVs) to take into account this duration. As shown in Figure 2, if a packet arrives at an empty queue and if the medium has been found idle for an interval of time longer than a distributed interframe space called DIFS, the source station can transmit the packet immediately. Meanwhile, other stations defer their transmissions by adjusting their NAVs, and start the backoff process. More precisely, stations compute a random time interval, called *backoff timer*, selected from the contention window (CW): *backoff timer* = $rand[0, CW] \cdot slot\ time$, where $CW_{min} < CW < CW_{max}$ and *slot time* depends on the PHY layer type. The *backoff timer* parameter is decreased only when the medium is idle; it is frozen when another station is transmitting. Each time the medium becomes idle, stations wait for a DIFS and continuously decrement their *backoff timer*. Once the backoff timer expires, the station is authorized to access the medium. Collisions occur when at least two stations start transmission simultaneously. On this purpose, a positive acknowledgement (ACK) is used to notify the sender that the transmitted frame has been successfully received, see Figure 2. If the ACK is not received, the sender assumes that there is a collision, and it schedules a retransmission by entering the backoff process again. To reduce the probability of collisions, after each unsuccessful transmission attempt, the CW value is doubled until a predefined maximum value CW_{max} is reached. After each successful transmission, the CW is reset to a fixed minimum value CW_{min}.

Hidden terminals can also induce collisions. These terminals are stations that the receiver can hear but that cannot be detected by other senders. Consequently, frames sent from different senders will collide at the same receiver. To solve this problem, the RTS/CTS scheme can optionally be used: the source sends a short RTS frame before each data frame transmission, see Figure 2, and the receiver replies with a CTS frame if it is ready to receive. Once the source receives the CTS frame, it transmits a frame. All other stations hearing a RTS, a CTS, or a data frame in the BSS update their NAVs, and will not start transmissions before the updated NAV timers reach zero. The RTS/CTS scheme improves significantly the performance of the basic DCF scheme when data frame sizes are large. DCF is mandatory in the standard and can be used both in ad-hoc and infrastructure modes.

PCF: Point Coordination Function

Priority-based access can also be used to access the medium. For example, PCF is a synchronous service that implements a polling-based contention-free access scheme. It can be used with the infrastructure mode only. Unlike DCF, its implementation is not mandatory. The reason is that the hardware implementation of PCF was thought to be too complex at the time the standard was finalized. Furthermore, PCF itself relies on the asynchronous service provided by DCF and the beacon interval must allow at least one DCF data frame to be transmitted during the CP. PCF uses a centralized polling scheme, which uses the AP as a point coordinator (PC). When a BSS is set up with PCF-enabled, the channel access time is divided into periodic intervals named beacon intervals, see Figure 3. The beacon interval is composed of a contention-free period (CFP) and a contention period (CP). During the CFP, the PC maintains a list of registered stations and polls each of them according to the list. When a station is polled, it starts to transmit data frames, where the size of each data frame is bounded by the maximum MAC service data unit size. Assuming that the PHY rate of every station is fixed, the maximum CFP duration for all the stations, which is called *CFP_max_duration*, is then decided by the PC. However, the link-adaptation (multirate support) capability makes the transmission time of a frame variable and may induce large delay jitters, which degrades the QoS performance of PCF (see Section §3.2). The time used by the PC to generate beacon frames is called target beacon transmission time (TBTT). The next TBTT is announced within the beacon frame by the PC to inform all other stations in the BSS. To give PCF higher priority of access than DCF in a beacon interval, the PC waits for a shorter interframe space than DIFS (called PIFS standing for PCF interframe space), before starting the PCF. But PCF is not allowed to interrupt any ongoing frame transmissions in DCF. Then, all other stations set their NAVs to the values of *CFP_max_duration*, or the remaining duration of CFP in case of delayed beacon. A typical medium access sequence during PCF is shown in Figure 3.

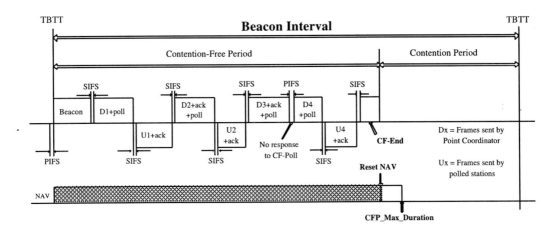

Figure 3: PCF and DCF cycles

Once PCF obtains access to the wireless medium, SIFS timing is used for frames exchanges during CFP except if the polled station does not respond the PC within a PIFS period. When a PC polls a station, it can piggyback the data frames to the station together with the CF-Poll, then the station sends back a data frame piggybacked with an ACK after a SIFS interval. When the PC polls the next station, it piggybacks not only the data frame to the destination, but also the ACK corresponding to the previous successful transmission. Silent stations are removed from the polling list after several periods and may be polled again at the beginning of the next CFP. Note that at any time, the PC can decide to terminate the CFP by transmitting a CF-End frame. Usually, PCF uses a round-robin scheduler to poll each station sequentially in the order of the polling list, but priority-based polling mechanisms can also be used if different QoS levels are requested by different stations.

3 QoS Limitations of 802.11 WLANs

Maintaining QoS is one of the most challenging functions a MAC layer should support. In particular, wireless links have specific characteristics such as high loss rates, bursts of frame loss, high latency and jitter. Furthermore, wireless link characteristics vary over time and location. There are several ways to characterize QoS in WLANs such as parameterized or prioritized QoS as proposed in [12]. Generally, QoS is the ability of a network element (such as an application, a host or a router) to provide some levels of assurance for consistent network data delivery. Parameterized QoS is a strict QoS requirement that is expressed in terms of quantitative values, such as data rate, delay bound, and jitter bound. In a traffic specification (TSPEC), these values are expected to be met within the MAC data service in the transfer of data frames between peer stations. Prioritized QoS is expressed in terms of relative delivery priority, which is to be used within the MAC data service in the transfer of data frames between peer stations. With a prioritized QoS scheme, the values of QoS parameters such as data rate, delay bound, and jitter bound, can vary during the transfer of data frames, without renegotiating the TSPEC between the station and the AP. According to the above definitions of QoS, this section presents the QoS limitations of IEEE 802.11 MAC functions.

3.1 Limitations of DCF

DCF does not provide any QoS guarantees, only a best-effort service is provided. Typically, time-bounded applications such as Voice over IP (VoIP), or videoconferencing require specified bandwidth, low delay and jitter, but can tolerate some losses. The point is that in DCF, all the stations compete for the channel with the same priorities. There is no differentiation mechanism to guarantee bandwidth, packet delay and jitter for high-priority multimedia flows. To illustrate the problem, we have made the following simulation using the ns-2 [22] simulator. A variable number of stations are located within the same IBSS, they use the ad-hoc mode and all hear each other (1-hop distance). Moreover, there is no mobility in the system. Each station uses the IEEE 802.11a PHY transmission mode-6 [11] and transmits three types of traffic (audio, video, and background flows) to each other. The audio packet size is equal to 160 bytes and the inter-packet arrival interval is 20ms, which corresponds to 8KBytes/s PCM audio flow. The video transmission rate is 80KBytes/s with a packet size equal to 1280 Bytes. The background transmission rate is 128 KBytes/s, and the corresponding packet size is 1600 bytes. The RTS/CTS option is not used. The main simulation parameters are summarized in Table 3.1, the three types of flows use CBR/UDP ns sources. We vary the load rate from 9.6% to 90% by increasing the number of stations from 2 to 18. Figure 4 shows the simulation results for the throughput and delay.

We can observe that the average throughput of the three flows for a station is quasi-stable when the channel load rate is less than 70% (i.e. the number of stations is up to 10): the mean throughput of audio, video and background is about 7.8 KBytes/s, 80KBytes/s, and 125KBytes/s respectively; and the delay is lower than 4ms. When the number of stations is larger than 10, the throughput of all three flows decrease very fast: it is reduced by 40%

Table 1: Simulation parameters for 802.11a mode 6

SIFS	$16\mu s$	MAC header	28Bytes
DIFS	$34\mu s$	PLCP header length	$4\mu s$
ACK size	14Bytes	Preamble length	$20\mu s$
PHY rate	36Mbps	CW_{min}	15
slot time	$9\mu s$	CW_{max}	1023

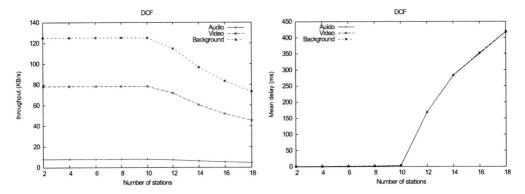

Figure 4: Throughput (left) and delay (right) performance for DCF

when the number of stations is 18 (corresponding to 90% load). Moreover, the mean delays are almost the same for the three flows and increase up to 420ms. This simulation clearly shows that there is neither throughput nor delay differentiation between the different flows. The reason is that these three flows share the same queue, thus they all experience the same delay. Unless admission control is used, there is no way to guarantee the QoS requirements for high-priority audio and video traffic in DCF.

3.2   Limitations of PCF

Although PCF has been designed to support time-bounded multimedia applications, this mode has three main problems that lead to poor QoS performance [16, 18, 27]. First, the central polling scheme is questionable. All the communications between two stations in the same BSS have to go through the AP. Thus, when this kind of traffic increases, a lot of channel resources are wasted. Second, the cooperation between CP and CFP modes may lead to unpredictable beacon delays [18],[27]: the AP schedules the next beacon transmission at next TBTT but it has to contend to access the channel, the beacon can then be transmitted when the medium has been found idle for an interval of time longer than a PIFS. Hence, depending on whether the wireless medium is idle or busy around the TBTT, the beacon frame may be delayed. In the current 802.11 legacy standard, stations are allowed to transmit even if the frame transmission cannot terminate before the upcoming TBTT [10]. The duration of the beacon to be sent after the TBTT defers the transmission of data frames during CFP, which may severely impact the QoS performance of multimedia applications. In the worst case, the maximum delay of a beacon frame can be 4.9 ms in 802.11a, and the average delay of a beacon frame can reach up to 250 μs [18]. Third, it is difficult to predict the transmission time of a polled station. A polled station is allowed to send a frame of any length between 0 and 2304 Bytes (the maximum MAC service data unit size), which may introduce variable transmission time. Furthermore, the PHY rate of the polled station can change according to the varying characteristics of the channel, so the AP is not able to predict in a precise manner the transmission time. This prevents the AP to provide guaranteed delay and jitter performance for other stations present in the polling list during the rest of the CFP.

4   QoS Enhancements for 802.11 WLANs

All the limitations for DCF and PCF we have described in the previous section can explain why so many research activities have been launched to enhance the performance of 802.11 MAC. When the bandwidth is not scarce, such as in wired LANs, QoS issues are not so important (1Gbps is now a common link speed in company LANs while 10Gbps 802.3ae Ethernet will appear soon). However, a WLAN have a higher bit error rate, a higher delay and a lower bandwidth than a wired LAN. Thus, they have been originally designed for best-effort, low data rate applications. Characteristics of wireless channels make high data rate transmission very difficult to achieve: The bit error rate (BER) is more than three orders of magnitude larger than in wired LANs. Moreover, high collision rate provoking frequent retransmissions cause unpredictable delays and jitters, which degrade the quality of real-time voice and video transmission. Enhanced QoS-aware MAC aims to reduce overhead, prioritize frames, and limit collisions to meet delay and jitter requirements. Different kinds of QoS enhancement schemes for both infrastructure and ad-hoc modes have been proposed for 802.11. First of all, QoS enhancement can be supported by adding service differentiation into the MAC layer. This can be achieved by modifying the parameters that define how a station or a flow should access the wireless medium. Current service differentiation based schemes can be classified with respect to a multitude of characteristics. A possible classification criterion is whether the schemes provide only one priority for one station (we refer to *station-based*) or introduce multiple priority queues in each station (refer to *queue-based*). Another classification depends on whether they are *DCF-based* or *PCF-based* enhancements. Figure 5 shows a classification in two levels. We distinguish between station-based and queue-based schemes at the top-level and DCF-based versus PCF-based enhancement at the second level. Previous research works mainly focus on the station-based DCF enhancement schemes [1],[4],[24],[25],[26]. Other recent works, including efforts done within the IEEE 802.11e task group, focus on queue-based hybrid coordination (combined PCF and DCF) enhancement schemes [2],[9],[12],[17],[18],[20],[23].

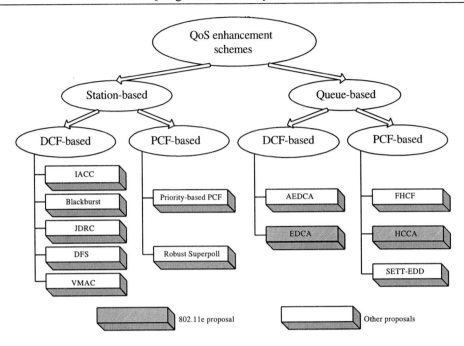

Figure 5: Classification of QoS enhancement schemes

4.1   Station-Based QoS Enhancement Schemes

We will use the classification shown above to present the main QoS enhancement schemes proposed in the literature. In the case schemes have no specific names, we have labelled them using initials of their respective authors.

4.1.1   DCF-Based Schemes

The IACC Scheme

The IACC scheme [1] aims to introduce priorities in the IEEE 802.11 standard under the DCF access method. Three techniques are used: the first one assigns different contention windows to stations with different priorities. Experiments show that this scheme performs well with UDP traffic while it performs badly with TCP traffic. The reason is that all TCP ACKs are sent with the same priorities, which affects the differentiation mechanism. In the second technique, each station sets the DIFS parameter according to its priority level. The main problem of this scheme is that low priority traffic suffers as long as high priority frames are queued. Contrary to the first scheme, there is no backoff problem with TCP, but TCP ACKs also reduce the effects of service differentiation because all ACKs have the same priorities. With the third technique, each station is assigned a different maximum frame length according to its priority level, therefore, a high priority station can transmit more information per medium access than low priority stations. This mechanism is used to increase both transmission reliability and differentiation, and works well for TCP and UDP flows. However, in a noisy environment, long packets are more likely to be corrupted than short ones, which decreases the efficiency of service differentiation.

The Blackburst Scheme

Blackburst [24] aims to minimize the delay of real-time traffic. Unlike other schemes, it imposes certain requirements on high priority stations: (1) the use of equal and constant intervals to access the medium, and (2) the ability to jam the medium for a period of time. When a high priority station wants to send a frame, it senses the medium. If it is idle, it sends its frame after a PIFS interval of time; if the medium is busy, it waits for the medium to be idle for another PIFS and then enters a black burst contention period in which the station sends a so-called black burst to jam the channel. The length of the black burst is determined by the time the station has waited to access the medium, and is calculated as a number of black slots. This has the nice effect that real-time flows will synchronize, and share the medium in a time division multiple access (TDMA) fashion. Simulation results show that Blackburst can support more real-time nodes than CSMA/CA, with stable data and real-time traffic operation, due to the absence of collisions. The main drawback of Blackburst is that it requires constant access intervals for high-priority traffic, otherwise the performance degrades considerably.

The JDRC Scheme

The JDRC scheme [4] is a service differentiation scheme which requires minimal modifications of the basic 802.11 DCF. It uses two parameters of the 802.11 MAC, IFSs and random backoff time between each data transmission to provide the service differentiation: two different backoff time algorithms are combined with two different IFS lengths PIFS and DIFS. Thus, four classes of priorities can be supported. A station that uses PIFS and short backoff time algorithm gets the highest priority, where a station that uses DIFS and long backoff time algorithm obtains the lowest priority. Using the JDRC scheme, high priority stations have short waiting time when accessing the medium. When a collision occurs, high priority stations have more chances to access the medium than the low priority ones. On the other hand, when none of the high priority stations wants to transmit packets, low priority stations still use long backoff time. Thus, an additional delay is imposed by long backoff time.

The DFS Scheme

The distributed fair scheduling (DFS) scheme [25] utilizes the ideas of self-clocked fair queueing (SCFQ) [8] to introduce both priority and fairness in the wireless domain. In DFS, the backoff process is always initiated before transmitting a frame. Contrary to 802.11 DCF, the backoff interval is computed as a function of packet size and weight of the station, which can be linear, exponential, or square-root function. With this scheme, stations with low weights generate longer backoff intervals than those with high weights, thus get low priority. Fairness is achieved by considering the packet size in the calculation of the backoff interval, causing flows with smaller packet size to be sent more often. If a collision occurs, a new backoff interval is calculated using the original backoff algorithm of the IEEE 802.11 DCF. However, the high complexity implementation of this scheme limits its deployment.

The VMAC Scheme

The virtual MAC (VMAC) scheme [26] uses a distributed service quality estimation, radio monitoring, and admission control mechanisms to support service differentiation. It monitors the radio channel and estimates locally MAC level statistics related to service quality such as delay, jitter, packet collision, and packet loss. The VMAC algorithm operates in parallel to the MAC within a station but it does not handle real packet transmission like the MAC. This is why it is called virtual MAC. The virtual source (VS) algorithm can utilize the VMAC to estimate application-level service quality. This allows application parameters to be tuned in response to dynamic channel conditions based on "virtual delay curves". VMAC is based on DCF, but uses different CW_{min} and CW_{max} values to support service differentiation. Simulation results show that: (1) when these distributed virtual algorithms are applied to the admission control of the radio channel, then a globally stable state can be maintained without the need for complex centralized radio resource management; (2) delay differentiation can be increased by increasing the gap between $CW_{min}^{high\_pri}$ and $CW_{max}^{low\_pri}$. The main drawback of this scheme is the high complexity introduced to allow interactions between the application and the MAC layers.

4.1.2   PCF-Based Schemes

Because PCF is optional in the 802.11 standard, only a few research works focused on PCF enhancements to transmit multimedia flows and the three main problems of PCF (as mentioned in §3.2) have not been solved.

The Priority-Based PCF Scheme

In PCF, the AP sends priority-based polling packets to a succession of stations in the wireless BSS, which can assign stations different priorities. IEEE 802.11 does not specify how the AP determines the polling sequence. In [28], four different polling schemes are evaluated to provide service differentiation support in PCF: Round-Robin (RR), First-In-First-Out (FIFO), Priority, and Priority-Effort Limited Fair (ELF) [5]. Simulations show that all these schemes have better performance than DCF and can support real-time traffic in some cases. The FIFO scheme achieves the highest throughput although some traffic behave badly. The priority scheme can support at low cost QoS of traffic but may severely affect low priority and best-effort traffic to compensate the losses of high priority traffic. The Priority-ELF scheme is fairer than other schemes and achieves high utilization of the wireless channel link.

The Robust SuperPoll Scheme

The Robust SuperPoll protocol [7] aims to improve performance of the PCF access scheme. Actually, PCF is very sensitive to lost polls. Instead of polling individually stations as in PCF, the SuperPoll mechanism sends polls (called "SuperPolls") to a group of stations. To make the scheme more robust against frame loss, each packet includes identities of remaining stations to be polled in the list. Therefore, stations have multiple opportunities to receive the poll. The observed increase in bandwidth and decrease in channel access time provide a better support for multimedia applications, especially in noisy environments.

4.2 Queue-Based QoS Enhancement Schemes

In order to provide queue-based QoS support, IEEE 802.11e proposed a new MAC layer coordination function called HCF (Hybrid Coordination Function). HCF uses a contention-based channel access method, also called the enhanced distributed channel access (EDCA), that operates concurrently with an HCF controlled channel access (HCCA) method. In HCF, contention-based EDCA and polling-based HCCA are no longer separated, and EDCA is defined as a part of HCF. The AP and stations that implement the QoS facilities are called QAP (QoS-enhanced AP) and QSTAs (QoS-enhanced stations) respectively.

One main new feature of HCF is the concept of transmission opportunity (*TXOP*), which refers to an instance during which a given QSTA has the right to send data frames. The aim of introducing *TXOP* is to limit the time interval during which a QSTA is allowed to transmit frames. Thus, the problem of unpredictable transmission time of a polled station in PCF (as mentioned in Section §3.2) is solved. A *TXOP* is called either *EDCA TXOP*, when it is obtained by winning a successful EDCA contention; or *HCCA TXOP*, when it is obtained by receiving a QoS CF-poll frame from the QAP. In order to limit delay, the maximum value of a *TXOP* is bounded by a value, namely *TXOPLimit*, which is determined by the QAP. A QSTA can transmit packets as long as its *TXOPLimit* has not expired. QAP allocates an uplink *TXOP* to a QSTA by sending a QoS CF-Poll frame, while no specific control frame is required for the downlink *TXOP*. Now we describe queue-based 802.11e HCF (EDCA/HCCA) and some enhanced schemes, such as AEDCA, FHCF and SETT-EDD respectively.

4.2.1 DCF-Based Schemes

The EDCA Scheme

EDCA is designed to provide prioritized QoS by enhancing DCF. Before entering the MAC layer, each data packet received from higher layers is assigned a specific user priority value. How to tag such a priority value for each packet is an implementation issue. At the MAC layer, EDCA introduces 4 different FIFO queues, namely, access categories (ACs). As specified in the 802.11e draft [12], each data packet from higher layers along with a specific user priority value should be mapped into a corresponding AC using a mapping table [12]. The user priority value is defined in the IEEE 802.1d bridge specification [13]. As

Table 2: Mapping between user priorities and Access Categories (ACs)

user priorities	ACs	Designation
1	AC_BK	Background
2	AC_BK	Background
0	AC_BE	Best Effort
3	AC_VI	Video
4	AC_VI	Video
5	AC_VI	Video
6	AC_VO	Voice
7	AC_VO	Voice

shown in Table 2, different kinds of applications such as background traffic, best-effort traffic, video traffic and voice traffic [13] can be mapped to different AC queues (i.e. AC_BK, AC_BE, AC_VI, AC_VO respectively). Every AC behaves as a single DCF contending entity and each entity has its own contention parameters ($CW_{max}[AC]$, $CW_{min}[AC]$, $AIFS[AC]$ and $TXOPLimit[AC]$) which are announced by the QAP periodically via beacon frames. Basically, the smaller values of $CW_{max}[AC]$, $CW_{min}[AC]$, $AIFS[AC]$ and $TXOPLimit[AC]$, the shorter channel access delay for the corresponding AC, and thus the higher priority to access the medium. Different from most station-based schemes which only use DIFS and PIFS for differentiation, EDCA introduces a new type of IFS, called arbitrary IFS (AIFS). Each AIFS is an IFS interval with arbitrary length (Figure 6) and is determined by

$$AIFS[AC] = SIFS + AIFSN[AC] \cdot slot\ time,$$

where $AIFSN[AC]$, called the arbitration inter frame space number, represents the number of *slot time* for an AC. For example, DCF uses $AIFSN = 2$ to compute DIFS (i.e. $DIFS = SIFS + 2 \cdot slot\ time$, see Figure 6). The default EDCA parameters used by QSTAs are suggested in Table 3 [12]. After waiting for an idle time interval of $AIFS[AC]$, each AC has to wait for a random backoff time ($CW_{min}[AC] \leq$ backoff time $\leq CW_{max}[AC]$). The purpose of using different contention parameters for different queues is to give low-priority traffic a longer backoff time than high-priority traffic. High-priority traffic is likely to access to the medium earlier than low-priority traffic. A potential problem is that the backoff times of different ACs overlap and reduce the effect of service differentiation. Furthermore, in EDCA, backoff timers of different ACs in one QSTA are random values and may reach zero at the same time, thus causing internal collisions. In order to avoid those internal collisions, EDCA introduces a scheduler inside every QSTA to allow only the highest priority AC to transmit a packet. As a result, EDCA aims to support prioritized QoS for multimedia applications.

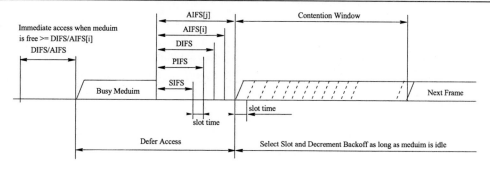

Figure 6: IEEE 802.11e interframe space (IFS) relationship [12]

Table 3: Default EDCA parameters

ACs	CW_{min}	CW_{max}	AIFSN	TXOPLimit (802.11b)	TXOPLimit (802.11a/g)
BK	CW_{min}	CW_{max}	7	0	0
BE	CW_{min}	CW_{max}	3	0	0
VI	$(CW_{min}+1)/2-1$	CW_{min}	2	6.016ms	3.008ms
VO	$(CW_{min}+1)/4-1$	$(CW_{min}+1)/2-1$	2	3.008ms	1.504ms

Adaptive EDCA (AEDCA) Schemes

While EDCA service differentiation is an important QoS enhancement for DCF, it is not enough to provide strict QoS support for delay-bounded multimedia applications. Moreover, EDCA is known to perform poorly during high channel load because of the excessively high contention rate [20, 23]. Based on the EDCA framework, several adaptive schemes [17, 23] have been proposed recently. In [23], after each successful transmission, the CWs of different ACs do not reset to CW_{min} as in EDCA. Instead, the CWs are updated according to the estimated channel collision rate which takes into account the varying traffic conditions. Furthermore, [17] proposes the adaptation of backoff timers according to the channel load rate, i.e. a backoff threshold is introduced upon which backoff timers are reduced exponentially fast. AEDCA computes the backoff threshold for each AC based on some analytical observations [17]. AEDCA can provide better QoS support for multimedia applications than EDCA in medium and high load cases. It achieves a high degree of fairness among applications of the same priority level.

4.2.2 PCF-Based Schemes

The HCCA Scheme

In order to provide strict and parameterized QoS support regardless the traffic conditions, the HCF controlled channel access (HCCA) mechanism has been proposed by the 802.11e working group. HCCA uses a poll-and-response mechanism similar to PCF, but there are many differences between the two mechanisms. For example, HCCA is more flexible than PCF, i.e., QAP can start HCCA during both CFP and CP where PCF is only allowed in CFP. In addition, HCCA solves the three main problems of PCF. (1) A direct link between peer stations is allowed in 802.11e, where stations can communicate each other without going through AP in HCCA. (2) An 802.11e QSTA is not allowed to transmit a packet if the frame transmission cannot be finished before the next beacon, which solves the beacon delay problem with PCF. (3) A *TXOPLimit* is used to bound the transmission time of a polled station. Figure 7 shows an example of an 802.11e beacon interval (the duration between two consecutive beacons), composed of alternated modes of optional CFP and mandatory CP. During CP, QAP is allowed to start several contention-free bursts, called controlled access period (*CAP*), at any time after detecting channel as being idle for a time interval of PIFS. As shown in Figure 6, PIFS is shorter than DIFS and AIFSs, which gives a QAP a higher probability to start HCCA at any instant during a CP than other contending QSTAs. HCCA is more flexible than PCF because the latter must occur periodically after a beacon frame, while a QAP can initiate an HCCA whenever it wishes. Even if PCF is still allowed in 802.11e [12], the flexibility of HCCA makes PCF useless. Thus, PCF is defined as optional in the 802.11e draft. After an optional period of CFP, the mechanisms of EDCA and HCCA which is used in CAP durations, alternate in a beacon interval (see Figure 7). Although HCCA can provide more strict QoS support than EDCA, the latter is still mandatory in 802.11e for supporting QoS specification exchange between QTSAs and QAP. For this purpose, the maximum duration of HCCA in an 802.11e beacon interval is bounded by a variable, $T_{CAPLimit}$.

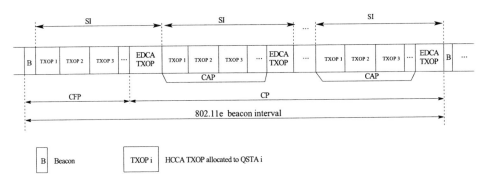

Figure 7: An example of 802.11e beacon interval used in HCF scheduling algorithm

A simple HCF scheduling algorithm is suggested as a reference design in the 802.11e specification [12], providing a parameterized QoS support based on the contract between QAP and corresponding QSTA(s). Before any data transmission, a traffic stream has first to be established and each QSTA is allowed to have no more than eight traffic streams with different priorities. Note that traffic streams and ACs are separated and use different MAC queues. In order to setup a traffic stream connection, a QSTA must send a QoS request frame containing the corresponding traffic specification (TSPEC) to the QAP[1]. A TSPEC describes the QoS parameter requirement of a traffic stream such as mean data rate, the maximum MAC service data unit (MSDU) size, the delay bound and the maximum Required Service Interval (RSI). The maximum RSI refers to the maximum time duration between the start of successive *TXOPs* that can be tolerated by the application. Intuitively, there is a link between maximum RSI and the delay bound for a given traffic stream. Consequently, the IEEE 802.11e draft suggests that if both the maximum RSI and the delay bound are specified by a QSTA, the HCF simple scheduler only uses the maximum RSI for the calculation of *TXOP* schedule. The simple 802.11e HCF scheduling algorithm is summarized as follows:

On receiving all these QoS requests, the QAP scheduler first determines the minimum value of all the maximum RSIs required by the different traffic streams. Second, it chooses the highest submultiple value of the 802.11e beacon interval duration as the selected service interval (SI), which is less than the minimum of all the maximum RSIs[2]. Third, the 802.11e beacon interval is cut into several SIs and QSTAs are polled accordingly during each selected SI. The selected SI refers to the time between the start of successive *TXOPs* allocated to a QSTA, which is the same for all the stations. As soon as the SI is determined, the QAP scheduler computes the different $TXOP$ values allocated to the different traffic streams for different QSTAs, which are $TXOP_1$, $TXOP_2$, etc., shown in the Figure 7. Suppose the mean data rate request of the applications from traffic stream j in the QSTA i is $\overline{\rho}_{i,j}$ and the nominal MSDU size for this queue is $M_{i,j}$, then the number of packets arriving in the traffic stream during the selected SI can be approximately computed as follows:

$$N_{i,j} = \lceil \frac{\overline{\rho}_{i,j} SI}{M_{i,j}} \rceil. \tag{1}$$

Thus the QAP scheduler computes the allocated *TXOP*, $T_{i,j}$ for the traffic stream j in QSTA i as follows:

$$T_{i,j} = max(\frac{N_{i,j} M_{i,j}}{R} + O, \frac{M_{max}}{R} + O), \tag{2}$$

where R is the PHY layer transmission rate and M_{max} is the maximum MSDU size (i.e. 2304 bytes). O refers to the transmission overheads due to PHY/MAC layer frame headers, IFSs, ACKs and poll frames. O is in time units and is computed as $2SIFS + T_{ACK}$ in this chapter.

Fourth, the QAP scheduler sums all the *TXOP* values of different traffic streams in a QSTA i as: $TXOP_i = \sum_{j=1}^{J_i} T_{i,j}$, where J_i is the number of active traffic streams in QSTA i. Then, the QAP scheduler allocates the time interval of $TXOP_i$ to QSTA i and allows the QSTA to transmit multiple frames during this time interval. In this way, the QAP scheduler

---

[1]This request frame is called an ADDTS QoS Action frame in [12].

[2]For example, if the beacon interval is $500ms$ and the three maximum RSI values are $150ms$, $275ms$ and $200ms$, the QAP scheduler will choose $125ms$ as selected SI, which is the highest submultiple of beacon interval ($500ms$) and is smaller than the minimum value of the three maximum RSIs, i.e. $150ms$ in this example.

is supposed to allocate the corresponding *TXOP* for transmitting all the arriving frames during the selected SI. Thus, the QAP scheduler is expected to control the delays.

An admission control algorithm is also suggested in the simple HCF scheduler: Using the above scheduling algorithm, the total fraction of transmission time reserved for HCCA of all *K* QSTAs in an 802.11e beacon interval can be computed as: $\sum_{i=1}^{K} \frac{TXOP_i}{SI}$. In order to decide whether or not a new request from a new traffic flow can be accepted in HCCA, the QAP scheduler only needs to check if the new request of $TXOP_{K+1}$ plus all the current *TXOP* allocations are lower than or equal to the maximum fraction of time that can be used by HCCA:

$$\frac{TXOP_{K+1}}{SI} + \sum_{i=1}^{K} \frac{TXOP_i}{SI} \leq \frac{T_{CAPLimit}}{T_{Beacon}}, \tag{3}$$

where $T_{CAPLimit}$ is the maximum duration bound of HCCA and T_{Beacon} represents the length of a beacon interval.

In Figure 7, each QSTA is polled once per SI according to the HCF scheduling algorithm. This scheduling algorithm assumes that all types of traffic are CBR, so the queue length increases linearly according to the constant application data rate. However, a lot of real-time applications, such as videoconferencing, have variable bit rate (VBR) characteristics. The simple HCCA scheduler may cause the average queue length to increase and may possibly drop packets. Even if the mean transmission rate of the application is lower than the rate specified in QoS requirements, peaks of transmission rate may not be absorbed by *TXOPs* allocated according to the QoS requirements. Some adaptive schemes that take into account fluctuation of traffic transmission rates are thus necessary. In the following sections, we describe two different schemes, FHCF and SETT-EDD which enhance the performance of the IEEE 802.11e scheduler.

The FHCF Scheme

FHCF [2] is composed of two schedulers: a QAP scheduler and a node scheduler. The QAP scheduler estimates the varying queue length of each traffic stream in every QSTA before the next SI. Considering that traffic is VBR and the estimation may be incorrect, the QAP scheduler uses an estimation of errors from the real queue length to adjust the prediction. Then the QAP scheduler compares the adjusted estimated queue length with the ideal queue length before allocating *TXOP* to a QSTA. Here, the ideal queue length refers to the queue size at the beginning of the next SI which is equal to zero at the end of the current *TXOP*. Actually, the HCF reference scheduling algorithm makes this assumption, but this is only valid when the transmission rate of the application is strictly CBR. Based on the difference between estimated and ideal queue lengths, the QAP scheduler of FHCF computes the value of additional time required to fit the variation of the traffic. When it is time for the QAP to poll a QSTA, the QAP scheduler computes the sum of all the required *TXOPs* of different traffic streams in the QSTA based on ideal queue length distribution and the additional time required to compensate the difference between estimated and ideal queue lengths. On the other hand, the node scheduler in each QSTA performs almost the same computation as the

QAP scheduler after receiving the *TXOP* allocation from the QAP, since each QSTA knows exactly its own traffic stream queue sizes before the transmission. Then it can redistribute the time allocation among its different traffic streams according to the new computation. Section §5 will show the performance comparisons between FHCF and HCF through the simulations.

The SETT-EDD Scheme

The SETT-EDD scheme [9] uses the same admission control algorithm rather than the one described in 802.11e [12]. It uses the delay bounded earliest due date (Delay-EDD) scheduling algorithm [6] which polls each queue in every QSTA. Furthermore, the SETT-EDD scheduler aims to consider the impact of bursty errors and link adaptation. Each QSTA selects an independent service interval (SI) and a token bucket of time units (or *TXOP timer*) is used. The *TXOP timer* of each QSTA increases at a constant rate corresponding to the total fraction of time the QSTA can spend in the HCCA *TXOP*. The *TXOP timer* is bounded by the $TXOPLimit$ value defined in 802.11e [12]. A QSTA can be polled only when the value of *TXOP* timer is greater than or equal to the minimum value of *TXOP*. This ensures the transmission of at least one frame using the minimum PHY data rate. The SETT-EDD improves the performance of the HCF scheduler by reducing the packet loss ratio and delay of video streams. In [9], it is also demonstrated that the widely-used two-states Markov chain model cannot capture the channel characteristics of 802.11 WLAN with link-adaptation implementations, because the station experiencing a bad channel (with a low signal to noise ratio) can still transmit and receive packets with a lower bit rate. There is a scalability problem in the SETT-EDD scheduler implementation because the QAP needs to calculate the deadline for each traffic stream in every QSTA. When the number of QSTAs increases, this scheduling algorithm becomes inefficient.

5   Simulation Analysis

We analyze several QoS enhancement schemes through *ns-2* simulations. Due to limited space, we only provide comparisons between AEDCA and EDCA, and between FHCF and HCF in this section.

5.1   AEDCA versus EDCA

We vary the channel load by increasing the number of active QSTAs, see Table 4. Each QSTA transmits three types of flows (audio, video, and data streams) to the same destination, QSTA0. We select 802.11a as PHY layer, the PHY data rate is set to 36 Mbps and other parameters for the three flows are shown in Table 5. Every simulation lasts 15 seconds. Most simulation results are averaged over 5 simulations with random flow starting time except that the fairness curves are averaged over 20 simulations.

Figure 8 shows that AEDCA improves significantly the total goodput of EDCA, mainly in high load situations (around 33% total goodput gain when the channel is fully loaded).

This is because AEDCA reduces the number of collisions a lot in both moderate and high
load rate cases as shown in Figure 8. Moreover, we observe in Figure 9 that AEDCA provides constant goodput for multimedia flows (both voice and video streams) whatever the
channel load while the goodput of video flow degrades in moderate load case with EDCA.
Figure 10 shows the latency distribution for different flows with AEDCA and EDCA for a
channel load equal to 80%. Recall that on a cumulative latency distribution plot, a perfect
result would coincide with the y-axis, representing 100% of packets with zero latency. Although a zero latency for all the packets is impossible in reality, the scheme that provides
an almost vertical line close to the y-axis will be the best one. We observe that AEDCA
delivers 90% of voice stream packets within $1.5ms$, 90% of video packets within $4ms$, and
90% of background packets within $1.7s$. While delays are much larger with EDCA, it can
transmit only about 41% of voice packets within $1.5ms$, 5.7% of video packets within $4ms$,
and 3% of background packets within $1.7s$. Improvements of delay performance come from
the fact that AEDCA obtains lower collision rate and less idle backoff time than EDCA.

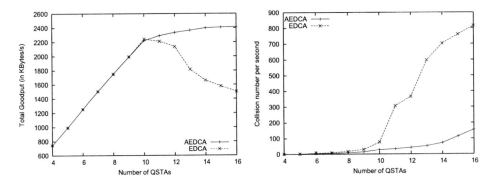

Figure 8: AEDCA versus EDCA: total goodput (left) and collision rate (right)

Table 4: Load rate versus number of QSTAs

Number of QSTAs	4	6	8	10	12	14	16
Load rate (%)	19	31	44	55	68	80	100

Table 5: Simulation parameters for the three ACs

	Audio	Video	Background
Transport protocol	UDP	UDP	UDP
AC	VO	VI	BE
CW_{min}	7	15	31
CW_{max}	15	31	1023
AIFSN	2	2	3
Packet Size	160 bytes	1280 bytes	1500 bytes
Packet Interval	20 ms	10 ms	12.5 ms
Flow Sending Rate	8 Kbytes/s	128 Kbytes/s	120 Kbytes/s

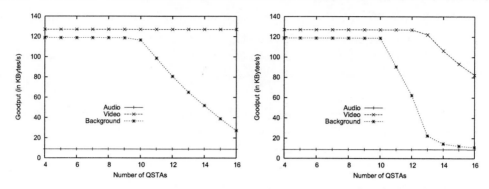

Figure 9: Goodput of different flows: AEDCA (left) versus EDCA (right)

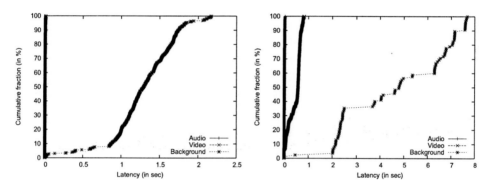

Figure 10: Latency distribution: AEDCA (left) versus EDCA (right)

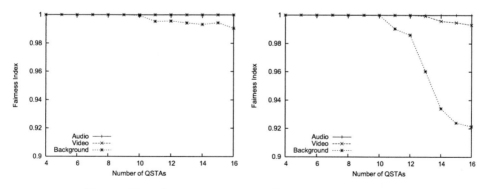

Figure 11: Fairness: AEDCA (left) versus EDCA (right)

While service differentiation and QoS support for multimedia applications are very important, fairness between applications with the the same priority is also an important issue in the design of 802.11 MAC protocols. In order to evaluate the fairness performance of AEDCA and EDCA, we choose the well-known Jain's fairness index [15]:

$$J = \frac{(\sum_{i=1}^{n} g_i)^2}{n \sum_{i=1}^{n} (g_i)^2},\qquad(4)$$

where n represents the total number of the flows with the same priority in a BSA, and g_i is the goodput of flow i. We recall that $J \leq 1$, and it is equal to 1 if all g_i are equal which corresponds to the highest degree of fairness between different stations. As shown in Figures 11, AEDCA is fairer than EDCA whatever the channel load and the type of traffic. The reason mainly comes from the fact that AEDCA performs the adaptive fast backoff algorithm, which resolves collisions efficiently and provides fair transmission opportunities for all the QSTAs.

5.2   FHCF versus HCF

FHCF has been implemented in *ns-2* simulator and source code is available at [3]. To evaluate the performance of both the QAP scheduler and the node scheduler, two kinds of simulation topologies are used. The first topology contains 18 mobile QSTAs and 1 fixed QAP with only one traffic stream per station (see Section 5.2.1), and aims to evaluate the performance of the QAP scheduler. The second topology is composed of 6 QSTAs and 1 QAP (see Section 5.2.2), which is used to evaluate the performance of the node scheduler. Each station has three traffic streams with different priorities.

5.2.1   Scenario 1

In Scenario 1, 6 QSTAs send highest priority on/off PCM audio streams ($64Kbps$), another 6 QSTAs send VBR video streams ($200Kbps$ in average) with medium priority and 6 QS-TAs send CBR MPEG4 video streams ($3.2Mbps$) with low priority. Table 6 and Table 7 summarize the main simulation parameters. All flows use UDP as transport layer protocol. PCM Audio flows are mapped to the 6th traffic stream of the MAC layer whereas VBR H.261 and CBR MPEG4 video flows are respectively mapped to the 5th and 4th traffic stream. The different VBR flows have been obtained with the VIC [19] videoconferencing tool using the H.261 coding and QCIF format for typical "head and shoulder" video sequences. The mean transmission rate of 6 traces is close to $200Kbps$ with a mean packet size of $660bytes$ and a mean interarrival time of $26ms$ [3]. A simple analysis of the trace files shows that the transmission rate distribution follows a Gaussian law and its mean value belongs to a window of $80Kbps$ around the mean value of $200Kbps$. The mean packet size varies between 600 and $700bytes$. Packet sizes of these flows belong to a large range of values between 20 and 1024 bytes.

Figure 12 shows that with FHCF, the maximum latency of all flows is bounded by the selected SI from all traffic streams (chosen equal to $50ms$). Whereas for HCF, some flows may not meet their QoS requirements. For example, the delays of the VBR flows are completely uncontrolled (see Figure 12) because the queue lengths increase dramatically

Table 6: Description of different traffic streams

Node	Application	Arrival period (ms)	Packet size (bytes)	Sending rate (Kbps)
$1 \rightarrow 6$	PCM Audio	4.7	160	64
$7 \rightarrow 12$	VBR video	$\simeq 26$	$\simeq 660$	$\simeq 200$
$13 \rightarrow 18$	MPEG4 video	2	800	3200

Table 7: PHY and MAC layer parameters

SIFS	$16\mu s$
DIFS	$34\mu s$
ACK size	$14bytes$
PHY rate	$36Mbps$
Minimum Badwidth	$6Mbps$
SlotTime	$9\mu s$
CCA Time	$4\mu s$
MAC header	$38bytes$
PLCP header length	$4bits$
Preamble length	$20bits$

during some time period. Note that the maximum delay of HCF can be controlled if *TXOPs* are allocated according to the maximum transmission rate of the VBR flows. In this case, fewer flows with HCF than with FHCF can be accepted in HCCA.

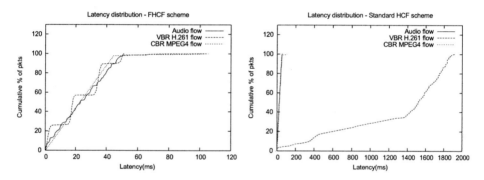

Figure 12: Latency distribution for FHCF and standard HCF

Figure 13 shows the fairness comparison between FHCF and HCF when the HCCA load rate is modified by increasing the transmission rate of the CBR MPEG4 traffic. The Jain's fairness index [15] is also used to compare fairness for different schemes between the same kinds of traffic:

$$J = \frac{(\sum_{i=1}^{n} d_i)^2}{n \sum_{i=1}^{n} d_i^2}$$

where d_i is the mean delay of the flow i and n is the number of flows with the same priority.

For both VBR and CBR video flows, FHCF is much fairer than HCF since the QAP scheduler of FHCF can estimate the varying queue length and allocate the *TXOP* fairly between different flows.

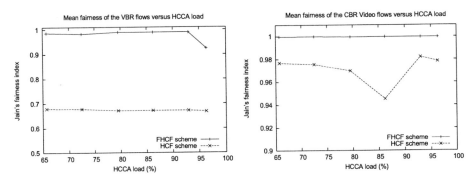

Figure 13: Fairness versus load for FHCF and standard HCF

5.2.2   Scenario 2

In Scenario 2 (see Table 8), each QSTA sends on/off PCM audio, VBR video (H.261), and CBR video (MPEG4) flows simultaneously through three traffic streams with different priorities. The HCCA load rate has been changed by increasing the packet size of the CBR MPEG4 flow from $600bytes$ ($2.4Mbps$) to $1000bytes$ ($4Mbps$) using a $100bytes$ increment and keeping the same inter-arrival period of $2ms$.

Figures 14 and 15 show respectively the mean delays and the fairness of several types of flows obtained with the various schemes for different loads of the network (see Table 8).

Table 8: Description of different traffic streams

Node	Application	Arrival period (ms)	Packet size $(bytes)$	Sending rate $(Kbps)$
$1 \rightarrow 6$	Audio	4.7	160	64
$1 \rightarrow 6$	VBR video	$\simeq 26$	$\simeq 660$	$\simeq 200$
$1 \rightarrow 6$	CBR video	2	$600 \rightarrow 1000$	$2400 \rightarrow 4000$

Audio and VBR H.261 Video Flows

Figure 14 shows that with FHCF, delay curves are almost horizontal lines which means that delays do not strongly depend on the network load. For the same reason as in Scenario 1, the delays of VBR flows sent using the standard HCF scheme are very high (the mean delays for the VBR flows are almost $300ms$).

As shown in Figure 15, Jain's fairness index between audio flows obtained with HCF and FHCF, is very high. The reason is that both of them allocate excessive *TXOPs* to these audio flows. Concerning VBR flows, FHCF is always fairer than HCF.

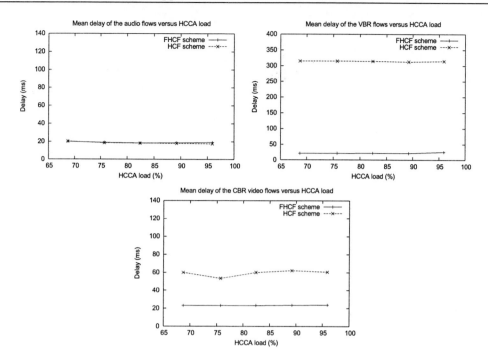

Figure 14: Mean delays versus load

CBR MPEG4 Video Flows

Figure 14 shows that the mean delays of both FHCF and HCF are not affected by the traffic load, while the delay of FHCF is smaller than that of HCF. As seen in Figure 15, we observe that FHCF is fair between the different CBR flows on a large range of loads since node schedulers succeed in redistributing time among the different traffic streams up to a very high network load (96%). However, with HCF fairness performance is poor since the schedulers are not able to absorb traffic fluctuations.

6   Conclusion

In this chapter we describe the QoS issues at the IEEE 802.11 MAC layer. We summarize different QoS-enhanced techniques proposed for 802.11 WLAN, including the upcoming IEEE QoS-enhanced standard, 802.11e. We also provide different criteria to classify different enhanced schemes. The performance evaluations of some QoS-enhancement schemes (including 802.11e) are conducted through computer simulations. The simulation results show that the upcoming 802.11e standard can offer certain QoS support, but it cannot provide good quality for real-time multimedia applications in some cases. Adaptive schemes are shown to perform well and need to be investigated further in future work. Moreover, good 802.11e analytical models and real testbed experiments are required to optimize the performance of 802.11e networks.

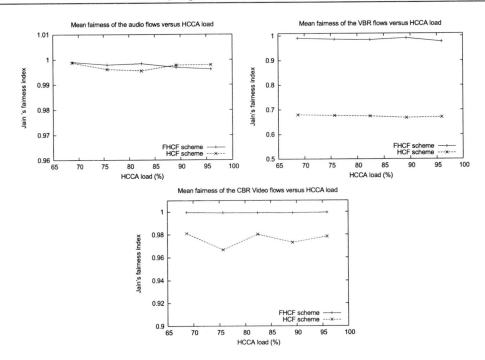

Figure 15: Fairness versus load

Acknowledgments

The authors would like to thank Prof. Torsten Braun (from University of Bern), Mr. Mathieu Lacage and Dr. Wen-Shin Lee (from INRIA) for reading the draft of this chapter and providing helpful comments.

References

[1] I. AAD, AND C. CASTELLUCCIA, *Differentiation mechanisms for IEEE 802.11*, Proc. of IEEE Infocom, Anchorage, Alaska, USA, April 2001, pp. 209-218.

[2] P. ANSEL, Q. NI, AND T. TURLETTI, *An efficient scheduling scheme for IEEE 802.11e*. Proc. of WiOpt (Modeling and Optimization in Mobile, Ad Hoc and Wireless Networks), Cambridge, UK, March 24-26, 2004.

[3] P. ANSEL, Q. NI, AND T. TURLETTI, *FHCF: A fair scheduling scheme for 802.11e WLAN*. INRIA Research Report No 4883, July 2003. Implementation and simulations available from *"http://www-sop.inria.fr/planete/qni/fhcf/"*.

[4] J. DENG, AND R. S. CHANG, *A priority scheme for IEEE 802.11 DCF access method*, IEICE Trans. in Com. 1999, pp. 96-102.

[5] D. A. ECKHARDT, AND P. STEENKISTE, *Effort-Limited Fair (ELF) scheduling for wireless networks*, Proc. of Infocom 2000.

[6] D. FERRARI, D. VERMA, *A scheme for real-time channel establishment in wide-area networks*, IEEE JSAC, Vol. 8, No. 3, April 1990, pp. 368-379.

[7] A. GANZ, A. PHONPHOEM, AND Z. GANZ, *Robust superpoll with chaining protocol for IEEE 802.11 wireless LANs in support of multimedia applications*, Wireless Networks 2001, pp. 65-73.

[8] S. J. GOLESTANI, *A self-clocked fair queueing scheme for broadband applications*, Proc. of Infocom 1994.

[9] A. GRILO, M. MACEDO, M. NUNES, *A scheduling algorithm for Qos support in IEEE802.11E Networks*. IEEE Wireless Communications Magazine, Vol.10, No.3, June 2003, pp. 36-43.

[10] IEEE 802.11 WG, *International Standard [for] Information Technology - Telecommunications and information exchange between systems-Local and metropolitan area networks-Specific Requirements - Part 11:Wireless LAN Medium Access Control (MAC) and Physical Layer (PHY) specifications, Reference number ISO/IEC 8802-11:1999(E)*, 1999.

[11] IEEE WG, *802.11a, Part 11: Wireless LAN Medium Access Control (MAC) and Physical Layer (PHY) Specifications: High-speed Physical Layer in the 5Ghz Band*, September 1999.

[12] IEEE 802.11 WG, *Draft Supplement to STANDARD FOR Telecommunications and Information Exchange Between Systems-LAN/MAN Specific Requirements - Part 11: Wireless Medium Access Control (MAC) and Physical Layer (PHY) specifications: Medium Access Control (MAC) Enhancements for Quality of Service (QoS)*, IEEE 802.11e/Draft 5.0, July 2003.

[13] IEEE 802.11 WG, *IEEE 802.11d, Part 3: MAC bridges, ANSI/IEEE Std. 802.1D*, 1998 edition, 1998.

[14] ITU-T RECOMMENDATION H.261, *Video codec for audiovisual services at $p \times 64$ kb/s*. 1993.

[15] R. JAIN, *The art of computer systems performance analysis*. John Wiley & Sons, 1991.

[16] A. LINDGREN, A. ALMQUIST, AND O. SCHELEN, *Evaluation of quality of service schemes for IEEE 802.11 wireless LANs*, Proc. of the 26th Annual IEEE Conference on Local Computer Networks, Florida, USA, November 15-16, 2001, pp. 348-351.

[17] M. MALLI, Q. NI, T. TURLETTI, AND C. BARAKAT. *Adaptive fair channel allocation for QoS enhancement in IEEE 802.11 wireless LANs*. IEEE ICC 2004 (International Conference on Communications), Paris, June 20-24, 2004.

[18] S. MANGOLD, S. CHOI, P. MAY, O. KLEIN, G. HIERTZ, AND L. STIBOR, *IEEE 802.11e wireless LAN for quality of service*, Proc. of European Wireless, Florence, Italy, February 2002.

[19] S. MCCANNE, V. JACOBSON, *Vic: a flexible framework for packet video*. ACM Multimedia, 1995.

[20] Q. NI, L. ROMDHANI, AND T. TURLETTI, *A survey of QoS enhancements for IEEE 802.11 wireless LAN*, Journal of Wireless and Mobile Computing, John Wiley & Sons Publisher, Vol. 4, Issue 5 August 2004, pp. 547-566.

[21] D. D. PERKINS, AND H. D. HUGHES, *A survey on quality-of-service support for mobile ad hoc networks*, Journal of Wireless Communications and Mobile Computing 2002, pp. 503-513.

[22] NS-2 SIMULATOR, *http://www.isi.edu/nsnam/ns/*.

[23] L. ROMDHANI, Q. NI, AND T. TURLETTI, *Adaptive EDCF: enhanced service differentiation for IEEE 802.11 wireless ad hoc networks*, Wireless Communications and Networking Conference, New Orleans, Louisiana, USA, March 16-20, 2003.

[24] J. L. SOBRINHO, AND A. S. KRISHNAKUMAR, *Real-time traffic over the IEEE 802.11 medium access control layer*, Bell Labs Technical Journal 1996, pp. 172-187.

[25] N. H. VAIDYA, P. BAHL, AND S. GUPA, *Distributed fair scheduling in a wireless LAN*, Proc. of the Sixth Annual International Conference on Mobile Computing and Networking, Boston, USA, August 2000, pp. 167-178.

[26] A. VERES, A. T. CAMPBELL, M. BARRY, AND L. H. SUN, *Supporting service differentiation in wireless packet networks using distributed control*, IEEE JSAC, Special Issue on Mobility and Resource Management in Next-Generation Wireless Systems 2001, pp. 2094-2104.

[27] M. A. VISSER, AND M. E. ZARKI, *Voice and data transmission over an 802.11 wireless network*, Proc. of PIMRC, Toronto, Canada, September 1995.

[28] J. Y. YEH AND C. CHEN, *Support of multimedia services with the IEEE 802.11 MAC protocol*, Proc. of IEEE ICC, May 2002, pp. 600-604.

In: Wireless LANs and Bluetooth
Editors: Yang Xiao and Yi Pan, pp. 51-76

ISBN 1-59454-432-8
©2005 Nova Science Publishers, Inc.

Chapter 3

PERFORMANCE LIMITATIONS OF IEEE 802.11 NETWORKS AND POTENTIAL ENHANCEMENTS

Fabrizio Granelli, *Dzmitry Kliazovich*[†]
DIT - Univ. of Trento, Via Sommarive 14,
I-38050, Trento (ITALY)
Nelson L. S. da Fonseca[‡]
Institute of Computing, State University of Campinas,
Av. Albert Einstein 1251, Campinas, SP (BRASIL)

Abstract

The IEEE 802.11 standard is a significant milestone in the provisioning of network connectivity for mobile users. However, due to the time-variant characteristics of wireless links, interference from other devices and terminal mobility, 802.11-based WLANs suffer from performance drawbacks in relation to wired networks. This chapter surveys the performance issues related to throughput and delay in 802.11 networks and describes proposals to overcome such shortcomings.

Keywords: IIEEE 802.11, WLAN, Performance Evaluation, TCP over Wireless

1 Introduction

Wireless networks are becoming increasingly popular in tele-communications, especially for the provisioning of mobile access to wired network services. As a consequence, efforts have been devoted to the provisioning of reliable data delivery for a wide variety of applications over different wireless infrastructures. In wireless network, regardless of the location, users can access services available to wired-network users.

---

[*]E-mail address: granelli@ing.unitn.it
[†]E-mail address: klezovic@dit.unitn.it
[‡]E-mail address: nfonseca@ic.unicamp.br

In this scenario, the IEEE 802.11 standards represent a significant milestone in the provisioning of network connectivity for mobile users. However, the 802.11 medium access control strategy and physical variability of the transmission medium leads to limitations in terms of bandwidth, latency, information loss, and mobility. Moreover, the deployment of the Transmission Control Protocol (TCP) over IEEE 802.11 networks is constrained by the low reliability of the channel, node mobility and long Round Trip Times (RTTs).

This chapter aims at providing a comprehensive analysis of the performance limitations and potential enhancements to 802.11 networks. Proposals to overcome such limitations are compared and their suitability for specific deployment scenarios is presented.

The structure of this chapter is as following: Section 2 provides an overview of the IEEE 802.11 standards and its extensions. Section 3 surveys the performance issues related to throughput and delay in 802.11 networks. Section 4 introduces existing proposals to overcome those problems. Sections 5 and 6 provide comparisons of the different solutions. Finally, Section 7 draws some conclusions.

2   The 802.11 Standards

The IEEE 802.11 Wireless Local Area Network (WLAN) standards were first adopted in 1997 and revised in 1999 [1]. It aims at "providing wireless connectivity to automatic machinery, equipment or stations that require rapid deployment, which may be portable or hand-held, or which may be mounted on moving vehicles within a local area" [1]. The IEEE 802.11 specification provides "wireless standards that specify an "over-the-air" interface between a wireless client and a base station or access point, as well as among wireless clients" [2].

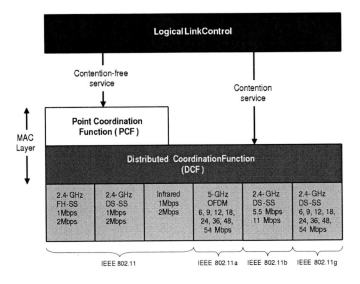

Figure 1: Overview of the IEEE 802.11 Protocol Stack.

Figure 1 presents an overview of the IEEE 802.11 protocol stack. The standards specify the Medium Access Control (MAC) sublayer, the MAC management protocol and services as well as different physical layers (PHY). A key issue is transparency. Above the MAC layer, 802.11 appears as any other 802.x LAN and offers similar services. The protocols are specified for communicating stations with and without the support of a specific infrastructure (Infrastructure Mode and Ad Hoc Mode, respectively). Furthermore, the standards describe the procedures for preserving privacy of user information.

The MAC protocol provides two medium access methods: Distributed Coordination Function (DCF) and Point Coordination Function (PCF). The DCF is a contention protocol based on the Carrier Sense Multiple Access Protocol (CSMA), known as CSMA/CA, with CA standing for collision avoidance. It also uses small RTS/CTS (Request To Send / Clear To Send) packets to reserve the medium in order to avoid collisions due to problems involving a hidden terminal. The exchange of such control messages allows all the terminals within the receiving range of both the source and the destination terminals to defer transmission in order to allow successful delivery of a data frame.

Figure 2 illustrates the RTS/CTS mechanism. The Network Allocation Vector, NAV, represents the duration stations sensing RTS/CTS signals which have to leave the medium idle to allow successful delivery of both a data frame and the corresponding acknowledgement. When the traffic of a station is backlogged, Request-To-Send messages are sent to notify the other stations that it wants to transmit a packet to a specific receiver. The receiver then notifies the sender that it can transmit by sending a Clear-To-Send message. No other stations transmit any packet in a period corresponding to the transmission time of the packet to be sent.

The small size of RTS/CTS control frames makes the probability of collision during their transmission lower than that of the collision of data frames, since these frames are usually larger than those involving RTS/CTS frames.

The joint usage of DCF and PCF presents obvious advantages in BSS infrastructure when the Base Station (BS) coordinates access to the wireless medium. However, experimental evidence shows that the performance of the PCF tends to be poor under certain conditions, such as during the simultaneous transmission of multimedia streams and best effort traffic [36].

The hierarchy of the IEEE 802.11 standards for wireless local area networks is presented in Fig. 3. Three physical layers are defined by these standards:

- Infra Red (IR), which supports bitrates of 1 or 2 Mbps;

- Frequency Hopping Spread Spectrum (FHSS), operating at 2.4 GHz, which supports bitrates of 1 or 2 Mbps;

- Direct Sequence Spread Spectrum (DSSS), operating at 2.4 GHz, which supports bitrates 1 or 2 Mbps.

In order to improve the wireless channel capacity, physical layer extensions to the original IEEE 802.11 standard have been proposed.

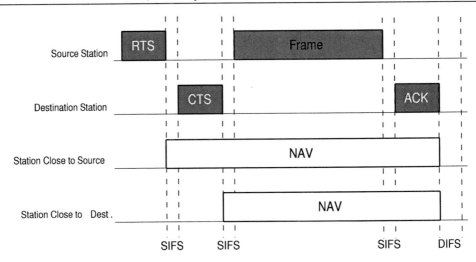

Figure 2: 802.11 RTS/CTS mechanism.

The IEEE 802.11a extension adopts Orthogonal Frequency Division Multiplexing (OFDM) and works in the 5 GHz band to provide PHY data rates ranging from 6 Mbps up to 54 Mbps.

The IEEE 802.11b extension, a High Data Rate Extension, is the most frequently used nowadays. It defines requirements for the extension of the DSSS at 2.4 GHz to achieve data rates of 5.5 Mbps and 11 Mbps. An important feature of this extension is a rate shift mechanism which makes it possible for high data rate networks to slow the rate down to 1 or 2 Mbps.

The IEEE 802.11g extension is similar to the 802.11a extension and specifies a physical layer for wireless LANs in both 2.4 GHz and 5 GHz bands, with a maximum rate of 54 Mbps. Such a rate is achieved by using OFDM. This provides backward compatibility with the 802.11b extension, but is not compatible with the 802.11a extension. The drawbacks involve the complexities of implementation since the latter involves a less complex implementation. This backward compatibility in the 802.11g extension can be considered as a disadvantage, since an Access Point (AP) running at the high data rate of 802.11g will switch down to the 802.11b rate upon the logging of any 802.11b device, thus reducing the transmission rate of all other devices in a cell [41].

The IEEE 802.11e protocol is an extension of the original MAC protocol aimed at providing Quality of Service (QoS) support for a variety of multimedia services over 802.11a, 802.11b and 802.11g physical layer specifications. In this extension, classes for service differentiation are defined. It introduces certain enhancements of the basic functions of the MAC operation: Enhanced DCF (EDCA) and the Hybrid Coordination Function (HCF), which operate in Contention and Contention Free periods, respectively.

The IEEE 802.11n task group was created at the end of 2003. The purpose of this group is to develop an extension of the IEEE 802.11 standards that produces a throughput greater

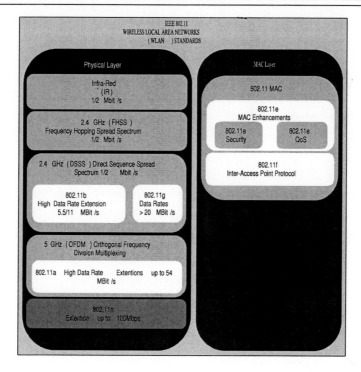

Figure 3: IEEE Wireless Local Area Network (WLAN) standards.

than 100Mbps. For this extension, throughput will be measured in the region between the 802.11 MAC and higher layers rather than at the physical layer. This measurement procedure should reveal the real throughput available for applications. A discussion of the differences between the actual data rate available for an application and that reported by standard specifications is presented in the next section. According to the estimated schedule of the 802.11n task group the publication of the standards release is expected for October 2005.

For additional details about IEEE 802.11 extensions, the reader is referred to the website of the IEEE 802.11 Working Group [3].

3   Performance Bounds and Limitations

Although the IEEE 802.11 standards provide mobile broadband access to the Internet, it suffers significant performance limitations. This section provides an overview of these drawbacks, both from the theoretical as well as from the implementational point-of-view.

The performance of the IEEE 802.11 standards depend on both throughput and delay considerations when the CSMA/CA (with the RTS/CTS mechanism) is employed. Actually, the main goal of the proposed mechanisms is the provision of both high throughput on the wireless channel and low delay in packet delivery.

The most relevant issues are discussed next:

- *Bandwidth* – The IEEE 802.11 standards specify the rates available for data transmission at the physical layer. The total link capacity is shared by all nodes which can operate within transmission range, including hidden terminals. Since collisions dramatically decrease the throughput, it is desirable to have knowledge of the total available bandwidth. Thus, various predictive algorithms have been proposed for that [33].

   Moreover, the IEEE 802.11 standards have certain theoretical limitations, due to the MAC policy, and these cannot be eliminated by simply raising the channel capacity. In [4], these limitations are identified as the Throughput Upper Limit (TUL) and the Delay Lower Limit (DLL).

- *Latency* – Latency in a wireless medium is greater than in a wired one. The factors that influence latency are propagation delay, overhead added by both physical layer and link layer protocols and the retransmission policy implemented at the link layer.

- *Channel losses* – Wireless channels suffer from fading caused by interference with other sources. While the Bit Error Rate (BER) varies from 10^{-6} to 10^{-8} in wired channels, it varies from 10^{-3} to 10^{-1} in wireless channels [7]. The typical scheme used to recover from losses is the link layer ARQ (Automatic Response reQuest).

- *Mobility* – The most common network setting is the infrastructured BSS connected to a fixed network via a Base Station (BS). Handoff (Switching between these BSs) require that all the information associated with user activities be transferred from BS to the next to prevent the termination of service provided to the mobile user.

- *TCP* – The problems that arise in the usage of TCP over wireless networks are due to their low reliability, as well as time-variant characteristics such as fading, shadowing, node mobility, hand-offs, limited available bandwidth and large RTTs. TCP performs poorly in such environments [10], [39] since they were originally designed for use on wired networks, which are characterized by stable links in which packet losses are mainly limited to congestion.

The IEEE 802.11 standards specify different rates for data transmission, ranging from 2 Mbps to 54 Mbps. However, a relatively large portion of the channel capacity is wasted due to the high overhead required for the transmission of data frames on the wireless channel. Each message coming from the application layer needs to be encapsulated into lower layer Protocol Data Unit (PDU) in order to be transmitted on the physical layer. Figure 4 provides a graphical representation of the process of packet encapsulation when TCP is used.

Most overhead due to packet encapsulation is related to the PLCP Preamble, which is necessary for the synchronization of the wireless receiver. This preamble, as well as the PLCP header, are transmitted at basic rate - regardless of the actual link speed. This makes it possible to operate at different speeds, since the information about the rate of

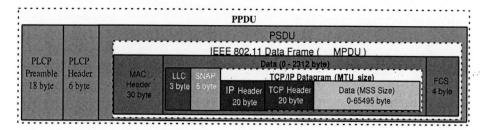

Figure 4: Packet encapsulation in TCP over 802.11 networks.[11]
Legend:
FCS = Frame Check Sequence
MSS = Maximum Segment Size
MTU = Maximum Transmission Unit
SNAP = SubNetwork Access Protocol
LLC = Logical Link Control
MPDU = MAC Protocol Data Unit
PLCP = Physical Layer Convergence Protocol
PSDU = PLCP Service Data Unit (SDU)
PPDU = PLCP Protocol Data Unit (PLCP + MPDU)

the remaining portion of the PPDU is included in the PLCP header. The PLCP preamble and header always take 192 microseconds (for 802.11b), regardless of the actual bitrate of the channel. An optional part of the 802.11 standards specifies the possibility of using a reduced, shorter preamble to decrease this overhead.

Table 1: Throughput Efficiency of 802.11 with long and short PLCP Preambles.

Link speed, Mbps	Long Preamble (18 bytes)		Short preamble (9 bytes)	
	TCP Throughput, Mbps	Efficiency, %	TCP Throughput, Mbps	Efficiency, %
1	0.75	74.9	0.77	76.9
2	1.41	70.7	1.49	74.3
5.5	3.38	61.5	3.83	69.6
11	5.32	48.4	6.52	59.3

Table 1 displays the maximum throughput obtained under the hypotheses of non-occurence of collisions, no fragmentation and no sending of RTS/CTS frames [11] (for a frame size of 1500 bytes, which is the maximum transfer unit (MTU) commonly allowed in Ethernet networks). A high percentage of the wireless link capacity is clearly wasted in transmitting supplementary information, which recudes the bandwidth available for data transmission to a level well below the reported capacity. For the widely used IEEE

802.11b extension, which operates at a rate of 11Mbps and employs a long PLCP preamble, the throughput is reduced to less than half of the reported capacity. This value may be further decreased by exponential backoff and RTS/CTS mechanisms.

4 Available Enhancement Schemes

Various approaches have been proposed to optimize the performance of IEEE 802.11 wireless networks. These can be broadly categorized into three groups:

- *Link Layer solutions* – The principle of this approach is to solve problems locally, with the transport layer not being made aware of the characteristics of the individual links. Such protocols attempt to hide losses in the wireless link to make it appear to be a highly reliable one. Link layer solutions require no changes in existing transport layer protocols.

- *Transport Layer solutions* – The theory underlying this approach is the modification of the transport protocol in order to achieve high throughput on wireless links. Since some packets may be lost, the modified transport protocol should implement congestion control as a reaction to packet losses, moreover, other schemes should be implemented to consider the peculiarities of the wireless environment.

- *Cross-Layer solutions* – Cross-layer solutions break the principles of layering by allowing interdependence and joint development of protocols involving various differents layers of the protocol stack.

A graphical representation of this classification is presented in Fig. 5.

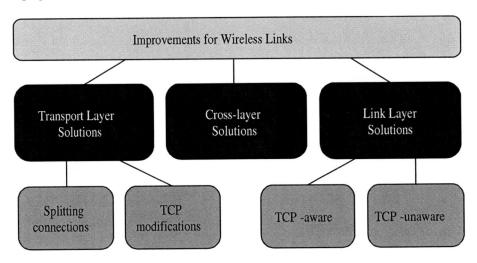

Figure 5: Graphical classification of possible improvements for 802.11 wireless networks.

4.1   Link Layer Solutions

TCP was originally designed and optimized for wired networks and, the performance problems related to its use and involve in the nature and characteristics of the wireless medium, as such. Hence, attempts to make wireless links resemble wired ones for high-level protocols are reflected in various approaches. The proposed solutions for the link layer can be classified into two groups on the basis of the awareness of the transport layer protocol. TCP-unaware protocols optimize the link layer by hiding existing differences between the wireless medium and the transport layer so that the transport layer can operate as if it were installed in a wired network. This method does not violate the modularity of the protocol stack, however, since the necessary adaptations improve the reliability independent of higher-layer protocols. Nonetheless, this lack of awareness can affect performance under certain specific conditions. For instance, a link layer retransmission technique may trigger a considerable number of TCP time outs, greatly decreasing the throughput of TCP. TCP-aware link layer solutions attempt to prevent unnecessary changes in the behavior of the transport protocol.

4.1.1   TCP-aware Link Layer Protocols

The TCP-aware link layer protocol presents certain advantages since knowledge of the protocol operating at the transport level allows fine tuning of the performance. For instance, an approach without awareness of the transport protocol may cause local link layer retransmission of a packet, as well as duplicate acknowledgement, since retransmissions can be performed on both layers.

Snoop Protocol   Snoop protocol [12] is used to handle connections in which most of the data are transferred from the Fixed Host (FH) to the Mobile Host (MH) (see Fig. 6). The mobile node runs a snoop protocol while snoop agents are located at the base station, which is the most common place for bridging the wired and wireless parts of a network. Snoop agents are implemented in the routing module of the protocol stack of the base station in order to allow inspection of the packet headers. These snoop agents maintain caches of TCP packets that have not yet been acknowledged by the MH. In case of duplication of FH packets, the cache is updated without sending further packets to the MH. Retransmission of cached packets is based on the reception of duplicate acknowledgements from the mobile node. Upon successful retransmission, duplicate acknowledgements are dropped at the Base Station (BS) to avoid the execution of the TCP fast retransmission mechanism.

A negative acknowledgement scheme has been added to improve the error recovery mechanism in case most of the data are sent from the MH to the wired network. In this way, the BS keeps track of all packets lost in any window and generates negative acknowledgements to the MH. These negative acknowledgements are typically based on the Selective Acknowledgement (SACK) option of the TCP [22].

The main disadvantages of Snoop protocols [13] are:

- Required changes in the base station protocol stack, demanding base station resources;

- No consideration of packet loss and delay during handoff;

- Failure in Snoop operation for encrypted traffic when there is no access to the packet header. The only possibility for handling encrypted traffic is to have part of the TCP header unencrypted, which is not feasible according to existing IP SEC standards specifications [37].

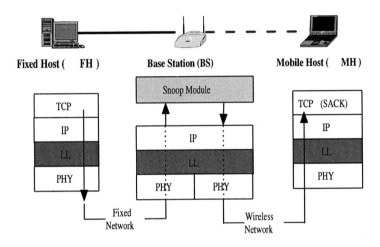

Figure 6: Snoop protocol scenario.

WTCP   WTCP [6] performs local retransmission on the wireless link between the base station and the mobile node without the need for modification of TCP for the fixed nodes. WTCP running on a base station buffers all unacknowledged packets coming from a fixed sender, maintaining its own flow control over the wireless link. When an arriving segment is the next expected one, it is stored in the WTCP buffer along with information about its arrival time. The sequence number of the next expected packet is then increased by the number of bytes included in the received segment. When a duplicate packet is received, it is dropped, since it has either been delivered to the wireless host or has already been buffered.

WTCP maintains the state of the information about the wireless part of the connection, such as the transmission window, sequence number of the last acknowledgement received from mobile hosts, and sequence number of the last segment sent to a mobile host.

Inaccurate Round Trip Time (RTT) estimation at the sender can lead to unnecessary retransmissions triggered by timeouts, since the sender writes the time stamp of the generation of the segment and the receiver echoes it back without any modification. If the segment is retransmitted, this RTT estimation may be affected. To avoid this, in WTCP the timestamp of the packet is incremented by the length of time the packet spent in the BS buffer. With this mechanism, the WTCP conceals the existence of wireless link errors and the difference in round trip time (RTT) from the FH sender, thus avoiding timeouts caused by local retransmissions.

WTCP does not change the basic end-to-end TCP semantics, since acknowledgements to the fixed node are generated only after a successful packet delivery to the mobile node.

4.1.2 TCP-unaware Link Layer Protocols

In early studies, enhanced link layer performance was achieved by the implementation of error correction techniques such as forward error correction (FEC) or the implementation of various Automatic Repeat ReQuest (ARQ) schemes for the retransmission of lost packets at the link layer. The combined implementation of these two techniques is considered in the AIRMAIL protocol.

AIRMAIL   Asymmetric Reliable Mobile Access In Link Layer [14] is a protocol designed for both indoor and outdoor wireless networks. The combined usage of FEC and local retransmissions provided by ARQ aims at obtaining enhanced end-to-end throughput and latency by correcting errors in an unreliable wireless channel, as well as on an end-to-end basis. The asymmetry in the design of the protocol reduces the processing load at the mobile node, since mobile terminals involve limited power and fewer computational resources than do base stations. The key idea in the asymmetric protocol design approach consists of empowering the base station with a certain degree of intelligence. The mobile terminal is required to combine several acknowledgements into a single acknowledgement to conserve power. The BS is required to send periodic status messages, making the acknowledgement from the mobile terminal event-driven. FEC implemented in AIRMAIL incorporates three levels of channel coding with adaptive interaction. The coding overhead is adaptively changed so that bandwidth expansion from forward error correction is minimized. However, sending large packets of data through the wireless link to save power results in reduced error correction possibilities for the TCP [15].

TULIP   Transport Unaware Link Improvement Protocol [15] is designed for half-duplex radio links. The TULIP provides a reliable link for higher layer protocols. It is service-aware, i.e. it provides reliable service for TCP data traffic, although it is unreliable for UDP traffic. On the receiver side, this protocol buffers packets, passing only in-order packets to the upper-layer and thus preventing the recept of duplicate acknowledgements (by the TCP). Another important feature implemented in the TULIP is the local link layer retransmission of lost packets, which effectively prevent retransmissions over the entire path.

Delayed Duplicate Acknowledgements (DDA)   DDA involve an attempt to approximate the behavior of Snoop protocols. The BS implements a local link layer retransmission scheme for packets lost on wireless links. Such retransmissions are triggered by link layer acknowledgements, rather than by the TCP-duplicated acknowledgements of the Snoop protocol scheme. As specified in [16], each TCP data packet, as well as ACKs, are encapsulated into a single link layer data packet, with its successful reception acknowledged by the link layer ACK. This ACK contains the sequence number of the link layer packet received, which is independent of the TCP sequence number. Although it maintains sequence numbers at the link layer, DDA does not attempt in-order delivery of the TCP data packets. This is differente from what happens with the Snoop protocol, for which duplicate acknowledgements are not dropped immediately but rather delayed a certain length of time. At the same time, the packet lost previously is retransmitted locally at the link layer. Upon the reception of an ACK, all delayed acknowledgements are dropped. If the retransmission is not successful and the time for which duplicate acknowledgements are delayed has expired, they will be released in the direction of the TCP sender to trigger retransmission at the TCP level. DDA provides results equivalent to those produced by the Snoop protocol, although the technique does not perform well on slow wireless links [16].

DAWL   Delayed-ACK Scheme on Wireless Link (DAWL) [17], [18] is a technique designed for the enhancement of link layer performance. It modifies the standard IEEE 802.11 MAC Stop & Wait ARQ by implementing the technique of native TCP delayed acknowledgement. The main idea is the lack of a need for immediate acknowledgement of packet receipt. DAWL assumes the existence of data in transit in the opposite direction. The possibility of encapsulating acknowledgements into data packets at the link level leads to the reduction of the traffic load in the wireless link. Moreover, DAWL implements a negative acknowledgement scheme for fast retransmission of lost packets.

Like the Delayed-ACK option of TCP, DAWL provides certain advantages in the presence of bi-directional traffic over wireless links. DAWL implementation requires a set of timers, which must be carefully tuned in order to optimize throughput, together with delay insertion for a packet delivery. Although this approach provides advantages for operation on a single-hop wireless link, it is also problematic due to the:

- Difficulty in tuning timer values in the multi-hop environment;

- The insertion of delay in packet acknowledgements;

- Increased buffer requirements at all wireless node, and

- Poor performance for links with high error rates.

4.2   Transport Layer Solutions

As mentioned above, TCP was originally designed for wired networks, where packet losses are caused mostly to network congestion, rather than errors resulting from noisy channels, handoffs and node mobility. A reduction in the congestion window is thus the TCP reaction to packet loss of any kind.

Despite the inadequacies of TCP implementation for wireless environments, changes can be avoided by adopting Link Layer solutions.

A reasonable number of solutions designed to achieve better performance through the modification of the TCP itself is available. These are logically divided into two groups according to the technique they introduce: connection splitting approach and TCP modifications.

4.2.1   Connection Splitting Solutions

In this scheme, the end-to-end TCP connection is divided into fixed and wireless parts, so that more degrees of freedom are available for the optimization of the TCP over both wired and wireless links.

The disadvantages of this solution mainly involve the attempt to perform transparent splitting (of the TCP) from the point of view of the TCP layer of the wired host. This leads to greater complexity in Base Station (BS) procedures, which is the most common and suitable place for splitting; the greater complexity involves not only the handling of hand-offs but also, prevention of end-to-end semantics of the TCP connection and, also greater software overhead caused by the TCP part of the stack involved at the intermediate point.

I-TCP   Indirect-TCP (I-TCP)[19] was one of the firt proposals for using such a connection-splitting approach. I-TCP is based on the indirect protocol model proposed in [20]. In this approach, (on the transport layer) the end-to-end connection between an FH and a mobile network is split into two separate connections: one between the FH (with regular TCP) and the Mobility Support Router (MSR), commonly the base station which serves the MH, and the other between the MSR and the MH.

The creation of two separate connections makes it possible to optimize transmission over the wireless link, concealing the loss recovery process on the wireless link from the fixed sender by implementing a modified version of TCP. The flow (control) and congestion control mechanisms used by I-TCP allow faster reactions to wireless link problems such as communication interruption and mobility.

Whenever an MH moves to another cell (or BSS), all the information associated with the entire connection is handed over to the new MSR. The fixed host is completely unaware of such indirection, although it maintains the end-to-end TCP connection alive while the mobile node moves from one cell to another.

This I-TCP approach, however, presents certain drawbacks:

- End-to-end TCP connection semantics cannot be preserved;

- Base Station addition of increased overhead for each packet;

- Decrease in complexity of the base station;

- Additional overhead during hand-offs related to connection state transfer;

- Not applicable to encrypted traffic.

METP   Mobile End Transport Protocol (METP) is a special transport protocol designed to use the connection-splitting approach on wireless links. The authors [21] propose the elimination of the TCP, as well as IP layer from the TCP/IP protocol stack of the wireless node, in order to reduce the overhead due to TCP and IP headers of the packet, as well as to their processing. The splitting point (BS) acts as a proxy for the TCP connection, providing for conversion of the packets received from the fixed network. Assuming that the wireless link is the only wireless hop within the end-to-end connection, the METP approach shifts IP datagram reception from the MH to the BS, which means that the packet passes through the IP and the Transport layer of the protocol stack of the BS. After the reception of a datagram, the BS then delivers the data to the MH by using the METP protocol, which involves a reduced packet header containing only minimal information (link source and destination addresses, port- and connection-related information).

METP provides reliable data delivery across the wireless link by introducing a special local retransmission scheme to link layer ARQ. It can also keep the overall TCP connection alive while dealing with handoffs. For this reason, all information, including states and sending and receiving windows, has to be handed over to the new BS. The authors report a throughput enhancement of up to 37% over TCP Reno and of 23% over other approaches [21]. However, this approach also has drawbacks:

- End-to-end semantics are not preserved;

- Great increase in complexity of the BS due to increased packet processing through the BS protocol stack since it must be handled twice, once when it is received (by using the TCP/IP stack) at the fixed host and again when it is transmitted to the wireless part of the network by the METP;

- Additional overhead related to the transfer of large amount of information during handoffs.

4.2.2   TCP Modifications

TCP Modification invloves a group of solutions which promote small changes on the behavior of TCP, such as the mechanics of acknowledgement generation used by TCP. The modifications to the TCP make it unnecessary to modify the Base Station, thus avoiding overhead in packet delivery and the increase in BS complexity. The major proposals in this framework are summarized below.

Selective Acknowledgements (SACK)   TCP selective acknowledgements (SACKs) is one option [22] for the efficient handling of multiple losses within a single window. The SACK acknowledgement algorithm enables the receiver to inform the TCP sender when packets are received out of order. The sender can then retransmit only those packets which have not reached the receiver. This technique is designed as an improvement of the standard cumulative ACK schemes in which retransmission is triggered by the reception of duplicate ACKs.

TCP using SACK provides a technique which performs better than standard TCP for multiple losses in a single window [10]. However, the window size must be "large enough" to take advantage of the SACK characteristics. The main drawback of this selective acknowledgement is the modification of acknowledgement procedures required at both sender and receiver.

TCP Santa Cruz   TCP Santa Cruz [23] employs the option field of the TCP header for the implementation of new congestion control and error recovery strategies. The congestion control algorithm is based on relative delays, both that between packets transmitted by a sender and that other between packets received at the receiver. This information is calculated by the TCP Santa Cruz using timestamps added to the packet at both ends, a technique originally presented in TCP Vegas [24]. An increase in the amount of information available about the TCP flow provides for more accurate RTT estimations at the sender side, while losses ACKs on their way back do not influence the forward throughput. As an acknowledgement strategy, the TCP Santa Cruz can be used to SACK. This scheme leads to an improvement in performance in relation to both TCP Reno and TCP Vegas. The main drawback is the increased complexity at the sender side.

Explicit Notification Schemes   ECN (Explicit Congestion Notification) allows the sender to become aware of problems not related to congestion. Knowledge about why packets are lost on the wireless link can help senders, identify those instances where congestion avoidance is not the proper reaction when losses have occurred. Different explicit notification schemes are available, as summarized in Table 2 [38] and described briefly below.

Table 2: Summary of explicit loss notification schemes.

Name	Mobile host is	Generated by	What it indicates	Carried by	Path
EBSN	destination	BS	Bad channel	New signal	To source
ELN	source	BS	loss	dupack	To source

Explicit Bad State Notification (EBSN) [25] notifies the sender whenever a BS is unsuccessful in delivering a packet over the wireless network. To do this, it sends an EBSN message when a message is receveid, the TCP sender restarts its timer to avoid execution of the slow start algorithm. This scheme requires minor modifications in the TCP sender code.

Explicit Loss Notification (ELN) [26] makes a sender aware of errors unrelated to congestion while have occurred on the wireless link. The Base Station monitors TCP packets in both directions. When a duplicate acknowledgement is received from the TCP receiver, the BS can encapsulate the ELN message by setting the ELN bit in the TCP acknowledgement header and forwarding it back to the sender. The sender can then choose a type of reaction based on the type of loss. ELN does not, however, provide local retransmission, so no caching is necessary. However, the required checking of all TCP headers represents an increase in complexity and additional overhead associated with each packet.

4.3   Cross-Layer Design

All of these approaches optimize a single parameter at a time, but when several different variables are to be considered they should be taken into account at the same time in order to achieve a truly optimal solution for the adaptation of a TCP developed for a wired environment to a wireless scenario.

Such joint optimization can be included in the wide range of recently-proposed solutions for optimizing wireless network design that are collectively labeled "Cross-Layer Design" [27], [28]. This approach breaks the ISO/OSI layering principles by allowing interdependence and joint design of protocols for passing from one layer to another.

ILC-TCP   The most promising approach, Interlayer Collaboration Protocol (ILC-TCP) [29], was designed to improve the performance of the TCP in wireless environments, involving long and frequent disconnections. The main modification is introduction of a State Manager (SM) in parallel with the protocol stack for gathering information about TCP, IP and Link/Physical layers, if necessary, this information can be furnished upon the request of the TCP layer. Each layer (Link/Physical or IP) periodically reports its state to the SM. If conditions are not appropriate for the flow of the TCP, the SM suggests that the TCP sender stop sending packets. When conditions have improved, the TCP can proceed with regular data delivery.

This approach tries to optimize performance in a scenario in which mobile hosts act as TCP senders. It is an end-to-end approach which requires no changes in the fixed TCP receiver.

The authors [24] report an improvement up to 25% in throughput in relation to standard TCP when disconnections and varied mobility patterns are present. However, in the absence of problems, ILC-TCP offers no improvement in TCP operation over an end-to-end connection.

ATCP   In this approach, feedback between the network and the transport layers is allowed as well as between the application and transport layers [30]. On the application level, information about priority is specified by the user and interpreted by the transport layer so that priorities can be established. This approach provides a throughput improvement of up to 40% over the Reno TCP.

LLE-TCP   Link-Layer ARQ Exploitation TCP (LLE-TCP) [31] introduces cross-layer collaboration, achieved by the utilization of link layer knowledge about successful and unsuccessful packet delivery. LLE-TCP introduces an ARQ Snoop agent in the protocol stack, and this agent keeps track of all TCP packets passing through the stack. For each TCP packet, the Snoop agent receives a message from the link layer indicating the result of delivery over the wireless medium. Whenever a packet reaches its destination, the ARQ Snoop agent at the sender side generates a TCP ACK packet for the transport layer in order to acknowledge this delivery. On the receiver side, the corresponding TCP acknowledgement is then dropped.

In summary, this technique provides the TCP layer with acknowledgements derived from local link layer acknowledgements, thus avoiding transmission of such acknowledgements over the wireless medium. Overhead can thus be reduced significantly.

The throughput achieved by this technique is strongly dependent on the size of the TCP data packets. One important advantage of this technique is that it does not lead to delay when packets are delivered over the wireless link.

The LLE-TCP does present certain drawbacks:

- Increased complexity of the sender node required for the tracing of TCP packets and generation of acknowledgement;

- Difficulty in preserving TCP end-to-end semantics in multi-hop networks.

5   Comparisons

In this section, the available proposals are compared since these proposals act at different layers, there is no one proposal that outperforms the others in all possible scenarios. The best way to compare them is to underline their differences through a comparison of their characteristics. A brief summary of the existing solutions and their advantages and disadvantages is presented in Table 5.1.

Certain features, however, are shared by all of the approaches belonging to the same group. These characteristics and their limitations are described for each of the layers.

Link Layer solutions. The main advantage of Link Layer solutions is the maintenance of end-to-end semantics, without modification of higher protocol layers. This makes it possible to leave untouched the existing implementations of the protocol stack in the various operating systems and limit the introduction of modifications to the link layer.

Most of the approaches which operate at this level rely on some intermediate point within the end-to-end connection for the introduction of performance improvements. For example, the Snoop protocol agent performs local retransmissions from a cache of monitored packets, and WTCP, although operating in a similar way introduces more accurate RTT estimations, thus preventing a reduction in TCP throughput. Both Snoop and WTCP must, however, have access to the header of TCP packets in order to function, which reduces their usefullness value if traffic is encrypted. DDA solves this problem by introducing a local retransmission scheme based solely on information transferred at the link layer; by delaying duplicate acknowledgements, it prevents the TCP source from duplication of efforts in retransmissions, since packets are produced locally at the link layer. The TCP-unaware protocols AIRMAIL and TULIP also rely on link layer retransmissions, but both also employ techniques for enhancement, the FEC for AIRMAIL and in-order delivery for TULIP.

Table 3: Brief summary of existing solutions (advantages and disadvantages).

Name	Advantages	Disadvantages
Link Layer solutions		
Snoop	Designed for BSS infrastructure. Performance of local retransmissions. No changes in TCP.	Modification of base station stack. No consideration of handoffs. Non-functional for encrypted traffic.
WTCP	Performance of local retransmissions. Maintenance of more accurate RTT estimation.	Greatly increased BS complexity. Mandatory maintenance state of information for TCP connections. Costly management of handoff.
AIRMAIL	MH acknowledgements combined. Event-driven MS acknowledgement. Power saving. Adaptive FEC implementation.	TCP timeout caused at high error rates.
TULIP	Provision of in-order delivery; local retransmissions. Useful on half-duplex radio links.	Can cause TCP timeout.
DDA	Provision of local retransmissions on link layer. Dupacks delayed before dropping. Performance poor on slow links. Functional for encrypted traffic.	Difficulty in choosing delay value (d). Can cause TCP timeout.
DAWL	ARQ enhancements with Delayed-ACK scheme. Performance good for one-hop, low error rate link in presence of bi-directional traffic.	Difficulty in tuning timers in multi-hop environment. Increased delay of packet delivery acknowledgement. Increased buffer requirements.
Transport Layer solutions		
I-TCP	Useful in BSS infrastructure. Connection splitting for faster reaction to loss over wireless link.	End-to-end semantics not prevented. Increased overhead from BS stack. Increased complexity of BS. Overhead for state transfer during handoffs. Not applicable in asymmetric networks.
METP	Elimination of TCP and IP layers, thus reducing header transmission overhead. Simplified headers on wireless link. Designed for BSS infrastructure.	No end-to-end prevention. Greatly increased BS complexity. Handoff handling costly.
SACK	Good Performance when window size is satisfactorily large. Selective TCP ACK scheme.	Modification of TCP acknowledgement scheme required.
TCP-SC	Modification of congestion control and error recovery mechanisms. Improved RTT calculation.	Increased complexity of TCP sender. TCP modification
EBSN	Notification of TCP sender about problems on the wireless link to prevent slow starts.	Minor modifications of TCP. BS overhead.
ELN	Notification of TCP sender about errors occurring on wireless links.	Increased complexity of TCP. BS overhead.
Cross-Layer solutions		
ILC-TCP	Useful in wireless environments with frequent and long disconnections.	Additional layer added to sender protocol stack.
ATCP	Prioritization of applications from upper layers. Optimization of operation on basis of link state and RTO estimation from lower layers.	Modification of TCP, as well as other layers, for feedback.
LLE-TCP	Utilization of link layer ACK information for local generation of TCP ACK	Increased sender complexity. Not truly end-to-end.

The maintenance of information related to the connection at intermediate nodes brings an increased complexity of IR, especially when transport layer per flow support is required (Snoop and WTCP), as well as a reduction in handoff performance when a large amount of information needs to be transferred to another IR to prevent the termination of an end-to-end connection.

DAWL tries to simplify the system by introducing modifications only in the ARQ scheme at the link layer and does not consider local retransmission at the IR. This design is advantageous in case of an IR crash. When this happens, all the information stored on the IR is lost, in the other schemes, and this would likely cause the termination of the end-to-end connection.

Transport Layer solutions propose modifications to TCP in order to improve the performance on wireless links. The modifications in the transport layer can be adopted for within the entire connection (SACK) or, separated by sender or receiver (EBSN and ELN). Moreover, the modification can focus directly on the wireless link, as in connection-splitting solutions (I-TCP, METP).

The main requirement for the modification of the TCP for running on wireless links is the allowance of the separation of losses due to congestion from those related to the nature of the wireless link (increased error rate, handoffs, etc.). The connection splitting solutions (I-TCP and METP) do not preserve the end-to-end semantics of the TCP while localizing the problem of the wireless link. At the same time, they introduce an increased complexity to the IR, as in the case of Link layer solutions.

The other approaches within this group preserve the end-to-end TCP semantics. SACK modifies the retransmission scheme of TCP in order to reduce unnecessary retransmissions for non-continuous losses within a single TCP window, while TCP-SC modifies the TCP sender and receiver to improve the congestion control algorithm on the basis of relative delay information. Neither SACK nor TCP-SC require IR support and the increased complexity of the sender does not accumulate at a single point, but is rather distributed among the several nodes of the network.

The explicit notification schemes EBSN and ELN require support from an IR in order to provide information either about the state of the wireless link (EBSN) or about the type of loss to the TCP sender (ELN). The crash of an IR does not have a significant impact on the functionality of these solutions since there is no connection-related information stored at this point.

Cross-Layer solutions. All the solutions mentioned try to optimize the performance of IEEE 802.11 networks within a single link, without the support of the IR.

ILC-TCP provides the framework for TCP to obtain information about long and frequent disconnections. From the lower layers of the protocol stack. More extensive feedback is introduced by ATCP, in which the TCP obtains information not only from the lower layers, but also from the application layer, depending of the level of priority of the applications running above it. ATCP introduces a modified version of TCP mechanisms considering information gathered from lower layers, such as link state and RTO estimation.

The differences between LLE-TCP, ILC-TCP and ATCP are mostly related to the optimization approach adopted. None of these tries to preserve the E2E semantics and leave the TCP unmodified. Increased performance is in fact obtained through the local generation of TCP acknowledgements based on packet delivery information provided by the link layer.

Table 4 provides a more detailed comparison of the existing protocols in relation to the following parameters:

- *Protocol Layer*: Solutions at the Link layer try to localize a problem and to the optimization they perform from the Transport layer. Solutions presented at the Transport layer, which are aware of the existence of wireless link, try to optimize TCP performance for conditions typical of the wireless link. Cross-layer solutions provide for joint optimization at both levels.

- *End-to-end (E2E) semantics*: This parameter identifies whether or not a solution preserves the end-to-end semantics of the TCP. Preservation means that the reception of an acknowledgement by the TCP sender provides for the notification of successful data packet delivery to the TCP receiver throughout the entire end-to-end connection.

- *TCP modification*: This parameter indicates whether a solution requires modifications to the TCP layer of the protocol stack. Since there are numerous implementations of TCP in various operating systems from different vendors, a modification of TCP may require a huge effort. For this reason, solutions which include TCP modifications may find implementation in very limited number of cases, even if the improvement achieved is usually high.

- *Intermediate Router (IR) support*: The overwhelming majority of solutions use an intermediate point within the end-to-end connection for performance optimization, such as splitting the connection at that point, or using to notify about network conditions (ELN and EBSN). In BSS infrastructure, the Base Station commonly plays the role of an IR. The rest of the parameters are connected with the existence of an intermediate point along the transmission path.

- *Retransmit at*: The most commonly used technique for performance enhancement is the local retransmission of lost packets only on the wireless link, rather than throughout the entire end-to-end connection. The "Retransmit at" parameter indicates the point where retransmissions are performed, as well as the protocol layer in which a solution handles retransmission.

- *IR crash impact*: When a solution relies on the IR, the crash of that intermediate point can lead to the termination of the TCP connection. In some cases, there is no possibility of maintaining the data flow when state information is lost.

Table 4 underlines the wide range of existing solutions, the differences in functionality implemented and their impact on network design. As can be seen, there is no single solution which will perform well in all scenarios.

Table 4: Comparison of existing solutions.

Scheme	E2E	TCP modification	IR support	Retransmit at	IR crash impact
Link Layer solutions					
Snoop	Present	Absent	TL/LL	BS	Limited
WTCP	Present	Absent	TL/LL	BS	Limited
AIRMAIL	Present	Absent	LL	BS	Minimal
TULIP	Present	Absent	LL	BS	Minimal
DDA	Present	Absent	LL	BS	Minimal
DAWL	Present	Absent	None	Sender	None
Transport Layer solutions					
I-TCP	Absent	Present	TL	BS	Present
METP	Absent	Present	TL	BS	Present
SACK	Present	Present	None	Sender	None
TCP-SC	Present	Present	None	Sender	None
EBSN	Present	Present	LL	Sender	None
ELN	Present	Present	TL	Sender	None
Cross-Layer solutions					
ILC-TCP	Present	Present	None	Sender	None
ATCP	Present	Present	None	Sender	None
LLE-TCP	Absent	Absent	None	Sender	None

6   Deployment Scenario

Focusing on the different scenarios for deployment of the schemes presented makes it possible to define different architectures involving IEEE 802.11 wireless technology:

- *single-hop wireless connections*: This scenario involves transmission between two mobile stations equipped with 802.11 wireless network cards, and by far is the simplest scenario.

    IEEE 802.11 networks rely mostly on link layer ARQ to provide the reliable delivery of packets to transport protocols. If the link layer abandons the transmission of a packet after all possible retransmissions, that packet will be transmitted by the TCP. This does not, however, lead to much of an increase in overhead, since there is only a single hop between the sender and the receiver. DAWL takes advantage of improvements derived from the use of an ARQ scheme for relatively low channel error rates in the presence of bi-directional traffic.

    The E2E solutions for the Transport layer, such as SACK and TCP-SC, improve the mechanism for TCP acknowledgement and congestion control, as well as recovery from error, and these will be reflected in performance improvements. All three solutions within the Cross-Layer area (ILC-TCP, ATCP and LLE-TCP) have been designed with this scenario in mind.

- *multi-hop scenario*: In this scenario, transmission occurs via multiple hops; there is no stationary infrastructure installed in multi-hop networks. Note that the MAC protocol specified by the IEEE 802.11 standard does not perform well in such an environment. Due to problems such as hidden nodes, exposed nodes and the unfairness of the exponential back off algorithm, this protocol "can not perform well in multi-hop networks" [32]. The analysis of existing solutions shows that the design of most proposals does not consider their operation in this scenario. In the best possible situation, only the final hop of a multi-hop connection is taken into account. Transport layer solutions (I-TCP, METP and Explicit loss notification schemes) require the support of a IR within a connection. In a multi-hop scenario, there is no centralized point for splitting (like BS), which makes the implementation of such schemes difficult. The usage of Cross-Layer schemes is more realistic. All methods reviewed introduce modifications performed in the protocol stack of the sender node. In a multi-hop network, the LLE-TCP is introduced only during the last hop [31].

- *Wireless-cum-wired scenario*: This is a more general and diffused scenario where a network is only partially wireless (802.11-based). The sender is located on the wired part of the network, which communicates with the mobile host through the gateway (the BS, in BSS infrastructure). Almost all solutions consider this scenario in their design. Moreover, some of them (such as Snoop, and WTCP) are especially designed to enhance performance in this case. All solutions in the Transport and Cross-Layer approaches can be implemented in a wireless-cum-wired scenario.

- *WLAN-only scenario*: In this scenario, all devices belong to the same WLAN, with a single Access Point. This scenario is similar to the Wireless-cum-wired scenario described above, the sender is a mobile host which communicates with a mobile receiver through an Access Point.

7 Conclusions

Wireless networks are becoming increasingly popular due to the growing use of mobile access to network services. As a consequence, significant efforts have been devoted to providing reliable data delivery for a wide variety of applications over a variety of wireless infrastructures.

In this scenario, the IEEE 802.11 standard and its extensions have gained worldwide diffusion, providing reasonable performance with reduced infrastructure and deployment costs. However, performance bounds and limitations of 802.11 WLANs exist. This chapter has provided an overview of the various solutions available for coping with these limitations.

From the analysis of existing improvements to the IEEE 802.11 standards, it is clear that there is no single best solution for all deployment scenarios.

Link layer solutions work on the wireless link without affecting higher-level protocols, but they increase the complexity of the base station and require the modification of the

MAC protocol on the wireless link (usually implemented in the hardware). Transport layer solutions aim at adapting the transport protocol to the characteristics of the wireless network, thus implying modification of the transport protocol in the protocol stack at both the sender and receiver ends. An alternate novel approach is represented by cross-layer solutions, which establish interdependence and collaboration between protocols in different layers of the stack.

References

[1] *IEEE Standard for Wireless LAN Medium Access Control (MAC) and Physical Layer (PHY) Specifications*, ISO/IEC 8802-11::1999(E), August 1999.

[2] http://standards.ieee.org/wireless/overview.html#802.11

[3] *IEEE 802.11 Working Group Web Site*, http://grouper.ieee.org/groups/802/11/

[4] Y. Xiao and J. Rosdahl, Throughput and Delay Limits of IEEE 802.11, *IEEE Communications Letters*, Vol. 6, No. 8, August 2002, pp. 355-357.

[5] P. Chatzimisios, A.C. Boucouvalas, V. Vitsas, *IEEE 802.11 Packet Delay - A Finite Retry Limit Analysis*, GLOBECOM 2003, pp. 950-654, 2003.

[6] K. Ratnam and I. Matta, WTCP: An efficient Mechanism for Improving TCP Performance over Wireless Links, *Proceedings of the Third IEEE Symposium on Computers and Communications*, p. Athens, Greece, June 1998, p. 74-78.

[7] K. Pentikousis, TCP in Wired-Cum-Wireless, *IEEE Communications Surveys*, 2000.

[8] J.B. Postel, *Transmission Control Protocol*, RFC 793, September 1981.

[9] G.J. Miller, K. Thompson, and R. Wilder, Wide-area Internet traffic patterns and characteristics, *IEEE Network*, November/December 1997, p. 10-23

[10] K. Fall and S. Floyd, *Simulation-based Comparisons of Tahoe, Reno, and SACK TCP*, Computer Communication Review 1996.

[11] *The Norwegian academic and research data network*, http://www.uninett.no/wlan/throughput.html

[12] H. Belakrishnan, S. Seshan, E. Amir, and R. Katz, Improving TCP/IP Performance over Wireless Networks, *Proceedings of the 1st ACM International Conference on Mobile Computing and Networking* (MOBICOM), Berkeley, CA, November 1995, pp. 2-11.

[13] H. Balakrishnan, V. Padmanabhan, S. Seshan, and R. Katz, A Comparison of Mechanisms for Improving TCP Performance over Wireless Links, *IEEE/ACM Transactions on Networking*, December 1997, pp. 756-769.

[14] E. Ayangolu, S. Paul, T. LaPorta, K. Sabnani, and R. Gitlin, AIRMAIL: A Link Layer Protocol for Wireless Networks, *Wireless Networks*, vol. 1, 1995, pp. 47-60.

[15] C. Parsa and J.J. Garcia-Luna-Aceves, Improving TCP Performance over Wireless Networks at the Link Layer, *Wireless Communications and Networking Conference, IEEE WCNC*, p. 1253 - 1257 vol. 3, September 1999.

[16] N.H. Vaidya, M. Mehta, C. Perkins, and G. Montenegro, Delayed Duplicate Acknowledgements: A TCP-unaware Approach to Improve Performance of TCP over Wireless, *Technical Report 99-003*, Computer Science Department, Texas A&M University, February 1999.

[17] D. Kliazovich and F. Granelli, DAWL: A Delayed-ACK Scheme for MAC-Level Performance Enhancement of Wireless LANs, *ACM/Kluwer Journal on Mobile Networking and Applications (MONET)*, August 2005.

[18] D. Kliazovich and F. Granelli, A Delayed-ACK Scheme for MAC-Level Performance Enhancement of Wireless LANs, *11th International Conference on Telecommunications (ICT'2004)*, Fortaleza (Brasil), August 2004.

[19] A. Bakre and B.R. Badrinath, I-TCP: Indirect TCP for mobile hosts, Distributed Computing Systems, *Proceedings of the 15-th International Conference*, June 1995, pp. 196 - 143.

[20] A. Bakre, Design and Implementation of Indirect Protocols for Mobile Wireless Environments, Rutgers University, New Brunswick, NJ, USA, October 1996.

[21] K. Wang and S.K. Tripathi, Mobile-end transport protocol: an alternative to TCP/IP over wireless links, *Seventeenth Annual Joint Conference of the IEEE Computer and Communications Societies. Proceedings. IEEE*, Vol. 3, April 1998, pp. 1046-1053.

[22] M. Mathis, J. Mahdavi, S. Floyd, and A. Romanow, *TCP Selective Acknowledgment Options*, RFC 2018, April 1996.

[23] C. Parsa and J.J. Garcia-Luna-Aceves, Improving TCP Congestion Control over Internets with Heterogeneous Transmission Media, in *Proceedings of IEEE ICNP '99*, Toronto, October 1999.

[24] L. S. Brakmo, S. W. O'Malley, and L. Peterson, TCP Vegas: New Techniques for Congestion Detection and Avoidance, In *Proc. of ACM SIGCOMM '94*, London, October 1994, pp. 24-35.

[25] B.S. Bakshi, P. Krishna, N.H. Vaidya, and D.K. Pradhan, Improving performance of TCP over wireless networks, in *Proc. of the 17th International Conference on Distributed Computing Systems '97*, Baltimore, Maryland, May 1997.

[26] H. Balakrishnan and R. Katz, Explicit Loss Notification and wireless web performance, in *Proc. IEEE Globecom Internet Mini-Conference*, Sydney, Australia, Nov. 1998.

[27] Z.H. Haas, Design Methodologies for Adaptive and Multimedia Networks, Guest Editorial, *IEEE Communications Magazine*, Vol. 39, No. 11, pp. 106-107, November 2001.

[28] Q. Wang and M.A. Abu-Rgheff, Cross-layer signalling for next-generation wireless systems, *IEEE Wireless Communications and Networking Conference (WCNC 2003)*, Vol. 2 , pp. 1084-1089, March 2003.

[29] M. Chinta and S. Helal, ILC-TCP: An Interlayer Collaboration Protocol for TCP Performance Improvement in Mobile and Wireless Environments, *Proceedings of the Trird IEEE Wireless Communications and Networking Conference (WCNC)*, New Orleans, Louisiana, March 2003.

[30] V.T. Raisinghani, A.K. Singh, and S. Iyer, Improving TCP performance over mobile wireless environments using cross layer feedback, *IEEE International Conference on Personal Wireless Communications*, pp. 81-85, 15-17 Dec. 2002.

[31] D. Kliazovich and F. Granelli, A Cross-layer Scheme for TCP Performance Improvement in Wireless LANs, *IEEE Global Communications Conference, GLOBECOM'04*, Dallas, December 2004.

[32] S. Xu and T. Saadawi, Does the IEEE 802.11 MAC Protocol Work Well in Multihop Wireless Ad Hoc Networks?, *IEEE Communi.Magazine*, pp.130-137, June 2001.

[33] L. Cheng and I. Marsic, Lightweight Models for Prediction of Wireless Link Dynamics in Wireless/Mobile Local Area Networks, in *Proceedings of the IEEE 2002 Sarnoff Symposium on Advances in Wired and Wireless Communications*, pp. 98-101, NJ, USA, March 13, 2002.

[34] G. J. Miller, K. Thompson and R. Wilder, Wide-area Internet traffic patterns and characteristics, *IEEE Network*, November /December 1997, pp. 10-23.

[35] S. Choi and J. Prado, 802.11g CP: A Solution for IEEE 802.11g and 802.11b Inter-Working, in *Proc. IEEE VTC'03-Spring*, Jeju, Korea, April 2003.

[36] M.A. Visser and M. El Zarki, Voice and data transmission over an 802.11 wireless network Personal, Indoor and Mobile Radio Communications, *PIMRC* Vol. 2, September 1995 pp. 648 - 652.

[37] S. Kent and R. Atkinson, Security Architecture for the Internet Protocol, *RFC 2401*, 1998.

[38] T. Moors, *TCP over Wireless*, Lecture notes, http://subjects.ee.unsw.edu.au/tele4363/2003/, 2003.

[39] D. Vardalis and V. Tsaoussidis, On the Efficiency and Fairness of Protocol Recovery Strategies in Networks with Wireless Components, *International Conference on Internet Computing CSREA Press*, Las Vegas, June 2001.

[40] S. Dawkins, G. Montenegro, M. Kojo, V. Magret, and N. Vaidya, End-to-end Performance Implications of Links with Errors, *RFC 3155*, IETF, August 2001.

[41] D. Robb, *Although Newer, 802.11g Not Necessarily Better*, Tutorial, http://www.wifiplanet.com/tutorials/article.php/3332691, 2004.

In: Wireless LANs and Bluetooth
Editors: Yang Xiao and Yi Pan, pp. 77-96

ISBN: 1-59454-432-8

Chapter 4

SATURATION PERFORMANCE ANALYSIS OF IEEE 802.11 DISTRIBUTED COORDINATION FUNCTION

Yang Xiao[*]

Department of Computer Science, The University of Memphis,
373 Dunn Hall Memphis, TN 38152 USA.

Abstract

With the popularity of the IEEE 802.11 standards, many analytical saturation throughput studies have been reported. In this chapter, under more realistic assumptions, we propose an improved analytical model to derive some new performance metrics: frame-dropping probability, frame-dropping time, saturation limits, and number of retransmissions, as well as previous performance metrics: saturation throughput and saturation delay. All performance metrics have been studied over various parameters. Our results show that when the retry limit or the initial window size is large enough, frame-dropping probability is almost zero. Studies further show that optimal initial window sizes exist for the optimal throughput and the optimal delay, and saturation limits exist for IEEE 802.11 protocols.

Key words. IEEE 802.11 protocol, Medium access control, Performance evaluation

Introduction

IEEE 802.11 employs a carrier sense multiple access with collision avoidance (CSMA/CA) medium access control (MAC) protocol with binary exponential backoff, called Distributed Coordination Function (DCF) [1]. The DCF defines a basic access mechanism and an optional request-to-send/clear-to-send (RTS/CTS) mechanism. In the DCF, a station (STA) with a frame to transmit shall invoke the carrier-sense mechanism to determine the busy/idle state of the wireless medium (WM). If the WM is busy, the STA shall defer until the WM is idle without interruption for a period of time equal to a distributed inter-frame space (DIFS) when the last frame detected on the WM was received correctly [1]. After the DIFS WM idle

---

[*] E-mail address: yangxiao@ieee.org

time, the STA shall generate a random backoff period for an additional deferral time before transmitting, unless the backoff timer already contains a nonzero value. The backoff time counter is decremented in terms of slot time as long as the WM is sensed idle. The counter is stopped when the WM is detected busy, and reactivated when the WM is sensed idle again for more than a DIFS. The STA transmits its frame when the backoff time reaches zero. At each transmission, the backoff time is uniformly chosen in the range $(0, CW-1)$, where CW is the current backoff window size. At the very first transmission attempt, CW equals the initial backoff window size CW_{min} (also denoted as W_0 in this chapter). After each unsuccessful transmission, CW is doubled until a maximum backoff window size value CW_{max} is reached. Once it reaches CW_{max}, CW shall remain at the value CW_{max} until it is reset. CW shall be reset to CW_{min} after every successful attempt to transmit, or the retransmission counter reaches the retry limit L_{retry}. In the later case, the frame will be dropped. After the destination station successfully receives the frame, it transmits an acknowledgment frame (ACK) following a short inter-frame space (SIFS) time. If the transmitting station does not receive the ACK within a specified ACK Timeout, or it detects the transmission of a different frame on the channel, it reschedules the frame transmission according to the previous backoff rules. In the optional RTS/CTS mechanism, before transmitting a data frame, a short RTS frame is transmitted. If the RTS frame succeeds, the receiver station responds with a short CTS frame. Then a data frame and an ACK frame will follow. All four frames (RTS, CTS, data, ACK) are separated by an SIFS time.

There have been many performance studies for the original IEEE 802.11 MAC [2-13]: both simulation [2] and analytical [3] studies. Chhaya and Gupta [4] calculated the throughput of CSMA/CA using a simple model with the probabilities of capture and the presence of hidden stations. Bianchi [5-6] proposed a simple and accurate analytical model to compute the saturation throughput. Ziouva and Antonakopoulos (ZA) [7] improved Bianchi's model by deriving saturation delay. Wu et al. [19] improved Bianchi's model by considering the retry limit. Huang, Ho, and Chen [3, 8] gave approximate models that account for hidden terminals and capture effects. Cali, Conti and Gregori [9-10] improved the performance by tuning the backoff strategies, and provided an excellent performance analysis. Tay and Chua [11] provided a good approximation of saturation throughput. Bing and Subramanian [13] adopted a quantitative performance approach. Kwon, Fang, and Latchman improved the MAC with a fast collision resolution scheme for Wireless LANs [18].

In this chapter, we improve Bianchi's model and ZA's model under more realistic assumptions. Difference of our analytic model from Bianchi's model and ZA's model is summarized as follows.

(1)   Bianchi's model assumes that the backoff counter is always decremented during a busy slot. This assumption is not consistent with the IEEE 802.11 standards since the backoff counter is stopped when a transmission is detected on the channel, and reactivated when the channel is sensed idle again [1]. Both our model and ZA's model improve Bianchi's model by removing this assumption.

(2)   ZA's model assumes that after every successful transmission, a station can transmit if the medium is idle without entering the backoff stage. Therefore, ZA's model introduces a non-backoff stage. This assumption is not consistent with the IEEE 802.11

standards [1]. Bianchi's model has not such an assumption. Our model has not such an assumption either.

(3)   Both Bianchi's model and ZA's model assume infinite retransmissions. This assumption is not consistent with the IEEE 802.11 standards: there exists a finite retransmission limit L_{retry} [1]. Furthermore, some new performance metrics, frame-dropping probability, frame-dropping time, saturation throughput limit, and saturation delay limit, can be derived and studied in this chapter.

(4)   Bianchi's model does not provide a delay model. ZA's provides a complex delay model. In this chapter, we provide a new and accurate delay model other than ZA's model. The delay model is much simpler, more accurate, and easier to understand.

Many studies [7, 14-15, 19] had been reported based on Bianchi's model, but none of them derived all these new performance metrics, as well as these old metrics. Furthermore, none of them consider all aspects listed in above. For an example, Wu et al. [19], based on Bianchi's model, also adopts a finite retry limit, but their model also has the problem of (1) in the above, does not provide a delay model, and does not derive all these new performance metrics such as frame-dropping probability, frame-dropping time, number of retransmissions, and saturation delay. Our work becomes important and meaningful in the sense that our work improves not only Bianchi's model and ZA's model, but also those work based on Bianchi's model.

The rest of the chapter is organized as follows. The improved analytic model is proposed in Section 2, where new and old performance metrics will be derived. Section 3 presents the numerical results to study performance metrics over different parameters. We conclude this chapter in Section 4.

An Improved Analytic Model

We proposed an improved analytical model in this section.

Improved Analytic Model

Let $j \left(j = 0,1,...,L_{retry} \right)$ denote the j-th backoff stage and let W_j denote CW in the j-th retry/retransmission (or the j-th backoff stage). The relationships among W_j, W_0, CW_{max}, and L_{retry} are given as follows.

$$
W_j = \begin{cases} 2^j CW_0 & \text{for } j = 0,1...,m-1, \text{ if } L_{retry} > m \\ 2^m W_0 = CW_{max} & \text{for } j = m,...L_{retry}, \text{ if } L_{retry} > m \\ 2^j W_0 & \text{for } j = 0,1..., L_{retry}, \text{ if } L_{retry} \leq m \end{cases}
\tag{1}
$$

where $m = \log_2 \left(CW_{max} / CW_0 \right)$ and $CW_0 = CW_{min}$

As Bianchi's model [5-6] and ZA's model [7], $b(t)$ is defined as a random process representing the value of backoff counter at time t, and $s(t)$ is defined as the random process representing the backoff stage j, where $0 \leq j \leq L_{retry}$ and $b(t)$ is uniformly chosen in the range $(0,1,...W_j - 1)$. Let p denote the probability that a transmitted frame collides. p also equals to the probability that a station in the backoff stage senses the channel busy. The bi-dimensional random process $\{s(t), b(t)\}$ is discrete-time Markov chain under the assumptions that the probability p is independent to the backoff procedure [5-7]. Therefore, the state of each station is described by $\{j, k\}$, where j stands for the backoff stage, and k stands for the backoff delay and takes values $(0,1,...W_j - 1)$.

The state transition diagram is shown in Fig. 1. As illustrated in the Fig. 1, in the L_{retry}-th backoff stage, the frame is dropped if a collision occurs. From Fig. 1, observe that our model is different from Bianchi's model [6-7] and ZA's model [8] in many aspects as follows.

- Bianchi's model assumes that the backoff counter is always decremented during a busy slot. Both our model and ZA's model improve Bianchi's model by removing this assumption.
- ZA's model assumes that after every successful transmission, a station can transmit if the medium is idle without entering the backoff stage. Our model has not such an assumption.
- Our model assumes that there is a finite retransmission limit (retry limit), whereas Bianchi's model and ZA's model assume an infinite retry limit.

In Fig. 1, the non-null transition probabilities are listed as follows.

$$\Pr\{(0,k) \mid (j,0)\} = \frac{1-p}{W_0} \text{ for } 0 \leq k \leq W_0 - 1 \text{ and } 0 \leq j < L_{retry}$$

$$\Pr\{(0,k) \mid (L_{retry}, 0)\} = 1/W_0, \text{ for } 0 \leq k \leq W_0 - 1$$

$$\Pr\{(j,k) \mid (j,k)\} = p \text{ for } 1 \leq k \leq W_j - 1 \text{ and } 0 \leq j \leq L_{retry}$$

$$\Pr\{(j,k) \mid (j,k+1)\} = 1-p, \text{ for } 0 \leq k \leq W_j - 2 \text{ and } 0 \leq j \leq L_{retry}$$

$$\Pr\{(j,k) \mid (j-1,0)\} = \frac{p}{W_j} \text{ for } 0 \leq k \leq W_j - 1 \text{ and } 1 \leq j \leq L_{retry}$$

In the above, we have $\Pr\{(j,k) \mid (j,k)\} = p$ since the backoff counter is stopped when the station senses the channel busy, and this is the same as ZA's model, but different from Bianchi's model. Let $b_{j,k} = \lim_{t \to \infty} \Pr\{s(t) = j, b(t) = k\}$ be the stationary distribution of the Markov chain. In steady state, we can derive following relations through chain regularities. We have

$$b_{j,0} = p^j b_{0,0} \quad 0 \leq j \leq L_{retry} \tag{2}$$

$$b_{j,k} = \frac{W_j - k}{W_j} \frac{1}{1-p} b_{j,0} \quad 0 \le j \le L_{retry}, 1 \le k \le W_j - 1 \tag{3}$$

$$\sum_{j=0}^{L_{retry}} \sum_{k=0}^{W_j-1} b_{j,k} = 1 \tag{4}$$

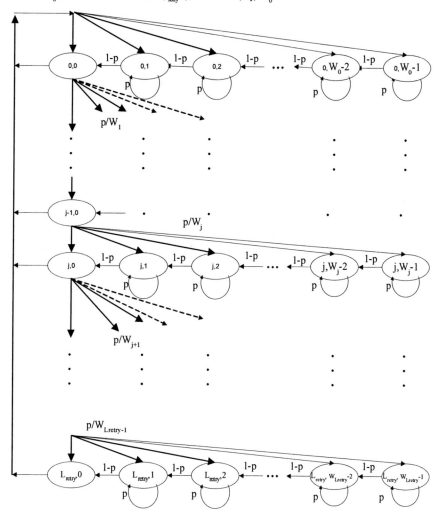

Fig. 1 State transmission diagram

From (2)~(4), we have,

$$b_{0,0} = \frac{1}{\sum\limits_{j=0}^{L_{retry}} \left[1 + \frac{1}{1-p} \sum\limits_{k=1}^{W_j-1} \frac{W_j - k}{W_j}\right] p^j} \tag{5}$$

Let τ be the probability that a station transmits during a generic slot time. A station transmits when its backoff counter reaches zero, i.e. the station is at any of states $\{j,0\}$.

$$\tau = \sum_{j=0}^{L_{retry}} b_{j,0} = b_{0,0}\frac{1-p^{L_{retry}+1}}{1-p} \tag{6}$$

Let n denote the number of stations. The probability p that a station in the backoff stage senses the channel busy is given

$$p = 1-(1-\tau)^{n-1} \tag{7}$$

p is also the probability that a transmitted frame collides. Substituting (1), (5), and (7) to (6), we can solve unknown parameters numerically. Then, we can calculate p from (7). Let p_{Tb} denote the probability that the channel is busy. It happens when at least one station transmits during a slot time. Please note that p_{Tb} is different from p. Therefore, we have

$$p_{Tb} = 1-(1-\tau)^n \tag{8}$$

Saturation Throughput

Let p_s denote the probability that a successful transmission occurs in a slot time. We have

$$p_s = n\tau(1-\tau)^{n-1} \tag{9}$$

Let S denote the normalized saturation throughput. Let δ, $T_{E(L)}$, T_s, and T_c denote the duration of an empty slot time, the time to transmit the average payload, the average time that the channel is sensed busy because of a successful transmission, and the average time that the channel has a collision, respectively. The probability that the channel is idle for a slot time is $(1-p_{Tb})$, and the probability that the channel is neither idle nor successful for a slot time is $[1-(1-p_{Tb})-p_s]=(p_{Tb}-p_s)$. We have,

$$S = \frac{E(\text{payload transmission time in a slot time})}{E(\text{length of a slot time})} = \frac{p_s T_{E(L)}}{(1-p_{Tb})\delta + p_s T_s + [p_{Tb}-p_s]T_c} \tag{10}$$

Let T_H, T_{ACK}, $SIFS$, $L*$, $T_{E(L*)}$, and γ denote the time to transmit the header (including MAC header, PHY header, and/or tail), the time to transmit an ACK, SIFS time, the length of the longest frame in a collision, the time to transmit a payload with length $E(L*)$, and the time of the propagation delay, respectively. For the basics access method, we have,

$$T_s^{basic} = T_H + T_{E(L)} + SIFS + \gamma + T_{ACK} + DIFS + \gamma \tag{11}$$

$$T_c^{basic} = T_H + T_{E(L^*)} + DIFS + \gamma \tag{12}$$

Please refer to [7] for calculating $T_{E(L^*)}$. Let T_{RTS} and T_{CTS} denote the time to transmit an RCS frame and the time to transmit a CTS frame, respectively. For the RTS/CTS access model, we have,

$$\begin{aligned} T_s^{rts/cts} &= T_{RTS} + SIFS + \gamma + T_{CTS} + SIFS + \gamma \\ &\quad + T_H + T_{E(L)} + SIFS + \gamma + T_{ACK} + DIFS + \gamma \end{aligned} \tag{13}$$

$$T_c^{rts/cts} = T_{RTS} + DIFS + \gamma \tag{14}$$

Frame-Dropping Probability, Frame-Dropping Time, and Number of Retransmissions

Let P_{drop} denote the frame-dropping probability. From Fig. 1, we observe that a frame can be dropped only in state $\{L_{retry}, 0\}$ if a collision occurs. In other words, a frame can be dropped when the retransmission counter reaches the retry limit L_{retry}. Therefore, we have

$$P_{drop} = p^{L_{retry}+1} \tag{15}$$

The frame-dropping time is a performance metric that shows how long a frame in backoff/collision stages before the frame is dropped. Since other frames in the queue of a station need to wait the first frame to finish (by either being dropped or completing a successful transmission), the frame-dropping time provide a worst-case waiting time for the next frame in the queue.

Let $E(FDT)$ denote the mean of the frame-dropping time (FDT) if the frame will be dropped. Note that a frame is dropped only in state $\{L_{retry}, 0\}$ if a collision occurs. Let $E(BS)$ denote the mean of the backoff slots (BS) for a dropping frame. We have

$$E(BS) = \sum_{j=0}^{L_{retry}} \frac{W_j - 1}{2} \tag{16}$$

$$E(FDT) = E(BS) \bullet E(\text{length of a slot time}) = E(BS)\left[(1-p_b)\delta + p_s T_s + [p_{Tb} - p_s]T_c\right] \tag{17}$$

Let $E(N_{retry})$ denote the average number of retries. The probability that the frame is successfully transmitted after the j-th retry (which is the (j+1)-th transmission) is $\dfrac{p^j(1-p)}{1-P_{drop}} = \dfrac{p^j(1-p)}{1-p^{L_{retry}+1}}$, which uses conditional probability on a successful transmission with probability $1 - P_{drop}$. We have,

$$E(N_{retry}) = \sum_{j=0}^{L_{retry}} j \frac{p^j(1-p)}{1-P_{drop}} = \sum_{j=0}^{L_{retry}} j \frac{p^j(1-p)}{1-p^{L_{retry}+1}} \tag{18}$$

Saturation Delay

Saturation delay is the average delay under the saturation condition, and it includes the medium access delay (due to backoff, collisions, etc.), transmission delay, and inter-frame spaces (such as SIFS). The average backoff delay depends on the value of a station's backoff counter and the duration when the counter freezes due to others' transmissions. Let X denote the random variable representing the total number of backoff slots, which a frame encounters without considering the case when the counter freezes. The average number of backoff slots after the j-th retry is $\sum_{h=0}^{j} \frac{W_h - 1}{2}$. Note that only successful transmissions are considered.

$$E(X) = \sum_{j=0}^{L_{retry}} \frac{p^j(1-p)}{1-p^{L_{retry}+1}} \sum_{h=0}^{j} \frac{W_h - 1}{2} \tag{19}$$

Let B denote the random variable representing the total number of slots when the counter freezes, which a frame encounters. The portion of idle slots is $(1-p)$, which is used to decrease $E(X)$. We have,

$$E(B) = \frac{E(X)}{(1-p)} p \tag{20}$$

We can treat $E(X)$ and $E(B)$ are the total number of idle slots and the total number of busy slots, which the frame encounters during backoff stages, respectively.

Let D denote the random variable representing the frame delay. Let T_o denote the time that a station has to wait when its frame transmission collides before sensing the channel again. Let $T_{ACK\_timeout}$ and $T_{CTS\_timeout}$ denote the duration of the ACK timeout and the duration of the CTS timeout, respectively. Note that $E(N_{retry})$ is one less than the number of transmissions. The average slot lengths are δ, $\left[p_sT_s + (p_{Tb} - p_s)T_c\right]$, $(T_c + T_o)$, and T_s for a idle slot at states $\{j,k\}$ $(k>0)$, a busy slot at states $\{j,k\}$ $(k>0)$, a failed transmission slot for this station at states $\{j,0\}$, and a successful transmission at states $\{j,0\}$, respectively. We have

$$E(D) = E(X)\delta + E(B)\left[p_sT_s + (p_{Tb} - p_s)T_c\right] + E(N_{retry})(T_c + T_o) + T_s \tag{21}$$

$$T_o^{basic} = SIFS + T_{ACK\_timeout} \tag{22}$$

$$T_o^{rts/cts} = SIFS + T_{CTS\_timeout} \tag{23}$$

Note that (21) counts only successful transmissions since $E(X)$, $E(B)$, and $E(N_{retry})$ are all considered with the conditional probability of success.

Saturation Limits

The IEEE 802.11, 802.11b, and 802.11a specifications provide up to 2, 11, and 54 Mbps data rates [1, 16-17], respectively, whereas the industry is seeking data rates over 100Mbps [12]. We proved that a theoretical throughput upper limit and a theoretical delay lower limit exist for IEEE 802.11 protocols [12] for the best-case scenario. The existence of such limits indicates that the overhead must be reduced to get good performance for higher data rates. In this chapter, we further prove that under the saturation scenario, a saturation throughput limit and a saturation delay lower limit exist for IEEE 802.11 protocols. When the data rate goes infinite high, we can derive the saturation limits. Since the backoff procedures are independent to the transmission rates, p_s and p_b remain the same when the data rates to infinite high. Therefore, it is easier to see that both the saturation throughput and the saturation delay are decreasing functions of the data rate. When the data rate goes infinite, from (10)-(19), we have

Lemma: A saturation throughput limit (STL) and an average saturation delay lower limit (SDLL) exist for IEEE 802.11 protocols. They are independent of data rates (even when the data rate goes to infinite high), fixed for a given payload size and a given set of overhead parameters, and given as follows:

$$STL = 0 \tag{24}$$

$$SDLL = E(X)\delta + E(B)\left[p_s A + (p_{Tb} - p_s)B \right] + E(N_{retry})(B + T_o) + A \tag{25}$$

Where T_P is the physical layer's preamble, T_{PHY} the physical layer's header overhead transmission time, $A^{basic} = 2T_P + 2T_{PHY} + SIFS + DIFS + 2\gamma$, $A^{rts/cts} = 4T_P + 4T_{PHY} + DIFS + 3*SIFS + 4\gamma$, and $B = T_P + T_{PHY} + DIFS + \gamma$.

For IEEE 802.11a, we have $T_P = 16\mu s$ and $T_{PHY} = 4\mu s$. The reasons that the saturation throughput limit (STL) is zero are stated as follows. The saturation throughput is a normalized throughput. When the data rate goes into infinite high, the normalized throughput should become zero. Furthermore, mathematically, when the data rate goes into infinite high, we have $T_{E(L)} = 0$. In other words, the nominator of the equation (10) goes zero, whereas the denominator goes to a constant positive value. Therefore, STL is zero.

The existence of such limits indicates that the overhead must be reduced to get good performance for higher data rates. Otherwise, the enhanced performance of higher data rates is limited and bounded even when the data rate goes into infinite high. Both reducing overhead and pursuing higher data rates are therefore necessary and important.

Numerical Results

In this section, we study the new and old performance metrics under various parameters. We adopt IEEE 802.11a [17]. The data rate is 6Mbps and the control rate is 6Mbps unless stated otherwise. We will study effects of the number of active stations, the retry limit, the payload size, and the initial window size on saturation throughput, saturation delay, frame-dropping probability, frame-dropping time, and number of retransmissions. We will study saturation limits at the last.

Effects of the Number of Active Stations, and Metric Values under Different Numbers of Active Stations

In this section, we study the effects of the number of active stations on saturation throughput, saturation delay, frame-dropping probability, frame-dropping time, and number of retransmissions. An additional purpose of this subsection is to show performance metric values with different number of active stations under our new improved model. We have following parameters: $L_{retry} = 7$, $CW_{min} = 8$, $CW_{max} = 1024$, and frame payload size=1024 bytes.

Fig. 2 shows throughput and delay over the number of active stations. We observe that throughput decreases and delay increases as the number of active stations increases. The reason is that the collision probability increases as the number of active stations increases.

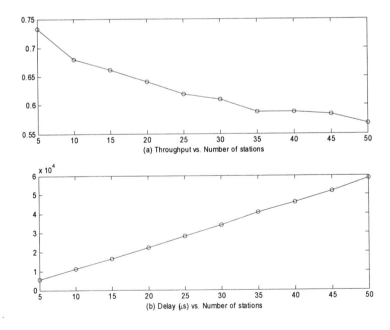

Fig. 2 Throughput and Delay vs. the number of active stations

Fig. 3 shows frame-dropping probability, frame-dropping time, and number of retransmissions over the number of active stations. We observe that all three metrics increase as the number of active stations increases. We observe that frame-dropping probability increases as the number of active stations increases since more active stations cause a higher probability of collisions that causes a higher probability of frame-dropping, a higher frame-dropping time, and a higher number of retransmissions.

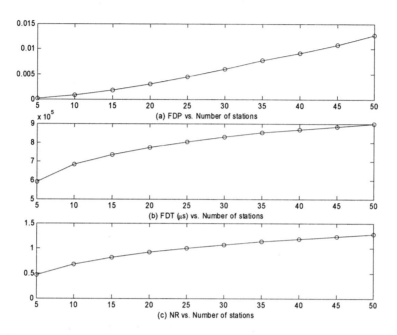

Fig. 3 Frame-dropping probability, frame-dropping time, and number of retransmissions vs. the number of active stations

Effects of the Retry Limit

In this section, we study the effects of the retry limit on saturation throughput, saturation delay, frame-dropping probability, frame-dropping time, and number of retransmissions. We have following parameters: $n = 10$, $CW_{min} = 8$, $CW_{max} = 1024$, and frame payload size=1024 bytes.

   Fig. 4 shows throughput and delay over the retry limit. Both throughput and delay increase as the retry limit increases. Throughput increases since the collision probability decreases a little bit due to the reason that some frames in the system may increase their backoff window size due to a larger retry limit. A larger retry limit has two effects on delay as follows. First, the collision probability decreases a little bit so that the delay should decrease for this aspect. On the other hand, a larger retry limit for a frame means a possible longer time to transmit for this frame, and therefore delay should increase. The overall result of the above two factors under our parameters is that delay increases. We also observe that throughput and delay both increase only a small amount. In other words, throughput and delay are a little bit insensitive to the retry limit.

   Fig. 5 shows frame-dropping probability, frame-dropping time, and number of retransmissions over the retry limit. As the retry limit increases, the frame-dropping probability decreases since frames have better chances to be successfully transmitted. The frame-dropping time increases since a frame if dropped will take a larger number of retries before being dropped. Number of retransmissions decreases since the collision probability decreases. We also observe that when the retry limit is large enough, frame-dropping probability is almost zero.

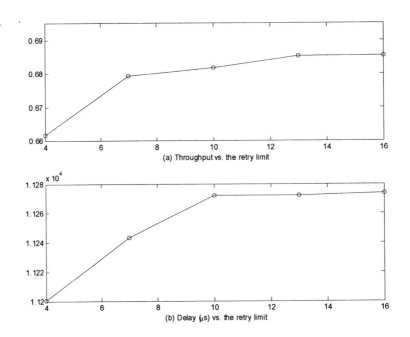

Fig. 4 Throughput and Delay vs. the retry limit

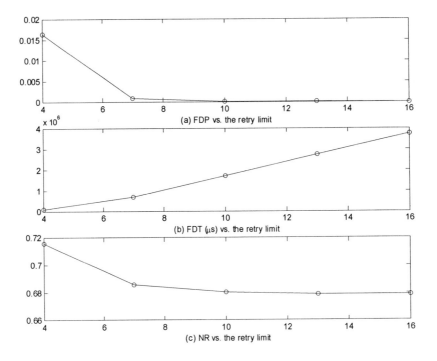

Fig. 5 Frame-dropping probability, frame-dropping time, and number of retransmissions vs. the retry limit

Effects of the Payload Size

In this section, we study the effects of the payload size on saturation throughput, saturation delay, frame-dropping probability, frame-dropping time, and number of retransmissions. We have following parameters: $n = 10$, $CW_{min} = 8$, $CW_{max} = 1024$, and $L_{retry} = 7$.

Fig. 6 shows throughput and delay over the payload size. Throughput increases as the payload size increases since more data are included in each transmission. Delay decreases as the payload size increases since delay is calculated when the whole frame is received.

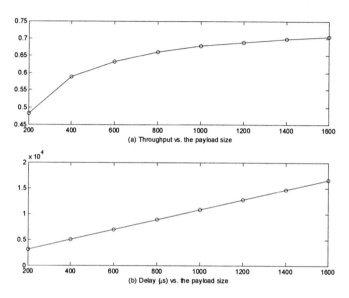

Fig. 6 Throughput and delay vs. the payload size (byte)

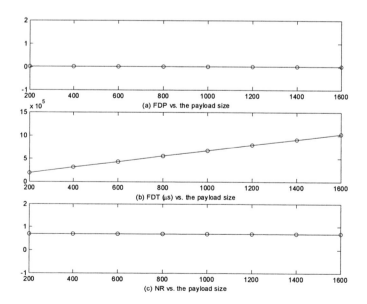

Fig. 7 Frame-dropping probability, frame-dropping time, and number of retransmissions vs. the payload size (byte)

Fig. 7 shows frame-dropping probability, frame-dropping time, and number of retransmissions over the payload size. Both frame-dropping probability and number of retransmissions are constant as the payload size changes. Frame-dropping time decreases as the payload size increases since larger packets take more time for transmissions no matter whether they are successfully transmitted or not.

Effects of the Initial Window Size

In this section, we study the effects of the initial window size on saturation throughput, saturation delay, frame-dropping probability, frame-dropping time, and number of retransmissions. We have following parameters: $n = 10$, $CW_{max} = 1024$, $L_{retry} = 7$, and frame payload size=1024 bytes.

Fig. 8 shows throughput and delay over the initial window size. As illustrated in the figure, as the initial window size increases, throughput first increases and then decreases. We observe that there is an optimal initial window size for throughput. When the initial window size increases, the collision probability decreases, and therefore throughput increases. On the other hand, when the initial window size is too large, there will be a lot of wasted empty slots, and therefore throughput decreases. The balance point of collisions and wasted slots is the optimal initial window size for throughput.

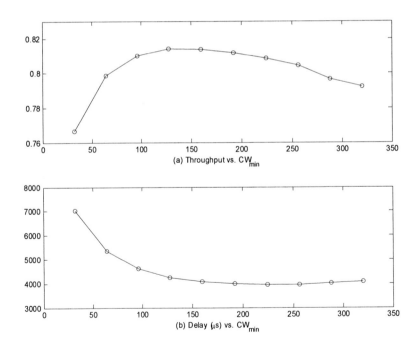

Fig. 8 Throughput and delay over the initial window size.

Fig. 9 shows frame-dropping probability, frame-dropping time, and number of retransmissions over the initial window size. As illustrated in the figures, all three metrics decrease as the initial window size increases. We also observe that as the initial window size is large enough, the frame-dropping probability is almost zero.

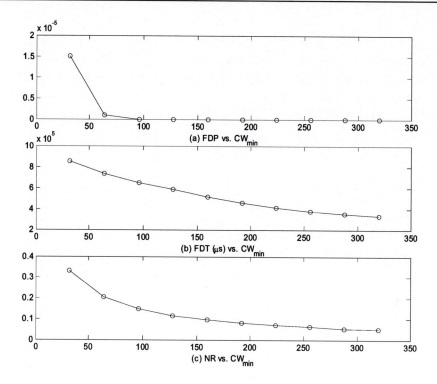

Fig. 9 Frame-dropping probability, frame-dropping time, and number of retransmissions vs. the initial window size

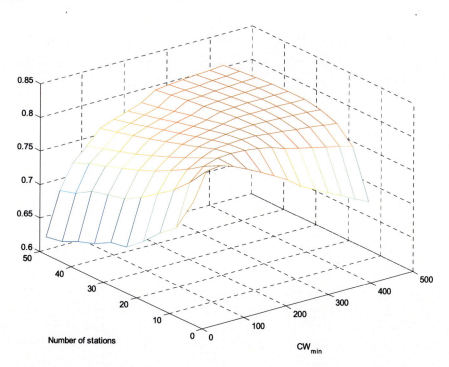

Fig. 10 Throughput vs. CW_{min} and the number of active stations

Fig. 8 shows that the optimal window sizes exist for a fixed number of active stations. Fig. 10 and Fig. 11 show throughput and delay, respectively, over both the number of active stations and the initial window size using 3D-figures. As illustrated in Fig. 10, the optimal window size for throughput increases as the number of active stations increases. The optimal window size for throughput is defined as the window size that makes the highest throughput for a fixed number of active stations.

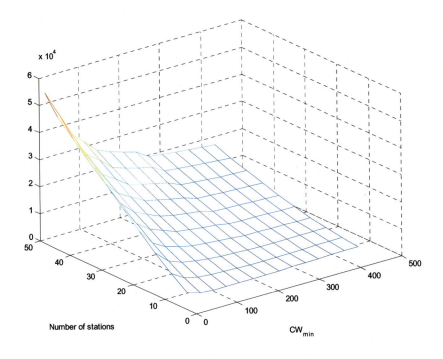

Fig. 11 Delay (μs) vs. CW_{min} and the number of active stations

Saturation Limits

In this subsection, we study the performance of saturation limits: STL and SDLL. Fig. 12 (a) shows the saturation throughput and STL over the number of active stations. The frame size is 1024 bytes. As illustrated in the figure, when the data rate increases, the saturation throughput decreases since it is a normalized throughput. When the data rate goes infinite high, the saturation throughput becomes zero. When the number of active stations increases, the saturation throughput deceases. Fig. 12 (b) shows the saturation delay and SDLL over the number of active stations. The frame size is 1024 bytes. As illustrated in the figure, when the data rate increases, the saturation delay decreases. When the number of active stations increases, the saturation delay increases. However, the delay difference of the data rate of 54Mbps and the date rate of infinite high is small: there is not much room available to improve the saturation delay. In other words, the saturation delay will not benefit a lot by increasing the data rate.

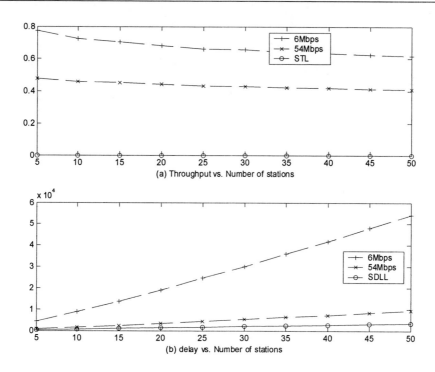

Fig. 12 Saturation Throughput, STL, Saturation Delay, and SDLL (μ sec.) over the number of stations for different data rates

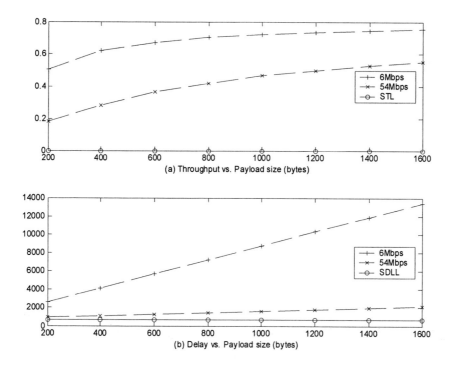

Fig. 13 Saturation Throughput, STL, Saturation Delay, SDLL (μ sec.) over the payload size for different data rates

Fig. 13 (a) shows the saturation throughput and STL over the payload size. The number of active stations is 10. As illustrated in the figure, when the data rate increases, the saturation throughput decreases since it is a normalized throughput. When the data rate goes infinite high, the saturation throughput becomes zero. When the payload size increases, the saturation throughput increases. Fig. 13 (b) shows the saturation delay and SDLL over the number of active stations for IEEE 802.11a. The number of active stations is 10. As illustrated in the figure, when the data rate increases, the saturation delay decreases. When the number of active stations increases, the saturation delay increases. However, the delay difference of the data rate of 54Mbps and the date rate of infinite high is small: there is not much room available to improve the saturation delay. In other words, the saturation delay will not benefit a lot by increasing the data rate. We observe that the SDLL is constant. In other words, no matter how high the data rate becomes, as long as the overhead is compatible with IEEE 802.11a, the saturation delay is lower bounded by SDLL that is a constant.

Summary

In this chapter, we propose an improved analytical model for IEEE 802.11 MAC to derive frame-dropping probability, frame-dropping time, saturation throughput limit (STL), saturation delay lower limit (SDLL), and number of retransmissions as well as saturation throughput and saturation delay under more realistic assumptions. The newly proposed delay model is simple and easy to understand. Performance metrics are studied over different performance parameters. Our study shows

- As the number of active stations increases, saturation throughput decreases, whereas saturation delay, frame-dropping probability, frame-dropping time, and number of retransmissions all increases.
- As the retry limit increases, saturation throughput, saturation delay, and frame-dropping time all increase, whereas frame-dropping probability and number of retransmissions all decrease. We also observe that when the retry limit is large enough, frame-dropping probability is almost zero.
- As the payload size increases, saturation throughput, saturation delay, and frame-dropping time all increase, whereas frame-dropping probability and number of retransmissions all remain constant.
- As the initial window size increases, throughput first increases and then decreases. We observe that there is an optimal initial window size for throughput. The balance point of collisions and wasted slots is the optimal initial window size. The optimal window size for throughput increases as the number of active stations increases. Similarly, as the initial window size increases, delay first decreases and then increases.
- As the initial window size increases, frame-dropping probability, frame-dropping time, and number of retransmissions all decrease. We also observe that as the initial window size is large enough, the frame-dropping probability is almost zero.
- Saturation limits exist for IEEE 802.11 protocols. The existence of such limits indicates that the overhead must be reduced to get good performance for higher data rates, i.e. if industry pursues higher data rate such as 100Mbps.

References

[1] IEEE 802.11 WG, Part 11: Wireless LAN Medium Access Control (MAC) and Physical Layer (PHY) specification, Standard, *IEEE*, Aug. 1999.

[2] G. Bianchi, L. Fratta, and M. Oliveti, "Performance evaluation and enhancement of the CSMA/CA MAC protocol for 802.11 Wireless LANs," *Proc. of PIMRC 1996*, pp. 392-396.

[3] T. S. Ho and K. C. Chen, "Performance evaluation and enhancement of the CSMA/CA MAC protocol for 802.11 wireless LAN's", in *Proc. IEEE PIMRC*, 1996, pp. 392-396.

[4] H. S. Chhaya and S. Gupta, "Performance modeling of asynchronous data transfer methods of IEEE 802.11 MAC protocol", Wireless Networks, vol. 3, pp. 217-234, 1997.

[5] G. Bianchi, "IEEE 802.11--Saturation Throughput Analysis," *IEEE Communications Letters* Vol. 2, No. 12, Dec.1998, pp. 318-320.

[6] G. Bianchi, "Performance Analysis of the IEEE 802.11 Distributed Coordination Function," *IEEE Journal on Selected Areas in Communications* Vol. 18, No. 3, March 2000, pp. 535-547.

[7] E. Ziouva and T. Antonakopoulos, "CSMA/CA performance under high traffic conditions: throughput and delay analysis," *Computer Communications*, **25** (2002), pp.313-321.

[8] K. C. Huang and K.-C. Chen, "Interference analysis of nonpersistent CSMA with hidden terminals in multicell wireless data networks", in *Proc. IEEE PIMRC*, Toronto, Canada, Sept. 1995, pp.907-911.

[9] F. Calì, M. Conti, and E. Gregori, "Dynamic Tuning of the IEEE 802.11 Protocol to Achieve a Theoretical Throughput Limit," *IEEE/ACM Trans. Networking*, Vol. 8, No. 6, Dec. 2000, pp. 785-790.

[10] F. Cali, M. Conti, and E. Gregori, "IEEE 802.11 Protocol: Design and Performance Evaluation of an Adaptive Backoff Mechanism," *IEEE J-SAC*, Vol. 18, No. 19, Sep. 2000, pp. 1774-1786.

[11] Y. C. Tay and K. C. Chua, "A Capacity Analysis for the IEEE 802.11 MAC Protocol," *Wireless Networks* 7, 2001, pp. 159-171.

[12] Y. Xiao and J. Rosdahl, "Throughput and Delay Limits of IEEE 802.11," *IEEE Communications Letters*, Vol. 6, No. 8, Aug. 2002, pp. 355-357.

[13] B. Bing and R. Subramanian, "A novel technique for quantitative performance evaluation of wireless LANs," *Computer Communications*, Vol. 21, No. 9, July 1998, pp.833-838.

[14] S.-T. Sheu and T.-F. Sheu, "A Bandwidth Allocation/Sharing/Extension Protocol for Multimedia Over IEEE 802.11 Ad Hoc Wireless LANs," *IEEE J-SAC*, Vol. 19, Oct. 2001, pp. 2065-2080.

[15] Y. Xiao, "A Simple and Effective Priority Scheme for IEEE 802.11," *IEEE Communications Letters*, Vol. 7, No. 2, Feb. 2003, pp. 70-72.

[16] IEEE 802.11b WG, Part 11: Wireless LAN Medium Access Control (MAC) and Physical Layer (PHY) specification: High-speed Physical Layer Extension in the 2.4 GHz Band, Supplement to IEEE 802.11 Standard, *IEEE*, Sep. 1999.

[17] IEEE 802.11a WG, Part 11: Wireless LAN Medium Access Control (MAC) and Physical Layer (PHY) specification: High-speed Physical Layer in the 5GHz Band, Supplement to IEEE 802.11 Standard, *IEEE*, Sep. 1999.

[18] Y. Kwon, Y. Fang, H. Latchman, "A Novel Medium Access Control Protocol with Fast Collision Resolution for Wireless LANs," *IEEE INFOCOM* 2003.

[19] H. Wu, Y. Peng, K. long, S. Cheng, and J. Ma, "Performance of reliable Transport protocol over IEEE 802.11 WLAN: Analysis and Enhancement", *IEEE INFOCOM* 2002.

In: Wireless LANs and Bluetooth
Editors: Yang Xiao and Yi Pan, pp. 97-117

ISBN 1-59454-432-8
©2005 Nova Science Publishers, Inc.

Chapter 5

DYNAMIC RANDOM ACCESS FOR WIRELESS LAN WITH MULTIPACKET RECEPTION[*]

Qing Zhao[†]
Department of Electrical and Computer Engineering,
University of California, Davis, CA 95616
Lang Tong[‡]
School of Electrical and Computer Engineering,
Cornell University, Ithaca, NY 14853

Abstract

We consider the dynamic queue protocol and its steady-state performance analysis. This protocol is proposed for wireless LAN with multipacket reception (MPR). It divides the time axis into transmission periods (TPs) where the ith TP is dedicated to the transmission of the packets generated in the $(i-1)$th TP. At the beginning of each TP, the state (active or idle) of each user is estimated based on the length of the previous TP and the incoming traffic load. By exploiting the information on the state of users and the channel MPR capability, the number of users who can simultaneously access the channel in the current TP is chosen so that the expected length of this TP is minimized. As a result, the MPR capability is more efficiently utilized by the proposed protocol as compared to, for example, the slotted ALOHA with optimal retransmission probability. Furthermore, this protocol requires little on-line computation. Its simplicity is comparable to that of slotted ALOHA.

Keywords: Medium Access Control, Wireless LAN, Multipacket Reception.
AMS Subject Classification.

[*]This work was supported in part by the Multidisciplinary University Research Initiative (MURI) under the Office of Naval Research Contract N00014-00-1-0564, Army Research Laboratory CTA on Communication and Networks under Grant DAAD19-01-2-0011.
[†]E-mail address: qzhao@ece.ucdavis.edu
[‡]E-mail address: ltong@ece.cornell.edu

1 Introduction

The design of medium access control (MAC) protocols has traditionally been separated from that of the physical layer. To a MAC protocol designer, the physical layer is a black box satisfying the so-called collision model: when only one user transmits, the packet arrives at the receiving node error-free. But when transmissions are simultaneous, packets are lost due to collision. Until recently, the theory of random access was based on such an idealized model, and random access protocols were viewed as collision resolution or collision avoidance techniques. Numerous protocols, such as ALOHA [1, 25], the tree algorithm [5], the first-come first-serve (FCFS) algorithm [9], and a class of adaptive schemes [18, 4, 15, 14], have been proposed and their performance studied.

In practice, the collision model is both optimistic and pessimistic: optimistic for it ignores channel effects such as fading and noise on reception, and pessimistic because it does not accommodate the possibility that packets may be successfully decoded in the presence of simultaneous transmissions. Given the advances in multiuser communications at the physical layer, the collision model no longer represents all the characteristics of the physical layer, missing some of its most important properties.

Is there a need to go beyond the collision model for wireless networks? Should the MAC layer assume a multiuser physical layer and be designed with a cross layer principle in mind? Is the gain of cross-layer design significant enough to justify replacing a well-tested protocol with a more sophisticated one? Will the cross-layer design be too complicated to implement, and too sensitive to channel changes to be useful?

The idea of cross-layer design has been brought to the fore by the phenomenal growth in wireless applications and a continuing push for broadband access. The fundamental challenge, as noted by Gallager in 1985 [10] and more recently by Ephremides and Hajek [8], lies in the choice of a proper model that interfaces the physical layer and network upper layers. From an information theoretic viewpoint, multiaccess communications can be made error-free via error control so long as the rates fall within the capacity region. The multiaccess channel is "smooth" in the sense that bits continuously flow from each user to the receiver; retransmissions are not necessary. From a network theoretic perspective, on the other hand, there is the basic notion of a packet. The multiaccess channel is "hard" in the sense that a packet either gets through or is lost in a collision; collision needs to be resolved by retransmissions. A major point of Gallager's paper [10] is that, in his words, "a better set of models and approaches are needed for multiaccess communication than collision resolution or information theory alone."

In this chapter, we consider the interactions between the physical (PHY) and the medium access control (MAC) layers where there are reasonable models that interface the two. Specifically, we focus on how a multiuser physical layer enabled by advanced signal processing affect the design of MAC protocols. We consider a small network (such as wireless LAN) where a few nodes with bursty arrivals communicate with an access point. The design objective is to achieve the highest throughput among users with variable rate and delay constraints. We examine the design of the MAC layer to fully exploit the MPR capability at the physical layer.

Extensive work has been done to address the impact of the MPR capability at the physical layer on the performance of existing MAC protocols. Being the first random access protocol, the application of ALOHA to networks with MPR capability has been thoroughly studied. In [21, 2, 13, 28, 33, 32, 7] and references therein, slotted ALOHA is applied to networks with capture effect. In [11, 12], a general model for channels with MPR capability is developed and the performance of slotted ALOHA analyzed for infinite population case. Other random access protocols such as the FCFS algorithm and the window protocol [23] have also been extended to networks with capture effect and their performance evaluated [27, 20, 29, 3]. The application of contention free scheme TDMA to networks with MPR capability is another interesting research topic. In [6, 17], the authors address the use of TDMA in fully connected half-duplex ad hoc networks with MPR provided by multiple independent collision channels. In [26], dynamic time slot allocation is introduced for cellular systems with antenna arrays. Given a set of active users (users with packets to transmit), the proposed dynamic slot allocation scheme assigns an appropriate number of active users to each time slot to utilize the MPR capability provided by the antenna array.

The design of the MAC layer explicitly based on a multiuser physical layer, however, has rarely been touched. The Multi-Queue Service Room (MQSR) protocol proposed in [30] is perhaps the first MAC protocol designed explicitly for networks with MPR capability. By optimally exploiting all available information up to the current slot, this protocol grants access to the channel to an appropriate subset of users so that the expected number of successfully received packets is maximized in each slot, leading to the optimal utilization of the channel MPR capability. The difficulty of the MQSR protocol, however, lies in its computational complexity which grows exponentially with the number of users in the network. In [31], the dynamic queue protocol is proposed that offers a performance comparable to that of the MQSR protocol with a much simpler implementation. In this chapter, we focus on the performance analysis of the dynamic queue protocol.

2   The Model

We consider a wireless network with M users who transmit data to an access point through a common wireless channel. Each user generates data in the form of equal-sized packets. Transmission time is slotted, and each packet requires one time slot to transmit. With probability p, a user independently generates a packet within each slot.

The common wireless channel is characterized by the probability of having k successes in a slot when there are n transmissions as denoted by

$$C_{n,k} = \text{P}[k \text{ packets are correctly received} \mid n \text{ are transmitted}] \ (1 \leq n \leq M, 0 \leq k \leq n).$$

The multipacket reception matrix of the channel in a network with M users is then defined as

$$\mathbf{C} = \begin{bmatrix} C_{1,0} & C_{1,1} & & & \\ C_{2,0} & C_{2,1} & C_{2,2} & & \\ \vdots & \vdots & \vdots & & \\ C_{M,0} & C_{M,1} & C_{M,2} & \cdots & C_{M,M} \end{bmatrix}. \tag{1}$$

By choosing $C_{1,0} > 0$, this channel model can easily accommodate a noisy environment. Let

$$c_n \overset{\Delta}{=} \sum_{k=1}^{n} k C_{n,k} \tag{2}$$

denote the expected number of correctly received packets when total n packets are transmitted. We then define the capacity of an MPR channel as

$$\eta \overset{\Delta}{=} \max_{n=1,\cdots,M} c_n. \tag{3}$$

Note that the channel capacity we define here differs from that defined by Shannon in information theory. As defined in (3), η is the maximum number of packets that we can expect to successfully receive within one time slot. It is the maximum throughput the MPR channel can offer, independent of MAC protocols. Let

$$n_0 \overset{\Delta}{=} \min\{\arg \max_{n=1,\cdots,M} c_n\}. \tag{4}$$

We can see that at heavy traffic load, n_0 packets should be transmitted simultaneously to achieve the channel capacity η. Noticing that the number of simultaneously transmitted packets for achieving η may not be unique, we define n_0 as the minimum to save transmission power. For MPR channels with n_0 greater than 1, contention should be preferred at any traffic load in order to fully exploit the channel MPR capability.

This general model for MPR channels was first proposed by Ghez, Verdú and Schwartz [11, 12] in 1988. It applies to the conventional collision channel and channels with capture as special examples.

Access to the common wireless channel is controlled by the access point. At the beginning of each slot, the access point chooses and broadcasts an access set which contains users allowed to access the channel in this particular slot. Users and only users in this access set transmit packets if they have any. At the end of this slot, the access point observes the channel outcome which contains information on whether this slot is empty and whose packets are successfully received. Here we assume that the access point can distinguish without error between empty and nonempty slots. Furthermore, if some packets are successfully demodulated at the end of a slot, the access point can identify the source of these packets. However, if at least one packet is successfully demodulated at the end of a slot, the access point does not assume the knowledge whether there are other packets transmitted in this slot but not successfully received.

After observing the channel outcome, the access point acknowledges the sources of successfully received packets (if any). Users who transmit but do not receive acknowledgment assume their packets are lost and will retransmit the next time they are enabled.

3   The Dynamic Queue Protocol

In this section, we give a brief review of the dynamic queue protocol. A detailed description of the protocol can be found in [31].

3.1   The Structure of Transmission Period

In the dynamic queue protocol, the time axis is divided into transmission periods (TPs). Each TP is dedicated to the transmission of packets generated in the previous TP and ends when the access point can assert that all packets generated in the previous TP have been successfully transmitted.

We assume that besides the packet waiting for transmission in the current TP, each user can hold at most one packet newly generated in the current TP and to be transmitted in the next one. Thus, in each TP, each user has at most one packet to transmit. Let q_i denote the probability that a user has a packet to transmit in the ith ($i \geq 1$) TP. Recall that p denotes the probability that a user generates a packet within one time slot. We have

$$q_i = 1 - (1-p)^{L_{i-1}}, \tag{5}$$

where L_{i-1} ($i \geq 2$) denotes the length of the $(i-1)$th TP defined as the number of slots it contains; L_0 specifies the network initial condition and is known to the access point. Thus, q_i carries our knowledge on the state of each user at the beginning of the ith TP. Based on q_i and the channel reception matrix $\mathbf{C}$, the size N_i of the access set which contains users who can simultaneously access the channel in the ith TP is chosen optimally (see Section 3.3). Packets generated in the $(i-1)$th TP are then transmitted according to the procedure specified in Section 3.2.

3.2   The Structure of the Dynamic Queue Protocol

The basic structure of the dynamic queue protocol is a waiting queue. At the beginning of the ith TP, all M users are waiting in a queue for the transmission of their packets generated in the $(i-1)$th TP. A user is said to be processed if the access point detects either it does not generate packet in the $(i-1)$th TP or its packet generated in the $(i-1)$th TP has been successfully transmitted. Based on q_i given by (5), N_i, the size of the access set for this TP, is chosen. Then, the first N_i users in the queue are enabled to access the channel in the first slot of the ith TP. At the end of this slot, the access point detects whether this slot is empty or not. If it is empty, all these N_i users are processed and the next N_i users in the queue are enabled in the next slot. On the other hand, if this slot is not empty and k ($k \geq 0$) packets are successfully received, the sources of these k packets are processed and removed from the waiting queue; the rest $N_i - k$ users along with the next k users in the queue are enabled to access the channel in the next slot. This procedure continues until all M users are processed.

With this structure, the only parameter to be designed is N_i, the size of the access set for the ith $(i \geq 1)$ TP, which we discuss in Section 3.3.

We point out that the order of a user in the waiting queue affects its average packet delay. While all users generate packets simultaneously, users in the front of the queue access the channel before users in the end of the queue unless $N_i = M$. If priority among users is desired, users with higher priority should be in the front of the queue in each TP. Otherwise, the order of a user in the queue needs to be randomized at the beginning of each TP to ensure fairness.

3.3   The Optimal Access Set

The optimal size N_i of the access set for the ith TP is chosen so that the expected length of this TP is minimized, ie, the expected number of slots for processing all M users, each with probability q_i having a packet, is minimized. Specifically, N_i is determined by

$$N_i = \arg \min_{N=1,\cdots,M} E[L_i \mid q_i, N], \tag{6}$$

where $E[L_i \mid q_i, N]$ is the expected length of the ith TP when each user with probability q_i has a packet to transmit and the size of the access set is N.

In order to determine N_i, we calculate $E[L_i \mid q_i, N]$ as the absorbing time of a finite state discrete Markov chain. It can be shown that the number of unprocessed users at the beginning of a slot along with the number of packets that will be transmitted in this slot forms a Markov chain. Specifically, at the beginning of a slot in the ith TP, the network is in state (j, k) if there are j $(j = 0, \cdots, M)$ unprocessed users and k $(k = 0, \cdots, \min\{N, j\})$ packets to be transmitted in this slot when the size of access set is chosen to be N. The transition probability from state (j, k) to state (l, m) is given by

$$r_{(j,k),(l,m)} = \begin{cases} B(m, \min\{N, l\}, q_i) \\ \quad (\text{if } k = 0, l = \max\{j - N, 0\}, 0 \leq m \leq \min\{N, l\}) \\ C_{k,j-l} B(m - k + j - l, \min\{j - l, \max\{j - N, 0\}\}, q_i) \\ \quad (\text{if } 1 \leq k \leq \min\{N, j\}, j - k \leq l \leq j, k - (j - l) \leq m \leq \min\{k, l\}) \\ 0 \quad (\text{otherwise}) \end{cases}, \tag{7}$$

where $B(u, U, s)$ denote the probability mass at the value u of a Binomial random variable with total U trials and a success probability s, ie,

$$B(u, U, s) \triangleq \binom{U}{u} s^u (1-s)^{U-u}. \tag{8}$$

The initial condition of this Markov chain is given by

$$P[X_0 = (M, k)] = B(k, N, q_i), \quad k = 0, \cdots, N, \tag{9}$$

where X_0 denote the initial state of the Markov chain. With state $(0,0)$ defined as the absorbing state, $E[L_i \mid q_i, N]$ is the absorbing time of this Markov chain, which is defined as the expected number of transitions until the first hit of state $(0,0)$. Define $e_{(j,k)}$ as the expected remaining time until absorption given that the current state is (j,k). Let

$$\mathbf{e} \triangleq [e_{(M,0)}, \cdots, e_{(M,N)}, e_{(M-1,0)}, \cdots, e_{(1,0)}, e_{(1,1)}, e_{(0,0)}]^t. \tag{10}$$

We then have

$$(\mathbf{I} - \mathbf{P})\mathbf{e} = \mathbf{1}, \tag{11}$$

where $\mathbf{P}$ is the transition probability matrix (after removing the absorbing state $(0,0)$) with entries specified by (7), $\mathbf{I}$ and $\mathbf{1}$ denote, respectively, an identity matrix and a vector with all entries equal to 1.

From (11), we can solve for $e_{(M,k)}$ for $k = 0, \cdots, N$. Thus, considering the initial condition of the Markov chain given by (9), we can calculate $E[L_i \mid q_i, N]$ as

$$E[L_i \mid q_i, N] = \sum_{k=0}^{N} B(k, N, q_i) e_{(M,k)}. \tag{12}$$

With $E[L_i \mid q_i, N]$ computed for all possible N, the optimal size N_i of the access set for the ith TP can be easily obtained from (6).

We point out that the optimal size of the access set can be computed off line. By varying q_i from 0 to 1, we can construct a table that specifies the interval of q_i in which a size $N \in \{1, \cdots, M\}$ of the access set is optimal (a typical look-up table is illustrated in Figure 2). Thus, when the network starts, the optimal size of the access set for each TP can be obtained from this table; little on-line computation is required to implement the dynamic queue protocol.

4   Steady-State Performance Analysis

Our main concern with MAC protocols is their long term behavior (when the initial condition of the network becomes irrelevant). Thus, steady-state performance measures such as throughput and average delay are commonly used for evaluating a MAC protocol. In this section, we study the steady-state performance of the dynamic queue protocol using throughput and average delay as our measures. First, we show that the network employing the dynamic queue protocol eventually reaches a steady state, regardless of the initial condition L_0. We then derive, in Section 4.2, formulas for throughput and average delay provided by the dynamic queue protocol at an arbitrary traffic load.

4.1   The Existence of Steady State

Given the channel reception matrix $\mathbf{C}$ and the incoming traffic load p, the optimal size N_i of the access set for the ith TP is a function of L_{i-1}, ie,

$$N_i = f_{\mathbf{C}, p}(L_{i-1}). \tag{13}$$

In general, $f_{C,p}(\cdot)$ is a monotonically decreasing [1] function as illusrated in Figure 6 of [31]. It is completely determined by C and p and can be computed off line. Suppose that the range of $f_{C,p}(\cdot)$ is $\{\underline{n}_1, \cdots, \underline{n}_J\}$ with $\underline{n}_1 > \underline{n}_2 > \cdots > \underline{n}_J$. We then define

$$\underline{l}_j \triangleq \min\{l : f_{C,p}(l) = \underline{n}_j\}, \quad j = 1, \cdots, J. \tag{14}$$

It can be shown (see Appendix A) that $\{L_i\}_{i=0}^{\infty}$ is a homogeneous Markov process with infinite state space $s = z^+$ (z^+ denotes the set of positive integers) and transition probability

$$p_{l,m} \triangleq P[L_i = m \mid L_{i-1} = l]. \tag{15}$$

The steady state of a network using the dynamic queue protocol is then defined as the stationary distribution of $\{L_i\}_{i=0}^{\infty}$. Before using steady-state performance measures such as throughput and average delay, questions about the existence and uniqueness of the network steady states must be resolved.

Theorem 1 *Suppose that $f_{C,p}(\cdot)$ is a monotonically decreasing function with range $\{\underline{n}_1, \cdots, \underline{n}_J\}$. Let*

$$Q_1 = \{1, 2, \cdots, \lceil \frac{M}{\underline{n}_w} \rceil - 1\}, \quad Q_2 = \{\lceil \frac{M}{\underline{n}_w} \rceil, \lceil \frac{M}{\underline{n}_w} \rceil + 1, \cdots\} \tag{16}$$

be a partition of the state space s, where

$$w \triangleq \max\{j : \lceil \frac{M}{\underline{n}_j} \rceil \geq \underline{l}_j, 1 \leq j \leq J\}. \tag{17}$$

Consider a noisy environment with $0 < C_{1,0} < 1$. We have, for $p \in (0,1)$,

T1.1 all states in Q_1 are transient;

T1.2 if the initial distribution of $\{L_i\}_{i=0}^{\infty}$ is such that $P[L_0 \in Q_2] = 1$, then $\{L_i\}_{i=0}^{\infty}$ is ergodic;

T1.3 $\{L_i\}_{i=0}^{\infty}$ has a limiting distribution $\{\pi_l\}_{l \in s}$ satisfying

$$\pi_l \begin{cases} > 0 & \text{if } l \in Q_2 \\ = 0 & \text{if } l \in Q_1 \end{cases}. \tag{18}$$

The proof of Theorem 1 is based on the following properties of $\{L_i\}_{i=0}^{\infty}$ (proved in Appendix B).

---

[1] A heuristic argument for $f_{C,p}(\cdot)$ being monotonic decreasing is as follows. In order to process all packets generated in the $(i-1)$th TP within a minimum number of slots, n_0 (as defined in (4)) packets should be transmitted simultaneously in each slot. With a smaller L_{i-1}, the probability that a user has a packet to transmit in the ith TP is smaller. Hence, the access set for the ith TP need to be enlarged so that the total number of packets held by users in the access set approaches n_0.

Property 1 *Let $l \rightarrow m$ denote that state l leads to state m. Under the same assumptions in Theorem 1, The Markov process $\{L_i\}_{i=0}^{\infty}$ has the following properties.*

P1.1 For $l, m \in s$ with $m \geq \lceil \frac{M}{\underline{n}_j} \rceil$, $l < \underline{l}_{j+1}$, where $j = 1, \cdots, J$ and $\underline{l}_{J+1} \triangleq \infty$, we have

$$l \rightarrow m. \tag{19}$$

P1.2 For $l, m \in s$ with $m < \lceil \frac{M}{\underline{n}_w} \rceil$, $l \geq \lceil \frac{M}{\underline{n}_w} \rceil$, we have

$$l \nrightarrow m. \tag{20}$$

Proof of Theorem 1:

T1.1: Consider a state $l \in \varrho_1$. Since $l < \underline{l}_{J+1} \triangleq \infty$, we have, from *P1.1*,

$$l \rightarrow \lceil \frac{M}{\underline{n}_J} \rceil. \tag{21}$$

Since $\underline{n}_w \geq \underline{n}_J$, we have,

$$\lceil \frac{M}{\underline{n}_J} \rceil \geq \lceil \frac{M}{\underline{n}_w} \rceil. \tag{22}$$

Hence, by the fact that $l < \lceil \frac{M}{\underline{n}_w} \rceil$ and *P1.2*,

$$\lceil \frac{M}{\underline{n}_J} \rceil \nrightarrow l. \tag{23}$$

We then conclude from (21,23) that there is a positive probability of the chain leaving state l and never coming back, ie, state l is transient.

T1.2: Consider a state $l \in \varrho_2$, ie, $l \geq \lceil \frac{M}{\underline{n}_w} \rceil$. By *P1.2*,

$$l \nrightarrow m \tag{24}$$

for any $m \in \varrho_1$. Hence, when we restrict the initial state to ϱ_2, the state space of $\{L_i\}_{i=0}^{\infty}$ becomes ϱ_2. To show $\{L_i\}_{i=0}^{\infty}$ is ergodic under this initial condition, we need to show it is irreducible, aperiodic, and positive recurrent.

Since $l < \underline{l}_{J+1} \triangleq \infty$ holds for any l, *P1.1* implies that any state leads to a state no smaller than $\lceil \frac{M}{\underline{n}_J} \rceil$. Hence, any two states no smaller than $\lceil \frac{M}{\underline{n}_J} \rceil$ communicate. It then follows that when $w = J$, the chain is irreducible. When $w < J$, we only need to show that for any $\lceil \frac{M}{\underline{n}_w} \rceil \leq m < \lceil \frac{M}{\underline{n}_J} \rceil$, we have m as a consequence of $\lceil \frac{M}{\underline{n}_J} \rceil$. Since $\lceil \frac{M}{\underline{n}_J} \rceil < \underline{l}_j$ for $w < j \leq J$ by the definition of w, we have, from *P1.1*,

$$\lceil \frac{M}{\underline{n}_j} \rceil \rightarrow \lceil \frac{M}{\underline{n}_{j-1}} \rceil, \quad w < j \leq J. \tag{25}$$

Thus,

$$\lceil \frac{M}{\underline{n}_J} \rceil \to \lceil \frac{M}{\underline{n}_{J-1}} \rceil \to \cdots \to \lceil \frac{M}{\underline{n}_w} \rceil. \tag{26}$$

Since $\lceil \frac{M}{\underline{n}_w} \rceil \leq \lceil \frac{M}{\underline{n}_{w+1}} \rceil < \underline{l}_{w+1}$, and $m \geq \lceil \frac{M}{\underline{n}_w} \rceil$, we have, by $P1.1$,

$$\lceil \frac{M}{\underline{n}_w} \rceil \to m. \tag{27}$$

This completes the proof of the chain being irreducible. $\{L_i\}_{i=0}^{\infty}$ being aperiodic follows directly from the self loop at state $\lceil \frac{M}{\underline{n}_J} \rceil$.

We now show, through Pakes Lemma [22], that this irreducible and aperiodic Markov chain is ergodic. Let d_l be the drift at state l defined as

$$d_l \triangleq E[L_i - L_{i-1} \mid L_{i-1} = l]. \tag{28}$$

We have, for any $l \in \varrho_2$,

$$
\begin{aligned}
d_l &= E[L_i \mid L_{i-1} = l] - l \\
&\leq \frac{M}{C_{1,1}} - l,
\end{aligned}
\tag{29}
$$

where (29) follows from the fact that

$$E[L_i \mid L_{i-1} = l] \leq E[L_i \mid N_i = 1] = \frac{M}{C_{1,1}}. \tag{30}$$

Thus,

$$\limsup_{l \to \infty} d_l < 0. \tag{31}$$

By Pakes Lemma, we conclude that $\{L_i\}_{i=0}^{\infty}$ is ergodic.

T1.3: This statement follows directly from *T1.1* and *T1.2*.

□□□

Theorem 1 shows that a network which employs the dynamic queue protocol will eventually reach a unique steady state, regardless of the initial condition L_0. Thus, we can use measures such as throughput and average delay to study the long term behavior of the dynamic queue protocol.

4.2   Throughput and Packet Delay

4.2.1   Throughput

The throughput U is defined as the average number of packets successfully transmitted within one time slot. Let S_i denote the number of packets generated in the ith TP. Recall that packets generated in the ith TP are all successfully transmitted in the $(i+1)$th TP. We have

$$U = \lim_{i \to \infty} \frac{S_0 + S_1 + \cdots + S_{i-1}}{L_1 + L_2 + \cdots + L_i}. \tag{32}$$

By Theorem 1, $\{L_i\}_{i=0}^{\infty}$ is an ergodic process with limiting distribution $\{\pi_l\}_{l \in s}$ given by (18). Hence, at steady state, we have, for any $p \in (0,1)$,

$$
\begin{aligned}
U &= \frac{E[S_i]}{E[L_i]} \\
&= \frac{\sum_{l \in Q_2} (\sum_{n=0}^{M} nB(n, M, 1 - (1-p)^l)) \pi_l}{\sum_{l \in Q_2} l \pi_l} \\
&= \frac{\sum_{l \in Q_2} (1 - (1-p)^l) M \pi_l}{\sum_{l \in Q_2} l \pi_l}.
\end{aligned} \tag{33}
$$

4.2.2 Average Packet Delay

The average packet delay D is defined as the average number of slots from the time a packet is generated to that it is successfully transmitted. Since a packet generated in the ith TP is transmitted in the $(i+1)$th TP, the average packet delay is determined by the lengths of two consecutive TPs. Based on the Markovian property of $\{L_i\}_{i=0}^{\infty}$, we can show that $\{(L_i, L_{i+1})\}_{i=0}^{\infty}$ is a homogeneous Markov process with infinite state space $\hat{s} \in z^+ \times z^+$. Its transition probability is given by

$$
\begin{aligned}
\hat{P}_{(j,k),(l,m)} &\overset{\Delta}{=} P[(L_i, L_{i+1}) = (l,m) \mid (L_{i-1}, L_i) = (j,k)] \\
&= \begin{cases} 0 & \text{if } l \neq k \\ p_{l,m} & \text{if } l = k \end{cases}.
\end{aligned} \tag{34}
$$

Furthermore, if $\{L_i\}_{i=0}^{\infty}$ has a limiting distribution $\{\pi_l\}_{l \in s}$ given by (18), then $\{(L_i, L_{i+1})\}_{i=0}^{\infty}$ has a limiting distribution $\{\hat{\pi}_{(l,m)}\}_{(l,m) \in \hat{s}}$ given by

$$
\hat{\pi}_{(l,m)} = \pi_l p_{l,m} \begin{cases} > 0 & \text{if } l, m \in Q_2 \\ = 0 & \text{otherwise} \end{cases}, \tag{35}
$$

which follows from

$$
\hat{\pi}_{(l,m)} \overset{\Delta}{=} \lim_{i \to \infty} P[(L_i, L_{i+1}) = (l,m)] = \lim_{i \to \infty} P[L_i = l] p_{l,m} = \pi_l p_{l,m}.
$$

Based on the limiting distribution of $\{(L_i, L_{i+1})\}_{i=0}^{\infty}$, the average delay provided by the dynamic queue protocol can be calculated as follows.

In the steady state, with probability $\hat{\pi}_{(l,m)}$, a packet is generated in a TP with length l and successfully transmitted in a TP with length m. Without loss of generality, we assume these two transmission periods are the first and the second TP. Let t_g and t_s denote, respectively, the time instance that the packet is generated and that the packet is successfully received. Assuming that the first TP starts at time 0 and each slot lasts one time unit, we have

$$
\begin{aligned}
D &= \sum_{l,m \in Q_2} E[t_s - t_g \mid L_1 = l, L_2 = m] \hat{\pi}_{(l,m)} \\
&= \sum_{l,m \in Q_2} (E[t_s \mid L_1 = l, L_2 = m] - E[t_g \mid L_1 = l]) \hat{\pi}_{(l,m)}.
\end{aligned}
\tag{36}
$$

Assuming that t_g is uniformly distributed in the slot in which the packet is generated, we have,

$$
E[t_g \mid L_1 = l] = \frac{p \sum_{k=1}^{l} k(1-p)^{k-1}}{1 - (1-p)^l} - 0.5,
\tag{37}
$$

where the first term is the probability that the packet is generated in the kth slot of the first TP which has length l. Furthermore,

$$
E[t_s \mid L_1 = l, L_2 = m] \le l + m,
\tag{38}
$$

we thus have, from (36),

$$
\begin{aligned}
D &\le \sum_{l,m \in Q_2} (l + m - \frac{p \sum_{k=1}^{l} k(1-p)^{k-1}}{1 - (1-p)^l} + 0.5) \hat{\pi}_{(l,m)} \\
&= \sum_{l,m \in Q_2} (l + m - \frac{p \sum_{k=1}^{l} k(1-p)^{k-1}}{1 - (1-p)^l} + 0.5) \pi_l p_{l,m}.
\end{aligned}
\tag{39}
$$

From (33,39) we see that the throughput and average delay provided by the dynamic queue protocol are given by the limiting distribution $\{\pi_l\}_{l \in s}$ and the transition probability $\{p_{l,m}\}_{l,m \in s}$ of $\{L_i\}_{i=0}^{\infty}$. In general, these two quantities are difficult to obtain even numerically. For simple examples, however, they may be studied analytically as shown in Section 5.1. Another special case where the throughput and average delay can be computed numerically is when $p = 1$, which we discuss in Section 4.2.3.

4.2.3   Throughput and Average Delay at $p = 1$

At $p = 1$, we have $q_i = 1$ for any i. It then follows that $\{L_i\}_{i=0}^{\infty}$ is an i.i.d. sequence. The throughput and average delay for $p = 1$ are given by

$$
U = \frac{M}{\min_{N=1,\cdots,M} E[L_i \mid q_i = 1, N]},
\tag{40}
$$

$$
D \le 2 \min_{N=1,\cdots,M} E[L_i \mid q_i = 1, N] - 0.5.
\tag{41}
$$

As shown in Section 3.3, $E[L_i \mid q_i = 1, N]$ can be obtained by analyzing the absorbing time of a finite state Markov chain. With $q_i = 1$ for all i, we can simply the state of this Markov chain to the number j of unprocessed users. The transition probability then becomes

$$r_{j,l} = \begin{cases} C_{\min\{N,j\}, j-l} & \text{if } 0 \leq l \leq j \\ 0 & \text{otherwise} \end{cases} . \tag{42}$$

The initial condition of this Markov chain is given by

$$P[X_0 = M] = 1. \tag{43}$$

With state 0 defined as the absorbing state, $E[L_i \mid q_i = 1, N]$ can be obtained as

$$E[L_i \mid q_i = 1, N] = e_M, \tag{44}$$

where e_M is the absorbing time of the Markov chain. With $E[L_i \mid q_i = 1, N]$ computed for all possible N, the throughput and an upper bound on the average delay at $p = 1$ can be easily obtained from (40,41).

5   Numerical and Simulation Examples

5.1   A Numerical Example

We first study a simple numerical example with $M = 2$. The channel reception matrix is given by

$$\mathbf{C} = \begin{bmatrix} 1 - p_1 & p_1 & 0 \\ 1 - p_2 & p_2 & 0 \end{bmatrix}, \tag{45}$$

where $0 < p_1, p_2 \leq 1$. By analyzing the absorbing time of the Markov chain with transition probability given by (7), we have

$$\begin{aligned} E[L_i \mid q_i, N_i = 1] &= 2 + 2(1 - p_1)q_i/p_1, \\ E[L_i \mid q_i, N_i = 2] &= 1 + \frac{2}{p_1}q_i + \frac{p_1 - p_2 - p_1 p_2}{p_1 p_2}q_i^2. \end{aligned} \tag{46}$$

Thus, to minimize $E[L_i]$, we have, for the case of $p_2 < p_1$,

$$N_i = \begin{cases} 2 & \text{if } q_i \leq q^* \\ 1 & \text{if } q_i > q^* \end{cases}, \tag{47}$$

where

$$q^* = \begin{cases} \dfrac{1}{2} & \text{if } p_2 = \dfrac{p_1}{1+p_1} \\ \dfrac{\sqrt{p_1 p_2 (p_1 - p_2)} - p_1 p_2}{p_1 - p_2 - p_1 p_2} & \text{otherwise} \end{cases} . \tag{48}$$

However, when $p_2 \geq p_1$, we have $N_i = 2$ for all q_i, ie, when the MPR capability is sufficiently strong, contention is desirable at any traffic load. In this example, we consider $p_2 < p_1$ which is usually the case.

By taking into account the incoming traffic load $0 < p < 1$, N_i as a function of L_{i-1} can be obtained from (47) as

$$N_i = \begin{cases} 2 & \text{if } 1 \leq L_{i-1} < l_2 \\ 1 & \text{if } L_{i-1} \geq l_2 \end{cases}, \tag{49}$$

where

$$l_2 = \lceil \frac{\ln(1-q^*)}{\ln(1-p)} \rceil. \tag{50}$$

Suppose that $p \geq 1 - \sqrt{1-q^*}$. In this case, we have $l_2 \leq 2$. From Theorem 1 we conclude that

$$\mathcal{Q}_1 = \{1\}, \quad \mathcal{Q}_2 = \{2,3,\cdots\} \tag{51}$$

contain, respectively, the transient states and positive recurrent states of $\{L_i\}_{i=0}^{\infty}$. It can be shown that the transition probability for states in $\mathcal{Q}_2$ is given by

$$p_{l,m} = \begin{cases} (1-(1-p)^l)^2 p_1^2 + 2(1-p)^l(1-(1-p)^l)p_1 + (1-p)^{2l} & \text{if } m = 2 \\ (1-(1-p)^l)^2(m-1)p_1^2(1-p_1)^{m-2} + 2(1-p)^l(1-(1-p)^l)p_1(1-p_1)^{m-2} & \text{if } m > 2 \end{cases}. \tag{52}$$

The limiting distribution of $\{L_i\}_{i=0}^{\infty}$ is then given by

$$\pi_l = \begin{cases} ap_1^2 + bp_1 + (1-a-b) & \text{if } l = 2 \\ a(l-1)p_1^2(1-p_1)^{l-2} + bp_1(1-p_1)^{l-2} & \text{if } l > 2 \end{cases}, \tag{53}$$

where a and b are, respectively, the probability that both users have packet and that only one user has packet at the beginning of a TP in the steady state. It is difficult to obtain them in close form. However, by estimating them through simulations, we can easily obtain the limiting distribution of $\{L_i\}_{i=0}^{\infty}$. The throughput can then be calculated from (33).

We now consider an example with $p_1 = \frac{3}{4}$ and $p_2 = \frac{1}{2}$. The limiting distribution of $\{L_i\}_{i=0}^{\infty}$ at $p = 0.4$ and $p = 0.9$ are shown in Figure 1, where we see that π_l decays exponentially in l, as promised by (53). Comparing the limiting distribution at $p = 0.4$ and that at $p = 0.9$, we see that $E[L_i]$ increases with the incoming traffic load p. The calculated and the simulated throughput of this 2-user system are shown in Figure 1 as a function of p. In both cases, the theoretical results match well with the simulation results.

5.2   Simulation Examples: MPR via Spread Spectrum

In this example, we consider a CDMA network with M users. Each transmitted packet is spread by a randomly generated code with length P. At the access point, the spreading code of each transmitted packet is assumed known, and a bank of matched filters are used as the

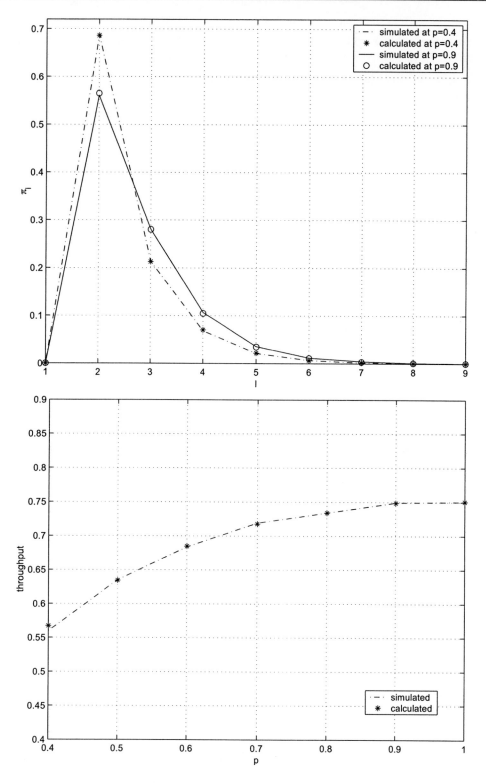

Figure 1: The limiting distribution and the throughput for the 2-user example.

receiver. We assume that each packet contains L_p bits. A block error control code is used which corrects up to t errors in each received packet. We consider a noisy environment where the variance of the additive white Gaussian noise is denoted by σ^2.

We first construct the reception matrix $\mathbf{C}$ for such a network. Under the Gaussian assumption on the multiaccess interference from users with equal power, the bit-error-rate (BER) p_e of a packet received in the presence of $n-1$ interfering packets is given by [19]

$$p_e(n-1) = Q(\sqrt{\frac{3P}{n-1+3P\sigma^2}}). \tag{54}$$

Assuming that errors occur independently in a packet, we then have the packet success probability in the presence of $n-1$ interfering packets as

$$p_s(n-1) = \sum_{i=0}^{t} B(i, L_p, p_e). \tag{55}$$

Under the assumption that each matched filter works independently at the receiver, we have

$$C_{n,k} = B(k, n, p_s(n-1)). \tag{56}$$

We compare the throughput performance of the dynamic queue protocol with that of the MQSR protocol and the slotted ALOHA with optimal retransmission probability. We considered a network with $M = 10$. The packet length L_p, spreading gain P, and the number of correctable errors in a packet were, respectively, 200, 6, and 2. The noise variance was given by $10\log_{10}\frac{1}{\sigma^2} = 10dB$. The capacity of the MPR channel in such a network is 1.7925, which can be achieved by transmitting $n_0 = 2$ packets in each slot.

We first construct the look-up table that specifies the q_i intervals in which a possible size (from 1 to 10) of access set is optimal. The result is shown in Figure 2. This result demonstrates clearly the trend that the heavier the traffic is (larger q_i), the smaller the access set should be, as intuition suggests. Note that the optimal size of access set equals to n_0 which is greater than 1 at the heaviest traffic load ($q_i = 1$), indicating that contention is preferable at any traffic load for this MPR channel.

In Figure 3, the throughput performance of the dynamic queue protocol at different incoming traffic load p is compared to that of the multi-queue service room (MQSR) protocol [30] and the delayed first transmission ALOHA with optimal retransmission probability. Comparing the performance of the dynamic queue protocol with that of the slotted ALOHA with optimal retransmission probability, we see a 55% throughput gain at medium and heavy traffic load. Compared to the MQSR protocol which aims to determine the access set for each slot by optimally exploiting all available information, the dynamic queue protocol achieved comparable performance with a much simpler implementation. Note that the throughput provided by the dynamic queue protocol at heavy traffic load approached to the channel capacity 1.7925.

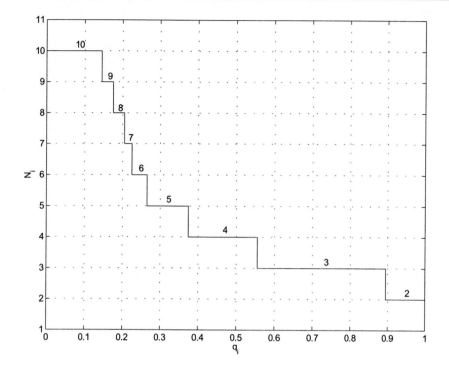

Figure 2: The optimal size of access set.

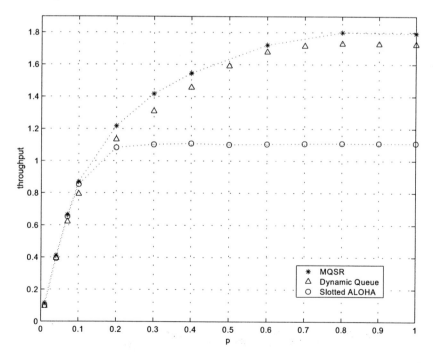

Figure 3: Throughput comparison.

6   Conclusion

We consider the dynamic queue protocol and its steady-state performance analysis. According to the traffic load and the channel MPR capability, the dynamic queue protocol adaptively controls the number of users who gain access to the channel in the same slot. As a consequence, unnecessary empty slots at light traffic and excessive collision events at heavy traffic are avoided simultaneously, leading to efficient channel utilization at any incoming traffic load. Furthermore, this protocol is particularly attractive in its simple implementation.

Appendix A

On the Markovian Property of $\{L_i\}_{i=0}^{\infty}$

Given the channel reception matrix $\mathbf{C}$ and the traffic load p, the distribution of L_i is completely determined by q_i and N_i (see Figure 3), which in turn, are determined by L_{i-1} through (5) and (13). We thus have

$$P[L_i = l_i \mid L_{i-1} = l_{i-1}, \cdots, L_0 = l_0] = P[L_i = l_i \mid L_{i-1} = l_{i-1}] \overset{\Delta}{=} p_{l_{i-1}, l_i}, \qquad (57)$$

ie, $\{L_i\}_{i=0}^{\infty}$ form a Markov chain. Since the transition probability $\{p_{l,m}\}$ is independent of the TP index i, this Markov chain is homogeneous. We consider here an initial condition L_0 which can take any positive integers, resulting in an infinite state space $s = z^+$.

□□□

Appendix B

Proof of Property 1

We start with *P1.2*, which follows directly from the following two facts.

1. If $N_i = \underline{n}_j$ ($j = 1, \cdots, J$), the minimum value that L_i can take is $\lceil \frac{M}{\underline{n}_j} \rceil$.

2. Based on $f_{\mathbf{C},p}(\cdot)$ being monotonically decreasing, when $L_{i-1} = l \geq \underline{l}_j$, we have $N_i \leq \underline{n}_j$.

Consider $L_{i-1} = l \geq \lceil \frac{M}{\underline{n}_w} \rceil \geq \underline{l}_w$. By the second statement above, we have $N_i \leq \underline{n}_w$. Then by the first statement, we have

$$L_i \geq \lceil \frac{M}{N_i} \rceil \geq \lceil \frac{M}{\underline{n}_w} \rceil, \qquad (58)$$

ie, starting with a state no smaller than $\lceil \frac{M}{\underline{n}_w} \rceil$, the chain can never hit a state smaller than $\lceil \frac{M}{\underline{n}_w} \rceil$. This proves *P1.2*.

We now consider *P1.1*. Similar to the second statement above, when $L_{i-1} = l < \underline{l}_{j+1}$, we have $N_i \geq \underline{n}_j$. Hence,

$$\lceil \frac{M}{\underline{n}_j} \rceil \geq \lceil \frac{M}{N_i} \rceil. \tag{59}$$

For $m \geq \lceil \frac{M}{\underline{n}_j} \rceil$, we have $m \geq \lceil \frac{M}{N_i} \rceil$. When equality holds, by considering the event that no packet has been generated in the $(i-1)$ TP, we have

$$p_{l,m} \overset{\Delta}{=} P[L_i = m \mid L_{i-1} = l] \geq (1 - q_i)^M > 0, \tag{60}$$

where

$$0 < q_i = 1 - (1 - p)^l < 1. \tag{61}$$

When $m > \lceil \frac{M}{N_i} \rceil$, we consider the event that only the first user in the queue has generated a packet in the $(i-1)$th TP. Thus,

$$p_{l,m} \geq q_i(1 - q_i)^{M-1} C_{1,0}^{m - \lceil \frac{M-1}{N_i} \rceil} C_{1,1} > 0, \tag{62}$$

which completes the proof of *P1.1*.

□□□

References

[1] N. Abramson. "The Aloha System - Another Alternative for Computer Communications". In *Proc. Fall Joint Comput. Conf., AFIPS Conf.*, page 37, 1970.

[2] N. Abramson. "The Throughput of Packet Broadcasting Channels". *IEEE Trans. Comm*, COM-25(1):117–128, January 1977.

[3] D.E. Ayyildiz and H. Delic. "Adaptive Random Access Algorithm with Improved Delay Performance". *Int. J. Commun. Syst.*, 14:531–539, 2001.

[4] J.I. Capetanakis. "Generalized TDMA: The Multi-Accessing Tree Protocol". *IEEE Trans. Communications*, **27**(10):1476–1484, Oct. 1979.

[5] J.I. Capetanakis. "Tree Algorithms for Packet Broadcast Channels.". *IEEE Trans. Information Theory*, **25**(5):505–515, Sept. 1979.

[6] I. Chlamtac and A. Farago. "An Optimal Channel Access Protocol with Multiple Reception Capacity". *IEEE Trans. Computers*, **43**(4):480–484, April 1994.

[7] G. del Angel and T.L. Fine. "Randomized Power Control Strategies for Optimization of Multiple Access Radio Systems". In *Proc. 38th Allerton Conference on Communication, Control and Computing*, October 2000.

[8] Anthony Ephremides and Bruce Hajek. Information Theory and Communication Networks: An Unconsummated Union. *IEEE Trans. Inform. Theory*, **44**(6):2416–2434, October 1998.

[9] R. Gallager. "Conflict Resolution in Random Access Broadcast Networks". In *Proc. of AFOSR Workshop on Comm. Theory and Appl.*, pages 74–76, Sept. 1978.

[10] R.G. Gallager. A Perspective on Multiaccess Channels. *IEEE Trans. Information Theory*, IT-31(2):124–142, March 1985.

[11] S. Ghez, S. Verdú, and S.C. Schwartz. "Stability Properties of Slotted Aloha with Multipacket Reception Capability" . *IEEE Trans. Automat. Contr.*, **33**(7):640–649, July 1988.

[12] S. Ghez, S. Verdú, and S.C. Schwartz. "Optimal Decentralized Control in the Random Access Multipacket Channel". *IEEE Trans. Automat. Contr.*, **34**(11):1153–1163, Nov. 1989.

[13] I.M.I. Habbab and *et al.* "ALOHA with Capture over Slow and Fast Fading Radio Channels with Coding and Diversity". *IEEE Journal on Select. Areas in Comm.*, 7:79–88, January 1989.

[14] M.G. Hluchyj. "Multiple Access Window Protocol: Analysis for Large Finite Populations". In *Proc. IEEE Conf. on Decision and Control*, pages 589–595, New York, NY, 1982.

[15] M.G. Hluchyj and R.G. Gallager. "Multiaccess of A Slotted Channel by Finitely Many Users". In *Proc. Nat. Telecomm. Conf.*, pages D4.2.1–D4.2.7, New Orleans, LA., Aug. 1981.

[16] R.K. Morrow Jr. and J.S. Lehnert. "Packet Throughput in Slotted ALOHA DS/SSMA Radio Systems with Random Signature Sequences". *IEEE Trans. Comm.*, **40**(7):1223–1230, July 1992.

[17] S. Kim and J. Yeo. "Optimal Scheduling in CDMA Pakcet Radio Networks". *Computers and Operations Research*, **25**:219–227, March 1998.

[18] L. Kleinrock and Y. Yemini. "An Optimal Adaptive Scheme for Multiple Access Broadcast Communication". In *Proc. International Conference on Communications*, pages 7.2.1–7.2.5, June 1978.

[19] J. Lehnert and M. Pursley. "Error Probabilities for Binary Direct-Sequence Spread-Spectrum Communications with Random Signature Sequences". *IEEE Trans. on Communications*, COM-35(1):87–98, January 1987.

[20] D.F. Lyons and P. Papantoni-Kazakos. "A Window Random Access Algorithm for Environments with Capture". *IEEE Trans. on Communications*, **37**(7):766–770, July 1989.

[21] J.J. Metzner. "On Improving Utilization in ALOHA Networks". *IEEE Trans. Communications*, **24**:447–448, Apr. 1976.

[22] A.G. Pakes. "some conditions for ergodicity and recurrence of markov chains". *Operation Research*, **17**:1058–1061, 1969.

[23] M. Paterakis and P. Papantoni-Kazakos. "A Simple Window Random Access Algorithm with Advantageous Properties". *IEEE Trans. Information Theory*, **35**(5):1124–1130, September 1989.

[24] A. Polydors and J. Sylvester. "Slotted Random Access Spread-Spectrum Networks: An Analytical Framework". *IEEE Journal on Selected Areas in Communications*, SAC-5:989–1002, July 1987.

[25] L.G. Roberts. "Aloha Packet System with and without Slots and Capture". In *(ASS Note 8). Stanford, CA: Stanford Research Institute, Advanced Research Projects Agency, Network Information Center.*, 1972.

[26] F. Shad, T.D. Todd, V. Kezys, and J. Litva. "Dynamic Slot Allocation (DSA) in Indoor SDMA/TDMA Using a Smart Antenna Basestation". *IEEE/ACM Trans. on Networking*, **9**(1):69–81, February 2001.

[27] M. Sidi and I. Cidon. "Splitting Protocols in Presence of Capture". *IEEE Trans. Info. Theory*, IT-31:295–301, March 1985.

[28] C. Vanderplas and J.P.M. Linnartz. "Stability of Mobile Slotted ALOHA Network with Rayleigh Fading, Shadowing, and Near-far Effect". *IEEE Trans. Veh. Tech.*, **39**:359–366, November 1990.

[29] B. Yucel and H. Delic. "Mobile Radio Window Random Access Algorithm with Diversity". *IEEE Trans. Vehicular Technology*, **49**(6):2060–2070, November 2000.

[30] Q. Zhao and L. Tong. "A Multi-Queue Service Room MAC Protocol for Wireless Networks with Multipacket Reception". *IEEE/ACM Transactions on Networking*, February 2003.

[31] Q. Zhao and L. Tong. "A Dynamic Queue Protocol for Multiaccess Wireless Networks with Multipacket Reception". *IEEE Transactions on Wireless Communications*, November 2004.

[32] M. Zorzi. "Mobile Radio Slotted ALOHA with Capture and Diversity". *Wireless Networks*, **1**:227–239, May 1995.

[33] M. Zorzi and R.R. Rao. "Capture and Retransmission Control in Mobile Radio". *IEEE Journal on Select. Areas in Comm.*, **12**:1289–1298, Oct. 1994.

In: Wireless LANs and Bluetooth
Editors: Yang Xiao and Yi Pan, pp. 119-134

ISBN 1-59454-432-8
©2005 Nova Science Publishers, Inc.

Chapter 6

Wireless LAN MAC Protocols Using Busy Tones and Jamming Signals

Yu-Chee Tseng*and Shiang-Rung Ye†
Department of Computer Science and Information Engineering
National Chiao Tung University, Hsin-Chu, 30050, Taiwan

1 Introduction

With the proliferation of wireless communications, wireless local-area networks (WLANs) have been accepted as an attractive way for providing high-speed and low-cost wireless communications. Depending on the presence of a coordinating station or not, a WLAN can be classified as an *infrastructure* network or an *ad hoc* network. In an infrastructure network, the coordinator is in charge of allocating network resources and managing issues such as association, power, and security, etc. On the contrary, in an ad hoc network, there is no centralized control, and stations must rely on a distributed coordination function to cooperate with each other in the network.

In a WLAN, the medium access control (MAC) protocol plays a significant role on the efficient use of the wireless channel. ALOHA is the simplest MAC protocol that was developed in 1970 [1]. In this protocol, stations can immediately transmit their packets upon receiving them from the upper layer. Assuming that the transmission time of a frame is a fixed amount of time T and those frames arrive at the MAC layer following the Poisson process, ALOHA can achieve a channel throughput of Ge^{-2G} where G is the frame arrival rate [14]. The achievable maximum throughput is 0.184. A variant of the ALOHA, called slotted ALOHA, divides the transmission time into time slots, each of a length T, and allows transmission to take place only at the beginning of a time slot. Since the vulnerable time of

*E-mail address: yctseng@csie.nctu.edu.tw
†E-mail address: shiarung@csie.nctu.edu.tw

packet transmission is halved, the channel throughput of the slotted ALOHA is Ge^{-G} and the maximum channel throughput increases to 0.368 [14].

The vulnerability of the ALOHA protocol results from its high collision probability under heavy traffic load conditions. To reduce the collision probability, the carrier sense multiple access (CSMA) scheme [14] requires each station to sense carriers on the wireless medium before transmitting data. If the medium is busy, a station should defer its transmission and reschedule it at a future time. This prevents frames from colliding with ongoing transmissions of other stations. When the medium is busy, a station can persistently wait for the medium to become idle, and then transmit data with a probability of 1 or with a probability of p, $p < 1$. The former is called 1-persistent CSMA, and the latter is called p-persistent CSMA. Alternatively, a station can reschedule transmission at later time and stop monitoring the medium. Afterward, at the new scheduled time, it listens to the medium again and then transmits if the medium is idle. This access procedure is called nonpersisten CSMA.

Although the CSMA scheme significantly increases channel utilization, it still suffers from the hidden terminal problem and is incapable to support quality of service (QoS) for multimedia applications. The purpose of this chapter is to present MAC protocols that employ busy tones and/or jamming signals to further improve the network throughput [4, 6–10, 12, 15, 16, 19] and to provide QoS support [2, 5, 13, 18].

The rest of this chapter is structured as follows. In Section 2, we describe the concepts of busy tones and jamming signals. Section 3 presents several MAC protocols that utilize the busy tones or/and jamming signals to prevent the hidden terminal problem. In Section 4, some power control mechanisms based on busy tones are described, and Section 5 presents priority MAC protocols that support QoS for multimedia applications via busy tones.

2 Busy Tone Signaling and Jamming Signaling

Busy tone signaling is first proposed and studied in [15]. The goal is to prevent the hidden terminal problem in an infrastructure network. A busy tone is an out-of-band signal that is transmitted on a separate channel. There is no data carried in this signal, but its presence and strength serve as important information for MAC protocols to determine the current channel status. For example, stations may detect the presence of a busy-tone signal to determine whether they are hidden from other stations, or measure the strength of busy tones from other stations to control their own transmission power.

A busy tone is not a noise signal but a predefined wave such as a sine wave [15] that may be detected by neighboring stations. The presence or strength of a busy tone is to carry some special information for a MAC protocol. If a busy tone is transmitted on a wide-band channel, the detection time is minor and can be neglected. But if the tone is transmitted on a narrow-band channel, the detection time should be taken into consideration.

A jamming signal is an in-band signal that is usually transmitted on data channels or control channels. It doesn't carry any digital information but its presence makes other stations be aware of the busy status of the wireless channel. Because of its in-band nature, such signals may cause collisions at stations that are receiving frames. However, if a jamming signal is intelligently used, it can still be employed to prevent the hidden terminal problem in a MAC protocol. In addition, prioritized medium access can also be supported by transmitting different lengths of jamming signals. These possibilities will be reviewed in later sections.

3   Preventing the Hidden Terminal Problem Using Busy Tones and Jamming Signals

The CSMA protocols and its variants suffer from the hidden terminal problem. As shown in Fig. 1, station B is in the transmission range of station A and C, but station C is out of the transmission range of station A. During the transmission of frames from station A to station B, if station C transmits during this period, the frames from station A to station B will be corrupted at station B. In other words, since station C is hidden from station A, the hidden terminal problem may cause collisions for stations that are located in the intersection of station A's and station C's transmission ranges.

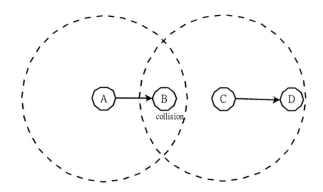

Figure 1: The hidden terminal problem.

There have been some research works on the prevention of the hidden terminal problem using busy tones or jamming signals [4, 6–10, 15, 19]. In an infrastructure network, the busy tone multiple access (BTMA) protocol [15] divides the whole wireless bandwidth into two channels: a data channel and a narrow-band busy-tone channel. When the base station detects a carrier on the data channel, it transmits a busy tone to inform other stations of the busy state of its receiver as shown in Fig. 2. Any station that detects the busy tone should defer transmission until the disappearance of the busy tone.

In [11], the multiple access with collision avoidance (MACA) protocol introduces RTS (request to send) and CTS (clear to send) frames to prevent the hidden-terminal problem. In this scheme, a source station transmits a RTS frame to a destination station to request for transmission. If the destination correctly receives the RTS frame, it admits the trans-

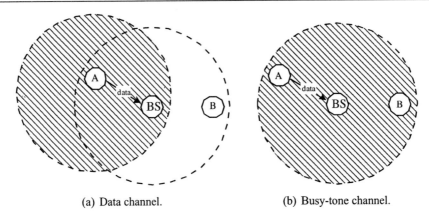

(a) Data channel.   (b) Busy-tone channel.

Figure 2: The busy tone multiple access (BTMA) protocol.

mission by sending back a CTS frame. Other stations that overhear the RTS or CTS frame
are required to keep silent during this period and reschedule their transmissions at later
time in order to prevent collision. Based on this RTS-CTS-DATA dialogue, the DBTMA
protocol [4, 8] uses two busy tones to convey channel states in a multihop ad hoc network.
The DBTMA protocol divides the communication bandwidth into a control channel, a data
channel, and two busy tones, namely BT_t and BT_r. Fig. 3 shows a possible bandwidth
allocation example for the DBTMA protocol. In the DBTMA protocol, when a source station has a frame to send, it first listens to the BT_r tone. If there is no BT_r, it transmits a
RTS frame on the control channel. When the intended destination station receives the RTS
frame, it listens to the BT_t tone. If there is no BT_t, it turns on the BT_r and sends a CTS
frame back to the source station on the control channel. On receiving the CTS frame, the
source station turns on the BT_t and starts transmission of its data frame on the data channel.
After the transmission and reception of the data frame, the source station and the destination station turn off their BT_t and BT_r, respectively. In this way, stations know whether
they are hidden from other stations by listening to the busy tones. Fig. 4 shows an example.
Suppose that station A is transmitting to station B. So station A turns on BT_t and station B
turns on BT_r. Because station C is under the coverage of station A's BT_t, it can not admit
the transmission request from station D. Also because station E is under the coverage of
station B's BT_r it can not initiate transmission to station F. However, station C is allowed
to transmit to station D and station E is allowed to receive from station F, as shown in the
figure.

In [3], it has been shown that the reliability of MAC layer has a significant impact on
the transport layer such as the TCP protocol. Unreliable data transmission at the MAC layer
may cause frame dropping and thus degrade the performance of the TCP protocol, which is
designed with the assumption that the dropping probability is quite small. To improve the
reliability of the MAC layer, an ACK frame is suggested after the transmission of a data
frame. Based on the RTS-CTS-DATA-ACK frame exchange sequence, a jamming-based
MAC (JMAC) protocol [19] is proposed that separates source stations' traffic from destina-

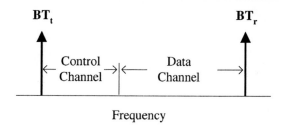

Figure 3: A bandwidth allocation example for the control channel, data channel, and two busy tones in the DBTMA protocol.

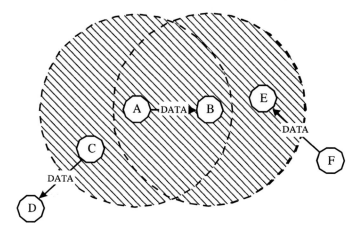

Figure 4: The dual busy tone multiple access (DBTMA) protocol.

tion stations' traffic into different channels. Specifically, it divides the wireless bandwidth into two channels, called S channel and R channel, and explicitly signals the channel status by jamming the S channel or the R channel.

In the JMAC protocol, transmission activities of source stations take place only on the S channel, and reception activities are on the R channel. By contrast, destination stations use the R channel to transmit frames back but receive source stations' frames on the S channel. Specifically, a source station transmits RTS frames, DATA frames, and jamming signals on the S channel, and the destination station transmits CTS, ACK, and jamming signals on the R channel. In this access scheme, a source station first listens to the R channel, and if the channel is idle, it transmits a RTS frame on the S channel and then jams the S channel while waiting for the destination's response on the R channel. The jamming signal prevents neighboring stations from admitting RTS frames of two-hop-away stations. If a CTS frame is received on the R channel, the source station stops jamming the S channel but sends a DATA frame on the S channel. After the transmission of the data frame, the source station jams the S channel again to protect the arriving ACK frame from the R channel. For the destination, after receiving a RTS frame on the S channel, it transmits a CTS frame on the R channel, and then jams the R channel while waiting for a DATA frame on the S channel. The jamming signal protects the arriving data frame at the destination station. Fig. 5 shows the access procedure.

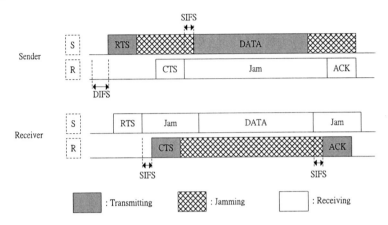

Figure 5: Medium access procedure of the JMAC protocol.

One important issue is the ratio of bandwidth that is allocated to the S channel to that allocated to the R channel. Assuming that the data rate of the wireless channel is proportional to the bandwidth of the wireless channel, we derive the allocation as follows. Let α be the ratio of total bandwidth allocated to the S channel, $0 < \alpha < 1$, and let $f(\alpha)$ be the time to complete a RTS-CTS-DAT-ACK frame exchange, not including interframe spaces, on the S channel. We have

$$f(\alpha) = \frac{RTS + DATA}{\alpha \times r} + \frac{CTS + ACK}{(1 - \alpha) \times r} , \tag{1}$$

where r is the channel rate. The optimal α is the one that minimizes $f(\alpha)$. We differentiate $f(\alpha)$ with respect to α,

$$\frac{df(\alpha)}{d\alpha} = \frac{\alpha^2 \times (CTS + ACK) - (1 - \alpha)^2 \times (RTS + DATA)}{\alpha^2 \times (1 - \alpha)^2 \times r} , \tag{2}$$

and set it to zero. Let $\hat{\alpha}$ denote the optimal α. Since $0 < \hat{\alpha} < 1$, we have

$$\hat{\alpha} = \frac{RTS + DATA - \sqrt{(RTS + DATA) \times (CTS + ACK)}}{RTS + DATA - CTS - ACK} \tag{3}$$

Fig. 6 shows the values of $\hat{\alpha}$ with respect to different frame sizes. As the frame size increases, more bandwidth should be allocated to the S channel.

The JMAC protocol enables concurrent transmissions which may not be allowed in the MACA and IEEE 802.11 protocols. In the MACA protocol, when a station is transmitting or

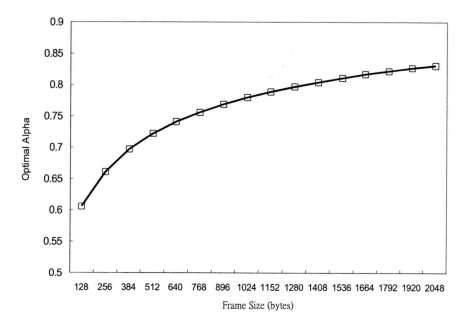

Figure 6: The $\hat{\alpha}$ with respect to different frame sizes for the JMAC protocol.

receiving data, neighboring stations should not initiate any transmission in order to prevent collision. If a neighboring station of the source station transmits during the time when the source station is receiving a CTS frame or a ACK frame, collision will occur at the source station. Similarly, if a neighboring station of a destination station transmits when the destination station is receiving DATA, collision will occur at the destination station. In the JMAC protocol, since transmission of RTS and DATA frames is separated from that of CTS and ACK frames, source stations that are in the transmission range of each other can concurrently transmit if no neighboring station is a destination station of other stations. Fig. 7 shows an example. In this example, station A and station C are source stations of the destination station B and station D, respectively. The shaded area in Fig. 7(a) represents an area where any station is allowed to initiate a new transmission by transmitting a RTS frame. Similarly, in Fig. 7(b), the shaded area is where any station is allowed to admit a RTS frame.

Fig. 8 and Fig. 9 compare the performance of the JMAC protocol to that of IEEE 802.11 DCF. Fig. 8 shows the mean saturation throughputs under different network sizes N. The saturation throughput is defined to be the limit of system throughput as the network traffic load increases. The figure shows that saturation throughput decreases as the number of stations N increases for both the JMAC and IEEE 802.11 DCF protocols. But the JMAC achieves a higher performance than the IEEE 802.11 DCF. Fig. 9 shows the mean throughputs for JMAC and IEEE 802.11 DCF under different traffic loads. At light loads, the

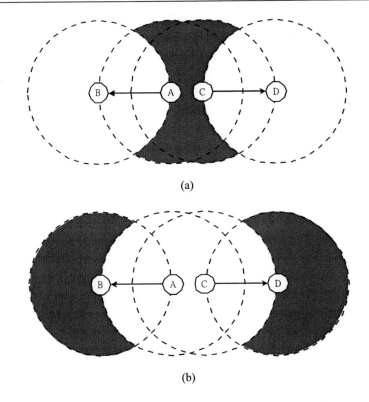

(a)

(b)

Figure 7: Concurrent transmission scenarios in the JMAC protocol.

mean throughputs of JMAC and IEEE 802.11 are very close. However, as the traffic load increases, JMAC will outperform IEEE 802.11.

4   Transmission Power Control Using Buy Tones

Reference [17] further improves the performance of the DBTMA protocol by taking the transmission power into consideration. Consider Fig. 10(a), where a transmission from A to B is ongoing. The transmission from C to D can not be granted because D can hear A's BT_t. Similarly, the transmission from E to F can not be granted because E can hear B's BT_r. However, as shown in Fig. 10(b), if we can properly tune each transmitter's power level, all communication pairs can coexist without causing interference.

The following discussion gives a basic idea to incorporate power control [17] into the DBTMA protocol. In the previous scenario, we first enforce A to transmit its data packet and BT_t at a minimal power level, but keep B's BT_r at the normal (largest) power level. When C wants to communicate with D, C senses no BT_r, so it can send a RTS to D. At this moment, D hears no BT_t, so D can reply a CTS to C. Now if C appropriately adjusts its transmission power, the communication from C to D will not corrupt the transmission from A to B. The communication from E to F deserves more attention. At this time, E

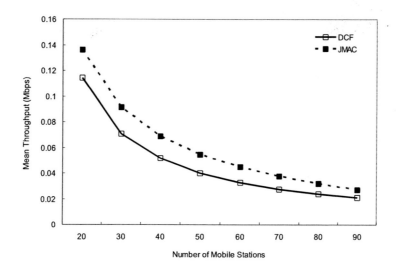

Figure 8: Mean saturation throughput versus network size.

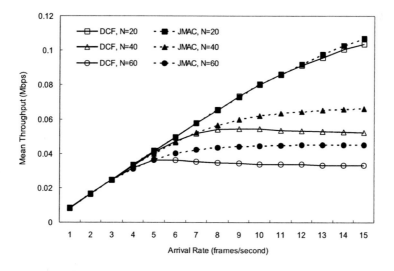

Figure 9: Mean saturation throughput versus frame arrival rate.

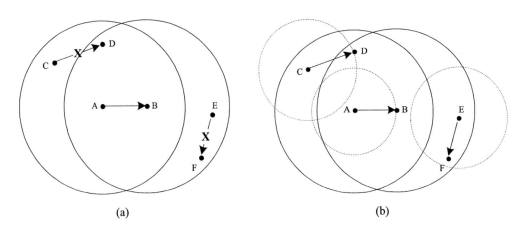

(a)   (b)

Figure 10: Transmission scenarios (a) when there is no power control, and (b) when there is power control.

can sense B's BT_r. Ideally, E should send a RTS to invite F with a power level that is sufficiently large to reach F but not B. The basic idea is that E's yet-to-be-transmitted data packet should not corrupt B's reception. Host F, which must be closer to E than B is, will reply with a CTS. This causes no problem as F hears no BT_t. Then the communication from E to F can be started. To summarize, the rules are: (i) data packet and BT_t are transmitted with power control based on the power level of the received CTS, (ii) CTS and BT_r are transmitted at the normal (largest) power level, and (iii) RTS is transmitted at a power level to be determined based on how strong the BT_r tones are around the requesting host.

The following discussion gives some idea about controlling transmission power. Suppose that a source host transmits a packet to a destination host. Let P_t and P_r be the power levels on which the packet is transmitted and received on the sender and receiver sides, respectively. Then the following equation holds:

$$P_r = P_t(\frac{\lambda}{4\pi d})^n g_t g_r, \tag{4}$$

where λ is the carrier wavelength, d is the distance between the sender and the receiver, n is the path loss coefficient, and g_t and g_r are the antenna gains at the sender and the receiver, respectively. Note that λ, g_t, and g_r are constants in normal situations. The value of n is typically 2, but may vary between 2 and 6 depending on the physical environment, such as existence of walls, cabinets, or obstacles. Suppose host X transmits a RTS with power P_t to host Y, who receives the packet with power P_r. If Y wants to reply a CTS to X at a certain power level P_{CTS} such that X's receiving power is the smallest possible, say P_{min}, then we have

$$P_{min} = P_{CTS}(\frac{\lambda}{4\pi d})^n g_t g_r. \tag{5}$$

Dividing Eq. (5) by Eq. (4), we have

$$\frac{P_{min}}{P_r} = \frac{P_{CTS}}{P_t}.$$

Thus, Y can determine the power level $P_{CTS} = P_t P_{min}/P_r$ even if d and n are unknown.

The main idea of [17] is to use the exchange of RTS/CTS packets to determine which power level to transmit. The following notations regarding power levels will be used.

- P_{max}: the maximum transmission power

- P_{min}: the minimum power level for a host to distinguish a signal from a noise

- P_{noise}: a power level under which an antenna will regard a signal as a noise (P_{noise} should be less than P_{min} by some constant; ideally, we assume that $P_{min} - P_{noise}$ is a very small value.)

The complete protocol is formally described below.

1. On a host X intending to send a RTS to host Y, host X should sense any receive busy tone BT_r around it and send a RTS on the control channel at power level P_x as determined below:

   - If there is no receive busy tone, then $x = P_{max}$.
   - Otherwise, let P_r be the power level of the BT_r that has the highest power among all BT_r's that X receives. We let

   $$P_x = \frac{P_{max} P_{noise}}{P_r}. \tag{6}$$

   That is, the RTS signal should not go beyond the nearest host that is currently receiving a data packet. Note that P_{max} is used in Eq. (6) because a receive busy tone BT_r is always transmitted at the maximum power level (see rule 2 below).

2. On host Y receiving X's RTS packet, it should sense any transmit busy tone BT_t around it. There are two cases:

   - If there is any such busy tone, then Y ignores the RTS (because collision would occur if X does send a data packet to Y).
   - Otherwise, Y replies with a CTS at the maximum power P_{max} and turns on its receive busy tone BT_r at the maximum power P_{max}.

3. On host X receiving Y's CTS, it turns on its transmit busy tone BT_t and starts transmitting its data packet, both at the power level

$$P_x = \frac{P_{min} P_{max}}{P_r},$$

where P_r is the level of the power at which X receives the CTS. This power level P_x is the minimum possible to ensure that Y can decode the data packet correctly.

The reader can verify that the above protocol will grant the transmissions from C to D and from E to F in Fig. 4(b). Performance evaluations of the protocol can be found in [17].

The power control multiple access (PCMA) protocol [12] takes a similar strategy as [17]. A source station and a destination station exchange their power information by using the request-power-to-send (RPTS) frame and the acceptable-power-to-send (APTS) frame before data transmission takes place. The source station measures the power level of the busy tone and transmits a RPTS frame to the destination if the allowable power level is higher than the minimum power at which a frame can be correctly received. On receiving the RPTS frame, the destination station computes a power level for the source station by measuring the signal to interference ratio (SIR) and channel gain and attaches the information in its APTS frame. After receiving the APTS frame, the source station checks whether the specified power level is allowed without interfering other ongoing transmissions. If this is allowed, it transmits a data frame with the power level. When the destination starts receiving the data frame, it turns on the busy tone.

5   Priority Access Using Jamming Signals

In many priority MAC protocols, priority access is implemented by using different sizes of minimum contention windows or/and different lengths of interframe spaces. This gives stations *soft* priority access because low-priority station still has chance to transmit during the backoff period of high-priority stations. The priority MAC protocols which are based on jamming signals can support *strict* priority access, in which high-priority stations can always transmit before low-priority stations.

In the black-burst contention access [13], real-time stations contend for the wireless medium by transmitting black burst (BB), i.e., pulses of energy. The transmission duration of BB is an increasing function of the contention delay experienced by real-time stations. Specifically, after the medium becomes idle and lasts for a predefined interframe space, a real-time station transmits BB for a duration depending on the delay that it has experienced. At the end of the BB transmission, the station listens to the wireless medium again. If the medium is busy, which implies there is another station with a longer delay being experienced by its real-time packets, the former station gives up the contention in this round and retries in the next round. But if the medium is idle, it can start transmission of its real-time data. Since the duration of BB is an increasing function of the contention delay, real-time stations that experience longer delays are given higher priorities to access the medium. Fig. 11 illustrates an example. Suppose that station A starts its transmission first. After station A's transmission, all stations A, B, and C contend for the next transmission opportunity using BBs. Since station B has experienced the longest delay, it contends with the longest BB and thus prohibits stations A and C from transmitting at this time. After B's transmission, again all stations contend with BBs. Since station C has the longest BB, it succeeds at this time.

The European Telecommunications Standards Institute (ETSI) defines the HIPERLAN standard for WLANs. The channel access mechanism in the HIPERLAN is based on

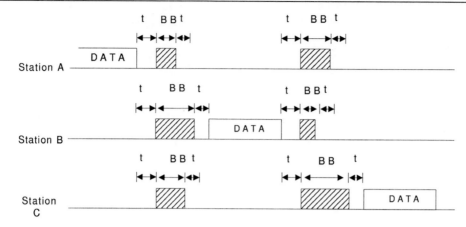

Figure 11: Black burst (BB) prioritization procedure.

the Elimination-Yield Non-preemptive Priority Multiple Access (EY-NPMA). In the EY-NPMA, the medium access procedure consists of three phases: a prioritization phase, a contention phase, and a transmission phase as shown in Fig. 12. In the prioritization phase, time is divided into priority slots which are assigned to different priority levels. A station with priority level h is assigned the $(h + 1)$-th priority slot. If it has frames to send, it is required to listen to the first h priority slots in the prioritization phase. If all these h priority slots are idle, it can transmit a burst in the $(h + 1)$-th priority slot and then steps to the contention phase. However, if the station detects any burst during the first h priority slots, it gives up in this round and retries in the next round. The contention phase further consists of two phases: an elimination phase and an yield phase. In the elimination phase, stations with the same priority level compete with each other by transmitting energy burst with different lengths as in the BB contention scheme. At the end of transmission, stations listen to the medium for a survival verification slot. If the medium is idle during this slot, they are admitted to the yield phase. Otherwise, it gives up in this round. Since there may be multiple stations which are admitted to the yield phase, these stations perform geometric backoff before transmitting their data. This procedure is illustrated in Fig. 12.

Based on the concept of prioritization scheme in the EY-NPMA, the MAC protocol proposed in [5] considers both priority and fair medium access. In this protocol, each station forms a tuple $(p, c, n, d_{n-1}, ..., d_0)$ according to its priority level, collision status, and a chosen backoff value. The ith element in the tuple is the number of slots that the station must listen to before transmitting an energy burst in the ith contention phase. Each phase is similar to the prioritization phase in the the EY-NPMA scheme, and there are multiple phases to prioritize stations. The element p is the priority level of a station. As in the EY-NPMA, if the medium is idle in the first p slots, a station transmits a energy burst in the $(p + 1)$ slots and then enters the next phase. If the medium is busy during any of the first p slots, it gives up in this round and retries in the next round. The operations in the rest of contention phases are the same. The c element is a flag with a value 0 or 1. This

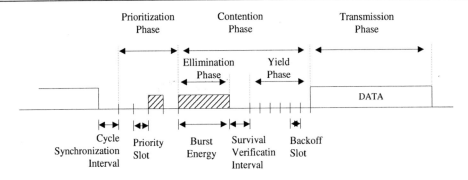

Figure 12: EY-NPMA access scheme.

indicates whether this is a retransmission. If a station fails to transmit in the previous round due to collision, this flag is set to 0, which gives priority to the stations that fail to transmit in the previous round. The remaining elements are formed according to a chosen backoff value, which is transformed into the base-N representation, where N is a predefined value. Element d_i is the i-th digit of the base-N representation. The third element n in the tuple is the number of digits when the base-N representation is used. The remaining phases use the values of $d_{n-1}, d_{n-2},...,d_0$.

6   Concluding Remarks

This chapter surveys MAC protocols that employ the busy tones and jamming signals to improve channel utilization as well as to support QoS for multimedia applications in wireless LANs. The first class of MAC protocols is aimed to prevent the hidden terminal problem by detecting the presence of busy tones or jamming signals. The second class of protocols tries to improve the channel utilization by controlling the transmission power. The power levels of busy tone signals serve as important reference for stations to choose a proper transmission power. The third class enables priority access by assigning different lengths of energy burst to different priority levels. These designs help remove some inherent limitations of wireless channels.

Acknowledgement

Y. C. Tseng's research is co-sponsored by the NSC Program for Promoting Academic Excellence of Universities under grant number 93-2752-E-007-001-PAE, by Computer and Communications Research Labs., ITRI, Taiwan, and by Intel Inc.

References

[1] N. ABRAMSON, *The Aloha System -Another Alternative for Computer communication*, in AFIPS Conf. Proc., 1970, pp. 281–285.

[2] G. ANASTASI, L. LENZINI, AND E.MINGOZZI, *Stability and performance analysis of HIPERLAN*, in IEEE INFOCOM, 1998, pp. 134–141.

[3] V. BHARGHAVAN, A. DEMERS, S. SHENKER, AND L. ZHANG, *MACAW: A media access protocol for wireless LAN's*, in ACM SIGCOM, 1994, pp. 212–225.

[4] J. DENG AND Z. J. HAAS, *Dual busy tone mulitple access (DBTMA): A new medium access control for packet radio networks*, in IEEE ICUPC, 1998, pp. 973–977.

[5] A. DUGAR, N. VAIDYA, AND P. BAHL, *Priority and fair scheduling in a wireless lan*, in IEEE MILCOM, 2001, pp. 993–997.

[6] A. C. V. GUMMALLA AND J. O. LIMB, *Wireless collision detec(wcd): Multiple access with receiver initiated feedback and carrier detect signal*, in IEEE ICC, 2000, pp. 397–401.

[7] Z. J. HAAS AND J. DENG, *Performance evaluation of the r-btma protocol in a distributed mobile radio network context*, (1992), pp. 24–34.

[8] ——, *Dual busy tone multiple access (DBTMA) - performance evaluation*, in IEEE VTC, 1999, pp. 314–319.

[9] ——, *Dual busy tone multiple access (DBTMA) - a multiple access control scheme for ad hoc networks*, IEEE TRANSACTIONS ON COMMUNICATIONS, (2002), pp. 975–985.

[10] Z. HUANG, C.-C. SHEN, C. SRISATHAPORNPHAT, AND C. JAIKAEO, *A busty-tone based directional mac protocol for ad hoc networks*, in IEEE MILCOM, 2002, pp. 1233–1238.

[11] P. KARN, *MACA - a new channel access method for packet radio*, in Proceedings of 9th Amateur Radio Computer Networking Conference, April 1990, pp. 134–140.

[12] J. P. MONKS, V. BHARGHAVAN, AND W. MEI W. HWU, *A power controlled multiple access protocol for wireless packet networks*, in IEEE INFOCOM, vol. 01, 2001, pp. 219 – 228.

[13] J. L. SOBRINHO AND A. S. KRISHNAKUMAR, *Quality of service in ad hoc carrier sense multiple access wireless network*, IEEE Journal on Selected Areas in Communications, 17 (1999), pp. 135–1368.

[14] F. A. TOBAGI AND L. KLEINROCK, *Packet switching in radio channels: Part I - carrier sense multiple-access modes and their throughput-delay characteristics*, IEEE Transactions on Communications, com-23 (1975).

[15] ——, *Packet switching in radio channels: Part II - the hidden terminal problem in carrier sense multiple-access modes and the busy-tone solution*, IEEE Transactions on Communications, com-23 (1975).

[16] C. WU AND V. O. K. LI, *Receiver-initiated busy-tone multiple access in packet radio networks*, in ACM SIGCOMM 87 Workshop: Frontiers in Computer Communications Technology, Aug. 1987.

[17] S.-L. WU, Y.-C. TSENG, AND J.-P. SHEU, *Intelligent medium access for mobile ad hoc networks with busy tones and power control*, IEEE Journal on Selected Areas in Communications, 18 (2000), pp. 1647–1657.

[18] X. YANG AND N. VAIDYA, *Priority scheduling in wireless ad hoc networks*, in ACM MOBIHOC, 2002.

[19] S.-R. YE, Y.-C. WANG., AND Y.-C. TSENG, *A jamming-based mac protocol to improve the performance of wireless multihop ad hoc networks*, Wireless Communications and Mobile Computing, 4 (2004), pp. 75–84.

In: Wireless LANs and Bluetooth
Editors: Yang Xiao and Yi Pan, pp. 135-156

ISBN 1-59454-432-8
©2005 Nova Science Publishers, Inc.

Chapter 7

MAC AND ROUTING PROTOCOLS FOR IEEE 802.11 WIRELESS MESH NETWORKS

Xudong Wang[*]
Kiyon, Inc., La Jolla, CA 92037

Abstract

IEEE 802.11 wireless technologies have been widely accepted as the de facto standards for wireless local area networks (WLANs). Most of the current deployments are based on infrastructure mode in which only single-hop and point-to-multipoint communications are concerned. However, as more and more wireless communications are being adopted to various application scenarios, wireless mesh networks (WMNs) with multi-hop and multipoint-to-multipoint communications are needed. Although an ad hoc mode has been specified by IEEE 802.11 standards, its throughput and delay performance is not scalable to a WMN. To support IEEE 802.11 WMNs based on IEEE 802.11 technologies, many research and development challenges still remain. In this chapter we study the current research and development advances in IEEE 802.11 WMNs. In particular, we focus on MAC and routing protocols for IEEE 802.11 WMNs. Network architecture, application scenarios, and implementation issues of IEEE 802.11 WMNs are also discussed.

Keywords: iIEEE 802.11, Ad hoc networks, Wireless mesh networks, Medium access control, Ad hoc routing

1 Introduction

IEEE 802.11 wireless networks have been undergoing rapid progress. The transmission speed of an IEEE 802.11 radio has jumped from the initial 2 Mbps to 54 Mbps [1], [2]. With more advanced physical layer techniques, much higher speed can be delivered [3].

---

[*]E-mail address: wxudong@ieee.org

Moreover, certain quality of service (QoS) can be provisioned in an IEEE 802.11 wireless network.

In parallel with these progresses, the price per Mbps of an IEEE 802.11 access point (AP) or network interface card (NIC) constantly decreases. Such advantages enable IEEE 802.11 wireless networks to penetrate and then quickly dominate the market of wireless local area networks (WLANs). To date IEEE 802.11 WLANs have been widely deployed in various application environments.

Despite the achieved success, IEEE 802.11 WLANs still have several limitations:

1. *Low MAC layer throughput.* Even though the physical transmission speed of an IEEE 802.11 radio is rather high, the MAC layer throughput is still low, especially when the node density is high.

2. *Single-hop and point-to-multipoint communications.* Currently most of the IEEE 802.11 WLANs consists of a set of basic service sets (BSSs). In each BSS, network nodes work in an infrastructure mode, i.e., one wireless client has to reply on an AP to communication with another wireless client. Although ad hoc mode is already specified in the existing IEEE 802.11 standards, its performance is not guaranteed for two reasons. First, the IEEE 802.11 MAC is not scalable to multi-hop multipoint-to-multipoint communications. With such an MAC protocol, the end-to-end throughput is extremely low. Second, IEEE 802.11 standards have not specified any routing protocols for ad hoc mode. Thus, the performance of ad hoc mode tightly depends on routing protocols outside of IEEE 802.11 standards.

3. *Low robustness to link failure.* In a BSS, once the AP fails, all communications have to be dropped.

4. *High deployment cost.* Due to limited transmission range of wireless radios, a single BSS only covers a small area. When a large area needs to be covered, multiple BSSs are needed, and Ethernet wires are needed to connect different BSSs. This usually increases the deployment cost by a significant percentage.

Such limitations hinder the penetration process of IEEE 802.11 technologies to many other promising application scenarios where multi-hop multipoint-to-multipoint communications are needed. To eliminate these restrictions, a new wireless networking technology, called wireless mesh networking, is being researched and developed by many companies and universities. Recently, IEEE 802.11 standards committee has also established a working group, i.e., IEEE 802.11s, to promote IEEE 802.11 based wireless mesh networks (WMNs).

IEEE 802.11 wireless mesh networking will be a convergence of IEEE 802.11 and ad hoc networking technologies. Compared with the conventional IEEE 802.11 WLANs, IEEE 802.11 WMNs have the following advantages:

1. *Self-formed mesh topologies.* Multi-hop multipoint-to-multipoint communications are established and maintained autonomically.

2. *Easy deployment and coverage extension.* Due to mesh connectivity and network self-organization, IEEE 802.11 WMNs can be easily deployed. Sophisticated site survey is not needed. Moreover, extending coverage can also be quickly achieved by just adding more mesh nodes. On the other hand, dead zones can be eliminated by adding mesh nodes.

3. *Robustness.* Due to mesh connectivity, single point of failure will not terminate the services. Robustness of the network is significantly improved.

4. *Resource sharing.* With mesh networking, expensive backhaul network access can be shared by many mesh nodes. Multiple available backhaul network access again improve the robustness.

However, to date, functions to realize these promising advantages have not been fully achieved for IEEE 802.11 WMNs. Many research issues need to be resolved. In this chapter, we focus on MAC and routing protocols for IEEE 802.11 WMNs. In order to give a clear comparison between IEEE 802.11 WMNs and IEEE 802.11 WLANs and ad hoc networks as well, we first discuss potential application scenarios and the network architecture of IEEE 802.11 WMNs. A brief analysis is then given to the existing issues of IEEE 802.11 WMNs. However, due to space limit, the detailed study is only focused on MAC and routing protocols.

2   Network Architecture and Applications of IEEE 802.11 WMNs

IEEE 802.11 WMNs have two distinct features:

1. IEEE 802.11 WMN is a wireless network that provides mesh connectivity for multi-hop multipoint-to-multipoint communications.

2. IEEE 802.11 WMN is also required to be compatible with existing IEEE 802.11 standards and support network access for conventional IEEE 802.11 wireless nodes.

These two features enable IEEE 802.11 WMNs to be deployed in many application scenarios. They also determine the network architecture of IEEE 802.11 WMNs, and bring many challenges in protocol design and implementation.

2.1   Application Scenarios

With mesh connectivity, IEEE 802.11 wireless networks can be applied to many applications. Since IEEE 802.11 WLANs have been widely deployed in home and enterprise networks, typical application scenarios of IEEE 802.11 WMNs are broadband home networking and enterprise networking. Due to the advantages of IEEE 802.11 WMNs as pointed out in Section 1, IEEE 802.11 WMNs will avoid existing issues with IEEE 802.11 WLANs, and provide better service quality in these application scenarios. For example, a scenario of broadband home networking is shown in Fig. 1, where multiple IEEE 802.11 mesh routers are deployed in different locations of a home. In this way, dead zones in a home can be eliminated. Moreover, comparing to the relationship between a conventional access point and client nodes, a shorter distance exists between mesh routers and client nodes, which prevents the transmission rate from dropping in a long distance. This feature is exactly desired by broadband applications such as video streaming among multiple video devices. Moreover, if a client node is mesh-enabled, it can directly communicate any other mesh-enabled clients and mesh routers, which significantly enhances the network access flexibility of the IEEE 802.11 client nodes.

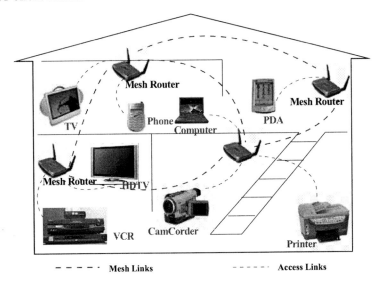

Figure 1: IEEE 802.11 WMNs for Broadband Home Networking

IEEE 802.11 WMN is also a promising solution to wireless metropolitan area networks (WMANs), because it can provide broadband service but without complicated network infrastructure, maintenance, and so on. WMANs via cellular networks needs complicated infrastructure but only provides much lower transmission rate. WMANs through other techniques such as IEEE 802.16 [4], wireless ATM networks [5], and high altitude long operation (HALO) networks [6], [7] will be much more expensive. As shown in Fig. 2, the WMAN based on IEEE 802.11 WMNs can be extended with coverage by adding more mesh routers in the desired locations.

Mesh routers are normally placed on power/phone-line poles or on top of a building, so no expensive towers are needed. Services provided to clients can be much more heterogeneous than a cellular network. For example, voice and any data services are inherently supported in IEEE 802.11 WMNs. Higher speed of Internet access can be also provided by adding more backhaul access to mesh routers.

As the techniques of IEEE 802.11 WMNs advance, they can be applied to many other applications such as building automation, transportation systems, medical and health systems, security surveillance systems, etc. [8].

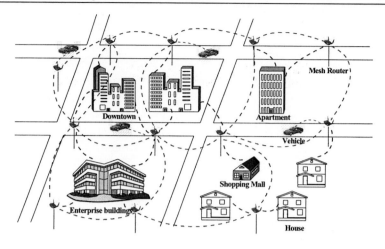

Figure 2: IEEE 802.11 WMNs for WMANs

2.2   Network Architecture

In an IEEE 802.11 WMN, wireless nodes consists of mesh routers and mesh clients. Mesh clients may not have ad hoc networking capability and have to rely on mesh routers to accomplish communications. Thus, an IEEE 802.11 WMN typically has a hybrid architecture in which both infrastructure and ad hoc modes are supported by mesh routers. Ad hoc mode enables mesh networking, while the infrastructure mode is needed in order to be compatible with legacy IEEE 802.11 client nodes. Thus, mesh routers and mesh clients in the hybrid IEEE 802.11 WMN work in a hierarchical architecture, as shown in Fig. 3.

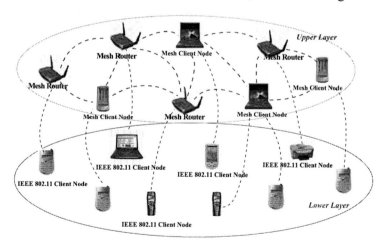

Figure 3: Architecture of IEEE 802.11 WMNs

The lower layer is comprised of conventional IEEE 802.11 wireless nodes. Communications in these nodes have to go through the mesh routers in the upper layer. In other words, the wireless nodes in lower layer and mesh routers in the upper layer work together in the infrastructure mode. No direct communication (or ad hoc networking) exists among nodes in the lower layer.

The upper layer consists of mesh routers and mesh clients with ad hoc networking capability. As a result, communications among wireless nodes in the upper layer are similar to ad hoc networking. However, two differences exist between the upper layer wireless network and a legacy ad hoc network:

1. Transmission rate of mesh routers can be much higher than mesh clients. Mesh routers provide network access for conventional IEEE 802.11 nodes in the lower layer. They may also provide backhaul access for mesh clients in both lower and upper layers. However, in a legacy ad hoc network, traffic in ad hoc nodes do not have such an obvious pattern.

2. Mobility of mesh routers is different from mesh clients. Usually mesh routers have minimal mobility or even fixed, while mesh clients are not fixed and may have high mobility. In a legacy ad hoc network, no difference of mobility exists in wireless nodes.

It should be noted that the mesh client in the lower layer is not necessarily a conventional IEEE 802.11 client. It can also be a conventional IEEE 802.11 access point or router. Similarly, one more layer can be added on top of the upper layer in Fig. 3. As a result, the network architecture becomes a multi-layer hierarchical network, as shown in Fig. 4.

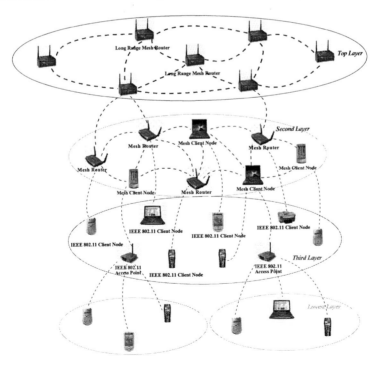

Figure 4: Multi-layer Hierarchical Architecture of IEEE 802.11 WMNs

The top layer in Fig. 4 usually consists of pure mesh routers with much longer transmission range than mesh clients and routers in the lower layers. The objective of having these mesh routers is to extend coverage of a WMN. In a WMAN scenario, these mesh routers are deployed outdoors with a much higher altitude and have line-of-sight (LOS) communications among them. The transmission power levels of these mesh routers are relatively high to prevent significant drop of transmission rate in a long distance.

2.3 Challenging Issues in IEEE 802.11 WMNs

Despite the promising future of IEEE 802.11 WMNs many challenging issues need to be resolved.

2.3.1 Communication Protocol Design

Communication protocols in the physical and MAC layers have been specified by IEEE 802.11 standards for IEEE 802.11 wireless LANs. However, the standards are focused on the infrastructure mode. Although ad hoc mode is also specified, it does not intend for a mesh network. The MAC protocol, i.e., carrier sense multiple access with collision avoidance (CSMA/CA) with optional request-to-send/clear-to-send (RTS/CTS), is not scalable to a network with high node density or with multi-hop communications. Considering a multi-hop ad hoc network, when CSMA/CA is applied, the end-to-end throughput drops significantly as the number of hops increases.

Several ad hoc routing protocols have been proposed as IETF drafts or RFCs [9]. However, their performance in a multi-hop mesh network still needs improvement. Moreover, how to carry out cross-layer design between ad hoc routing and IEEE 802.11 MAC protocol have not been studied in these IETF documents.

In the transport layer, varieties of TCP for wireless networks have been proposed, but special problems in an IEEE 802.11 WMNs have not been fully investigated. For example, in IEEE 802.11 WMNs, due to ad hoc architecture, the network topology may dynamically impact the calculation of round trip time (RTT). In addition, cross-layer design between TCP and IEEE 802.11 MAC is also needed in order for TCP to work more properly by taking into account the characteristics of the MAC protocol.

2.3.2 Security Mechanism

IEEE 802.11 WMNs are more vulnerable to security attacks than IEEE 802.11 WLANs because of larger wireless coverage areas, more nodes supported, and more distributed network architecture. To date no efficient comprehensive security mechanism exists for ad hoc networks, even though many schemes have been proposed from the perspective of different protocol layers [10]. In a WMN with ad hoc architecture, attacks may target at different protocols layers. Without a comprehensive scheme, the security will be compromised no matter how good performance can be achieved by a secure routing, secure MAC, encryption, or authentication schemes.

2.3.3   Network Maintenance and Management

To maintain an IEEE 802.11 WMN may become more complicated than a WLAN due to the ad hoc architecture. Charging, remote monitoring and configuration, authentication, and authorization are all much more difficult tasks. In addition, mobility management, location services, topology management are all necessary functions for an IEEE 802.11 WMN. They are much more difficult to be accomplished due to dynamic mesh connectivity.

Since many research issues are involved in the IEEE 802.11 WMNs, we will not conduct a comprehensive study on all of them in this chapter. In what follows, the detailed study will be focused on the issues in the MAC and routing protocols for IEEE 802.11 WMNs.

3   MAC Protocols

3.1   IEEE 802.11 MAC and Well-Known Problems

Distributed control function (DCF) is the standard MAC protocol for IEEE 802.11 wireless networks, which is briefly described as follows:

1. *Carrier sense multiple access (CSMA).* Before a node transmits packets, it needs to sense a channel. If the channel is idle for an period of DCF inter-frame space (DIFS) , the node starts its transmission. Otherwise, the node needs to select a random period in an interval $[W_{min}, W]$, where W_min is the minimum contention window, and W is the current contention window. The random period is a backoff timer for the node, and decrements when a channel is idle for one slot. Once the backoff timer expires, the node repeats the previous sensing process until the channel is idle for DIFS, and then starts transmission. The header of a MAC packet contains a field, called network allocation vector (NAV), to specify the transmission length of the packet. All other nodes that get NAV have to defer for a period equal to the length of the on-going packet. This deferral process is one of the two virtual carrier sense procedures of IEEE 802.11 (the other is RTS/CTS).

2. *Collision avoidance (CA).* Once a packet is transmitted by this node, collisions with other nodes may occur. During packet transmission in a wireless environment, there is no way for the node to detect collisions. Thus, MAC layer acknowledgement (ACK) is employed to determine if collisions have occurred. If an ACK has not been received within a given time limit, the node assumes that a collision has occurred with the transmitted packet. Under this situation, the node needs to increase the size of the contention window W (actually in IEEE 802.11 the size is doubled for each collision until the maximum window W_{max} is reached). Afterwards, the node selects a backoff timer with the new contention window, and then repeats the sensing process until the packet is successfully transmitted or timeout.

3. *Request-to-send/clear-to-send (RTS/CTS).* In CSMA/CA, collisions occurred under two scenarios. In one scenario, nodes can hear each other but happen to get the

same channel simultaneously due to the random process in the backoff procedure. In the other scenario, nodes *A* and *C* can hear node *B*, but *A* and *C* are hidden from each other. As a result, when node *A* is transmitting packets to *B*, node *C* can still transmit packets to *B* and cause packet collisions. This is the well-known hidden node problem. The backoff procedure helps to resolve the contention in the former scenario, but it has no effect on the latter scenario. In order to solve the hidden node problem, RTS/CTS is usually adopted. Before a node sends a packet, it first sends a RTS packet. The destination node must respond with a CTS packet. By applying this procedure, each node actually extends their sensing range so that the probability of hidden nodes is significantly reduced.

The above descriptions have addressed the key functions of DCF, although the actual operation procedures of DCF in the IEEE 802.11 standards are much more complicated.

The IEEE 802.11 MAC has been proposed for a long time. However, open issues still remain for both infrastructure and ad hoc mode. In both ad hoc and infrastructure modes, the MAC layer throughput significantly drops as the number of nodes per AP increases. In an ad hoc mode, the MAC layer throughput also drops quickly as the number of hops increases. In an IEEE 802.11 WMN, both infrastructure and ad hoc modes are supported, so both of the problems exist. The essential reasons for the low throughput performance are summarized as follows:

1. *Low efficiency of backoff procedure.* Once a channel is sensed busy, a random back-off timer is selected. This is a typical feature of a random process protocol, but its performance is usually low, especially when the number of nodes increases.

2. *Low efficiency of collision avoidance.* When a packet is sent, a collision may not be determined until a certain timeout occurs. Moreover, once a collision occurs, the exponential increment of contention window will significantly reduce the timely transmission of a packet. The entire process takes a long time and wastes a large amount of bandwidth.

3. *No efficient solution to hidden node issue.* Hidden nodes can be reduced by RTS/CTS. However, RTS/CTS results in large overhead, especially when IEEE 802.11g or 802.11a is considered; one small RTS or CTS needs a large OFDM preamble and wastes bandwidth. An engineering solution to hidden nodes is to make sure the sensing range is more than twice larger than the communication range, which is widely used in all wireless LAN NICs and APs.

4. *Exposed nodes by RTS/CTS, large sensing range, and NAV.* Either RTS/CTS or large sensing range solution may provide a solution to hidden nodes, but both of them make the exposed node issue more severe. When RTS/CTS is used, once a node is transmitting packets, more nodes will be prohibited from transmission. This is the same when a large sensing range is applied. Exposed nodes also exist when NAV is applied. One possible solution to exposed nodes is to use directional antenna or

smart antenna. However, there are two problems with such a solution. One is the complexity and cost. The other is that directional antenna or smart antenna will highly increase the number of hidden nodes.

3.2 State-of-the-Art Approaches

Considering the above problems, three types of approaches can help to improve the performance of IEEE 802.11 MAC.

1. Designing virtual MAC protocols. This approach does not have any impact to the hardware. In other words, it neither needs to change the hardware nor modifies the operation of the hardware. Usually, some scheduling algorithms are proposed beyond the MAC layer. Since the MAC mechanism is not touched, it will improve the behavior of the MAC protocol, but will not fundamentally improve the performance of the MAC.

2. Tuning MAC parameters. Several MAC parameters can be modified. For example, contention window, backoff timer, backoff procedure, etc. These changes may require modifications in the hardware operation. The performance improvement by this approach is limited, since the mechanism of the CSMA/CA is not changed.

3. Changing IEEE 802.11 MAC. This approach basically changes the mechanism of CSMA/CA. It will achieve significant performance improvement. However, the implementation becomes a rather challenging issue, because changes in hardware or firmware are usually needed, and this will needs a design of new chipsets. A scheme to change the mechanism of the MAC without designing new chipsets has recently proposed by the author and is being prototyped [11].

For the above three approaches, performance can be further improved by adding more channels into the MAC. However, for a multi-channel MAC, more challenges will be involved. For example, maintenance, coordination, and packet scheduling of multiple channels make protocol design be much more complicated. How to achieve fast channel switching is also a challenge.

In the following subsections, recent advances of both single-channel MAC and multichannel MAC are studied and analyzed.

3.2.1 Single-Channel MAC

Currently a few MAC protocols have been proposed for multi-hop ad hoc networks by enhancing the CSMA/CA protocol [12], [13]. These schemes usually adjust parameters of CSMA/CA such as contention window size and modify the backoff procedures. They may greatly improve throughput for one-hop communications. However, for multi-hop cases such as in IEEE 802.11 WMNs, these solutions only reach a low end-to-end throughput. The reason is that they cannot significantly reduce the probability of contentions among neighboring nodes. As long as contention occurs frequently, whichever method is taken to modify backoff, deferral, and contention resolution procedures, the end-to-end throughput will be significantly reduced due to the accumulating effect on the multi-hop path.

Cross-layer design with advanced physical layer techniques can be used to improve the performance of the IEEE 802.11 MAC. Two major schemes exist in this category: MAC based on directional antenna [14], [15] and MAC with power control [16]. The first set of schemes eliminates exposed nodes if antenna beam is assumed to be perfect. However, due to the directional transmission, more hidden nodes are produced in this case. Thus, new solutions must be developed which can reduce the number of hidden nodes. More-over, MAC protocols based on directional antennas also face other difficulties such as cost, system complexity, and practicality of fast steerable directional antennas. The second set of schemes is developed for the purpose of reducing power consumptions [17], [18], [19] and they do not address the throughput scalability problem. These schemes reduce exposed nodes problem, especially in a dense network, and thus, improve the spectrum spatial reuse factor in IEEE 802.11 WMNs [20]. However, hidden nodes still exist and may become worse because lower transmission power level reduces the possibility of detecting a po-tential interfering node [21]. In addition, power control has no way to ensure cooperative communication among different nodes.

In order to fundamentally resolve the issue of low end-to-end throughput in a multi-hop ad hoc environment such as IEEE 802.11 WMNs, innovative solutions are necessary. De-termined by their poor scalability in an ad hoc multi-hop network, random access protocols such as CSMA/CA are not a solution. Thus, revisiting the design of the IEEE 802.11 MAC protocol is necessary. Although TDMA or CDMA MAC protocols are more efficient than CSMA/CA, they are difficult to be applied to IEEE 802.11 WMNs for two reasons. One is the compatibility of TDMA (or CDMA) MAC with existing MAC chipsets. The other is the complexity and cost of developing a distributed and cooperative MAC with TDMA or CDMA.

3.2.2   Multi-channel MAC

A multi-channel MAC can be implemented on several different hardware platforms.

1. *Multi-Channel single-transceiver MAC.* If cost and compatibility are the concern, one transceiver on a radio is a preferred hardware platform. Since only one transceiver is available, only one channel is active at a time in each network node. However, different nodes may operate on different channels simultaneously in order to improve system capacity. To coordinate transmissions between network nodes under this situ-ation, protocols such as the multi-channel MAC in [22] and the seed-slotted channel hopping (SSCH) scheme [23] are needed. SSCH is actually a virtual MAC protocol, since it works on top of IEEE 802.11 MAC and does not need changes in the IEEE 802.11 MAC.

2. *Multi-channel multi-transceiver MAC.* In this scenario, a radio includes multiple par-allel RF front-end chips and baseband processing modules to support several simul-

taneous channels. On top of the physical layer, there is only one MAC layer to coordinate the functions of multiple channels. Engim multi-channel wireless LAN switching engine [24] belongs to this category. However, how to design an efficient MAC protocol for this type of physical layer platform is still an open research topic.

3. *Multi-Radio MAC.* In this scenario, a network node has multiple radios each with its own MAC and physical layers. Communications in these radios are totally independent. Thus, a virtual MAC protocol such as the multi-radio unification protocol (MUP) [25] is required on top of MAC to coordinate communications in all channels. In fact, one radio can have multiple channels. However, for simplicity of design and application, a single channel is usually used in each radio.

To give a detailed analysis on existing multi-channel MAC protocols, here we explain two protocols: *multi-channel MAC (MMAC)* [22] and *multi-radio unification protocol (MUP)* [25].

As far as MMAC is concerned, there are three main functions:

1. *Maintaining data structure of all channels in each node.* Channels of a node are classified into three types: *high preference* if it has been selected, *medium preference* if the channel has not yet been taken, and *low preference* if it is already taken by at least of one of the neighboring nodes.

2. *Negotiating channels during ad hoc traffic indication message (ATIM) window.* In the ATIM window, every node must listen to the default channel (pre-defined channel known to all nodes for sending control messages during ATIM window only). All beacons and ATIM packets are transmitted on this default channel. When node *A* has packets to be transmitted to node *B*, it sends an ATIM packet in which the preferred channel list is embedded. When node *B* receives this information, it selects the best channel based on node *A*'s preferable channel list, its own channel list, and a performance criterion (source-destination pair) as explained in the next item. After a channel is selected, node *B* informs node *A* by sending an ATIM-ACK packet. When node *A* receives this packet, it may have two scenarios: node *A* can or cannot select the channel. If node *A* can select the channel, it sends an ATIM-RES packet to node *B*, with the selected channel specified in the packet. However, if node *A* cannot select the same channel as node *B* did, node *A* cannot send packets during the current beacon interval.

3. *Selecting a channel according to the count of source-destination pairs for each channel.* The criterion for best channel is to select the channel with the least scheduled traffic. Specifically, a receiver must count the number of source-destination pairs that have selected a channel by overhearing the ATIM-ACK and ATIM-RES packets. The receiver selects the channel with the lowest count.

Several problems have not been solved in the MMAC [22].

1. It is assumed that RTS/CTS always work in IEEE 802.11 DCF. In reality, RTS/CTS is an optional function of DCF, and it may cause a large percentage of overhead. However, the MMAC frequently uses RTS/CTS messages, even after ATIM/ATIM-ACK/ATIM-RES has been done.

2. The network is assumed to be globally synchronized. Usually this is difficult to achieve in an ad hoc network with a large number of hops and nodes.

3. The channel switching time was assumed to be 224 μs. However, the channel switching time may be much larger than this number [25]. Then the performance of the proposed MAC protocol will be significantly degraded.

4. Channel selection is based on the number of source-destination pairs for each channel. This is not always true. It is pointed out in [22] that using pending packets as a metric to select a channel would improve performance.

5. The MMAC eliminates multi-channel hidden nodes, but it also generates many exposed nodes because of using RTS/CTS and ATIM/ATIM-ACK (for default channel) procedures.

The major functions of MUP [25] include:

1. *Discovering neighbors and classifying nodes.* The address resolution protocol (ARP) is used to record MAC addresses of all neighboring nodes. After this initialization, a MUP discovery process is started to see if a neighbor is a MUP-enabled node. This is done by sending a channel select (CS) message. A MUP-enabled node will respond with a CS-ACK message, while a legacy node will not. When this process is completed, a MUP neighbor table is maintained in each MUP-enabled node.

2. *Selecting communication channel relying on one-hop round trip time (RTT) measurements.* MUP selects the network interface card (NIC) with the best quality by sending a probe message and measuring the RTT after receiving a response from neighboring nodes. RTT measurement provides the overall quality estimation on both transmitting channels and receiving channels, which is the advantage of this scheme. In order to let probe messages be sent out first, a priority queue is formed. Thus, MUP relies on IEEE 802.11e to make it work.

3. *Utilizing selected channel for a long time period.* Once a channel is selected, MUP needs to stick with it for a long time period. This period is determined by a random process and on the order of 10-20 seconds.

4. *Switching channels after the randomized time interval.* After the random time period, all channels are measured again through one-hop probe messages. If a channel has a certain amount of quality improvement (e.g., > 10%) than the existing channel, then that channel is selected as the new one for sending packets. Re-ordering of packets may happen when packets in the old channel has not been finished. MUP does not contain a solution for this problem.

According to the procedures of MUP, we notice that several issues remain unresolved.

1. *Hidden node issue is not solved.* The channel quality measurement is based on one-hop RTT. However, measurements based on shortest RTT do not guarantee that there exists no hidden nodes. For example, suppose nodes A and C are hidden from each other and node B is a neighbor of both A and C. When Node A measures channels, it sends a CS message to neighbors, node C cannot hear it, but node B can receive it and send back a CS-ACK message. When node A receives the CS-ACK message, it selects channel 1 (as an example) to send packets. By this time, CS-ACK should have been received by node C. However, MUP does not have a procedure for node C to process the CS-ACK message for node A. Thus, node C has a very high probability to select channel 1 and send packets to node B. As a result, collisions occur at node B. Although RTS/CTS can be used to reduce collisions, it causes a large percentage of overhead. In order to eliminate this problem, the channel selection procedure needs to be revised.

2. *Channel switching mechanism is not justified.* MUP allocates a random time period for each selected channel. Performance of this scheme cannot be guaranteed, because the time of having the best quality in a channel is definitely not randomized. The time is related to the wireless channel characteristics and interference from nodes using the same channel.

3. *Packet re-ordering is needed when channels are switched.* MUP relies on TCP to handle this issue. This may not be appropriate for a multi-hop network, because it will cause low end-to-end throughput.

4. *Multiple channels per radio are not utilized in parallel.* Although multiple channels are available on each NIC, MUP does not try to utilize them in parallel. Each NIC has a fixed channel assignment.

4   Routing Protocols

4.1   Limitations of Ad Hoc Routing Protocols

Since IEEE 802.11 WMNs share common features with ad hoc networks, the routing protocols developed for them can be applied to IEEE 802.11 WMNs. For example, mesh routers of Firetide Networks [26] are based on topology broadcast based on reverse-path forwarding (TBRPF) protocol [27], Microsoft mesh networks [28] are built based on dynamic source routing (DSR) [29], and many other companies [30] are using ad-hoc on-demand distance vector (AODV) routing [31].

Despite the availability of several routing protocols for MANETS, the design of routing protocols for IEEE 802.11 WMNs is still an active research area because the existing routing protocols treat the underlying MAC protocol as a transparent layer. However, the cross-layer interaction must be considered to improve the performance of the routing protocols in IEEE 802.11 WMNs.

Some IEEE IEEE 802.11 WMNs do not have a strict constraint on power consumption as in ad hoc networks and high mobility is not a desired feature. Such differences imply that routing protocols designed for MANETs have different goals than for IEEE 802.11 WMNs.

4.2   Features of Routing Protocols for IEEE 802.11 WMNs

Based on the performance of the existing routing protocols for ad hoc networks and the specific requirements of IEEE 802.11 WMNs, we believe that an optimal routing protocol for IEEE 802.11 WMNs must capture the following features:

1. *Performance Metrics.* Many existing routing protocols use minimum hop-count as a performance metric to select the routing path. This has been demonstrated not to be valid in many situations. Suppose a link on the minimum hop-count path between two nodes has bad quality. If the minimum hop count is used as the performance metric, then the throughput between these two nodes will be very low. To solve this problem, performance metrics related to link quality are needed. If congestion occurs, then the minimum-hop count will not be an accurate performance metric either. Usually RTT is used as an additional performance metric. The bottomline is that a routing path must be selected by considering multiple performance metrics.

2. *Fault tolerance with link failures.* One of the objectives to deploy IEEE 802.11 WMNs is to ensure robustness in link failures. If a link breaks, the routing proto-col should be able to quickly select another path to avoid service disruption.

3. *Load Balancing.* One of the objectives of IEEE 802.11 WMNs is to share the network resources among many users. When a part of a WMN experiences congestion, new traffic flows should not be routed through that part. Performance metrics such as RTT help to achieve load balancing, but are not always effective, because RTT may be impacted by link quality.

4. *Scalability.* Setting up a routing path in a very large wireless network may take a long time, and the end-to-end delay can become large. Furthermore, even when the path is established, the node states on the path may change. Thus, the scalability of a routing protocol is critical in IEEE 802.11 WMNs.

In the rest of this section, we discuss various routing protocols for IEEE 802.11 WMNs and emphasize the open research issues.

4.3   State-of-the-Art Approaches

4.3.1   Routing Protocols with Various Performance Metrics

The impact of performance metrics on a routing protocol is studied in [32], where the link quality source routing (LQSR) is proposed on the basis of DSR. LQSR aims to select a routing path according to link quality metrics. Three performance metrics, i.e., expected transmission count (ETX) [33], per-hop RTT, and per-hop packet pair are implemented separately in LQSR.

The performance of the routing protocol with these three performance metrics is also compared with the method using the minimum hop-count. For stationary nodes in IEEE 802.11 WMNs ETX achieves the best performance, while the minimum hop-count method outperforms the three link quality metrics. The reason is that, as the sender moves, the ETX metric cannot quickly track the change in the link quality. This result illustrates that the link quality metrics used in [32] and the minimum-hop count are still not enough for IEEE 802.11 WMNs when mobility occurs. Better performance metrics need to be developed, and routing protocols integrating multiple performance metrics are necessary.

4.3.2   Multi-radio Routing

In IEEE 802.11 WMNs, multi-radio per node may be a preferred architecture, because the capacity can be increased without modifying the MAC protocol. A routing protocol is proposed in [34] for multi-radio IEEE 802.11 WMNs. A new performance metric, called weighted cumulative expected transmission time (WCETT) is proposed for the routing protocol. WCETT takes into account both link quality metric and the minimum hop-count. It can achieve good tradeoff between delay and throughput because it considers channels with good quality and channel diversity in the same routing protocol.

In IEEE 802.11 WMNs, multi-channel per radio is another alternative to improve the capacity. For this type of networks, the scheme proposed in [34] is not applicable because significant differences exist between a multi-channel node and a multi-radio node as explained in Section 3.2.2.

4.3.3   Multi-path Routing for Load Balancing and Fault Tolerance

The main objective of using multi-path routing is to perform better load balancing and to provide high fault tolerance [35]. Multiple paths are selected between source and destination. Packets flow in one of these selected paths. When link is broken on a path due to a bad channel quality or mobility, another path in the set of existing paths can be chosen. Thus, without waiting for setting up a new routing path, the end-to-end delay, throughput, and fault tolerance can be improved. However, the improvement depends on the availability of node-disjoint routes between source and destination.

A drawback of multi-path routing is its complexity and overhead. Whether or not the multi-path routing can be used for IEEE 802.11 WMNs needs to be investigated depending on applications. Another problem is that multi-path routing is not effective if the shortest path is taken as the routing performance metric [36]. Thus, how to design an effective multi-path routing protocol with appropriate performance metrics is an interesting research topic.

4.3.4 Scalable Hierarchical Routing

Numerous hierarchical routing protocols [37], [38], [39] have been proposed in recent years. Instead of addressing each of them, we describe the common principle of these routing protocols.

In hierarchical routing, a certain self-organization scheme is employed to group network nodes into clusters. Each cluster has one or more cluster heads. Nodes in a cluster can be one or more hops away from the cluster head. Since connectivity between clusters are needed, some nodes can communicate with more than one cluster and work as a gateway. Routing within a cluster and routing between clusters may use different mechanisms. For example, inter-cluster routing can be a proactive protocol, while intra-cluster routing can be on demand [37].

When the node density is high, hierarchical routing protocols tend to achieve much better performance because of less overhead, shorter average routing path, and quicker set-up procedure of routing path. However, the complexity of maintaining the hierarchy may compromise the performance of the routing protocol. In IEEE 802.11 WMNs, hierarchical routing actually may face the implementation difficulty, because a node selected as a cluster head may not necessarily have higher processing capability and channel capacity than the other nodes. Unless being intentionally designed so, the cluster head may become a bottleneck. Hierarchical routing provides a possible approach for scalability. However, whether or not these hierarchical schemes can really solve the scalability problem still remains a question.

5   Open Research Issues

In this section, the research challenges are summarized for both MAC and routing protocols.

5.1   Research Challenges in MAC Protocols

To the best of our knowledge, the scalability issue in multi-hop ad hoc networks has not been fully solved yet. Most of existing MAC protocols solve partial problems of the overall issue, but raise other problems. This is partly because CSMA/CA is used the basic multiple access scheme. In fact, both TDMA and CDMA can be applied to IEEE 802.11 WMNs, if a distributed scheme can be developed to locally eliminate the difficulties of implementing TDMA or CDMA in an ad hoc network. For example, a scheme has been proposed in [11] to implement a distributed TDMA MAC over an IEEE 802.11 radio. This scheme does not need a global timing synchronization scheme or a centralized scheduling scheme, and thus works in a distributed way. Many other interesting research problems related to the scalability issue of IEEE 802.11 WMNs still remain to be solved. When advanced techniques such as MIMO and cognitive radios are used in the physical layer, novel MAC protocols need to be proposed to utilize the agility provided by the physical layer.

Multi-channel MAC protocols for radios with multiple transceivers have not been thoroughly explored, possibly due to the relatively high cost of such radios. However, as the cost goes down, a multi-channel multi-transceiver MAC will be a rather promising solution for IEEE 802.11 WMNs. To really achieve spectrum efficiency, a multi-channel MAC protocol must include the single-channel solution that can fundamentally resolve the scalability issue of IEEE 802.11 WMNs. Otherwise, the throughput per node per channel will still be very low. How to apply the innovative single-channel solution to a multi-radio or multi-channel system is another research problem.

Most of the existing research efforts in MAC are focused on capacity, throughput, and fairness. However, many applications need to support broadband multimedia communication in IEEE 802.11 WMNs. Thus, the development of MAC protocols with multiple QoS metrics such as delay, packet loss ratios, and delay jitter is an important topic for IEEE 802.11 WMNs.

Another challenge related to MAC is its implementation, because both software and firmware may be involved when a MAC protocol is to be modified. As an example in IEEE 802.11 MAC, although chipset manufacturers have put efforts to pull up more functions in the firmware into the driver level as software, many timing critical functions remain in the firmware. Such a "thin" MAC solution provides little flexibility in changing MAC protocols. To avoid changing firmware, one approach is to design a MAC without coupling with firmware. For example, the virtual MAC protocols do not require any modification in firmware or hardware. However, in some circumstances key functions in the firmware need to be changed in order to significantly improve the performance of the MAC protocol. Changing firmware is a doable but not a viable solution due to its cost and complexity. A solution to this problem is to choose a more flexible MAC protocol architecture. To our knowledge, there are several IEEE 802.11 chipset manufacturers that have eliminated firmware in their MAC implementation architecture. With such an architecture, a true soft MAC or even a programmable MAC can be implemented.

5.2   Research Challenges in Routing Protocols

Although many routing protocols exist, several challenging research issues need to be resolved. Scalability is the most critical question in IEEE 802.11 WMNs. Hierarchical routing protocols can only partially solve this problem due to their complexity and difficulty of management. Thus, new scalable routing protocols need to be developed. Existing performance metrics incorporated into routing protocols need to be expanded. Moreover, how to integrate multiple performance metrics into a routing protocol so that the optimal overall performance is achieved is a challenging issue. Routing for multicast applications is another important research topic. Many applications of IEEE 802.11 WMNs need multicasting capability. For example, in a community or a city-wide network, video distribution is a common application. Without multicasting functionality, the network resources will be quickly occupied by video broadcasting or unicasting in IEEE 802.11 WMNs.

Cross-layer design between routing and MAC protocols is another interesting research topic. Previously, routing protocol research was focused on layer-3 functionality only. However, it has been shown that the performance of a routing protocol may not be satisfactory in this case. Adopting multiple performance metrics from layer-2 into routing protocols is an example. However, interaction between MAC and routing is so close that merely exchanging parameters between protocol layers is not adequate. Merging certain functions of MAC and routing is a promising approach.

When multi-radio or multi-channel wireless mesh nodes are considered, new routing protocols are needed for two reasons. First, the routing protocol not only needs to select a path in-between different nodes, it also needs to select the most appropriate channel or radio on the path. Second, cross-layer design becomes a necessity because change of a routing path involves the channel or radio switching in a mesh node. Without considering cross-layer design, the switching process may be too slow to degrade the performance of IEEE 802.11 WMNs.

6   Conclusion

IEEE 802.11 WMNs are widely gaining attentions from both industry and academia. To date, products of mesh routers and client nodes are already available on the market. Various deployments and application scenarios have demonstrated that IEEE 802.11 WMNs have many advantages over conventional IEEE 802.11 WLANs. More interestingly, IEEE 802.11 WMNs can complement the missing functions of other existing wireless networks such as cellular networks and wireless metropolitan area networks. IEEE 802.11 WMNs can even be applied to sensor networks. A typical example is that IEEE 802.11 WMNs have been applied to RFID networks. The promising advantages motivate the increasing demands of IEEE 802.11 WMNs in various application scenarios.

However, open research issues still exist in IEEE 802.11 WMNs, in particular, scalability, self-organization, and security are the most important problems. Without a solution to these problems, an IEEE 802.11 WMN will not be able to deliver the functions as what are expected; the advantages of IEEE 802.11 WMNs will be compromised. As we studied in this chapter, existing communications protocols can deliver a functional WMN, however, their performance is still not satisfactory. Considering the similarities between IEEE 802.11 WMNs and ad hoc networks, convergence of research results from ad hoc networks and IEEE 802.11 wireless LANs can contribute to a better protocol design for IEEE 802.11 WMNs. However, an IEEE 802.11 WMN also holds many differences than an ad hoc network. Thus, tremendous research and development efforts are still needed to promote IEEE 802.11 WMNs into a fully mature technology.

References

[1] IEEE 802 STANDARD WORKING GROUP, Wireless LAN Medium Access Control (MAC) and Physical Layer (PHY) specifications: Further Higher Data Rate Extension in 2.4 GHZ Band, *IEEE 802.11g Standard*, 2003.

[2] IEEE 802 Standard Working Group, Wireless LAN Medium Access Control (MAC) and Physical Layer (PHY) specifications: High-speed Physical Layer in the 5 GHz Band, *IEEE 802.11a Standard*, 1999.

[3] IEEE 802.11 Standard Group Web Site, http://www.ieee802.org/11/

[4] IEEE 802.16 Standard Group Web Site, http://www.ieee802.org/16/

[5] N. Passas, S. Paskalis, D. Vali, and L. Merakos, Quality-of-service Oriented Medium Access Control for Wireless ATM Networks, *IEEE Communications Magazine*, **35** (1997), pp. 42–50.

[6] I. F. Akyildiz, X. Wang, and M. J. Colella, HALO (High Altitude Long Operation): A Broadband Wireless Metropolitan Area Network, *Proc. IEEE International Workshop on Mobile Multimedia Communications*, (1999), pp. 271–275.

[7] M. J. Colella, J. N. Martin, and I. F. Akyildiz The HALO Network^{TM}, *IEEE Communications Magazine*, **38** (2000), pp. 142–148.

[8] I. F. Akyildiz, X. Wang, and W. Wang, Wireless Mesh Networks: State-of-the-Art and Research Challenges, *Elsevier Computer Networks*, to appear.

[9] IETF Mobile Ad Hoc Networks Charter, http://www.ietf.org/html.charters/manet-charter.html

[10] H. Yang, H. Luo, F. Ye, S. Lu, and L. Zhang, Security in Mobile Ad Hoc Networks: Challenges and Solutions, *IEEE Wireless Communications*, (2004), pp. 38–47.

[11] X. Wang, W. Wang, and M. Nova, A High Performance Single-Channel IEEE 802.11 MAC with Distributed TDMA, *Technical Report of Kiyon*, Inc. (submitted for patent application), Aug. 2004.

[12] F. Cali, M. Conti, and E. Gregori, Dynamic Tuning of the IEEE 802.11 Protocol to Achieve a Theoretical Throughput Limit, *IEEE/ACM Transactions on Networking*, **8** (2000), pp. 785-799.

[13] D. Qiao and K. Shin, UMAV: A Simple Enhancement to IEEE 802.11 DCF, *Proc. of Hawaii International Conference on System Science*, 2002.

[14] Y.B. Ko, V. Shankarkumar, and N.H. Vaidya, Medium Access Control Protocols Using Directional Antennas in Ad Hoc Networks, *Proc. IEEE INFOCOM*, 2000.

[15] R. R. Choudhury, X. Yang, R. Ramanathan, and N. H. Vaidya, Using Directional Antennas for Medium Access Control in Ad Hoc Networks, *Proc. ACM MOBICOM*, 2002.

[16] N. Poojary, S. V. Krishnamurthy, and S. Dao, Medium Access Control in A Network of Ad Hoc Mobile Nodes with Heterogeneous Power Capabilities, *Proc. IEEE ICC*, (2001), pp. 872–877.

[17] C. F. Chiasserini and R. R. Rao, A Distributed Power Management Policy for Wireless Ad Hoc Networks, *Proc. IEEE WCNC*, (2000), pp. 1209–1213.

[18] R. Zhong and R. Kravets, On Demand Power Management for Ad Hoc Networks, *Proc. IEEE INFOCOM*, (2003), pp. 481–491.

[19] Y.-C. Tseng, C.-S. Hsu, and T.-Y. Hsieh, Power-Saving Protocols for IEEE 802.11 Based Multi-Hop Ad Hoc Networks,*Proc. IEEE INFOCOM*, (2002), pp. 200–209.

[20] A. Acharya, A. Misra, and S. Bansal, High-Performance Architectures for IP-Based Multihop 802.11 Networks, *IEEE Wireless Communications*, (2003), pp. 22–28.

[21] K. Jain, J. Padhye, V. Padmanabhan, and L. Qiu, Impact of Interference on Multi-Hop Wireless Network Performance, *Proc. ACM MOBICOM*, 2003.

[22] J. So and N. Vaidya, Multi-Channel MAC for Ad Hoc Networks: Handling Multi-Channel Hidden Terminals Using A Single Transceiver, *Proc. ACM MOBIHOC*, 2004.

[23] P. Bahl, R. Chandra, and J. Dunagan, SSCH: Slotted Seeded Channel Hopping for Capacity Improvement in IEEE 802.11 Ad-hoc Wireless Networks, *Proc. ACM MO-BICOM*, 2004.

[24] Engim Inc., Multiple Channel 802.11 Chipset, http://www.engim.com/products_en3000.html

[25] A. Adya, P. Bahl, J. Padhye, A. Wolman, and L. Zhou, A Multi-radio Unification Protocol for IEEE 802.11 Wireless Networks, *Proc. BroadNets* 2004.

[26] Firetide Networks, http://www.firetide.com

[27] R. Ogier, F. Templin, and M. Lewis, Topology Dissemination Based on Reverse-Path Forwarding (TBRPF), *IETF RFC* **3684**, Feb. 2004.

[28] Microsoft Mesh Networks, http://research.microsoft.com/mesh/

[29] D. B. Johnson, D. A. Maltz, and Y.-C. Hu, The Dynamic Source Routing Protocol for Mobile Ad Hoc Networks (DSR), *IETF Internet-Draft*: work in progress, July 2004.

[30] Kiyon Autonomic Networks, http://www.kiyon.com

[31] C. Perkins, E. Belding-Royer, and S. Das, Ad hoc On-Demand Distance Vector (AODV) Routing, *IETF RFC* **3561**, July 2003.

[32] R. Draves, J. Padhye, and B. Zill, Comparisons of Routing Metrics for Static Multi-Hop Wireless Networks, *Proc. ACM SIGCOMM*, Aug. 2004.

[33] D. S. J. De Couto, D. Aguayo, J. Bicket, and R. Morris, A High-Throughput Path Metric for Multi-Hop Wireless Routing, *Proc ACM MOBICOM*, 2003.

[34] R. Draves, J. Padhye, and B. Zill, Routing in Multi-radio Multi-Hop Wireless Mesh Networks, *Proc. ACM MOBICOM*, 2004.

[35] S. Mueller and D. Ghosal, Multipath Routing in Mobile Ad Hoc Networks: Issues and Challenges, *Lecture Notes in Computer Science*, M. C.i Calzarossa and E. Gelenbe, eds., 2004

[36] Y. Ganjali, A. Keshavarzian, Load Balancing in Ad Hoc Networks: Single-path Routing vs. Multi-path Routing, *Proc. IEEE INFOCOM*, Mar. 2004.

[37] A. K. Saha and D. B. Johnson, Self-Organizing Hierarchical Routing for Scalable Ad Hoc Networking, Department of Computer Science Technical Report, TR04-433, Rice University.

[38] E. M. Belding-Royer, Multi-level Hierarchies for Scalable Ad hoc Routing, *ACM/Kluwer Wireless Networks (WINET)*, **9** (2003), pp. 461–478.

[39] K. Xu, X. Hong, and M. Gerla, Landmark Routing in Ad Hoc Networks with Mobile Backbones, *Journal of Parallel and Distributed Computing (JPDC), Special Issue on Ad Hoc Networks*, **63** (2002), pp. 110–122.

In: Wireless LANs and Bluetooth
Editors: Yang Xiao and Yi Pan, pp. 157-171

ISBN: 1-59454-432-8
© 2005 Nova Science Publishers, Inc.

Chapter 8

THROUGHPUT ANALYSIS OF THE IEEE 802.11E ENHANCED DISTRIBUTED CHANNEL ACCESS

Haitao Wu[1], Qian Zhang[2]
Microsoft Research Asia, China
Xin Wang[3],
Tsinghua University, China
Xuemin (Sherman) Shen[4]
Department of Electrical and Computer Engineering,
University of Waterloo, Waterloo, Ontario, Canada

Abstract

The upcoming standard IEEE 802.11e will provide Quality of Service (QoS) support in Wireless Local Area Network (WLAN). The contention based channel access method called the Enhanced Distributed Channel Access (EDCA) is considered as the mandatory mode for Medium Access Control (MAC) in IEEE 802.11e. This chapter presents an accurate analytical model of EDCA based on Markov Chain for average throughput achieved in the saturated situation. The analytical model is suitable for both basic access and RTS/CTS access mechanisms. It considers most of the new features in EDCA such as different Arbitration Inter-frame Space (AIFS) and contention window for different Access Category (AC), and virtual collision for different priority queue in the same station; and can be easily extended to other features such as Transmission Opportunity (TXOP), etc. The analytical model is evaluated by the extensive simulation results, and can provide deep understanding of the effect of different parameter setting to the throughput performance.

Keywords. Enhanced Distributed Channel Access (EDCA), IEEE 802.11e, Throughput analysis, Wireless Local Area Network (WLAN)

---

[1] E-mail address: t-hwu@microsoft.com.
[2] E-mail address: qianz@microsoft.com.
[3] E-mail address: wangxin02@mails.tsinghua.edu.cn.
[4] E-mail address: xshen@bbcr.uwaterloo.ca.

Introduction

It has been experiencing a tremendous growth in recent years for wireless local area network (WLAN) as evidenced by the fast increasing popularity of WLAN hotspots deployed in residence, enterprise and public areas such as airports, campuses, conference venues, shopping malls, and exhibitions. Meanwhile, WLAN services are evolving from the best effort data services to real-time applications with a certain level of quality-of-service (QoS) provisioning. IEEE Project 802 recommends an international standard 802.11[1-3] for WLAN. The standard includes detailed specifications both for Medium Access Control (MAC) Layer and Physical (PHY) Layer. To support Quality of Service (QoS) over WLAN, the standard IEEE 802.11e is being proposed.

In IEEE 802.11e, hybrid coordination function (HCF) is used as the MAC access method. It combines the contention-based Enhanced Distributed Channel Access (EDCA) and contention-free HCF controlled channel access (HCCA) to provide QoS stations (QSTAs) with prioritized and parameterized QoS access to the wireless medium, while continuing to support non-QoS STAs with best-effort services. It is compatible with the distributed coordination function (DCF) and the point coordination function (PCF) in IEEE 802.11. EDCA defines the prioritized carrier sense multiple access with collision avoidance (CSMA/CA) mechanism, and it is the mandatory mechanism in 802.11e. In this chapter, we focus on a complete and accurate average throughput analysis achieved in the saturated situation by modeling the EDCA.

Since 802.11e EDCA adopts most of the design principles in 802.11 DCF, such as exponential backoff, basic and RTS/CTS access method, etc., it is natural to leverage the modeling work for 802.11 DCF. In the literature, there have been extensive efforts to model 802.11 since the standard was proposed. The effect of capture and hidden terminal is considered in [8], and the theoretical throughput limit of 802.11 based on a p-persistent variant is given in [9]. However, none of them captures the effect of the Contention Window (CW) and binary exponential backoff procedure used by DCF in 802.11. In [10], a Markov model is developed to analyze the saturated throughput of 802.11. In [11], the Markov model is refined by considering the frame retry limits and timeout after collisions. All of these models have been applied to the legacy DCF in 802.11, and can be extended to the scenario with different packet size and channel modulation rate.

To provide service differentiation in 802.11e EDCA [3], different Arbitration Inter-frame Space (AIFS) and CW for different Access Category (AC), and virtual collision for different priority queue in the same station are introduced. Each station can maintain up to 4 packet queues corresponding to 4 ACs, respectively. Based on the Markov model for saturated condition [10-11], an analytical approach is proposed for throughput and delay of 802.11e EDCA with different CWs, retry limit and the backoff window-increasing factor for each AC [5-6]. In [12], a three-dimensional Markov model is developed for analyzing the performance of EDCA on AIFS and CW differentiation, but only the approximated performance can be obtained. Recently, a concise three-dimensional Markov model is proposed in [13] for EDCA. It partially gives the analysis for the effect of AIFS by introducing additional slot corresponding to the differentiation of AIFS as in [12]. Neither of them takes the different packet collision probability experienced by different AC into consideration. To address this issue, a novel notation called *contention zone* is introduced in [14], where the different collision probability for different AC in a random slot is analyzed by calculating the distribution for the location of the slot with last channel busy time. However, the calculation of the probability for contention zone in [14] does not take virtual collision into consideration. In addition, the analysis for the post collision period in [14] assumes a much less timeout value than that defined in standard [1] for stations experiencing collisions.

In this chapter, we propose a Markov Chain based model for each AC, and differentiate the collision probability experienced by different AC through the refined contention zone. Different CW for each AC and the virtual collision defined in EDCA are also taken into account. Other factors such as different packet length, modulation rate, and Transmission Opportunity (TXOP) in EDCA can be analyzed by extending our model straightforwardly. Our contribution is to address all the factors related to QoS introduced in EDCA and target at an accurate model.

The remainder of this paper is organized as follows. In Section 2, we briefly introduce 802.11 DCF and the major mechanism in EDCA for QoS support. In Section 3, we propose a Markov chain based model with contention zone [14] to analyze the average throughput performance of EDCA, taking all the QoS related factors in EDCA into consideration. The accuracy of our model is evaluated by extensive simulation results in Section 4. We conclude our chapter in Section 5

IEEE 802.11 EDCA

The basic service set (BSS) is the fundamental building block of IEEE 802.11 architecture, and it is called QoS BSS (QBSS) for 802.11e. DCF is the mandatory access method for 802.11 and EDCA can be considered as its QoS extension. In this section, we first briefly present DCF, then explain the QoS related factors introduced in EDCA.

Distributed Coordination Function (DCF)

DCF is based on CSMA/CA, and only provides asynchronous access for best effort data transmission. It consists of both a basic access method and an optional channel access method using RTS/CTS exchanges prior to data transmission. In 802.11, priority access to the wireless medium is controlled by the use of inter-frame space (IFS) time between the transmissions of frames, and Short IFS(SIFS), PCF-IFS(PIFS), and DCF-IFS(DIFS) are defined.

A source station may proceed with its transmission if the medium is sensed to be idle for an interval larger than the DIFS. If the medium is busy, the station defers until a DIFS is detected and then generates a random backoff period before transmission. The backoff timer is decreased as long as the channel is sensed idle, frozen when the channel is sensed busy, and resumed when the channel is sensed idle again for more than a DIFS. A source station can initiate a transmission when the backoff timer reaches zero. The backoff time is uniformly chosen in the range [0, w-1], and (w-1) is known as CW, which is an integer with the range determined by the PHY characteristics CW_{min} and CW_{max}. After each unsuccessful transmission, w is doubled, up to a maximum value $2^m W$, where W equals (CW_{min}+1) and $2^m W$ equals (CW_{max}+1). Upon having received a packet correctly, the destination station waits for a SIFS interval immediately following the reception of the data frame and transmits an ACK back to the source station, indicating that the data packet has been received correctly.

Enhanced Distributed Channel Access

In 802.11e EDCA, service differentiation is provided by assigning different contention parameters to different Access Categories (AC). A QoS station can support at most eight user priorities, which are mapped into four ACs. Each AC in a station is supported by a separate queue contending channel access with different AIFS and CW setting. Compared with DCF where DIFS is used as the common IFS for a station to access the channel, EDCF uses different AIFS for each AC to achieve the access differentiation, where the AIFS for a given AC is defined as

$$AIFS[AC] = AIFSN[AC] \times \delta + SIFS.$$

The AIFSN denotes the number to differentiate the AIFS for each AC, and δ is the time interval of a slot for 802.11 standard, which is determined according to the physical medium used. Table 1 shows the default parameter settings defined for different ACs in 802.11e draft standard [3], where AC1 for voice is assigned the highest priority while AC4 for background is given the lowest priority.

Table 1 Default EDCA parameter set

AC	CWmin	CWmax	AIFSN
AC_VO(Voice)	7	15	2
AC_VI(Video)	15	31	2
AC_BE(Best Effort)	31	1023	3
AC_BK(Background)	31	1023	7

To understand the service differentiation introduced by AIFS and CW, we use an example shown in Fig. 1, where there are two stations with packets in AC1 and AC4, respectively. The difference of AIFSN is 5, so the AC1 in STA1 will decrease its backoff counter 5 slots earlier than AC4 in STA2. In addition, the backoff counter of high priority AC may count to zero in this interval and transmit the packet, which results in channel busy due to high priority packet transmission and resynchronization after that. So the backoff counter of low priority AC will be decreased much slower than that of the high priority AC. An interesting behavior from this example is that, since the low priority AC can not access the channel in the interval introduced by AIFS difference, different AC experiences different channel busy probability, which makes AC with high priority beneficial. Most of the modeling development [12-13] for 802.11e EDCA do not take this effect into account except that in [14] with the novel notation of contention zone.

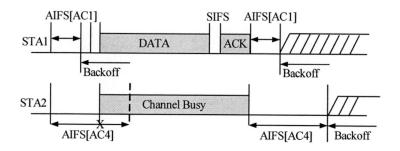

Fig.1 An example of channel access in EDCA

In a single QoS station supporting EDCA, each AC is implemented as a separate queue, as shown in Fig. 2. Each queue behaves like a virtual station and contends for the channel access independently. When a collision occurs among different queues of the same station, i.e., two backoff counters of the queues decreases to zero simultaneously, the highest priority queue always wins the contention, and the lower priority queues act as if a collision occurred.

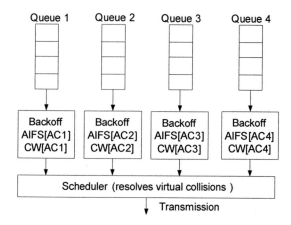

Fig.2 Single station with multiple priority queues & virtual collision resolution

By differentiating the IFS and CW of each AC and virtual collision solution, the traffic with high priority will have more chances to gain the channel access and suffer less delay. This chapter proposes a Markov chain based model to analyze the saturated throughput and channel access time. Note 802.11e EDCF also proposes the TXOP limit parameter allowing a transmission burst for different AC in contrast to a common restriction for one packet as in DCF, which can be analyzed by extending our model using similar methods proposed in [10, 15] for different packet size and modulation rate.

Analytical Model

In this section, we present an analytical model for EDCF based on Markov chain in [10-11]. We consider the saturated condition, i.e., if a station has packet arrival in a given AC, the AC will always have packets waiting for transmission. We also assume a perfect physical channel, i.e., we do not consider wireless transmission error, fading, capture effect, etc.

Packet Transmission Probability

The fundamental assumption from the original Markov chain for DCF is that each station will transmit with a stationary probability τ in a generic (i.e., random chosen) slot. In addition, the key approximation is that each station collides with constant probability p regardless of the number of retransmissions suffered. However, due to the difference in AIFS of each AC, the number of competing stations may vary at different time slots and the collision probability can not be simply assumed as constant. Therefore, we use separate Markov chain for each AC, and the collision probability is assumed as an average value $\overline{p_{[AC]}}$ for each AC, respectively. We also assume that each queue behaves as a virtual station, and it initiates a transmission in a random chosen slot available for this AC with a stationery conditional probability $\tau_{[AC]}$.

Let $b(t)$ be the stochastic process representing the backoff window size for a given station at slot time t, and the backoff stage is denoted as $s(t)$. A discrete and integer time scale is adopted, where t and $t+1$ denote the two consecutive slot times, and the backoff counter of each queue decreases at the beginning of each slot time. Note different AC will experience different slot time due to the difference in AIFS. Thus, for each AC, the bi-dimensional process $(s(t), b(t))$ is a discrete-time Markov chain, which is shown in Fig. 3. Here $W_i^{[AC]}-1$ denote the contention window of the AC at backoff stage i, and m denote the maximal backoff stage. Each backoff will double the value of $W_i^{[AC]}$ until the contention window is equal to the $CW_{\max}$ of the corresponding AC.

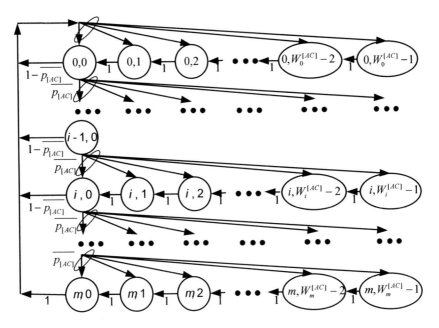

Fig 3. Markov chain model for each AC

The formation of the state transition in the Markov chain is similar to that in paper [11]. In the following, we briefly explain the formation procedure. The conditional transmission probability $\tau_{[AC]}$ can be represented as the sum of the probability,

$$\tau_{[AC]} = \sum_{i=0}^{m} b_{i,0}^{[AC]} = \frac{1 - (\overline{p_{[AC]}})^{m+1}}{1 - \overline{p_{[AC]}}} b_{0,0}^{[AC]} \qquad (1)$$

where $b_{i,k}^{[AC]}$ is the stationary distribution of the Markov chain in state (i, k) for AC respectively, and $b_{0,0}^{[AC]}$ can be represented by an equation of $\overline{p_{[AC]}}$ using $\sum_{i=0}^{m} \sum_{k=0}^{W_i^{[AC]}-1} b_{i,k}^{[AC]} = 1$. So we can figure out an equation for $\overline{p_{[AC]}}$ by the conditional transmission probability $\tau_{[AC]}$ respectively.

To solve the equation, the key issue is to obtain another formation for different collision probability $\overline{p_{[AC]}}$ with conditional probability $\tau_{[AC]}$, which is introduced to address the difference of AIFS for each AC. Thus, the difference of AIFS creates different *contention zones* for AC to differentiate the access probability, which is illustrated in Fig. 4 by an example for the differentiation for two ACs, where AC-*A* stands for high priority and AC-*B* stands for low priority. For each queue, the probability that any transmission experiences a collision is constant within a contention zone, regardless of the number of retransmissions suffered. Comparing with the work in [14] for contention zone, we take virtual collision into consideration in calculating the collision probability.

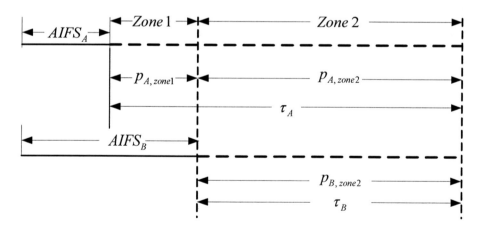

Fig. 4 Transmission probability and collision probability in different contention zones

To understand the effect of contention zone, we take two priority queues with different AIFS settings as an example. As shown in Fig. 4, in contention zone 1, only high priority queues contend for the channel access; while in contention zone 2, high priority queues contend with the low priority queues. In other words, a low priority queue never 'sees' contention zone 1. And due to virtual collision resolution, a high priority queue never 'sees' low priority queue in the same station. Under the saturated condition, the maximal slot number for all contention zones is $L_1 + L_2 = \min(CW_{\max}[AC])$, where L_j denote the number of slot in zone j. The transmission probability for a packet in each AC is restricted by the contention zones available for this AC, so it is a conditional probability. For example, $\tau_{B,zone2}$ is the conditional transmission probability given that the random chosen slot is in contention zone 2 since a low priority queue can only access the medium in contention zone 2.

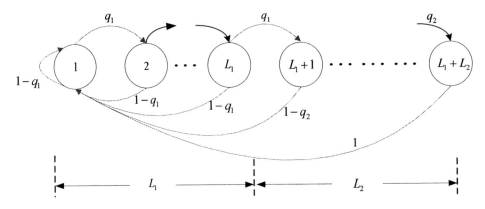

Fig.5 Transition of slots in contention zones

To calculate the stationary probability for the slot in each contention zone, we assume that it can be approximated by a Markov chain. Fig. 5 shows the relationship between different backoff slots for two ACs, where we use q_j to denote the probability that no stations transmit in contention zone j. There are n stations in competition for channel access, and among them, n_A stations have packets in AC A and n_B stations have packets in AC B. Let $\mu_{i,j}$ denote the transmission probability for station i $(1 \le i \le n)$ in zone j, then the transition probability for a slot in zone j to its adjacent slot can be represented as

$$q_j = \prod_{i=1}^{n}(1 - \mu_{i,j}) \cdot \tag{2}$$

For the two ACs scenario in our example, if we consider all the stations both have packet on the two ACs, i.e., $n = n_A = n_B$, for each station i we have

$$\begin{cases} \mu_{i,1} = 1 - (1 - \tau_A) \\ \mu_{i,2} = 1 - (1 - \tau_A)(1 - \tau_B) \end{cases} . \tag{3}$$

On the contrary, if each station only has one AC associated with packets, i.e., $n = n_A + n_B$, the transmission probability for the station is simply the transmission probability for that AC in each zone respectively. However, the transition probability in Fig.5 is in the same formation, independent of the pattern that ACs are associated with stations, i.e.,

$$\begin{cases} q_1 = (1 - \tau_A)^{n_A} \\ q_2 = (1 - \tau_A)^{n_A}(1 - \tau_B)^{n_B} \end{cases} . \tag{4}$$

Let z_k denote the stationary probability for slot k in contention zones, and let $zone(k)$ denote the zone that slot k is located, i.e., $zone(k) = j$ means slot k is in zone j, then the relationship between the backoff slots is

$$z_k = z_1 \prod_{l=2}^{k} q_{zone(l-1)}, k > 1.$$ (5)

Considering $\sum_{k=1}^{\min(CW_{max}[AC])} \pi_k = 1$, we have

$$z_1 = [1 + \sum_{k=2}^{\min(CW_{max}[AC])} \prod_{l=2}^{k} q_{zone(l-1)}]^{-1}.$$ (6)

For the case with two ACs, it can be simplified as

$$z_1 = [\frac{1-(q_1)^{L_1+1}}{1-q_1} + q_1^{L_1} q_2 \frac{1-(q_2)^{L_2-1}}{1-q_2}]^{-1}.$$ (7)

Let $\pi_{zone(j)}$ denote the stationary distribution for a random slot in zone j, it can be calculated as

$$\pi_{zone(j)} = \sum_{zone(k)=j} z_k$$ (8)

Therefore, with the distribution obtained for each zone, we can use the weighted collision probability by the distribution of contention zone to calculate the average conditional collision probability experienced by each AC

$$\overline{p_{[AC]}} = (\sum_{j} p_{[AC],zone(j)} \pi_{zone(j)}) / \sum_{j \in [AC]} \pi_{zone(j)}$$ (9)

where we use $j \in [AC]$ to denote that zone j is available for the transmission of packet belongs to [AC], and we use $p_{[AC],zone(j)}$ to denote the conditional collision probability of the AC in zone j.

For the two ACs we are examining, the high priority AC A can transmit packet in both zone 1 and zone 2, while low priority AC B can transmit packet only in zone2. The collision probability of high priority queue associated with AC A can be calculated by

$$\overline{p_A} = p_{A,zone1} \pi_{zone1} + p_{A,zone2} \pi_{zone2}.$$ (10)

Since there will be only high priority AC for transmission in zone 1, so the collision probability for high priority queue in zone 1 is,

$$p_{A,zone1} = 1 - (1 - \tau_A)^{n_A - 1}. \tag{11}$$

For zone 2, the calculation needs to take virtual collision into consideration, where a high priority AC will only collide with packet from other stations, not the low priority AC in the same station. Let $D = \{1,0\}$ denote whether there is AC B in the station with AC A, e.g., for $n = n_A = n_B$, we have $D = 1$, and for $n = n_A + n_B$ we have $D = 0$. Then the collision probability of AC A in zone 2 can be calculated by

$$p_{A,zone2} = 1 - (1 - \tau_A)^{n_A - 1}(1 - \tau_B)^{n_B - D} \tag{12}$$

While low priority queue can only access to the channel in contention zone 2, i.e., $p_{B,zone1} = 0$, and will collide with both the packets from other stations and packet from the same station belongs to high priority AC, so its collision probability is,

$$\overline{p_B} = p_{B,zone2} = 1 - (1 - \tau_B)^{n_B - 1}(1 - \tau_A)^{n_A}. \tag{13}$$

The calculated average collision probability for each AC is used in Markov chain in Fig.3, where the chain is ergodic and has a unique stationary solution. Therefore, combining (1)(4)(5)(8)(9) we can solve the variable $\tau_{[AC]}$. And the conditional transmission probability for each station in each zone $\mu_{i,j}$ can also be calculated.

Average Throughput Analysis

We calculate the average throughput with the numerical results obtained from Markov chain. Let $P_{tr}^{[AC]}$ be the probability that there is at least one transmission for a specific AC in the considered slot time, and $P_s^{[AC]}$ be the probability that a transmission is successful, given the probability $P_{tr}^{[AC]}$. Then, we have the conditional transmission probability for each AC in the slot that is available

$$\begin{cases} P_{tr}^A = 1 - (1 - \tau_A)^{n_A} \\ P_{tr}^B = 1 - (1 - \tau_B)^{n_B}. \end{cases} \tag{14}$$

Therefore, the channel idle probability for a slot in each zone can be calculated as

$$\begin{cases} P_{idle,zone1} = 1 - P_{tr}^A = (1 - \tau_A)^{n_A} \\ P_{idle,zone2} = (1 - P_{tr}^A)(1 - P_{tr}^B) = (1 - \tau_A)^{n_A}(1 - \tau_B)^{n_B}. \end{cases} \tag{15}$$

The conditional successful transmission probability for high priority packet transmitted in the slot is

$$\begin{cases} P_{s,zone1}^A = n_A \tau_A (1-\tau_A)^{n_A-1} / P_{tr}^A \\ P_{s,zone2}^A = n_A \tau_A (1-\tau_A)^{n_A-1} (1-\tau_B)^{n_B-D} / P_{tr}^A, \end{cases} \tag{16}$$

and the conditional successful transmission probability for low priority packet transmitted in the slot is

$$P_{s,zone2}^B = n_B \tau_B (1-\tau_B)^{n_B-1} (1-\tau_A)^{n_A} / P_{tr}^B \tag{17}$$

With the above equations, we can express the normalized system throughput S as

$$S = \frac{E[\text{Payload Information in a slot time}]}{E[\text{Length of a slot time}]} \tag{18}$$

The average slot time is calculated according to the distribution of slots in contention zones. Three types of events may happen in a slot, which determine the time costs for the slot, respectively: idle, a successful transmission, or a collision. Let δ, $T_s^{[AC]}$ and $T_c^{[AC]}$ denote the corresponding time costs. For instance, T_c^A is the time cost for collision happened between packets only in AC A, and $T_c^{\{A,B\}}$ is the time cost for collision happens between packets in AC A or B. Therefore, we have the following averaged slot time in zone 1 and zone 2, respectively

$$\begin{cases} \overline{\sigma_{zone1}} = P_{idle,zone1}\delta + P_{tr}^A P_{s,zone1}^A T_s^A + \left(1 - P_{idle,zone1} - P_{tr}^A P_{s,zone1}^A\right)T_c^A \\ \overline{\sigma_{zone2}} = P_{idle,zone2}\delta + P_{tr}^A P_{s,zone2}^A T_s^A + P_{tr}^B P_{s,zone2}^B T_s^B + \left(1 - P_{idle,zone2} - P_{tr}^A P_{s,zone2}^A - P_{tr}^B P_{s,zone2}^B\right)T_c^{\{A,B\}}, \end{cases} \tag{19}$$

and the averaged slot time is

$$\overline{\sigma} = \pi_{zone1}\overline{\sigma_{zone1}} + \pi_{zone2}\overline{\sigma_{zone2}} \tag{20}$$

The average payload information in a slot time can be calculated by the successful transmission probability for each AC, so the throughput for each AC can be represented as

$$\begin{cases} S_A = \left(\pi_{zone1}P_{tr}^A P_{s,zone1}^A + \pi_{zone2}P_{tr}^A P_{s,zone2}^A\right)E[P]/\overline{\sigma} \\ S_B = \left(\pi_{zone2}P_{tr}^B P_{s,zone2}^B\right)E[P]/\overline{\sigma} \end{cases} \tag{21}$$

where $E[P]$ denotes the average packet size. For simplicity, we assume all the packets have the same length, where the extension for different packet length can be referred to [10]. Therefore, the superscript of $T_s^{[AC]}$ and $T_c^{[AC]}$ can be removed. If basic access method is used, the successful transmission time T_s and collision time T_c for an AC can be represented by

$$\begin{cases} T_s = \min(AIFS_{[AC]}) + H + E[P] + SIFS + ACK + 2\varepsilon \\ T_c = \min(AIFS_{[AC]}) + H + E[P] + SIFS + ACK, \end{cases} \tag{22}$$

where ε denotes the propagation delay, H the time cost for both PHY and MAC header for a frame, and SIFS and ACK are the time cost for short inter-frame space and MAC acknowledgement, respectively. Note that according to the standard [3], after a collision, all the stations will contend the channel access using EIFS-DIFS+AIFS[AC], which effectively resynchronizes the backoff of all the stations again.

For the RTS/CTS access method, we have

$$\begin{cases} T_s = \min(AIFS_{[AC]}) + RTS + CTS + H + E[P] + 3 \times SIFS + ACK + 4\varepsilon \\ T_c = \min(AIFS_{[AC]}) + RTS + SIFS + CTS. \end{cases} \tag{23}$$

Although equations (22) and (23) do not consider fragmentation, where a payload will be fragmented and transmitted by several frame continuously [1], but the formation for considering fragmentation is straightforward and omitted here.

Analytical Model Evaluation

To evaluate the proposed model, we use the well-known simulation tool *NS*-2[16] from Lawrence Berkeley National Laboratory and the implementation of 802.11e EDCA in *NS*-2 from TKN group in Technical University of Berlin. Also, we make each station have enough data to send to obtain the saturated throughput performance of different AC. We vary the number of stations to evaluate the difference in each AC. All the parameters used follow the standard [1], and are summarized in Table 2. The CW and AIFS setting for each AC is based on Table 1.

Table.2 Parameters for MAC and PHY Layer

Packet Payload	8000bits
MAC header	224bits
PHY header	192bits
ACK	112bits+PHY header
RTS	160bits+PHY header
CTS	112bits+PHY header
Channel bit rate	11Mbps
Propagation delay	1us
Slot time	20us
SIFS	10us

To validate the accuracy of our model, we compare the numerical results with simulations. In the following figures, we use *model* to denote our analysis results and *sim* to denote the simulation results. And the results for both the basic access method and RTS/CTS access method have been presented. Each point for a simulation result shows the average of 10 simulation runs with different seeds and the statistics for each run are collected in an interval of 20 seconds. Each station is configured with two saturated queues associated with different ACs in all the simulations, i.e., the case for $n = n_A = n_B$.

First we show the effect of different AIFS introduced for different AC with the same backoff window. Each station is associated with two ACs, AC_BE and AC_BK, and we vary the number of stations to compare their throughput performance. From Fig. 6 we can see that our modeling results match the simulation results well. We observe that even with the same initial and maximal contention window setting from 31 to 1023, AC_BE with AIFSN 3 achieves overwhelming priority over AC_BK with AIFSN 7.

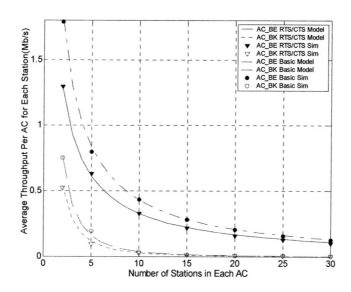

Fig. 6 Throughput of AC_BE vs. AC_BK with the same number of queues

Second we exam whether priority is provided to real time traffic such as video in AC_VI comparing with AC_BE. We also compare the throughput performance for different numbers of stations. From Fig.7, comparing with the results in Fig.6, we observe similar difference in priority for the throughput between AC_VI and AC_BE. AC_VI in Fig. 7 achieves higher throughput than AC_BE in Fig.6 when the number of stations is smaller, since the contention window range for AC_VI is much smaller. However, when the number of stations is large, AC_VI achieves smaller throughput than AC_BE in Fig.6 since smaller contention window leads to higher collision probability.

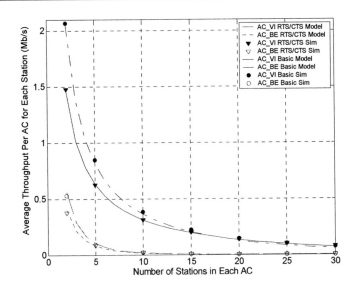

Fig. 7 Throughput of AC_VO (2 queues) vs. AC_BE with different number of queues

From the extensive simulation results, we can conclude that the proposed analytical model is accurate, and the priority between ACs in EDCF is effective which implies that high priority traffic load should be controlled carefully to avoid starvation to lower priority traffic. We have also evaluated the accuracy of our model for other cases, e.g., $n = n_A + n_B$, which are omitted due to space limitation.

Summary

In this chapter, an accurate and simple analytical model based on Markov chain has been proposed for average throughput performance of EDCA, where the new QoS-related features of EDCA (including different AIFS and CW, and virtual collisions) have been taken into account. The model can be used for both the basic access method and the RTS/CTS access method in EDCA. It is expected that the research work should be helpful for better understanding of IEEE 802.11e for QoS support over WLAN

References

[1]   IEEE standard for Wireless LAN Medium Access Control (MAC) and Physical Layer (PHY) Specifications, *ISO/IEC 8802-11:1999(E),* Aug. 1999

[2]   B.P. Crow and J.G. Kim. IEEE 802.11 Wireless Local Area Networks, *IEEE Comm.Mag.,* Sept. 1997

[3]   IEEE Draft for Wireless Medium Access Control (MAC) and Physical Layer (PHY) Specifications: Medium Access Control (MAC) Enhancements for Quality of Service (QoS), *IEEE Std 802.11e/ Draft 11.0,* October 2004

[4]   Q.Pattara-akikom and P.Krishnamurthy. Distributed Mechanism for Quality of Service in Wireless LANs, *IEEE Wireless Comm.,* June 2003

[5]   Y. Xiao. A Simple and Effective Priority Scheme for IEEE 802.11, *IEEE Comm. Letters*, V7, N2, Feb. 2003

[6]   Y. Xiao. Performance Analysis of IEEE 802.11e EDCF under Saturation Condition, *Proc. IEEE ICC 2004*

[7]   G.Gupta and P.R.Kumar. The Capacity of Wireless Network. *IEEE Trans. on Info. Theory*, V46, N2,: March 2002

[8]   H.S. Chhaya, and S. Gupta. Performance Modeling of Synchronous Data Transfer Methods of IEEE 802.11 MAC Protocol. *Wireless Networks*, V3, N3, 1997

[9]   F.Cali, M.Conti, and E.Gregori. Dynamic Tuning of the IEEE 802.11 Protocol to Achieve a Theoretical Throughput Limit, *IEEE/ACM Trans. on Networking*, V8, N6, Dec. 2000

[10] G.Bianchi. Performance Analysis of the IEEE 802.11 Distributed Coordination Function. *IEEE J. on Selected Area in Comm.*, V18, N3, March 2000

[11] H.Wu, Y.Peng, K. Long, *et al.*. Performance of Reliable Transport Protocol over IEEE 802.11 Wireless LAN: Analysis and Enhancement, *Proc. IEEE INFOCOM 2002*

[12] J.Zhao, Z.Guo, Q.Zhang and W.Zhu. Performance Study of MAC for Service Differentiation in IEEE 802.11, *Proc. IEEE Globecom* 2002

[13] Z.Kong, D.H.K.Tsang, B.Bensaou and D.Gao. Performance Analysis of IEEE 802.11e Contention-Based Channel Access, *IEEE J. on Selected Area in Comm.*, V22, N10, Dec. 2004

[14] J.W.Robbinson and T.S.Randhawa, Saturation Throughput Analysis of IEEE 802.11e Enhanced Distributed Coordination Function, *IEEE J. on Selected Area in Comm.*, V22, N5, June 2004

[15] G.R.Cantieni, Q.Ni, C.Barakat and T.Turletti. Performance Analysis under Finite Load and Improvements for Multirate 802.11, *Computer Comm.*, V28, N4, 2005, http://www.hamilton.ie/Qiang_Ni/

[16] NS-2, URL http://www-mash.cs.berkeley.edu/ns/

[17] S.Wiethölter and C.Hoene. Design and Verification of an IEEE 802.11e EDCF Simulation Model in ns-2.26, Telecommunication Networks Group, *Technical Report TKN-03-019*, Technical University of Berlin, Nov. 2003. http://www.tkn.tu-berlin.de/research/802.11e_ns2/

PART II: BLUETOOTH

In: Wireless LANs and Bluetooth
Editors: Yang Xiao and Yi Pan, pp. 173-193
ISBN 1-59454-432-8

Chapter 9

PICONET AND SCATTERNET MANAGEMENT
IN BLUETOOTH NETWORKS*

Wensheng Zhang,† Hao Zhu‡ and Guohong Cao§
Department of Computer Science & Engineering,
The Pennsylvania State University,
University Park, PA 16802

Abstract

This chapter summarizes our work on piconet and scatternet management in Bluetooth networks. It has two major parts: piconet management and scatternet management. In piconet management, we address two issues. First, dynamic role configuration protocols are proposed to reduce the access latency and increase the bandwidth
utilization. Second, power aware scheduling schemes and their effects on access delay
and bandwidth utilization are investigated. In scatternet management, we address issues such as scatternet-wide scheduling and routing. We present a switch-table based
scatternet-wide scheduling algorithm and present techniques to dynamically adjust the
switch-table based on the traffic pattern.

1   Introduction

Bluetooth [14, 15, 27] is a promising new technology which is aimed at supporting wireless
connectivity among mobile devices such as cell phones, headsets, PDAs, digital cameras,
laptop computers and their peripherals. The technology enables the design of low-power,
small-sized, low-cost radios that can be embedded in existing portable devices. Initially, the

---

*This work was supported in partby the National Science Foundation (CAREER CCR-0092770 and ITR-
0219711).
†E-mail address: wezhang@cse.psu.edu
‡E-mail address: hazhu@cse.psu.edu
§E-mail address: gcao@cse.psu.edu

technology will be used as a replacement for cables. Eventually, it will provide solutions for point-to-multipoint and multi-hop networking, and lead toward ubiquitous connectivity to truly connect everything to everything.

Due to the unpredictable interference of the existing 2.45 GHz ISM frequency band, Bluetooth relies on a psudorandom frequency hopping mechanism. A set of 79 hop carriers have been defined with a 1 MHz spacing. Each hop sequence defines a Bluetooth channel, which can support 1Mbps. A group of devices sharing a common channel is called a *piconet* [2, 5]. Multiple piconets can co-exist because each uses a different hopping sequence. Each piconet has a master unit, which controls the access to the channel, and at most seven slaves as group participants. Within a piconet, the channel is shared using a slotted time division duplex (TDD) protocol where the master uses a polling style protocol to allocate time slots to slave nodes; each polling epoch, called a *Bluetooth frame*, consists of two slots in which a packet can be exchanged between the master and the (polled) slave. Piconets can also be interconnected via *bridge* [4, 15] nodes to form a bigger ad hoc network known as a *scatternet*. However, the current specification does not describe the algorithms or mechanisms to create a scatternet due to a variety of unsolved issues.

Bluetooth networks are significantly different from other wireless networks [9, 24] in which ubiquitous computing has been explored. For example, in cellular networks [12] such as GSM, NA-TDMA, IS-95, a backbone infrastructure connects base stations; mobile terminals establish connections to the network through base stations according to control channel protocols. However, Bluetooth networks are formed spontaneously and they cannot rely on any infrastructure. Without control channels, Bluetooth adopts different medium access control protocols. The spontaneous nature of Bluetooth is similar to that of ad hoc networks [15, 20]. However, most ad hoc networks only support one channel, whereas Bluetooth networks support multiple channels. Moreover, Bluetooth networks are primarily designed for low-power and close-range, whereas most ad hoc networks consider scalability to much longer range communication.

Because of the difference, many existing solutions for wireless networks cannot be directly applied to Bluetooth. Since Bluetooth technology is still emerging, many technical details are not clearly specified. Though some computer manufactures are deploying Bluetooth technology at the piconet level, routing in scatternet and issues related to forming and maintaining scatternets are not yet specified. Although some techniques exist in the specification, these solutions are very simple and may not be the best choice when performance issues are considered. For example, using polling schemes to achieve medium access control is a simple and working solution, but it may not be the most efficient one. When some slaves do not have any data to send, polling them not only wastes the scarce bandwidth, but also wastes the power of the master and the slaves. Further, the active slaves may suffer from long waiting delay since some of the bandwidth is wasted on polling. Thus, many research issues need to be solved before Bluetooth can be used to connect everything to everything.

In this chapter, we summarize our recent work on piconet and scatternet management for Bluetooth networks. The relationship between piconet management (also called the link

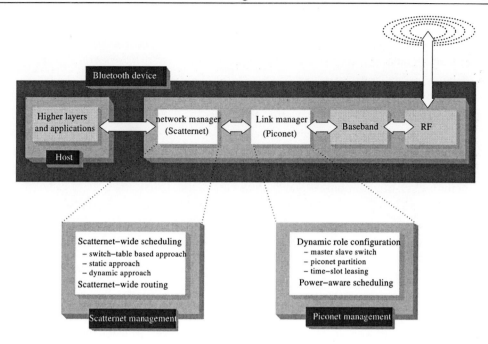

Figure 1: The relationship between piconet management, scatternet management, and other layers in Bluetooth networks

manager[1]), scatternet management, and other layers is shown in Figure 1. The RF layer [15] specifies the radio parameters. The baseband layer specifies the low-level operations at the bit and packet levels such as FEC operations, encryption, CRC calculations, and ARQ protocols. The link manager layer includes specifications such as connection establishment and release, authentication, connection and release of synchronous and asynchronous channels, traffic scheduling, and power management tasks. Higher layer protocols [10] include logical link control and adaptation protocols, service discovery protocols, and protocols to support serial interface. The scatternet management layer is not yet defined in the Bluetooth specification due to unresolved issues. However, to truly connect everything to everything using Bluetooth technology, scatternet is essential, and will be studied in this chapter.

The rest of the chapter is organized as follows. The next two sections present our work on piconet management. Specifically, Section 2 discusses dynamic role configuration, and Section 3 presents our power-aware scheduling algorithm. In Section 4, we present our work on scatternet-wide scheduling. Section 5 addresses issues on scatternet-wide routing. Section 6 concludes the chapter.

---

[1]*Link manager* is a Bluetooth terminology. It does not necessary correspond to the data link layer in the OSI protocol architecture.

2   Piconet: Dynamic Role Configuration

To facilitate communication between a group of devices (nodes), Bluetooth supports piconets. Each piconet consists of exactly one master node and up to seven slave nodes. The master and the slave nodes share the channel using a slotted time division duplex protocol. The master node is also responsible for controlling the allocation of the time slots. All master-slave pairs can communicate with each other, but slaves are not permitted to communicate with each other directly. This is because all slaves only listen during the master-to-slave transmission slot. When a slave node transmits, only the master listens to the medium. Lack of communication capability at the link layer, however, does not prevent two slave nodes from communicating. Using a higher layer forwarding protocol, a master node can always switch packets among all connected slave nodes. However, this may create some unpleasant scenarios when performance issues are considered. Consider a piconet with several slaves S_1 to S_7, and a master M. Due to traffic pattern changes, the following two scenarios may occur.

Scenario 1: Suppose slave S_1 needs to frequently communicate with several other slaves S_2, S_3, and S_4. Due to the restriction of the Bluetooth link management protocol, all the traffic must go through the master M. Since the protocol is based on time division duplex, sending data to the master also accounts for a time slot. As a result, the system throughput can be reduced by half since each packet must spend one time slot to reach the master, and another time slot to reach the destination.

Scenario 2: Suppose two slaves S_1 and S_2 need to set up a synchronous video transmission which may last for a long time. Similar to scenario 1, the communication between S_1 and S_2 may reduce the system throughput since they need the switch from the master.

The following schemes [35, 36, 8] can be used to deal with the performance degradation in the above scenarios. **Mater-slave switching (MSS):** In scenario 1, by switching the role of S_1 and M, most of the communication will happen between the master and the slaves, and the performance can be doubled without considering the master switch overhead. This can be implemented by using the *LMP_switch_req* PDU in the current Bluetooth specification. The role switch basically comprises the process of migrating from the master/slave transmit timing sequence in the piconet of the old master (the new slave) to the master/slave transmit timing sequence in the piconet of the new master (the old slave). Although the role switch can be implemented, when and under what situation to do the switch needs further investigation. Also, the role switching overhead needs to be considered. Obviously, if the communication between the new master and other slaves are very short, e.g. lasting only several time slots, this role switch may not be helpful. Thus, in order to find out when to do a role switch, the master of the piconet needs to monitor the traffic pattern in the network, and make a decision based on the observation.

Piconet partition (PP): In scenario 2, if two slaves S_1 and S_2 rarely communicate with other slaves, they should form a new piconet in order to increase the system throughput.

The master can name one of them as the master and the other as the slave. In general, if the master observes frequent traffic flow between some slave pairs, the master can ask these pairs of slaves to form new piconets. If some member of the newly formed piconet needs to communicate with old members of the old piconet, inter-piconet communication is required. Thus, before breaking a piconet into two or more piconets, the master should consider the breaking overhead and the subsequent inter-piconet communication overhead.

Time-slot leasing (TSL): Due to the inter-piconet communication overhead, we provide another solution to scenario 2. Instead of breaking the piconet into multiple piconets, the master can temporarily lease some time slots to the two slaves so that they can form a *temp-piconet* [36]. The master specifies one slave as the *temp-master* of the temp-piconet. This temp-piconet is synchronized with the old master and use the old frequency hop sequence. Thus, the temp-master can only use the assigned time slot to communicate with slaves in the temp-piconet. At the same time, the master can also communicate with the slaves in the temp-piconet on any time slot except those assigned to the temp-master. The master specifies a lease termination time. Before the lease terminates, slaves in the temp-piconet have the flexibility to use the leased time slots, and the old master cannot use these time slots. After the lease terminates, the temp-piconet is removed and slaves return to their original role. If necessary, the lease can be renewed when the master polls them after the lease terminates.

The TSL approach can improve the performance of a Bluetooth network without permanently modifying the scatternet/piconet structure. However, there is a drawback in this approach. Since all the temp-piconets share the same channel with the original piconet, once a slot is leased to a temp-piconet, any other node outside of the temp-piconet is not allowed to transmit during this slot unless it can switch to another piconet of which it is also a member. Consequently, the system throughput improvement is limited by the available bandwidth of a single channel. To address the problem, we propose an enhanced TSL (ETSL) approach. The ETSL approach allows each temp-piconet to use its dedicated channel defined by its temp-master, and all the temp-piconets are time-synchronized to the original piconet for easy coordination. With the ETSL approach, slots can be leased to multiple temp-piconets which have no common member. During the leased slots, both the temp-masters and the original master are allowed to transmit simultaneously, since they use different frequencies. In this way, the actual bandwidth of the piconet is increased. The ETSL approach is different from the PP approach in which a piconet is broken into two or more interconnected independent piconets. In the ETSL approach, the temp-piconets are not independent or permanent, they exist only during the leased slots specified by the original master. For other time slots, the members of the temp-piconet act as slaves of the original piconet.

Figure 2 shows some simulation results based on our work in [35]. In the simulation model, there are four slaves and five connections. Two of the connections are between the master and a slave; the other three connections are between slaves. The simulation evaluates the performance of four protocols: TSL, PP, MSS, and the standard TDD polling protocol. As can be seen, the TSL approach has the highest system throughput and the lowest packet

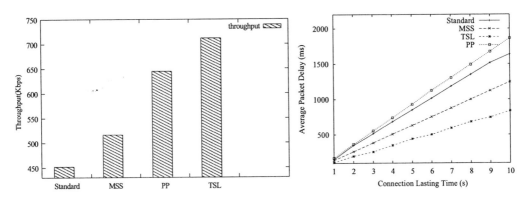

Figure 2: Comparisons of the system throughput and the average packet transmission delay

transmission delay. On the other hand, the standard TDD polling protocol has the lowest system throughput and a very high packet transmission delay. Intuitively, this is correct since the TSL approach can improve the performance of slave-to-slave communications and there are three slave-to-slave communication sessions in our simulation model. The MSS approach has better throughput than the standard master/slave model, but lower throughput than the PP approach. In our simulation model, one slave has more traffic density than the old master. Thus, letting it become the master can reduce the number of slave-to-slave communications and improve the system throughput. However, compared to the PP approach, the MSS approach still has many slave-to-slave communications, and hence the MSS approach has lower system throughput than the PP approach. It is interesting to see that the PP approach has the highest packet transmission delay. This is due to the fact that after the piconet partition, the inter-piconet communications slow down the packet transmission time. Details of the protocol and performance evaluations can be found in [36].

3 Piconet: Power Aware Scheduling

In this section, we first discuss some related work and background information, then present our power-aware scheduling protocol.

3.1 Related Work

Bluetooth supports two types of channels: synchronous and asynchronous. For synchronous communication, the master and slaves communicate with each other at regular intervals of time which are reserved in advance. For asynchronous communication, the master uses a polling style protocol to allocate time slots to the slaves [29]. That means the master polls a slave and the slave responses in the next time slot and so on. The main advantage of the polling based scheduling scheme is simplicity, which makes the bluetooth device simpler, lower power and lower cost compared to other wireless communication devices (e.g.

wireless LAN card). In most of the current Bluetooth products, the master polls the slaves in a round robin (RR) manner. Many new scheduling schemes [6, 25] have been proposed to improve the performance of the piconet. However, the polling based RR scheduling has another drawback when considering power consumption. The master polls each slave as quick as possible. If the slave being polled has no packet to send, two time slots will be wasted. As a result, if the slave's traffic density is low, a large amount of power will be wasted due to excessive polling. Meanwhile, since the slave does not know when it will be polled, it has to keep listening and wasting lots of power.

There has been a lot of research on low-power control for wireless devices. At the hardware level, the communication device can adjust the power level used by the mobile transmitter during active communication. At the software level, we can reduce the power consumed by communication devices [23] and non-communication devices such as displays, disks, and CPUs. The underlying principle is to estimate when the device will be used and suspend it for those idle intervals. Following this principle, some solutions [7] have been proposed to reduce the power consumption of slaves in a piconet by putting them to low-power mode periodically. Then, the slave stays in active only when it has packets to transmit or receive, which could significantly increases the power efficiency. These solutions work well when power consumption is the major concern. However, they may not be able to provide good QoS provision to each flow at the same time.

3.2 Background and Motivations

3.2.1 Bluetooth Operation Modes

A Bluetooth device has four operational modes [27]: *active, sniff, hold* and *park*. In the *Active mode*, a Bluetooth device actively participates on the channel. In the *Sniff mode*, the native clock cycle of a slave's listen activity is reduced to specified periodic time slots, which are called sniff slots, and the master will poll the slave every sniff slots. In the *Hold mode*, the slave goes into sleep mode for a specified amount of time: *holdTO*. After *holdTO* time, the slave returns to active mode. This means that the slave temporarily leaves the channel for a time interval of *holdTO*. Before entering the hold mode, the master and the slave agree on the time duration that the slave should remain in the hold mode. After the slave wakes up, it synchronizes to the traffic on the channel and waits for further information from the master. In the *Park mode*, the slave is in the sleep mode for an unspecified amount of time and gives up its active member address *AM_ADDR*. The master has to explicitly make the slave active at a future time by broadcasting through the *beacon channel* [14]. The parked slave wakes up at regular intervals to listen to the channel in order to re-synchronize and to check for beacon channel message.

3.2.2 The Guaranteed Service Model

Each unit of data transmission at the network level in a packet-switch network is a packet. We refer to the sequence of packets transmitted by a source as a *flow* [13]. We consider the *guaranteed service model* as following: before the communication starts, the source needs to specify its flow traffic characteristics and the desired performance requirements. When the network admits the request, it guarantees that the specified performance requirements will be met provided that the source follows its traffic specification [32]. In addition, the network has an admission mechanism that may reject the source's connection request due to lack of resource or administrative constraint. Thus, this service contract is settled before the real data transfer during a connection establishment process and is kept valid throughout the life time of the flow. The network meets the requirements of all flows by appropriately scheduling its resource. A scheduling algorithm can be classified as either *work-conserving* or *non-work-conserving*. For working-conserving scheduling, the server is never idle when there is a packet to send. For non-work-conserving scheduling, each packet is not served until it is eligible [32], even though the server is idle at that time.

3.2.3 Motivations

In current commercial Bluetooth products, the round-robin (RR) scheduling scheme is applied as well as specified in the Bluetooth specification. Under this scheduling policy, the master works in the work-conserving manner and keeps polling the slaves of the piconet in turns.

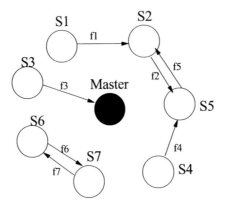

Figure 3: A piconet example

For example, as shown in Figure 3, there are seven slaves and seven flows in the piconet. Under the RR policy, the master's schedule sequence is: $S_1 - S_2 - S_3 - S_4 - S_5 - S_6 - S_7$. Suppose it is slave S_1's turn, the master has to poll S_1 no matter S_1 has a packet to send or not since it doesn't know S_1's real-time traffic situation. If S_1 doesn't have any packet to send, it will reply a NULL packet. Thus, a couple of time slots and some amount of power are wasted due to this polling. As a result, if flow f_1's rate is low, lots of power can be wasted due to the excessive polling toward S_1. Because the packet length might vary, other slaves cannot know the exact time when it will be polled. Therefore, they have to keep listening to the channel and waste a large amount of power. In order to fix these problems, we propose a MAC layer scheduling scheme and use the hold mode to optimize the power consumption while providing guaranteed service for the flows in the piconet. The basic idea is to let the master poll the slave when the slave has data to send and make the slave stay in the low power mode until the master wants to communicate with it. In order to maintain QoS guarantees, we use the *guaranteed service model* [32] as the underlying model of our approach and assume that every flow is allocated a flow rate (in bps). Based on this model, we propose a *non-work-conserving* MAC layer scheduling scheme in which the master arranges a power efficient polling sequence based on the current prediction of the flow data rate. We use the *hold* operation mode of Bluetooth to make the slave idle whenever there is no data addressed to it so that the slave can avoid unnecessarily staying in active. Intuitively, power conservation is achieved by reducing the number of unnecessary polling slots and unnecessary active periods. Since the prediction may not always be accurate, the slave may not have data to send while being polled, in which case, power will be wasted. In order to reduce this kind of mis-prediction, our scheme applies additive-increase multiplicative-decrease (AIMD) to adaptively adjust the predicted rate of the flow based on the power tuning knob and the flow attribute parameters. Next, we present some details of the algorithm.

3.3   An Adaptive Power-Conserving Service Discipline for Bluetooth (APCB)

Table 1: Notations

Notation	Description
L_i^k	the length of the kth packet of flow i
L_i^{max}	the maximum packet length of flow i
$EAT(p_i^k)$	the *expected arrival time* of the kth packet of flow i
r_i	the max rate admitted to flow i (in bps)
$r(p_i^k)$	the *expected data rate* of flow i (in bps), where the kth packet is the head-of-line packet. It is initialized to r_i

We adopt the idea of the virtual clock service model [33] and require each flow to provide its attribute parameters, such as flow rate and burstiness degree, before the communication starts. The sender/receiver of the flow and the master (if different) will keep these parameters. The flow has a queue at its sender side, and the master (if different) forwards the flow's packets to the receiver (if different) and doesn't buffer the packets. If the master is different from the sender of the flow, which is true in most cases, it can not get the real-time knowledge of the arrival time of a flow's packets; i.e., when the sender has the next packet to send. As a result, the master only uses the *expected arrival time* (EAT) of the packets of the flow to predict when the sender will have packet to send. Without loss of correctness, when the master is the sender of a flow, the master can still use EAT to indicate when the next packet will be sent. For clarity, we introduce some notations in Table 1.

In the APCB service model, the master works in non-work-conserving manner in our scheduling policy. It will try to serve the flow which has the packet with the smallest EAT, and use the node's address to break the tie. The whole algorithm is related to the master and the end nodes, which are $Sender_i$ and $Reciever_i$ of flow i. Applying the same algorithm, the master, $Sender_i$, and $Reciever_i$ can mutually agree on the next polling time based on the current packet length L_i^k and the current expected data rate $r(p_i^k)$. If there is a mis-prediction, which means $Sender_i$ does not have data to send while being polled, they will adaptively adjust $r(p_i^k)$ and prolong the interval of the next polling time to $L_i^{max}/r(p_i^k)$. We use L_i^{max} as the current packet length when a mis-prediction happens in order to let the scheme work more power efficiently. Because the end nodes also adjust $r(p_i^k)$ as the master does, mutual agreement can be established. Since the nodes apply the same algorithm, if the master is different from the end nodes, unlike the hold operation defined in the specification, no extra message is required to explicitly coordinate the hold period between the master and the end nodes under the APCB scheme, which is illustrated in Figure 4. As shown in the figure, $Sender_i$ and $Receiver_i$ calculate the EAT of flow i independently, and know that the master will not serve flow i until EAT_i. Therefore, the master, $Sender_i$ and $Receiver_i$ can agree on the hold period, which is equal to $holdTO$. If no other flow is connected to $Sender_i$ and $Receiver_i$, they can enter the hold mode and wake up at EAT_i. Since the master manages the piconet, it does not turn off to sleep at any time. Details of the protocol and performance evaluations can be found in [37, 38].

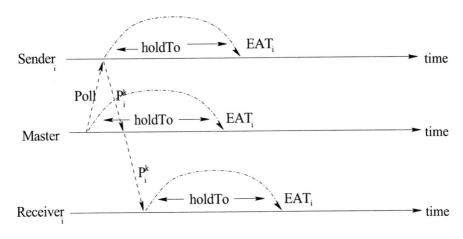

Figure 4: An example of mutual agreement among the nodes

4　Scatternet-Wide Scheduling

In this section, we first present related work, and challenges in scatternet scheduling. Then, we present a switch-table based scatternet-wide scheduling algorithm and present techniques to dynamically adjust the table based on the traffic pattern.

4.1   Related Work

Multiple piconets can co-exist in a common area because each piconet uses a different hopping sequence. Piconets can also be interconnected via bridge [4, 15] nodes to form a bigger ad hoc network known as a scatternet. Bridge nodes are capable of timesharing between multiple piconets, receiving data from one piconet and forwarding it to another.

To improve the performance of Bluetooth scatternet, two kinds of schedule are necessary: piconet and scatternet-wide schedule. Recent research on piconet schedule determines how the bandwidth capacity will be distributed among the slave nodes. As a simple solution, the master controls the traffic by means of polling the slaves according to a Round Robin scheme. As an improvement, Kalia *et al.* [21] proposed a dynamic weighted round-robin scheme in which the weights of the master-slave pairs depend on the queue status. Garg *et al.* [11] proposed schedule schemes to optimize the power. Johansson *et al.* [18] introduced an efficient fair exhaustive polling scheme to provide both high utilization and fair distribution of piconet capacity among the participating slaves.

At the scatternet level [19], the bridge node must schedule its presence in all the piconets of which it is a member. The main challenge for the scatternet-wide scheduling is to schedule the presence of the bridge node in its different piconets such that the traffic can flow within and between the piconets as efficiently as possible. Given that the bridge node is a single transceiver unit, it can only be active in one piconet at a time, and be blind in all other piconets. However, the master in a piconet always expects the slave to be present when it sends a data or (a poll) packet to it. If the slave is not present, the master may remove the slave from its piconet after some predefined timeout period. This is necessary since the slave may be out of range, in which case, polling the slave wastes bandwidth. However, in a scatternet, the slave may be a bridge node and it may be vising another piconet when the master sends it a packet. We call this phenomenon as *bridge conflict*. Thus, the main issue of scatternet-wide scheduling is to coordinate the simultaneous presence of bridge nodes and masters to avoid or reduce the bridge conflict, thus achieve higher performance in inter-piconet communication. Although many researchers have addressed the piconet scheduling problem, not much work [1, 18, 3] has been done on scatternet-wide schedule. These methods can not completely avoid bridge conflicts, since there is no explicit coordination between bridges and masters. Moreover, the current Bluetooth specification does not describe the algorithms or mechanisms to manage a scatternet due to a variety of unsolved issues. The research on scatternet formation [29, 31, 26], which is an important topic related to scatternet-wide scheduling, is also still in its nascent stage. These algorithms can only address the scenarios where nodes are within the communication range of each other.

4.2   Bluetooth Scatternet

Multiple piconets can be interconnected via bridge nodes to form a complicated topology called scatternet. A bridge node is a node belonging to two or more piconets. It can be a master in one piconet and a slave in other piconets, in which case it is called a M/S bridge. It can also be a slave in all piconets, in which case it is called a S/S bridge. Figure 5 illustrates these two kinds of topology.

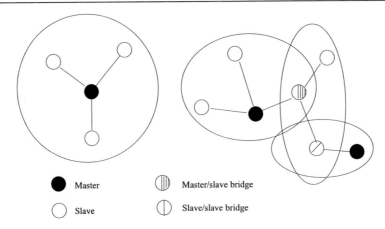

Figure 5: Illustration of a piconet (left picture) and a scatternet (right picture).

In default, a master assumes that its slaves are always present in the piconet. That is, whenever the master transmits to a slave, the slave must answer the packet unless the transmission fails. However, for the purpose of power saving, Bluetooth offers various modes which are used to reduce the duty cycle of devices: hold, park and sniff mode. Here, we only introduce the sniff mode which has often been proposed as the means to enable scatternet operations. In this mode, a slave arranges its presence in a piconet by negotiating specific slots which are called *sniff slots* with the master. Communication between the master and this slave may start at these sniff slots. If no communication takes place during these slots, both the nodes may spend the time freely until the next sniff slots. However, once the communication starts, it may be extended until one party quits the communication.

Even though the current Bluetooth specification defines scatternets, it focuses on operations within a piconet and does not describe the algorithms or mechanisms to form and manage a scatternet due to a variety of unsolved issues. Next, we discuss some challenges of scatternet-wide scheduling.

Bridge Conflicts: Piconets are interconnected via bridge nodes. We also assume that each node has only a single transceiver unit. Under such a model, a bridge node can switch between piconets to which it belongs, but can not be synchronized to two or more piconets simultaneously. If there is no coordination between these piconets, a bridge conflict occurs when two masters poll the same bridge at the same time, or when a master polls the bridge while the bridge shows up in another piconet. Bridge conflicts waste bandwidth. Scatternet-wide scheduling schemes should adopt some coordination to avoid or reduce bridge conflicts.

Bridge Switching Overhead: According to the Bluetooth specifications [14], the timing and frequency hopping pattern of a piconet are determined by the master node, and different piconet can not share a common master node. That is, the hop selection and timing of different piconets are typically independent of each other, unless certain inter-piconet timing synchronization mechanism is deployed. This may result in some bandwidth loss associated with the bridge node. Considering this overhead, bridge nodes should not switch too frequently between piconets. However, low switching frequency may increase packet forwarding delays since packets have to wait longer before passing through a bridge node. Thus, there is a tradeoff between system throughput and delay.

Adaptive on Load Variation: Workload variation is common in a scatternet scenario. A scatternet-wide scheduling scheme should address bridge conflicts, and be adaptive to workload variations. Intuitively, a bridge node should be present more frequently in the piconet with higher inter-piconet traffic load.

4.3   The Basic Idea of Switch-Table Based Scatternet-wide Scheduling

Piconets are interconnected via bridge nodes. A bridge node can be a M/S node or a S/S node. We only consider S/S bridge nodes in this work for simplicity, but we believe that the proposed technique can also be extended to M/S bridges. In fact, early work by Kalia *et al.* [22] has suggested that scatternets with only S/S bridge nodes have better performance. Figure 6(a) shows one scatternet example.

To avoid bridge conflicts, each bridge maintains a *switch-table*, which directs the bridge node how to switch between piconets, and notifies the master when it can poll the bridge node safely. Table 2 shows the switch-table of bridge B_4 corresponding to the topology of Figure 6(a). This switch table has four rows, each corresponds to one piconet. There are three parameters related to a piconet: the number of slots in each cycle, the start point and the end point of the slots when B_4 is synchronized to the piconet. Take the first row as an instance, three parameters together specify that B_4 is synchronized to piconet 0 during the slots from $26 * k$ to $26 * k + 5$, where k is a non-negative integer.

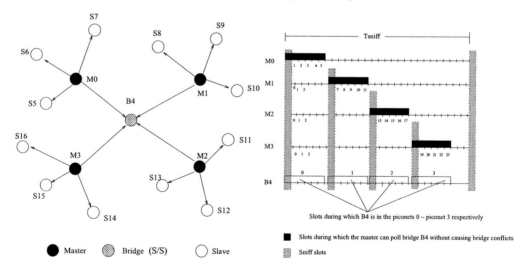

Figure 6: Illustration of the proposed scatternet-wide scheduling algorithm

The switch-table directed bridge switching can be implemented via the sniff mode. In this implementation, the cycle length is mapped to the sniff period, and the start slots correspond to the sniff slots. As an example, Figure 6(b) shows the switching path of

Table 2: Switch table for bridge B_4

Piconet#	Start slot	End slot	Cycle length (slots)
0	0	5	26
1	6	11	26
2	12	17	26
3	18	23	26

bridge B_4. At the start slot corresponds to piconet 0, B_4 switches to piconet 0. After that, it will stay in the piconet until another sniff slot (the start slot corresponds to piconet 1) approaches, at which point B_4 switches to piconet 1. A master should communicate with a bridge node only when the bridge is present in its piconet to avoid bridge conflicts. Figure 6(b) also shows the slots that each piconet can use to communicate with B_4 without causing bridge conflicts. Note that the switch-table directed bridge switching does not need any major change to the current specification, since it can be implemented using the sniff mode.

The switch-table of a scatternet can be constructed when the scatternet is formed. Taking the *Bluetooth Topology Construction Protocol (BTCP)* [29] as an example, BTCP has two phases: first, a leader is elected with a complete knowledge of all nodes; second, this leader tells other nodes how a scatternet should be formed. The switch-table is constructed after the first phase since the leader has the complete knowledge of the scatternet at this time. The results will be sent to other nodes in the second phase. Note that the bridge node can modify the entry about itself after the switch-table has been constructed, but the master nodes can not modify it. To be consistent, whenever a bridge node modifies an entry, it should notify the corresponding masters to make necessary updates.

4.4　The Static Scatternet-Wide Scheduling (SSS) Algorithm

In this subsection, we present the static scatternet-wide scheduling (SSS) algorithm, which solves the bridge conflict by using predefined switch-tables. The basic idea of the proposed algorithm is to let the master poll its slaves, including the bridge nodes, in a weighted round robin manner. For each frame, the master polls a bridge node only when the bridge node shows up in the piconet based on the switch-table, and the bridge node is polled according to its weight. This algorithm can solve the problem of bridge conflict, and can schedule traffic efficiently.

The weight of each slave is computed based on the estimated traffic load for each "master-slave" link. Hence, in each schedule cycle [21], only a subset of the slaves are polled. In order to decide the frequency for each slave to be polled, each slave has a polling weight which is represented by a tuple (P, R), where P indicates that the slave should be polled every P schedule cycles, and R represents the maximum times that the slave can be polled in a cycle if it is scheduled to be polled at the cycle. A master can dynamically change the polling weight of each slave based on its estimations of the traffic load carried by the link between itself and the slave. Note that a master can only directly monitor the length of the "master→slave" queues. A master estimates each link's traffic based on the polling results. The rules for adjusting the slave's polling weight (P,R) are as follows: If a poll is wasted in the sense that both slots allocated for polling are not used, the value of P associated with the offending slave is increased until it reaches a certain upper threshold; otherwise, the polling period is decreased until it reaches one. If the current p value for a slave is already one, the value of R will be adjusted as follows: If a poll is wasted, the value of R is decreased until it reaches one, and in this case, the value of P is increased; If a poll is not wasted, the value of R is increased until it reaches an upper bound. A formal description of the algorithm can be found in [34].

4.5   The Dynamic Scatternet-Wide Scheduling (DSS) Algorithm

In the SSS scheme, a static reservation schedule is determined centrally when the scatternet is constructed. Due to traffic pattern changes, using the statically determined reservation schedule may not be able to achieve high bandwidth utilization. In this section, we propose dynamic scatternet-wide scheduling (DSS) schemes to address this problem. In the DSS scheme, the switch-table can be dynamically adjusted based on the traffic pattern. Specifically, by monitoring the queue length, the bridge increases (decreases) the number of slots that a bridge appears in the piconet before it switches to another piconet if the traffic load between the master and the bridge is high (low). Similar to [10], we assume that the queues are maintained in the L2CAP layer. Since the information about queue length is very small, it can be piggy-backed in polling packets, instead of using extra packets, to save bandwidth.

The DSS algorithm contains two phases: First, the decision on how to adjust the switch-table is made by a bridge node. Second, the switch-table is updated through the coordination between bridge and master nodes.

Phase I: Decide how to adjust the switch-table

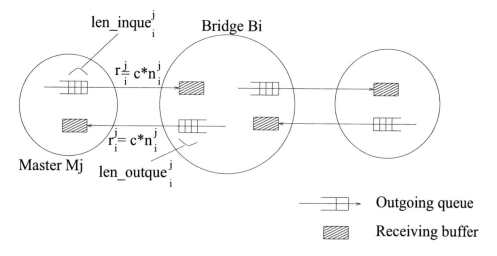

Figure 7: Illustration of the queue model

The traffic pattern change can be detected by monitoring the queue length. For this purpose, each master needs to notify the bridge about its queue length whenever it has a major change. At the bridge side, the bridge monitors the outgoing queue length and maintains the incoming queue length obtained from the master. Figure 7 shows the queue model considered in this paper. Here, $len\_inque_i^j$ represents the length of the queue which queues packets from M_j to B_i, and $len\_outque_i^j$ represents the length of the queue which queues packets from B_i to M_j. Bridge B_i maintains the maximum value of the outgoing queue length and the incoming queue length (denoted as $len\_que_i^j = max\{len\_inque_i^j, len\_outque_i^j\}$). r_i^j and r_j^i represent the output rates of these two queues respectively, and they are in proportion to the number of slots assigned to the link in the switch-table, which is denoted as n_i^j. Obviously, the master-bridge link with long incoming or outgoing queue indicates a heavy traffic, and it should get more slots in the switch-table than those with relatively low queue length. The following describes how to adjust the switch-table.

First, the bridge checks the queue length every n_c cycles. The selection of this interval has a significant impact on the system performance. In order to adjust the switch-table promptly when the traffic pattern changes, the interval should not be too long. However, the interval should not be too short in order to avoid unnecessary adjustments and keep the frequency of adjustments within an affordable scope.

Second, the goal of an adjustment is to balance the queue length among all links in the bridge. For this purpose, a balanced queue length should be calculated for each link. A simple way to calculate the balanced queue length is to average all the queue lengths. However, links assigned different number of slots in the switch-table should have different balanced queue length. As shown in Figure 7, the number of slots assigned to a link $M_j - B_i$, is proportional to the service rate r_i^j of link $M_j - B_i$'s outgoing/incoming queue. For two queues that have the same length but different service rate, the delay for passing a packet through the queue with high service rate will be smaller than the one with low service rate. Considering the number of slots assigned, the desired balanced queue length for the link $M_j - B_i$ is calculated as: $n_i^j * \sum_k len\_que_i^k$.

Third, potential borrowers and lenders should be found. For link $M_j - B_i$, if its current queue length is larger than the desired balanced queue length, i.e., $len\_que_i^j > avg\_qlen * n_i^j$, it is beneficial for it to borrow slots from others. Conversely, if $len\_que_i^j < avg\_qlen * n_i^j$, the link can lend slots to others as long as its queue length is still less than the balanced queue length after lending. This condition is heuristically expressed as $\lfloor \frac{avg\_qlen * n_i^j - len\_que_i^j}{n_c} \rfloor > 0$, which means that the queue length is still less than the balanced value even if the number of packets transmitted each cycle is reduced by one. Finally, in order to keep the TDD protocol work, the number of slots transferred from the lender to the borrower should be even.

Phase II: Update the switch-table

When the sniff slot positions of the lender and the borrower are next to each other, the switch-table is updated by changing the sniff slot position of the borrower or lenders. The procedure can also be explained by Figure 8. In order to avoid bridge conflicts, the bridge cannot immediately notify them about the modification. Instead, the bridge has to notify the lender first. After the lender has acknowledged the modification, the borrower is notified. Certainly, in case the lender cannot lend the slots, the update will be aborted.

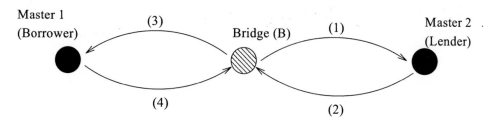

Figure 8: Illustration of a switch-table updating process

5   Scatternet-Wide Routing

In the Bluetooth architecture, multiple piconets with overlapping area of coverage can co-exist as long as their frequency hopping patterns are different. Multiple piconets can be connected to form a scatternet through bridge nodes. Bridge nodes can participate in multiple piconets through a time sharing basis, receiving data from one piconet and forwarding it to another. One problem in scatternets is how to set up a connection between two nodes [29]. This is similar to the routing problem in ad hoc networks [20]. However, two blue-tooth nodes cannot hear each other unless they form a master-slave pair. This is different form ad hoc networks where any two nodes within proximity can hear each other's transmissions. It is also anticipated that scatternets will differ from classical ad hoc networks in terms of applications, traffic characteristics, mobility patterns, and scaling requirements. In most application instances, scatternets will be quasi-static, short lived, and small. Therefore, the scalability and adaptivity features of ad hoc routing algorithms may not always be necessary.

Dynamic source routing protocols [20] have been proposed and evaluated in ad hoc networks. In this approach, the sender learns the complete ordered sequence of network hops necessary to reach the destination, and each packet to be routed carries this list of hops in its header. The key advantage of a source routing design is that intermediate nodes do not need to maintain up-to-date routing information in order to route the packets that they forward, since the packets themselves already contain all the routing decisions. As a result, it eliminates the need for the periodic route advertisement and neighbor detection packets present in other protocols [30]. However, specifying the whole route may lead to large overhead since each node is represented by a 48 bit bluetooth address. Since scalability is not the major issue, each node in Bluetooth may not be able to connect more than 8 piconets. As a result, we can assign three bits to each piconet for that bridge node. In this way, the route can be specified by the bridge node and the piconet name, next bridge node, next piconet name, etc. The routing overhead can thereby be reduced since 48 bit addresses are replaced by 3 bit addresses. Certainly, issues such as maintaining the map between logical address and physical address needs to be addressed.

In source routing, *route discovery* [20] is used to find a route from the source to the destination. Normally, this route discovery is done by a network flooding, which is an expensive operation since it may cause a large number of request packets to be transmitted and since it adds latency to the subsequent delivery of the data packet that initiated it. To reduce the cost of route discovery, caching techniques [16] can be used. The cached results of previous route discoveries may be useful in future routing decisions and allow the associated cost to be amortized. There are still many questions to be answered before applying these techniques to Bluetooth networks. For example, what is the effect of flooding (used in route discovery) on bluetooth networks? Can caching techniques be used to reduce the flooding overhead? How will the polling techniques affect the routing delay and route maintenance? All of these issues need further investigation.

Handling Mobility: When a node joins or leaves a piconet (or scatternet), the original route may be broken. In dynamic source routing, *route maintaince* [20] is used to address this problem. Route maintenance is used to detect whether the network topology has changed and the route used by this packet has broken. When transmitting the packet to the next hop, each node along the route is responsible for detecting if its link to the next hop has been broken. When a broken route is detected, the source node should be notified and find an alternate route to the destination. This alternative route can be a route which has been cached during the route discovery phase. Other optimization techniques can be used. For example, instead of notifying the source node, the node which discovers the broken route may be able to fix the problem locally.

The structure of Bluetooth scatternet has some similarity to the cellular networks since the master can be mapped to the base station. From this point of view, the mobility of Bluetooth nodes can be handled by applying handoff techniques in cellular networks, such as location tracking by pointer forwarding or by using anchors used in IS-41 or GSM [17, 28]. Following this strategy, when a bridge moves, the master should find a new bridge to replace it. However, since the master may also move, and the communication link between masters may also be broken, these techniques may not be directly applied to Bluetooth networks.

6   Conclusions

Bluetooth technology enables devices to communicate seamlessly without wires. Since Bluetooth technology is still emerging, many technical details are not clearly specified or specified without considering various performance factors. This chapter addressed the research issues in piconet and scatternet management. Our future work will focus on fine tuning some of the system parameters and addressing issues in scatternet formation, scatternet-wide scheduling and scatternet-wide routing.

References

[1] F. Kubinszky A. Racz, G. Miklos and A. Valko. A pseudo Random Coordinated Scheduling Aglrotihm for Bluetooth Scatternets. *MOBIHOC*, 2001.

[2] M. Albrecht, M. Frank, P. Martini, M. Schetelig, A. Vilavaara, and A. Wenzel. IP Services over Bluetooth: Leading the Way to a New Mobility. *Proc. Conf. on Local Computer Networks (LCN'99)*, pages 2–11, 1999.

[3] Simon Baatz, Matthias Frank, Carmen Kuhl, Peter Martini and Christoph Scholz. Bluetooth Scatternets: An Enhanced Adaptive Scheduling Scheme. *IEEE INFOCOM*, 2002.

[4] P. Bhagwat and A. Segall. A Routing Vector Method (RVM) for Routing in Bluetooth Scatternets. *The Sixth IEEE International Workshop on Mobile Multimedia Communications (MOMUC)*, 1999.

[5] J. Bray and C. Sturman. Bluetooth: Connect Without Cables. *Prentice-Hall, Englewood Cliffs*, 2000.

[6] A. Capone, M. Garla and R. Kapoor. Efficient Polling Schemes for Bluetooth Picocells. *IEEE ICC*, 2001.

[7] I. Chakraborty, A. Kashyap, A. Rastogi, H. Saran, R. Shorey and A. Kumar. Policies for Increasing Throughput and Decreasing Power Consumption in Bluetooth MAC. *IEEE International Conference on Personal Wireless Communications (ICPWC)*, 2000.

[8] C. Cordeiro, S. Abhyankar, and D. Agrawal. Design and Implementation of QoS-driven Dynamic Slot Assignment and Piconet Partitioning Algorithms over Bluetooth WPANs. *IEEE Infocom*, 2004.

[9] D. Cox. Wireless Personal Communications: What is It. *IEEE Personal Communication*, **2**(2), April 1995.

[10] A. Das, A. Ghose, A. Razdan, H. Saran and R. Shorey. Enhancing Performance of Asynchronous Data Traffic Over the Bluetooth Wireless Ad-hoc Network. *IEEE INFOCOM*, April 2001.

[11] S. Garg, M. Kalia, and R. Shorey. MAC Scheduling Policies for Power Optimization in Bluetooth: A Master Driven TDD Wireless System. *IEEE VTC*, pages 196–200, 2000.

[12] D. Goodman. Wireless Personal Communications Systems. *Addison-Wesley*, 1997.

[13] P. Goyal, H. Vin, and H. Cheng. Start-Time Fair Queuing: A Scheduling Algorithm for Integrated Services Packet Switching Networks. *ACM SIGCOMM*, August 1996.

[14] Bluetooth Special Interest Group. Specification of the Bluetooth System, 1.1. *http://www.bluetooth.com*, Feb. 2001.

[15] J. Haartsen. The Bluetooth Radio System. *IEEE Personal Communications*, **7**(1):28–36, Feb. 2000.

[16] Y. Hu and D. Johnson. Caching Strategies in On-Demand Routing Protocols for wireless Ad Hoc Networks. *Proceedings of the Sixth Annual ACM/IEEE International Conference on Mobile Computing and Networking (Mobicom)*, pages 231–242, 2000.

[17] R. Jain and Y. Lin. An Auxiliary User Location Strategy Employing Forwarding Pointers to Reduce Network Impacts of PCS. *ACM Wireless Networks*, pages 197–210, 1995.

[18] N. Johansson, F.Alriksson and U.Jonsson. JUMP Mode - A Dynamic Window-based Scheduling Framework for Bluetooth Scatternets. *MobiHoc*, 2001.

[19] P. Johansson, M. Kazantzidis, R. Kapoor, and M. Gerla. Bluetooth: An Enabler for Personal Area Networking. *IEEE Network*, **15**(5), Sep/Oct 2001.

[20] D. Johnson and D. Maltz. Dynamic Source Routing in Ad Hoc Wireless Networks. *Mobile Computing, Kluwer*, pages 153–181, 1996.

[21] M. Kalia, D. Bansal, and R. Shorey. Data Scheduling and SAR for Bluetooth MAC. *IEEE VTC*, pages 716–720, 2000.

[22] M. Kalia, S. Garg, and R. Shorey. Scatternet Structure and Inter-Piconet Communication in the Bluetooth System. *Technical Report, IBM India Research Lab*, 2000.

[23] R. Kravets and P. Krishnan. Power Management Techniques for Mobile Communication. *MobiCOM*, October 1998.

[24] R. Lamaire, A. Krishna, P. Bhagwat, and J. Panian. Wireless LANs and Mobile Networking: Standards and Future Directions. *IEEE Communications*, **34**(8):86–94, 1996.

[25] J-B. Lapeyrie and T. Turletti. FPQ: a Fair and Efficient Polling Algorithm with QoS Support for Bluetooth Piconet. *IEEE INFOCOM*, 2003.

[26] C. Law and K. Siu. A Bluetooth Scatternet Formation Algorithm. *GLOBECOM*, 2001.

[27] B Miller and C. Bisdikian. Bluetooth Revealed. *Prentice Hall*, 2000.

[28] S. Ramanathan and M. Steenstrup. A Survey of Routing Techniques for Mobile Communications Networks. *Mobile Networks and Applications*, pages 89–104, 1996.

[29] T. Salonidis, P. Bhagwat, L. Tassiulas, and R. LaMaire. Distributed Topology Construction of Bluetooth Personal Area Networks. *IEEE INFOCOM*, April 2001.

[30] R. Sivakumar, P. Sinha, and V. Bharghavan. CEDAR: A Core-Extraction Distributed Ad Hoc Routing Algorithms. *IEEE Journal on Selected Areas in Communications*, pages 1454–1465, Aug. 1999.

[31] G. Zaruba,S. Basagni and I. Chlamtac. Bluetrees - Scatternet Formation to Enable Bluetooth-based Ad Hoc Networks. *IEEE ICC*, 2001.

[32] H. Zhang. Service Disciplines for Guaranteed Performance Service in Packet-Switching Networks. *Proceedings of the IEEE*, **83**(10), October 1995.

[33] L. Zhang. Virtual clock: a new traffic control algorithm for packet switching networks. *ACM SIGCOMM*, September 1990.

[34] W. Zhang and G. Cao. A Flexible Scatternet-wide Scheduling Algorithm for Bluetooth Networks. *IEEE International Performance, Computing, and Communications Conference (IPCCC)*, 2002.

[35] W. Zhang, H. Zhu, and G. Cao. Improving Bluetooth Network Performance Through Dynamic Role Management. *Technical Report, CSE-01-018 Pennsylvania State University, also available at http://www.cse.psu.edu/~gcao/paper/bluetooth.ps*, May 2001.

[36] W. Zhang, H. Zhu, and G. Cao. Improving Bluetooth Network Performance Through A Time-Slot Leasing Approach. *IEEE Wireless Communications and Networking Conference (WCNC)*, March 2002.

[37] H. Zhu, G. Cao, G. Kesidis, and C. Das. An Adaptive Power-Conserving Service Discipline for Bluetooth. *IEEE ICC*, pages 303–307, April 2002.

[38] H. Zhu, G. Cao, G. Kesidis, and C. Das. An Adaptive Power-Conserving Service Discipline (APCB) for Bluetooth Wireless Networks. *Computer Communications*, to appear.

In: Wireless LANs and Bluetooth
Editors: Yang Xiao and Yi Pan, pp. 195-220
ISBN 1-59454-432-8
©2005 Nova Science Publishers, Inc.

Chapter 10

TCP PERFORMANCE IN BLUETOOTH PICONETS

Jelena Mišić, Vojislav B. Mišić
Department of Computer Science, University of Manitoba,
Winnipeg, Manitoba, Canada
Ka Lok Chan
The Hong Kong University of Science and Technology,
Hong Kong, China

Abstract

Recent updates of the Bluetooth specification have introduced significant changes in the Bluetooth protocol stack, including optional flow control. When the Bluetooth piconet is used to carry TCP traffic, complex interactions between TCP congestion control mechanisms and data link layer controls of Bluetooth will occur. In this work, we model the performance of the piconet with TCP traffic, expressed through segment loss probability, round-trip time, and goodput, through both probabilistic analysis and discrete-event simulations. We show that satisfactory performance for TCP traffic may be obtained through proper dimensioning of the Bluetooth architecture parameters.

Keywords: Bluetooth, Piconet, TCP protocol, Token bucket, Probabilistic analysis

1 Introduction

Bluetooth is an emerging standard for Wireless Personal Area Networks (WPANs) [1], originally intended as a simple cable replacement. Most performance analyses of data traffic in Bluetooth were focusing on scheduling techniques, and a number of proposals have been made [2, 3, 4, 5], usually under the assumption that the traffic consists of individual UDP datagrams, which is unrealistic. To the best of our knowledge, none of these proposals offers any quality of service (QoS) guarantees; only recently a polling scheme that can support negotiated delay bounds (but at the expense of efficiency) has been proposed [6].

However, the number of possible uses of Bluetooth has been steadily growing to include various networking tasks between computers and computer-controlled devices such as PDAs, mobile phones, smart peripherals, and the like. As a consequence, the majority of the traffic over Bluetooth networks will belong to different flavors of the ubiquitous TCP/IP family of protocols. In order to cater to such applications, the recently adopted version 1.2 of the Bluetooth specification allows each L2CAP channel to operate in Basic L2CAP mode (essentially the L2CAP mode supported by the previous version of the specification [7]), Flow Control mode, or Retransmission mode [8]. All three modes offer segmentation, but only the latter two control buffering through protocol data unit (PDU) sequence numbers, and control the flow rate by limiting the required buffer space. Additionally, the Retransmission Mode uses a go-back-n repeat mechanism with an appropriate timer to retransmit missing or damaged PDUs as necessary. The architectural blocks of the L2CAP layer are schematically shown in Fig. 1.

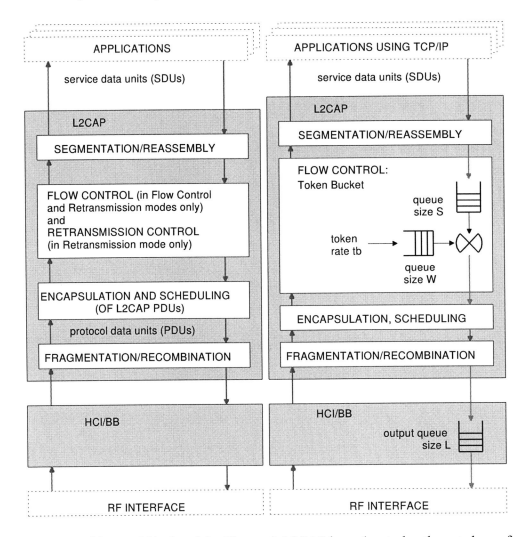

Figure 1: Architectural blocks of the Bluetooth L2CAP layer (control paths not shown for clarity)((a) Original specification from [8]. (b) Implementation of the Flow Control mode.).

It is clear that complex interactions between the TCP congestion control and the L2CAP flow control and baseband scheduling mechanisms may be expected in Bluetooth networks carrying TCP traffic. In this chapter, we will investigate those interactions, both analytically and through simulations. We will model the segment loss probability, probability distribution of TCP round trip time (including the L2CAP round trip time) and TCP sending rate. We also discuss the dimensioning of various parameters of the architecture with regards to the tradeoff between end-to-end delay and achievable throughput under multiple TCP connections from different slave devices.

The chapter is organized as follows. Section 2 describes the system model and the basic assumptions about the piconet operation under TCP traffic, and discusses some recent related work in the area of performance modeling and analysis of TCP traffic. Section 3 discusses the segment loss probability and the probability distribution of the congestion window size, and presents the analytical results. Section 4 presents simulation results for the performance of piconet with TCP connections running on slaves. Section 6 concludes the chapter. Detailed derivations of the probability density functions for the TCP segment and acknowledgment delay, as well as the blocking probability through the token bucket filter and the output queue serviced by the E-limited scheduler, are presented in Appendices A and B.

2 System Model and Related Work

2.1 The System Model

Bluetooth devices are organized in small centralized networks, or piconets, with $\mu \leq 8$ active nodes or devices [9, 10, 8]. One of the nodes acts as the master, while the others are slaves. All communications in the piconet take place under master's control: a slave can talk only when addressed by the master, and only immediately after being addressed by the master. As slaves can only talk to the master, hence all communications in the piconet, including slave-to-slave ones, must be routed through the master.

We consider a piconet in which the slaves create TCP connections with each other, so that each TCP connection will traverse two hops in the network. There are no TCP connections starting or ending at the master. We focus on TCP Reno [11], which is probably the most widely used variant of TCP as of now. We assume that the application layer at slave i (where $i = 1 .. \mu - 1$) sends messages of 1460 bytes at a rate of λ_i. This message will be sent within a single TCP segment, provided the TCP congestion window is not full. The TCP segment will be encapsulated in an IP packet with the appropriate header; this packet is then passed on to the L2CAP layer. We assume that the segmentation algorithm produces the minimum number of Bluetooth baseband packets [12], i.e., four DH5 packets and one DH3 packet per TCP segment [10]. We also assume that each TCP segment will be acknowledged with a single, empty TCP segment carrying only the TCP ACK bit; such acknowledgment requires one DH3 baseband packet. Therefore, the total throughput per piconet can reach a theoretical maximum of $0.5 \frac{1460 \cdot 8}{(4 \cdot 5 + 2 \cdot 3) \cdot 625 \mu s} \approx 360$ kbps. As we consider the case with $\mu - 1 \leq 7$ slaves with identical traffic, each slave can achieve a goodput of only about $360/i$ kbps.

Our analysis setup implements the L2CAP Flow Control mode through a token bucket [13], with the data queue of size S and a token queue of size W wherein tokens arrive at a constant rate of tb. Furthermore, there is an outgoing queue for baseband data packets of size L, from which the data packets are serviced by the scheduler using the chosen intra-piconet scheduling policy. This implementation is shown in Fig. 1. Note that the devices acting as slaves have one outgoing, or uplink, queue, whilst the device operating as the piconet master will maintain several downlink queues, one per each active slave, in parallel.

The parameters of this architecture, namely the sizes of the queues and the token rate in the token bucket, may be adjusted in order to achieve delay-throughput trade-off for each slave. This scheme can limit the throughput of the slave through the token rate, while simultaneously limiting the length of the burst of baseband packets submitted to the network. Depending on the token buffer size and traffic intensity, overflows of the token buffer can be detected through the TCP loss events such as three duplicate acknowledgments or time-outs. In the former case, the size of the congestion window will be halved and TCP will continue working in its Additive Increase-Multiplicative Decrease (AIMD) phase. In the latter case, the congestion window will shrink to one, and TCP will enter its slow-start routine.

2.2   Related Work

The performance of TCP traffic, in particular the steady-state send rate of the bulk-transfer TCP flows, has recently been assessed as the function of segment loss rate and round trip time (RTT) [14]. The system is modeled at the ends of rounds that are equal to the round trip times and during which a number of segments equal to the current size of the congestion window is sent. The model assumes that both the RTT and loss probability can be obtained by measurement, and derives average value of congestion window size.

The same basic model, but with improved accuracy with regard to the latency and steady state transmission rate for TCP Tahoe, Reno, and SACK variants, has been used in [15]. The authors have also studied the impact of correlated segment losses under three TCP versions.

In our approach, we will model the system at the moments of acknowledgement arrivals, instead of at the ends of successive rounds as in both papers mentioned above. In this manner, we are able to obtain more accurate information about performance, and to derive the TCP congestion window size and throughput in both non-saturated and saturated operating regimes. In addition, the blocking probabilities of all the queues along the path are known and each packet loss can be treated independently.

We note that both of the papers mentioned above consider RTT as a constant due to the large number of hops, whereas in our work there are two hops only, and RTT must be modeled as a random variable which is dependent on the current congestion window size.

Recently, the Adaptive Increase-Multiplicative Decrease (AIMD) technique was applied to control the flow over the combination of wireless and wireline path, by using the concept similar to the token bucket filter [16]. It is assumed that packets can be lost over the wireless link only, and that the all packet transmission times take exactly one slot. The system is modeled at the ends of the packet transmission times. This approach is orthogonal to ours, since we assume that the wireless channel errors will be handled through Forward Error Correction (FEC), and focus on finite queue losses at the data-link layer instead.

2.3   On the Choice of Intra-piconet Scheduling Scheme

Of course, the performance of Bluetooth networks is also affected by the intra-piconet scheduling policy. As the master cannot know the status of all slaves' queues at any time, simpler policies, such as limited or exhaustive service, are to be preferred [2]. Both limited and exhaustive service are limiting cases of a family of schemes known as E-limited service [17]. In this polling scheme, the master and a slave exchange up to M packets, or less if both outgoing queues are emptied, before the master moves on to the next slave. (Limiting cases of $M = 1$ and ∞ correspond to limited and exhaustive service policies, respectively.) Our previous work indicates that the E-limited service offers better performance than either limited or exhaustive service [18]. E-limited service does not require that the master knows the status of slaves' uplink queues, and does not waste bandwidth when there are no data packets to exchange. Furthermore, it provides fairness by default, since the limit on the number of frames exchanged with any single slave prevents the slaves from monopolizing the network. Of course, the TCP protocol itself provides mechanisms to regulate fairness among TCP connections from one slave, but the bandwidth that can be achieved in Bluetooth networks is too small to warrant a detailed analysis in this direction.

3   Analysis of the TCP Window Size

3.1   TCP Traffic in a Bluetooth Piconet

Under the assumptions outlined above, the probability generating function (PGF) for the burst size of data packets at the baseband layer is $G_{bd}(z) = z^5$. The corresponding PGF for the acknowledgment packet burst size is $G_{ba}(z) = z$. The PGF for the size distribution of baseband data packets is $G_{pd}(z) = 0.8z^5 + 0.2z^3$, while the PGF for the size distribution of acknowledgment packets is $G_{pa}(z) = z^3$. Therefore, the PGF for the packet size as $G_p(z) = 0.5G_{bd}(G_{pd}(z)) + 0.5G_{ba}(G_{pa}(z))$, and the mean packet size as $\overline{L_{ad}} = 0.5G'_{bd}(G_{pd}(z))|_{z=1} + 0.5G'_{ba}(G_{pa}(z))|_{z=1} = 3.8$. (All time variables are expressed in units of time slots of the Bluetooth clock, $T = 625\mu s$.) We will also assume that the receiver advertised window is larger than the congestion window at all times.

The paths traversed by the TCP segment sent from slave i to slave j and the corresponding acknowledgment sent in the opposite direction, are shown schematically in Fig. 2. A TCP segment or acknowledgment can be lost if any of the buffers along the path is full (and, consequently, blocks the reception of the packet in question). In Appendices A and B we have calculated the probability distributions of token bucket queue lengths and outgoing buffer queue lengths at arbitrary times, as well as the corresponding blocking

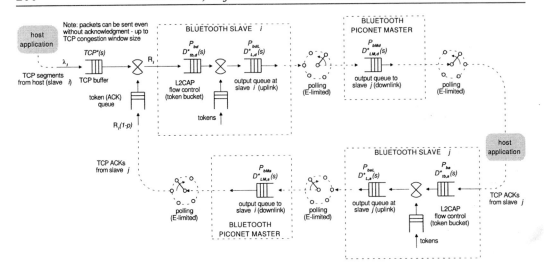

Figure 2: The path of the TCP segment and its acknowledgment, together with the blocking probabilities and LSTs of the delays in respective queues.

probabilities for TCP segments (P_{Bd}, P_{BdL}) and TCP acknowledgments (P_{Ba}, P_{BaL}). Segments/acknowledgments are also passing through the outgoing downlink queue at the master. However, we assume that this queue is much longer than the corresponding queues at the slaves, and the blocking probabilities P_{BMd}, P_{BMa} are much smaller and may safely be ignored in calculations. Then, the total probability p of losing a TCP segment or its acknowledgment is

$$p = 1 - (1 - P_{Bd})(1 - P_{BdL})(1 - P_{BMd})(1 - P_{Ba})(1 - P_{BaL})(1 - P_{BMa}) \qquad (1)$$

We will model the length of the TCP window at the moments of acknowledgments arrivals. Since TCP window of size w grows by $1/w$ after the successful acknowledgment, it is not possible to model the system using Probability Generating Functions – we have to find the probability distribution directly. This probability distribution is a hybrid function represented by the mass probability w_1 of window size being 1, and by the continuous probability density function $w(x)$ for window sizes from 2 to ∞. We also need to determine the probability distribution of the congestion window threshold $t(x)$ at the moments of acknowledgements arrivals. We will represent the probability of the time-out event as $P_{to} = p(1 - (1 - p)^3)$, and the probability of loss by three duplicate acknowledgements as $P_{td} =$

$p(1-p)^3$. These probability distributions can be described by following equations:

$$
\begin{aligned}
w_1 &= P_{to} + P_{td} \int_{x=2}^{3} w(x)dx, \text{ for } w = 1 \\
t(x) &= t(x)(1-p) + w(2x)p, \text{ for } w \geq 2 \\
w(x) &= \left(w(x) - w'(x)\frac{1}{x} \right)(1-p) \int_{0}^{x-1/x} t(y)dy \\
&\quad + w(x/2)(1-p) \int_{0.5x}^{\infty} t(y)dy + w(2x)P_{td}
\end{aligned}
\tag{2}
$$

where $\int_{0}^{x-1/x} t(y)dy$ denotes the probability that the current congestion window size $x - 1/x$ is above the threshold size (i.e., that TCP is working in the AIMD mode), and the probability that the current size $0.5x$ of the congestion window is lower than the threshold (i.e., that the system is in the slow start mode) is given by $\int_{0.5x}^{\infty} t(y)dy$.

The system (2) of integro-differential equations could be solved numerically, but it was found that sufficient accuracy may be obtained through the following approximation:

$$
w(x) = C_1 e^{-0.25px^2(1+3p-3p^2+p^3)/(1-p)}
\tag{3}
$$

where the normalization constant C_1 is determined from the condition $1 - w_1 = \int_{2}^{\infty} w(x)dx$. The probability density function of window size for various values of TCP window size and segment loss probability p is shown in Fig. 3.

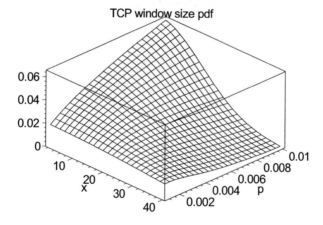

Figure 3: Probability density function of TCP window size versus window size and segment loss probability.

The mean TCP window size $\overline{w}$ and mean threshold size $\overline{t}$ are calculated as

$$
\begin{aligned}
\overline{w} &= w_1 + \int_{2}^{\infty} xw(x)dx \\
\overline{t} &= \int_{1}^{\infty} xw(2x)dx
\end{aligned}
$$

since $t(x) = w(2x)$. The dependency of mean window size on TCP window size and segment loss probability p is shown in Fig. 4.

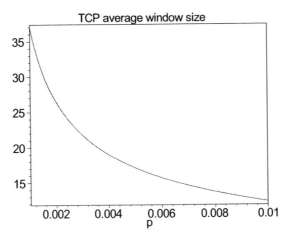

Figure 4: Mean value of the TCP window size versus the segment loss probability.

3.2   TCP Send Rate and Round-Trip Time Estimation

As shown in Appendices A and B, we can find the probability distribution of delays through all the token bucket filters and the baseband buffers along the path of the TCP segment and its acknowledgment. The delay is calculated from the moment when the TCP segment enters the token bucket filter at the source device until the acknowledgment is received by that same device. This delay is equal to the sum of delays in all the buffers from Bluetooth protocol stack along the path. We will refer to this delay as the L2CAP round trip delay, and its probability distribution can be described through the corresponding Laplace-Stieltjes transform:

$$D^*_{L2CAP}(s) = D^*_{tb,d}(s)D^*_{L,d}(s)D^*_{LM,d}(s)D^*_{tb,a}(s)D^*_{L,a}(s)D^*_{LM,a}(s) \tag{4}$$

We can also calculate the probability distribution of the number of outstanding (unacknowledged) segments at the moments of segment acknowledgement arrivals. This number for an arbitrary TCP segment is equal to the number of segment arrivals during the L2CAP round trip time of that segment. The PGF for the number of segment arrivals during the L2CAP round trip time can be calculated, using the approach from [17], as

$$A(z) = D^*_{L2CAP}(\lambda_i - z\lambda_i).$$

The probability of k segment arrivals during the RTT time is equal to

$$a_k = \frac{d^k}{dz^k}D^*_{L2CAP}(\lambda_i - z\lambda_i)|_{z=0}.$$

Using the PASTA property (Poisson Arrivals See Time Averages), we conclude that arriving segment will see the same probability distribution of outstanding segments as the incoming acknowledgement. Therefore, the probability P_t that the arriving segment will find a free token and leave the TCP buffer immediately, is equal to:

$$P_t = \sum_{k=1}^{\infty} a_k \int_{k+1}^{\infty} w(x)dx \tag{5}$$

and the probability that the segments will be stored in the TCP buffer is $1 - P_t$. Then, the rate at which TCP sends the segments to the token bucket filter, which will be referred to as the TCP send rate R_i, has two components. One of these is contributed by the segments that find acknowledgments waiting in the token queue, and thus can leave the TCP buffer immediately; another one comes from the segments that have to wait in the TCP buffer until an acknowledgement (for an earlier segment) arrives. The expression for TCP send rate, then, becomes $R_i = P_t\lambda_i + R_i(1-p)(1-P_t)$, which may be simplified to

$$R_i = \lambda_i \frac{P_t}{P_t + p - pP_t} \tag{6}$$

As both components of the previous expression can be modeled as Poisson processes, we argue that the TCP sending process can still be modeled as Poisson process.

In order to calculate the delay through the TCP buffer, we need to determine the probability distribution of the number of segments buffered by the TCP due to the insufficient size of the congestion window. (We assume that the TCP buffer has infinite capacity.) The probability that k segments are buffered is

$$q_k = \sum_{i=1}^{\infty} a_{i+k} \int_i^{i+1} w(x)dx + a_{k+1}w_1 \tag{7}$$

and the LST for the delay through the TCP buffer is

$$D_{TCP}^*(s) = \sum_{k=0}^{\infty} q_k e^{-sk} \tag{8}$$

The entire round trip time of the TCP segment, then, becomes

$$RTT^*(s) = D_{TCP}^*(s)D_{L2CAP}^*(s) \tag{9}$$

4   Simulation Results for TCP Performance in Bluetooth Piconet

We first consider a piconet with two slaves only, having two simultaneous (but independent) TCP connections: slave 1 to slave 2, and slave 2 to slave 1. In the first set of experiments we have varied token buffer queue size S and offered load per connection, while other parameters were fixed:

1. The value of the scheduling parameter was $M = 5$, so that the entire TCP segment can be transferred in one piconet cycle.

2. The token rate was fixed to $tb = 250kbps$.

3. The token buffer capacity was $W = 3$KB.

4. The output rate of the token bucket queue was set to $max\_rate = 1Mbps$.

5. The outgoing (uplink) queue size was $L = 20$.

The values of TCP goodput and RTT obtained through simulation, using the ns-2 network simulator [19] with Bluehoc extension [20], are shown in Fig. 5. The size of token bucket buffer varied from 5 to 25 baseband packets, and the offered load varied from 80 to 240kbps.

The topmost row of diagrams show the round-trip time RTT and goodput. We observe that only for $S = 25$ the goodput reaches the physical limit (for the given segment size) of approximately 180kbps per connection. At the same time, round trip delay reaches $400ms$.

As can be seen from the two diagrams in the middle row, the mean congestion window size grows with S, which is expected since larger S means lower buffer loss. Furthermore, the congestion window grows with the segment arrival rate under very low loads, since there are not enough packets to expand the window size. For moderate and high offered loads, the average window size experiences a sharp decrease with the offered load. This is consistent with analytical results, since the packet loss probability is directly proportional to the offered load.

Finally, the bottommost row of Fig. 5 shows the rate of TCP timeouts and fast retransmissions as functions of offered load and buffer size S.

The dependencies shown in Fig. 5 hint that the value of $S = 25$ leads to maximum achievable throughput and negligible time-out rate for the offered load equal to the maximum achievable goodput (180kbps).

The next set of experiments considered TCP performance as a function of the scheduling parameter M, with constant values of $S = 25$ and $L = 20$. The resulting diagrams are shown in Fig. 6. We observe that the value of $M = 5$, which is sufficient to carry a TCP segment of five baseband packets, gives maximum goodput, minimum timeout rate and maximum fast-retransmission rate, when compared to larger values of M. Therefore, the minimal value of M which is sufficient to transfer a TCP segment in one piconet cycle appears also to be optimal with respect to goodput and other measures of performance.

We have also investigated TCP behavior with varying offered load and varying token rate; the corresponding diagrams are shown in Fig. 7. We observe that increasing the token rate over the maximal achievable goodput per connection can result only in marginal increase of mean congestion window size and goodput, despite the fact that the blocking probability at the token bucket filter is decreased. However, the blocking probability at the outgoing buffer at the baseband will still increase, and this increase leads to increased time-out rate and increased overall segment loss probability. Therefore, the token rate should not be set to the value much larger than the physical throughput limit per slave.

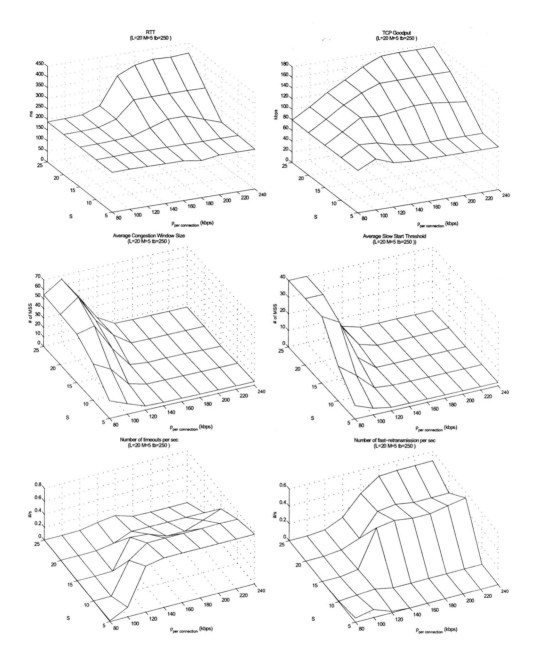

Figure 5: TCP performance as the function of the buffer size S, in the piconet with two slaves. ((a) Round-trip time (RTT). (b) Goodput. (c) Mean size of the congestion window. (d) Mean value of the slow start threshold. (e) Time-out rate. (f) Fast retransmission rate.)

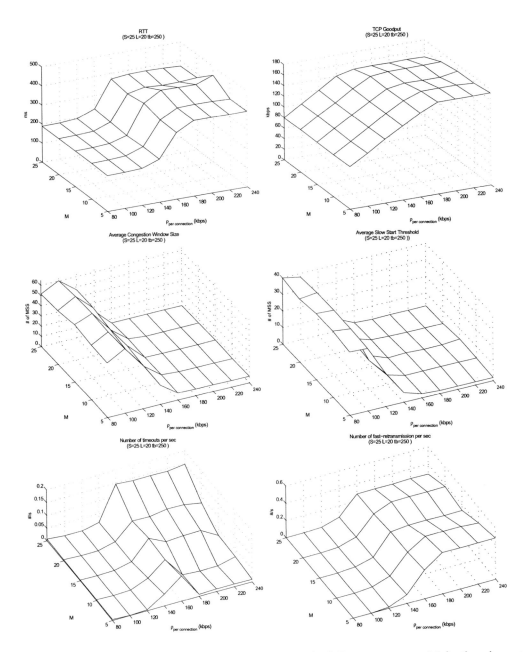

Figure 6: TCP performance as the function of the scheduling parameter *M*, in the piconet with two slaves. ((a) Round-trip time (RTT). (b) Goodput. (c) Mean size of the congestion window. (d) Mean value of the slow start threshold. (e) Time-out rate. (f) Fast retransmission rate.)

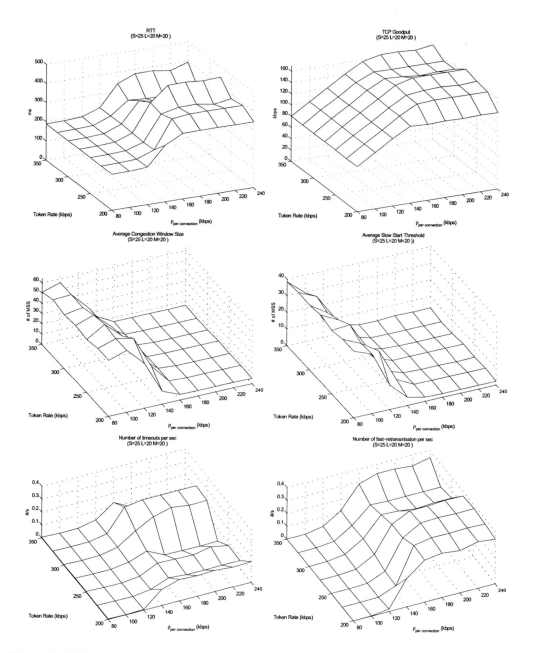

Figure 7: TCP performance as the function of token rate, in the piconet with two slaves. ((a) Round-trip time (RTT). (b) Goodput. (c) mean size of the congestion window. (d) Mean value of the slow start threshold. (e) Time-out rate. (f) Fast retransmission rate.)

5 TCP Performance in the Piconet with Seven Slaves

We have conducted a similar set of experiments in a piconet with seven active slaves. In this case, each slave i, $i = 1..7$ creates a TCP connection with another slave $j = (i+1) \bmod 7$, giving rise to a total of seven identical TCP connections. Consequently, the maximum goodput per slave is limited to $\frac{360}{7} \approx 50$ kbps.

The performance of TCP traffic, when the token buffer size varies from 5 to 25 baseband packets and the offered load varies 50% around the physical goodput limit, is shown in Fig. 8. Again, the value of $S = 25$ gives the goodput which is close to the limit under high load, as well as a low time-out rate. The shape of the time-out rate surface can be explained by the fact that packets do not arrive too frequently under low offered loads, and time-outs occur before three new packets are generated to provoke three duplicated acknowledgments.

Finally, Fig. 9 shows TCP performance with seven slaves under varying value of the scheduling parameter M and the token rate. We observe that this behavior is similar to that in the case of two slaves, although the optimality of the value $M = 5$ is much less pronounced. We again note that good performance is obtained if the token rate does not exceed about 50% of the maximum physical goodput.

6 Conclusion

We have analyzed the performance of the Bluetooth piconet carrying TCP traffic, assuming TCP Reno is used. We have analytically modeled the segment loss probability, TCP send rate, and the probability density functions of the congestion window size and the round trip time. We have investigated the impact of token bucket buffer size, token rate, outgoing baseband buffer size, and scheduling parameter on the goodput, round-trip time, congestion window size, time-out rate and fast-retransmission rate. Our results show that buffer sizes around 25 baseband packets are sufficient for achieving maximal goodput. Scheduling should be confined to the E-limited policy with scheduling parameter being equal to the number of baseband packets in the TCP segment. Token rate should be set to value only around 50% larger than the portion of the total piconet throughput dedicated to particular slave.

A Queueing Analysis of Token Bucket Filter under TCP Traffic

We consider the token bucket (TB) filter, the queueing model of which is shown in Fig. 10. We assume that the TCP segments arrive at the TCP sending rate R_i calculated in (6), while the TCP acknowledgements arrive at the rate of $R_i(1-p)$. The token arrival rate will be denoted as tb, which means that the token arrival period will be $T_b = 1/tb$. The queue which holds tokens has length of W baseband packet tokens. Packets leave the queue at max_rate, which is much larger than the token arrival rate. Using this model, we first derive the probability distribution function (PDF) of the number of the packets in the token bucket

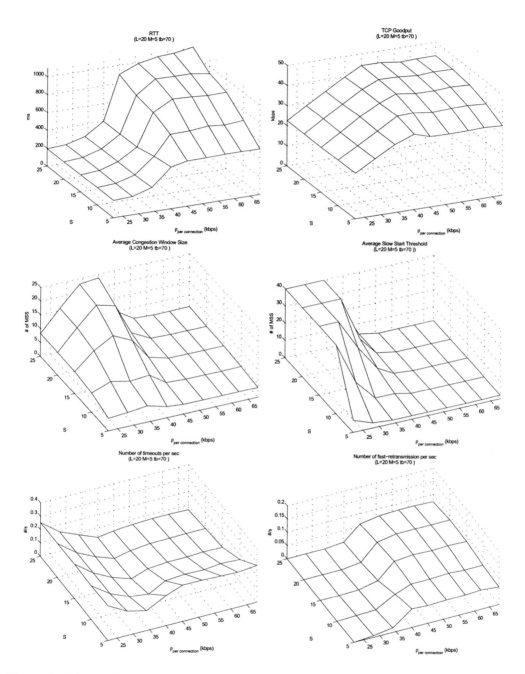

Figure 8: TCP performance as the function of the buffer size S, in the piconet with seven slaves. ((a) Round-trip time (RTT). (b) Goodput. (c) Mean size of the congestion window. (d) Mean value of the slow start threshold. (e) Time-out rate. (f) Fast retransmission rate.)

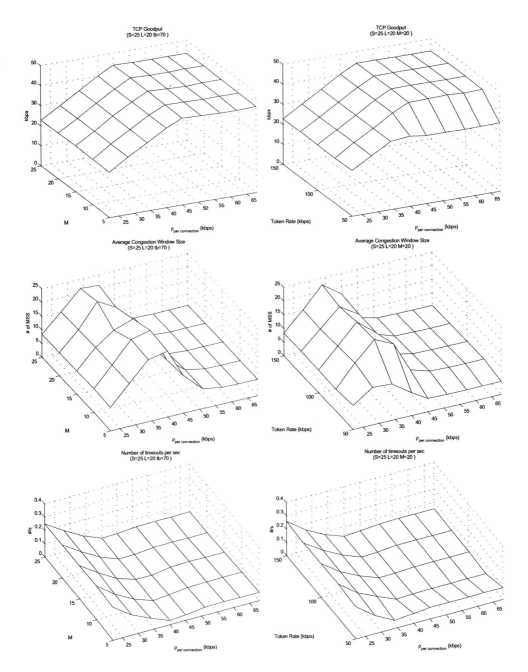

Figure 9: TCP performance in the piconet with seven slaves. ((a) Goodput as the function of the scheduling parameter *M*. (b) Goodput as the function of token rate. (c) Mean size of the congestion window as the function of the scheduling parameter *M*. (d) Mean size of the congestion window as the function of token rate. (e) Time-out rate as the function of the scheduling parameter *M*.(f) Time-out rate as the function of token-rate.)

queue at the moments of token arrival, and then proceed to calculate that same PDF at arbitrary time.

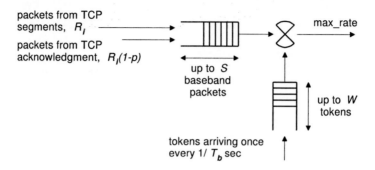

Figure 10: Queueing model of the token bucket with finite capacity, accepting two types of packets.

The probability of a_k baseband packet arrivals in the TB queue is equal to the sum of probabilities of data and acknowledgment packet arrivals:

$$
\begin{aligned}
a_k &= \sum_{i=1}^{k} \left[\frac{1}{i!} \frac{d^i}{dz^i} \left(e^{-R_i T_b (1-G_{bd}(z))} \right)_{|z=0} \right. \\
&+ \left. \frac{1}{(k-i)!} \frac{d^{k-i}}{dz^{k-i}} \left(e^{-R_i T_b (1-G_{ba}(z))} \right)_{|z=0} \right]
\end{aligned}
\tag{10}
$$

The TB can be modeled as a discrete-time Markov chain, in which the state i (when $0 \le i \le W$) corresponds to the situation when $W - i$ tokens are available in the token buffer, but no data packets are present in the data queue. The remaining states from $W + 1$ to $W + S$ correspond to the situation where there are data packets in the data queue, but the token queue is empty. Since both queues have finite lengths, the Markov chain, which is shown in Fig. 11, is finite as well. The balance equations for this Markov chain are

$$
\begin{aligned}
\pi_0 &= a_0 \pi_1 + (a_0 + a_1) \pi_0 \\
\pi_i &= \sum_{j=0}^{i+1} a_{i-j+1} \pi_j,, \text{ for } 0 < i < W + S - 1 \\
\pi_{W+S-1} &= \sum_{j=0}^{S-1} \pi_j \sum_{k=S-j}^{\infty} a_k
\end{aligned}
\tag{11}
$$

The PDF for the queue lengths at the moments of token arrivals can be found by solving this system with the condition $\sum_{k=0}^{S-1} \pi_k = 1$.

A.1 Analysis of the TB Queue Length at Arbitrary Times and the Derivation of Blocking Probability

By using the probability distribution of TB queue length at moments of token arrivals, we can derive the joint probability distribution of TB queue length and the remaining time

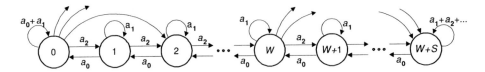

Figure 11: Token bucket may be represented as a discrete Markov chain.

before the token arrival. This will help us to obtain the blocking probability which is important since it determines the segment loss probability at the TCP level. We will introduce the following variables:

- The total queue length (including both token queue and data queue), L_q.

- The elapsed token time – from a given token arrival to the arbitrary time before the arrival of the next token, T_{b-}.

- The remaining token time – from the arbitrary time between two successive token arrivals till the next token arrival, T_{b+}.

- The number of packet arrivals (results of burst arrivals) during the elapsed token time, $A(T_{b-})$.

- The blocking probability at arbitrary time, P_B. Since the burst represents a TCP segment, we will adopt the total rejection policy for calculating the blocking probability. In other words, if there is not enough room for all baseband packets which belong to the burst (TCP segment), the entire burst will be rejected.

- Finally, the probability distribution function $T_b(x)$ of the token inter-arrival time, and the corresponding probability density function $t_b(x)$.

For the time between two successive token arrivals, the joint probability distribution of the TB queue length and remaining token time is

$$\Pi_k^* = \int_0^\infty e^{-sy} \mathrm{Prob}[L_q = k, y < T_{b+} < y + dy], \quad 1 \le k \le W + S \qquad (12)$$

By using the TB queue length distribution at the time of arrival of the previous token, we obtain

$$\Pi_k^*(s) = R_i(\overline{G_{bd}} + \overline{G_{ba}})T_b(1 - P_B)$$
$$\cdot \sum_{j=0}^{k} \pi_j E[e^{-sT_{b+}}|_{A(T_{b-})=k-j}]\mathrm{Prob}[A(T_{b-}) = k - j], \text{ for } 1 \le k < W + S \qquad (13)$$

$$\Pi_{W+S}^*(s) = \sum_{j=0}^{W+S-1} \pi_j \sum_{k=S-j}^{\infty} E[e^{-sT_{b+}}|_{A(T_{b-})=k-j}]\mathrm{Prob}[A(T_{b-}) = k - j] \qquad (14)$$

The system (13) and (14) can be simplified using the following expression:

$$\psi_k^*(s) = \sum_{l=0}^{\infty}\sum_{i=1}^{k}\left(\frac{1}{i!}\frac{d^i}{dz^i}G_{bd}(z)^l + \frac{1}{(k-i)!}\frac{d^{k-i}}{dz^{k-i}}G_{ba}(z)^l\right)_{|z=0}$$
$$\cdot \int_0^{\infty}\frac{(R_i x)^l}{l!}e^{-R_i x}\frac{1-T_b(x)}{T_b}dx\int_0^{\infty}e^{-sy}\frac{t_b(x+y)}{1-T_b(x)}dy \qquad (15)$$

Expression (15) can be further simplified to

$$\psi_k^*(s) = \frac{1}{T_b}\sum_{i=1}^{k}\left(\frac{1}{i!}\frac{d^i}{dz^i}\Big|_{z=0}\frac{e^{(R_i G_{bd}(z)-R_i)T_b}-e^{-sT_b}}{R_i G_{bd}(z)+s-R_i}\right.$$
$$\left. + \frac{1}{(k-i)!}\frac{d^{k-i}}{dz^{k-i}}\Big|_{z=0}\frac{e^{(R_i G_{pa}(z)-R_i)T_b}-e^{-sT_b}}{R_i G_{pa}(z)+s-R_i}\right) \qquad (16)$$

Now the system (13), (14) can be written as:

$$\Pi_k^*(s) = R_i(\overline{G_{bd}}+\overline{G_{ba}})T_b(1-P_B)\sum_{j=0}^{k}\pi_j\psi_{k-j}^*, \text{ for } 1\le k < W+S$$
$$\Pi_{W+S}^*(s) = R_i(\overline{G_{bd}}+\overline{G_{ba}})T_b(1-P_B)\sum_{j=0}^{W+S-1}\pi_j\sum_{k=S-j}^{\infty}\psi_{k-j}^* \qquad (17)$$

The probabilities that the TB filter has exactly k packets can be simply expressed as $P_k = \text{Prob}[L_q = k] = \Pi_k^*(0)$. Also, we note that the probability of the empty queue is equal to $P_0 = 1 - \lambda(\overline{G_{bd}}+\overline{G_{ba}})T_b(1-P_B)$. It should be observed that all queue state probabilities at arbitrary time are functions of P_B, therefore we need to express the blocking probability as the function of the queue state probabilities, and then solve this equation for P_B. The blocking probability under two types of packet bursts in the TB filter is

$$P_B = \sum_{k=0}^{W+S-1}P_k\sum_{j=W+S-k+1}^{\infty}0.5(g_{bd,j}+g_{ba,j})+P_{W+S} \qquad (18)$$

where $g_{bd,j} = \frac{1}{j!}\frac{d^j}{dz^j}G_{bd}(z)|_{z=0}$ and $g_{ba,j} = \frac{1}{j!}\frac{d^j}{dz^j}G_{ba}(z)|_{z=0}$ are mass probabilities of the burst size probability distribution for the TCP data segment and the TCP acknowledgment segment, respectively. Expression (18) can be rearranged to find the blocking probability P_B, which leads to the queue length distribution. After that, the individual blocking probabilities for each traffic type can be found as

$$P_{Bd} = \sum_{k=0}^{W+S-1}P_k\sum_{j=W+S-k+1}^{\infty}g_{bd,j}+P_{W+S}$$
$$P_{Ba} = \sum_{k=0}^{W+S-1}P_k\sum_{j=W+S-k+1}^{\infty}g_{ba,j}+P_{W+S} \qquad (19)$$

The delay through the token bucket filter should be calculated separately for the data segments and for the acknowledgments. The queueing delay of the entire TCP segment is equal to the queueing delay of the first baseband packet from the burst representing that TCP segment. The LST of the delay for the data segment is given with

$$
D_{tb,d}^*(s) = \frac{\left(P_0 + \sum_{l=1}^{W} \Pi_k^*(0)\right) \sum_{k=1}^{W+S-l} g_{bd,k} + \sum_{k=W}^{W+S-1} \Pi_k^*(s)[G_{pd}^*]^{k-1} \sum_{j=1}^{W+S-k} g_{bd,j}}{1 - P_{Bd}}
\tag{20}
$$

The LST for the delay of the acknowledgment, $D_{tb,d}^*(s)$, can be determined in an analogous manner.

B   Analysis of the Outgoing Queue at the Baseband Level

We will now derive the expressions for the delay and blocking probability for the other queue (buffer): the outgoing buffer at the baseband level. This buffer has finite length of L baseband packets, and it is fed by packets that pass through the token buffer filter. We assume that the TCP segment packets arrive at the rate of $\lambda_{i,d} = R_i(1 - P_{Bd})$, and that the TCP acknowledgment packets arrive at the rate of $\lambda_{i,a} = R_i(1 - p)(1 - P_{Ba})$. We again assume that each buffer has the total rejection policy, i.e., the entire burst is rejected if it cannot fit into the buffer.

The baseband queue is serviced by the baseband scheduler using the E-limited policy. The master sends a downlink packet to the slave, and receives an uplink packet from it. Empty (POLL or NULL) packets are sent if there are no data packets in the corresponding outgoing queue. Under the E-limited policy, the master stays with the slave (and services its outgoing queue) for at most M packet are transmitted, or less it if both outgoing queues are empty. Therefore, the operation of the outgoing queue has to be analyzed using the theory of $M^{[x]}/G/1$ queues with vacations, where vacation corresponds to the time when the master is serving other slaves. We will first determine the probability distribution of slave queue lengths in imbedded Markov points that correspond to vacation termination times and uplink transmission completion times [17]. Then, we will determine the PDF for the slave queue length at arbitrary point of time, and use it to derive the access delay and the blocking probability of the burst.

B.1   Analysis of Outgoing Queue Length Distribution in Markov Points

Let $q_{k,i,u}$ denote the joint probability that a Markov point in the uplink queue of slave i is a vacation termination time and that there are $k = 0, 1, 2 \ldots$ packets at the outgoing queue of the slave i at that time. Also, let $\pi_{k,i,u}^{(m)}$ denote the joint probability that a Markov point in the uplink queue i is the m-th uplink transmission completion time and that there are k packets in the queue, where $m = 1 .. M$ and $k = 0, 1, 2, \ldots$. The analogous probabilities for the corresponding downlink queue are denoted with $q_{k,i,d}$ and $\pi_{k,i,d}^{(m)}$.

Let $g_p(x)$ and $v_i(x)$ denote the probability density functions of the packet transmission time and vacation time, respectively, at the uplink queue of slave i; their LST transforms will be $G_p^*(s)$ and $V_i^*(s)$. The downlink packet transmission, immediately followed by the uplink transmission, will be denoted as a frame; the corresponding LST transform is $G_p^*(s)^2$. Let us also denote the probability of k packet arrivals at the uplink queue of slave i during the frame time as $a_{k,i,u}$, and the probability of k packet arrivals during the vacation time (i.e., while master is serving other slaves) as $f_{k,i,u}$. These probabilities may be calculated as

$$
\begin{aligned}
a_{k,i,u} &= \sum_{i=1}^{k} \frac{1}{i!} \frac{d^i}{dz^i} \left(G_p^*(\lambda_{i,d} - \lambda_{i,d} G_{bd}(z)) \right)^2 \Big|_{z=0} \\
&\quad + \frac{1}{(k-i)!} \frac{d^{k-i}}{dz^{k-i}} \left(G_p^*(\lambda_{i,a} - \lambda_{i,a} G_{ba}(z)) \right)^2 \Big|_{z=0} \\
f_{k,i,u} &= \sum_{i=1}^{k} \frac{1}{i!} \frac{d^i}{dz^i} \left(V^*(\lambda_{i,d} - \lambda_{i,d} G_{bd}(z)) \right)^2 \Big|_{z=0} \\
&\quad + \frac{1}{(k-i)!} \frac{d^{k-i}}{dz^{k-i}} \left(V^*(\lambda_{i,a} - \lambda_{i,a} G_{ba}(z)) \right)^2 \Big|_{z=0}
\end{aligned}
\tag{21}
$$

where $g_p * g_p(x)$ denotes the convolution of $g_p(x)$ with itself. Note that the expressions $(G_p^*(\lambda_{i,d} - \lambda_{i,d} G_{bd}(z)))^2$ and $G_p^*(\lambda_{i,a} - \lambda_{i,a} G_{ba}(z))$ denote the PGFs for the number of packet arrivals in the uplink queue from TCP data segments and acknowledgments, respectively, during the frame time. Also $(V^*(\lambda_{i,d} - \lambda_{i,d} G_{bd}(z)))^2$ and $V^*(\lambda_{i,a} - \lambda_{i,a} G_{ba}(z))$ denote the corresponding PGFs for the number of packet arrivals in the uplink queue, but during the vacation time.

For the packet departure times when the master polls the slaves, we note that the buffer occupancy can be between 0 and $L - 1$. The probabilities that the uplink queue contains k packets in Markov points are given by

$$
\begin{aligned}
\pi_{k,i,u}^{(1)} &= \sum_{j=1}^{k+1} q_{j,i,u} a_{k-j+1,i,u}, \ 0 \le k \le L-2 \\
\pi_{L-1,i,u}^{(1)} &= \sum_{j=1}^{L} q_{j,i,u} \sum_{k=L-j}^{\infty} a_{k,i,u} \\
\pi_{k,i,u}^{(m)} &= \sum_{j=1}^{k+1} \pi_{j,i,u}^{(m-1)} a_{k-j+1,i,u}, \ 0 \le k \le L-2, m = 2..M \\
\pi_{L-1,i,u}^{(m)} &= \sum_{j=1}^{L-1} \pi_{j,i,u}^{(m-1)} \sum_{k=L-j}^{\infty} a_{k,i,u}, \ m = 2..M \\
q_{k,i,u} &= \left(\sum_{m=1}^{M-1} \pi_{0,i,u}^{(m)} + q_{0,i,u} \right) f_{k,i,u} + \sum_{j=0}^{k} \pi_{j,i,u}^{(M)} f_{k-j,i,u}, \ 0 \le k < L \\
q_{K,i,u} &= \left(\sum_{m=1}^{M-1} \pi_{0,i,u}^{(m)} + q_{0,i,u} \right) \sum_{k=L}^{\infty} f_{k,i,u} + \sum_{j=0}^{L-1} \pi_{j,i,u}^{(M)} \sum_{k=L-j}^{\infty} f_{k,i,u}
\end{aligned}
\tag{22}
$$

Also, $\sum_{k=0}^{L} q_{k,i,u} + \sum_{m=1}^{M} \sum_{k=0}^{L-1} \pi_{k,i,u} = 1$. The distribution of the queue length in Markov points may be obtained.

Let us denote the probability that the vacation starts after the uplink transmission as $h_{i,u} = \sum_{m=1}^{M-1} \pi_{0,i,u}^m + \sum_{k=0}^{L-1} \pi_{k,i,u}^M$. Then, the probability that the vacation will start after an arbitrary Markov point is $q_{0,i,u} + h_{i,u}$. The average distance in time between two consecutive Markov points at slave i is

$$\eta_{i,u} = (q_{0,i,u} + h_{i,u})\overline{V_{i,u}} + (1 - q_{0,i,u} + h_{i,u})2\overline{L_{ad}} \tag{23}$$

B.2   Analysis of the Outgoing Queue Length Distribution at Arbitrary Time

By using the probability distribution of the uplink queue length in Markov points, we can derive the probability distribution of this queue length at arbitrary time between two Markov points, together with the PDF of the remaining vacation time (if the previous Markov point was the start of a vacation) or the PDF of the remaining frame service time (if the previous Markov point was the start of a packet service). We will introduce the following variables:

- The probability density function of the vacation time, $v_i(x)$, and its PDF, $V_i(x)$.

- The queue length at an arbitrary time, $L_{q,i,u}$.

- The elapsed vacation time, $V_{-,i,u}$.

- The remaining vacation time, $V_{+,i,u}$.

- The number of packet arrivals resulting from packet burst arrivals in the elapsed vacation time, $A(V_-)$.

- The probability density function of the frame service time, $g_p * g_p(x)$, and its PDF, $F_s(x)$.

- The elapsed frame service time, $X_{-,i,u}$.

- The remaining frame service time, $X_{+,i,u}$.

- The number of packet arrivals resulting from packet burst arrivals in the elapsed frame service time, $A(X_-)$.

For the time between the start and end of vacation, we define the joint probability of the queue length and the remaining vacation time as

$$\Omega_{k,i,u}^*(s) = \int_0^\infty e^{-sy} \text{Prob}[L_{q,i,u} = k, y < V_{+,i,u} < y + dy], 0 \leq k \leq L \tag{24}$$

For the time between the start and end of the frame service, for the frame $1 \leq m \leq M$, we define the joint probability of the queue length and remaining frame service time as

$$\Pi_{k,m,i,u}^*(s) = \int_0^\infty e^{-sy} \text{Prob}[L_{q,i,u} = k, y < X_{+,i,u} < y + dy], 1 \leq k \leq K, 1 \leq m \leq M \tag{25}$$

Then, by using the probabilities of the uplink queue state in the previous Markov point, we obtain

$$
\begin{aligned}
\Omega_{k,i,u}^*(s) &= \frac{\overline{V_{i,u}}}{\eta_{i,u}}\left(q_{0,i,u} + \sum_{m=1}^{M-1}\pi_{0,i,u}^m\right)E[e^{-sV_{+,i,u}}|_{A(V_{-,i,u})=k}]\mathrm{Prob}[A(V_{-,i,u})=k] \\
&\quad + \frac{\overline{V_{i,u}}}{\eta_{i,u}}\sum_{j=0}^{k}\pi_{j,i,u}^M E[e^{-sV_{+,i,u}}|_{A(V_{-,i,u})=k-j}]\mathrm{Prob}[A(V_{-,i,u})=k-j], \\
&\qquad\qquad\qquad\qquad\qquad\qquad\qquad\qquad\qquad\qquad\qquad \text{for } 0 \le k \le K-1 \\
\Omega_{L,i,u}^*(s) &= \frac{\overline{V_{i,u}}}{\eta_{i,u}}\left(q_{0,i,u} + \sum_{m=1}^{M-1}\pi_{0,i,u}^m\right)\sum_{k=L}^{\infty}E[e^{-sV_{+,i,u}}|_{A(V_{-,i,u})=k}]\mathrm{Prob}[A(V_{-,i,u})=k] \\
&\quad + \frac{\overline{V_{i,u}}}{\eta_{i,u}}\sum_{j=0}^{k}\pi_{j,i,u}^M\sum_{k=L-j}^{\infty}E[e^{-sV_{+,i,u}}|_{A(V_{-,i,u})=k}]\mathrm{Prob}[A(V_{-,i,u})=k]
\end{aligned}
$$

$$
\begin{aligned}
\Pi_{k,1,i,u}^*(s) &= \frac{2\overline{L}}{\eta_{i,u}}\sum_{j=1}^{k}q_{j,i,u}E[e^{-sX_{+,i,u}}|_{A(X_{-,i,u})=k-j}]\mathrm{Prob}[A(X_{-,i,u})=k-j], \\
&\qquad\qquad\qquad\qquad\qquad\qquad\qquad\qquad\qquad \text{for } 1 \le k \le L-1 \\
\Pi_{L,1,i,u}^*(s) &= \frac{2\overline{L}}{\eta_{i,u}}\sum_{j=1}^{L}q_{j,i,u}\sum_{k=K-j}^{\infty}E[e^{-sX_{+,i,u}}|_{A(X_{-,i,u})=k}]\mathrm{Prob}[A(X_{-,i,u})=k], \\
&\qquad\qquad\qquad\qquad\qquad\qquad\qquad\qquad\qquad \text{for } 1 \le k \le L-1 \\
\Pi_{k,m,i,u}^*(s) &= \frac{2\overline{L}}{\eta_{i,u}}\sum_{j=1}^{k}\pi_{j,i,u}E[e^{-sX_{+,i,u}}|_{A(X_{-,i,u})=k-j}]\mathrm{Prob}[A(X_{-,i,u})=k-j], \\
&\qquad\qquad\qquad\qquad\qquad\qquad\qquad\qquad \text{for } 1 \le k \le L-1,\, 2 \le m \le M \\
\Pi_{L,m,i,u}^*(s) &= \frac{2\overline{L}}{\eta_{i,u}}\sum_{j=1}^{L}\pi_{j,i,u}^m\sum_{k=K-j}^{\infty}E[e^{-sX_{+,i,u}}|_{A(X_{-,i,u})=k}]\mathrm{Prob}[A(X_{-,i,u})=k], \\
&\qquad\qquad \text{for } 2 \le m \le M
\end{aligned}
\tag{26}
$$

The system of equations (26) can be simplified using the following expressions:

$$
\begin{aligned}
\phi_k(s) &= E[e^{-sV_{+,i,u}}|A(V_{-,i,u})=k]\mathrm{Prob}[A(V_{-,i,u})=k] \\
&= \sum_{i=1}^{k}\left[\frac{1}{\overline{V_i}i!}\frac{d^i}{dz^i}|_{z=0}\left(\frac{V^*(-\lambda_i G_{bd}(z)+\lambda_{i,d})-V^*(s)}{\lambda G_{bd}(z)+s+\lambda_{i,d}}\right)\right. \\
&\quad \left. + \frac{1}{\overline{V_i}(k-i)!}\frac{d^{k-i}}{dz^{k-i}}|_{z=0}\left(\frac{V^*(-\lambda_i G_{ba}(z)+\lambda_{i,a})-V^*(s)}{\lambda G_{ba}(z)+s+\lambda_{i,a}}\right)\right]
\end{aligned}
$$

$$
\begin{aligned}
\psi_k^*(s) &= E[e^{-sX_{+,i,u}}|A(X_{-,i,u})=k]\mathrm{Prob}[A(X_{-,i,u})=k] \\
&= \sum_{i=1}^{k}\left[\frac{1}{2\overline{L}i!}\frac{d^i}{dz^i}|_{z=0}\left(\frac{G_p^*(-\lambda_{i,d}G_{bd}(z)+\lambda_i)^2-G_p^*(s)^2}{\lambda G_{bd}(z)+s+\lambda_{i,d}}\right)\right. \\
&\quad \left. + \frac{1}{2\overline{L}(k-i)!}\frac{d^{k-i}}{dz^{k-i}}|_{z=0}\left(\frac{G_p^*(-\lambda_{i,a}G_{ba}(z)+\lambda_{i,a})^2-G_p^*(s)^2}{\lambda G_{ba}(z)+s+\lambda_{i,a}}\right)\right]
\end{aligned}
$$

Then, (26) and (26) can be transformed to

$$
\begin{aligned}
\Omega_k^*(s) &= \frac{\overline{V}}{\eta_{i,u}}\left(q_{0,i,u} + \sum_{m=1}^{M-1} \pi_{0,i,u}^m\right)\phi_k^*(s) + \frac{\overline{V_{i,u}}}{\eta_{i,u}} \sum_{j=0}^{k} \pi_{j,i,u}^M \phi_{k-j}^* \\
\Omega_{L,i,u}^*(s) &= \frac{\overline{V_{i,u}}}{\eta_{i,u}}\left(q_{0,i,u} + \sum_{m=1}^{M-1} \pi_{0,i,u}^m\right) \sum_{k=K}^{\infty} \phi_k^*(s) \\
&\quad + \frac{\overline{V_{i,u}}}{\eta_{i,u}} \sum_{j=0}^{k} \pi_{j,i,u}^M \sum_{k=K-j}^{\infty} \phi_k^*(s)
\end{aligned}
\tag{27}
$$

$$
\begin{aligned}
\Pi_{k,1,i,u}^*(s) &= \frac{2\overline{L_{ad}}}{\eta_{i,u}} \sum_{j=1}^{k} q_{j,i,u} \psi_k^*(s), \; 1 \le k \le L-1 \\
\Pi_{L,1,i,u}^*(s) &= \frac{2\overline{L_{ad}}}{\eta_{i,u}} \sum_{j=1}^{L} q_{j,i,u} \sum_{k=K-j}^{\infty} \psi_k^*(s), \; 1 \le k \le L-1 \\
\Pi_{k,m,i,u}^*(s) &= \frac{2\overline{L_{ad}}}{\eta_{i,u}} \sum_{j=1}^{k} \pi_{j,i,u} \psi_{k-j}^*(s), \; 1 \le k \le L-1, 2 \le m \le M \\
\Pi_{L,m,i,u}^*(s) &= \frac{2\overline{L_{ad}}}{\eta_{i,u}} \sum_{j=1}^{L} \pi_{j,i,u}^m \sum_{k=L-j}^{\infty} \psi_k^*(s), \; 1 \le k \le L-1, 2 \le m \le M
\end{aligned}
\tag{28}
$$

The distribution of the size of the uplink queue at the slave, at arbitrary time, is given by

$$
\begin{aligned}
\text{Prob}[L_{q,i,u} = 0] &= \Omega_0^* = \frac{1}{\lambda_i \eta_{i,u}} \sum_{m=1}^{M} \pi_{0,i,u}^m \\
\text{Prob}[L_{q,i,u} = k] &= \Omega_k^*(0) + \sum_{m=1}^{M} \Pi_{k,m,i,u}^*(0) \\
&= \frac{1}{\lambda_i \eta_{i,u}} \sum_{m=1}^{M} \pi_{k,i,u}^m, \; 1 \le k \le K-1 \\
\text{Prob}[L_{q,i,u} = K] &= \Omega_L^*(0) + \sum_{m=1}^{M} \Pi_{L,m,i,u}^*(0)
\end{aligned}
\tag{29}
$$

With this distribution, we are able to calculate the burst blocking probability in the uplink queue at an arbitrary time. To that end, let us denote the mass probability of the burst size being exactly l packets as $g_l = \frac{1}{l!} \frac{d^l}{dz^l} G_b(z)|_{z=0}$. Then,

$$
P_{B,i,L} = \sum_{k=0}^{L} \text{Prob}[L_{q,i,u} = k]\text{Prob}[\text{burst} > L-k]
\tag{30}
$$

and the blocking probabilities for TCP segments and acknowledgments become

$$
P_{BdL} = \sum_{k=0}^{L} \text{Prob}[L_{q,i,u} = k] \sum_{l=L-k}^{\infty} g_{bd,l}
\tag{31}
$$

$$
P_{BaL} = \sum_{k=0}^{L} \text{Prob}[L_{q,i,u} = k] \sum_{l=L-k}^{\infty} g_{ba,l}
\tag{32}
$$

The delay of the entire TCP segment is equal to the delay of the first baseband packet from that segment:

$$
D_{L,d}^*(s) = \frac{1}{1 - P_{BdL}} \left(\sum_{k=0}^{K-1} \Omega_{k,i,u}^*(s) G_{pd}^*(s)^{2k} V_i^*(s)^{\lfloor k/M \rfloor} \right.
$$
$$
\left. + \sum_{k=1}^{K-1} \sum_{m=1}^{M} \Pi_{k,m,i,u}^*(s) G_{pd}^*(s)^{2(k-1)} V_i^*(s)^{\lfloor (k+m-1)/M \rfloor} \right)
$$

It should be noted that tis delay is not equal to the delay for acknowledgment segment $D_{L,a}^*(s)$, even though the expressions used to derive them are similar.

References

[1] "Wireless PAN medium access control MAC and physical layer PHY specification," IEEE, New York, NY, *IEEE standard 802.15*, 2002.

[2] A. Capone, R. Kapoor, and M. Gerla, "Efficient polling schemes for Bluetooth pic-ocells," in *Proceedings of IEEE International Conference on Communications ICC 2001*, vol. 7, Helsinki, Finland, June 2001, pp. 1990–1994.

[3] A. Das, A. Ghose, A. Razdan, H. Saran, and R. Shorey, "Enhancing performance of asynchronous data traffic over the Bluetooth wireless ad-hoc network," in *Proceedings Twentieth Annual Joint Conference of the IEEE Computer and Communications Societies IEEE INFOCOM 2001*, vol. 1, Anchorage, AK, Apr. 2001, pp. 591–600.

[4] N. Johansson, U. Körner, and P. Johansson, "Performance evaluation of scheduling algorithms for Bluetooth," in *Proceedings of BC'99 IFIP TC 6 Fifth International Conference on Broadband Communications*, Hong Kong, Nov. 1999, pp. 139–150.

[5] M. Kalia, D. Bansal, and R. Shorey, "MAC scheduling and SAR policies for Blue-tooth: A master driven TDD pico-cellular wireless system," in *Proceedings Sixth IEEE International Workshop on Mobile Multimedia Communications (MOMUC'99)*, San Diego, CA, Nov. 1999, pp. 384–388.

[6] J.-B. Lapeyrie and T. Turletti, "FPQ: a fair and efficient polling algorithm with QoS support for Bluetooth piconet," in *Proceedings Twenty-Second Annual Joint Conference of the IEEE Computer and Communications Societies IEEE INFOCOM 2003*, vol. 2, New York, NY, Apr. 2003, pp. 1322–1332.

[7] Bluetooth SIG, *Specification of the Bluetooth System*, Version 1.1, Feb. 2001.

[8] ——, *Specification of the Bluetooth System – Core System Package [Host volume]*, Version 1.2, Nov. 2003, vol. 3.

[9] ——, *Specification of the Bluetooth System – Architecture & Terminology Overview*, Version 1.2, Nov. 2003, vol. 1.

[10] ——, *Specification of the Bluetooth System – Core System Package [Controller volume]*, Version 1.2, Nov. 2003, vol. 2.

[11] V. Jacobson, "Modified TCP congestion avoidance algorithm," note posted on end2end-interest mailing list, Apr. 1990, available at ftp://ftp.isi.edu/end2end/end2end-interest-1990.mail.

[12] M. Kalia, D. Bansal, and R. Shorey, "Data scheduling and SAR for Bluetooth MAC," in *Proceedings VTC2000-Spring IEEE 51st Vehicular Technology Conference*, vol. 2, Tokyo, Japan, May 2000, pp. 716–720.

[13] D. P. Bertsekas and R. Gallager, *Data Networks*, 2nd ed. Englewood Cliffs, NJ: Prentice-Hall, 1991.

[14] J. Padhye, V. Firoiu, D. F. Towsley, and J. F. Kurose, "Modeling TCP Reno performance: A simple model and its empirical validation," *ACM/IEEE Transactions on Networking*, vol. 8, no. 2, pp. 133–145, Apr. 2000.

[15] B. Sikdar, S. Kalyanaraman, and K. S. Vastola, "Analytical models for the latency and steady-state throughput of TCP Tahoe, Reno, and SACK," *ACM/IEEE Transactions on Networking*, vol. 11, no. 6, pp. 959–971, Nov. 2003.

[16] L. Cai, X. Shen, and J. W. Mark, "Delay analysis for AIMD flows in wireless/IP networks," in *Proceedings Globecom'03*, San Francisco, CA, Dec. 2003.

[17] H. Takagi, *Queueing Analysis*. Amsterdam, The Netherlands: North-Holland, 1991, vol. 1: Vacation and Priority Systems.

[18] J. Mišić, K. L. Chan, and V. B. Mišić, "Performance of Bluetooth piconets under E-limited scheduling," Department of Computer Science, University of Manitoba, Winnipeg, Manitoba, Canada, Tech. report TR 03/03, May 2003.

[19] *The Network Simulator ns-2*. Software and documentation available from http://www.isi.edu/nsnam/ns/, 2003.

[20] Bluehoc, *The Bluehoc Open-Source Bluetooth Simulator, version 3.0*. Software and documentation available from http://www-124.ibm.com/developerworks/opensource/bluehoc/, 2003.

In: Wireless LANs and Bluetooth
Editors: Yang Xiao and Yi Pan, pp. 221-240

ISBN: 1-59454-432-8
© 2005 Nova Science Publishers, Inc.

Chapter 11

SCHEDULING IN BLUETOOTH NETWORKS

Ji Jun, Xiao Hong

Information Engineering Department, Changchun Institute of Technology,
Tongzhi Street No. 80, Changchun City, Jilin Province, 130021 P.R. China.

Yang Xiao [*]

Department of Computer Science, The University of Memphis,
373 Dunn Hall Memphis, TN 38152 USA.

Rakshit Patel, Zhijun Lu

Computer Science Division, The University of Memphis,
Memphis, TN 38152 USA.

Abstract

In this chapter, we first introduce Bluetooth technology, and then we provide a comprehensive survey and classification on scheduling algorithms in Bluetooth networks.

Keywords: Bluetooth, Scheduling, Wireless Personal Area Networks

Introduction

Bluetooth is a new wireless technology for short-range wireless communication. It is named after a King of Denmark, Harald Bluetooth (ruled between 940 and 986), to celebrate part of the Scandinavian heritage. Bluetooth technology is originally designed as a wireless replacement for cables between electronics devices such as Personal Data Assistants (PDA's), wireless headphones, MP3 players, cell phones, cordless phones, audio/visual equipment, laptops, personal computers, printers, and other potential devices. Bluetooth is one kind of Wireless Personal Area Network (WPAN), with a range as a circle with radius of 10 meters. Low power, short range, low cost, and ad hoc fashion are goals of Bluetooth. The Bluetooth

---

[*] E-mail address: yangxiao@ieee.org

specification was released in 1998 by the Bluetooth Special Interest Group (SIG) as a joint effort between Ericsson, IBM, Intel, Nokia, and Toshiba. Later on, the IEEE 802.15 working group for WPAN has approved a standard, IEEE 802.15.1, derived from the Bluetooth Specification in 2002.

One key issue in Bluetooth networking is the scheduling algorithm in a piconet and between two piconets. The Bluetooth standard only proposes a Round Robin scheduling algorithm [1] but has been proved wastage of bandwidth. Efficient scheduling algorithms are therefore needed since the Bluetooth standard leaves these areas open. There are many researches on these issues [2-26]. In this chapter, we provide a survey and classification on scheduling algorithms in Bluetooth networks.

The rest of this chapter is organized as follows. In Section 2, we give an introduction on Bluetooth technology. In Section 3, various scheduling schemes are categorized. Section 4 and Section 5 introduce intra-piconet scheduling schemes and inter-piconet scheduling schemes, respectively. Finally, Section 6 concludes this chapter.

Bluetooth

Bluetooth specifications include several functionality models, shown in Fig. 1, such as the Physical layer (PHY), Baseband (BB), Link Manager (LM), logical link control adaptation protocol layer (L2CAP), the control layer, and the audio layer [1].

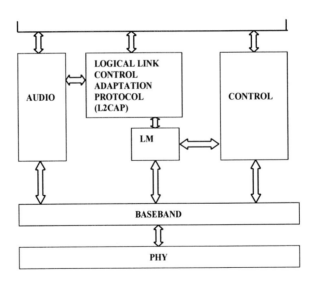

Fig. 1 The Bluetooth layer structure.

The PHY implements the physical links among the Bluetooth units, and operates in the 2.4 GHz unlicensed Industry, Science, and Medicine (ISM) band, which provides physical channel among the Bluetooth units with 79 radio frequency channels of 1 Mbps bit rate. Each channel is divided into 625us slots by Time Division Multiplexing (TDM) technique and has multiple units to transfer packets at same time. Each packet is transmitted in the frequency hop pattern with maximum frequency hopping rate of 1600 hops/s. The BB layer is built on the PHY layer to control the transport service of the packets, i.e., provides the packet transmission service upon the physical link. The LM layer is built on the BB layer and is responsible for the connection configuration and control, security, and power management. In other words, the LM performs the sep-up and management of physical links including setting the states of slave nodes, monitoring the status of the physical channel, guaranteeing the Quality of Service (QoS), and implanting the security capacities. The L2CAP layer is used to transmit and receive packets to/from higher level protocol and application, which implements the functions of protocol multiplexing, segmentation and reassembly (SAR), group management, and QoS. The control layer defines a command interface to the baseband controller, link manager, hardware status, and control registers. The MAC layer in OSI model includes a part of radio layer and baseband layer, and L2CAP.

A piconet is the smallest network unit specified in Bluetooth standard and consists of one master and up to seven active slaves. A piconet occurs in one frequency-hopping slotted channel and is controlled by the master unit. The master works at even-number slots and polls the slaves while the slave replies in odd-number slots. The transmission only happens between master and a slave. Interconnected multiple piconets form a scatternet, shown in Fig. 2, in which one unit is a member of two or more piconets.

The Physical Layer (PHY) - Radio Layer

The PHY layer receives a bitstream from the upper layer and transmits the stream via radio waves. Additionally, the PHY layer receives radio waves to form a bitstream to pass to the upper layer.

Each channel is divided into 625μs-slots using TDM, and each slot refers to radio hop frequency with maximum frequency hopping rate of 1600 hops/s. Each channel can only have one piconet which consists of one master and up to seven active slaves. Each slot is synchronized to the clock of the master. The master always polls the slaves with identification packets in even numbered slots while slaves send out data only when polled or immediately after polled by the master in odd numbered slots. The Bluetooth antenna has normal power which enables transmission range from 0m to 10m, and can be extended to 100m by increasing the power.

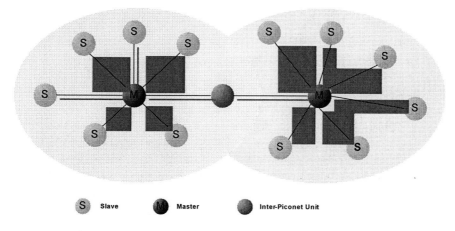

Fig. 2 Intra-piconet and Inter-piconet with Inter-piconet unit.

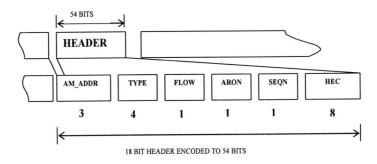

Fig. 3 The Header

The Baseband Layer

The Baseband layer has the following tasks: setting up the physical connections between the master and the slaves, transmitting different packets upon the physical channel, synchronizing the devices within one piconet based on the master, and managing different power saving states.

There are two type physical links among the Bluetooth devices, the Synchronous Connection-Oriented (SCO) Link and the Asynchronous Connection-Less (ACL) Link.

The SCO link is a point-to-point link between a master and a single slave in the piconet. The master maintains the link by using reserved slots at regular intervals and is considered to be circuit-switched. It supports time-critical data like voice and audio. The master can support up to three SCO links to a single slave or even to different slaves, while a single slave can support up to three SCO links from a single master, but only two SCO links if they originate from different masters in different piconets within a scatternet. The link is always established by the master, which sends an SCO setup message via the Link Manager Protocol (LMP). The message to setup a link contains timing parameters to specify reserved slots to inform the slave when to expect transmissions from the master as well as when the slave is permitted to transmit messages back to the master.

The ACL link is a link between a master and all slaves in the piconet. All packets and messages sent in an ACL link are read by all devices within the piconet (broadcast) only if the packets are not addressed to a specific device in the piconet. If there is no data to be sent, then no transmission takes place.

Each packet consumes one/three/five slots. A slot consists of a 68-72-bit access code, a 54-bit header, and 0-2745-bit payload. There are three types of Access Code: Channel Access Code (CAC), Device Access Code (DAC), and Inquiry Access Code (IAC). The Header, shown in Fig. 3, is composed of an Active Member Address (AM_ADDR), Type, Flow, Automatic Repeat Request (ARON), Sequential Numbering Scheme (SEQN), and Header Error Check (HEC). The AM_ADDR is a member address that distinguishes between active members on the piconet. Each device can identify which device is sending information. It is three bits in length, which means that there is a maximum of 8 participating active members on a piconet at any given point. An address with all 0's is reserved for the master of the piconet. The Type field is 4 bits in length and changes with the link type. Obviously, there are up to 16 different types of packets to be distinguished including two NULL and POLL packet types. Frequency Hop Synchronization (FHS) re-synchronizes the piconet and Data-Medium Rate (DM1) indicates a basic data packet. All four of these types are available to both SCO and ACL links, making a total of eight types. The ACL links have another two types: Data-High Rate (DH1) and AUX1. Four of them are available only to SCO links: High Quality Voice for 10, 20, and 30 bits of information (HV1, HV2, and HV3), and Data-Voice (DV). The last four are only available for ACL links when the packet size increases to three or to five slots in length, for medium and high data (DM3, DH3, DM5, and DH5), shown in Table 1 [1].

Table 1: Types

Type	Max. Payload (bytes)	FEC	CRC	Bandwidth Efficiency (bytes/slot)
DM1	17	2/3	Yes	17
DH1	27	No	Yes	27
DM3	121	2/3	Yes	40.3
DH3	183	No	Yes	61
DM5	224	2/3	Yes	44.8
DH5	339	No	Yes	67.8
AUX1	29	No	No	29

The Flow is a single bit to indicate that the transmitter buffer is full, and a return of FLOW=0 will stop transmission temporarily, until the buffer can once again resumes normal operation. The ARQN is a single bit used as an Acknowledgment key (ACK=1, NAK=0). The SEQN is a single bit used to order packet stream information sequentially for the purpose of filtering out retransmission due to a NAK by comparing the SEQN of later packets. The HEC is eight bits in length and is used to check for header integrity; if the header integrity has been compromised, the entire packet will be disregarded.

Link Manager Layer (LM) and Link Manager Protocol (LMP)

The LM is responsible for setting up the link, and ensuring security, basic control, and QoS information. The LMP packet has a higher priority than user data. The LM initiates the link and receives responses based on PIN's and Bluetooth Device Addresses (BD's). The shared key for all slaves is issued by the LMP, which also handles synchronization information and makes the switch between the master and a slave. The LMP handles hold mode, forced hold mode, and park mode. In the hold mode, the slave temporarily does not support ACL packets on the channel any more; capacity can be made free to do other things like scanning, paging, inquiring, or attending another piconet; and the slave unit enters a low-power sleep mode. In the park mode, a slave does not need to participate on the piconet channel, but still remains synchronized to the channel with a low-power mode and without AM_ADDR.

Logical Link Control Adaptation Protocol Layer (L2CAP)

The L2CAP provides connectionless data services to upper layers. It is responsible for multiplexing, providing segmentation and reassembly of data packets up to 64 Kilobits (Kb) in length from higher level protocols, which break packets down further for the L2CAP to process before transmissions. The goals of the L2CAP are simplicity and low overhead since Bluetooth-enabled devices have limited computational ability such as wireless headsets and wireless speakers. A typical L2CAP packet contains up to 65,567 individual bits, broken down into a 16-bit Length field, a 16-bit Channel ID, and a Payload. The Length field does not include itself or the header but only the size of the Payload. Channel ID identifies the channel of the destination endpoint.

The Control Layer

The control layer is referred to as a Host Controller Interface (HCI), and defines a physical interface for each externally-enabled Bluetooth device. The master's control layer is always the most active part, providing definitions for control functions for all Bluetooth implementations, whereas a slave's control layer is seldom in use.

Scheduling Scheme Classification

The master, the central controller, decides which slave can access the channel at a time. The scheduling algorithm that determines which slave is polled and in what order the slaves send or receive packets is very important for piconet efficiency. Therefore, the polling policy used by the master is the key point towards the efficiency of a piconet to manage the limited bandwidth.

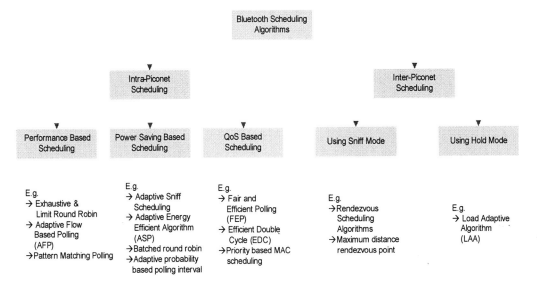

Fig. 4 Classification of Scheduling Algorithms

The Bluetooth specification has left the choice of scheduling policy open [1]. Only pure Round Robin (RR) algorithm is suggested in the Bluetooth specification [1] and is has been proved not to be efficient for bandwidth utilization [2].

Bluetooth scheduling algorithms can be classified into the intra-piconet scheduling and inter-piconet scheduling, shown in Fig.4. Intra-piconet scheduling is defined as the scheduling policy within one piconet, whereas inter-piconet scheduling is defined as the scheduling policy between two connected piconets, shown in Fig. 2.

We classify intra-piconet scheduling into performance-based scheduling [3, 6, 10-11, 14-15], power-saving-based scheduling [9, 22], and QoS-based scheduling [5, 13]. Inter-piconet scheduling [17-18] can be classified into schemes using the sniff mode, and schemes using the hold mode. Performance-based scheduling algorithms aim at improvement of the utilization of scarce bandwidth of piconet; QoS-based scheduling algorithms aim at satisfying the specific traffic demand for some real time applications such as video; power-based scheduling is mainly for the energy-saving purpose; inter-piconet scheduling considers the impact of piconet scheduling to the Scatternet when one unit of a piconet acts as the bridge to interconnect two piconets into one Scatternet, shown in Fig. 2.

Intra-piconet Scheduling

In this section we will present various intra-piconet scheduling algorithms which can enhance Bluetooth's performance. We will be presenting performance-based, power-saving-based, and QoS-based algorithms.

Performance-based Scheduling Algorithms

The performance-based scheduling algorithms aim to maximize the usage of bandwidth. In Bluetooth operation model, the master polls slaves, which response with/without data transmissions. The master controls the procedure of scheduling but doesn't know the status of a slave' queue, i.e., whether the slave queues have packets to transmit. A master's polling a slave with an empty queue wastes the bandwidth.

Round Robin Schemes

Capone et al. [8] study Pure Round Robin (PRR) scheduling suggested by Bluetooth specification and several different varied round robin scheduling algorithms described in the following subsections. Two approaches are used in [8]: exhaustive and partial exhaustive. The difference between the two schemes is whether it sends out all the packets in the queues of a master-slave queue one time or not.

Pure Round Robin (PRR)

PRR is originally suggested in Bluetooth specification. The master polls a slave in one time slot with a Poll packet or data packet. In the next time slot, the slave can send data packet to the master or send Null packet. In the next available slot, the master polls the next slave in a circular fashion. Therefore, each slave gets a chance to communicate one after another with the master. The scheme is not exhaustive, i.e., slaves are not given chance to send all the data queued up in their queue to be sent to the master but instead are given only single slot at a time to send data. The scheme is the simplest with less complexity among various round robin schemes.

Exhaustive Round Robin (ERR)

Based on the PRR, ERR is exhaustive and the master-slave pair will exhaust their queues before the control is switched to other pairs. In other words, the master and slave gets chance to send all the possible data to each other. This scheme is not like round robin where the slaves and the master had just single slot to send the data at a time. Instead, master polls a slave by sending poll packet or data packet and in the next slot the slave gets the chance to send data or reply with a null packet, the master keeps on polling the slave in every alternative slot until both master's and slave's queues are empty. However, this scheme may cause starvation for other slaves if one slave keeps having packets to transmit.

Exhaustive Pseudo-Cyclic Master Queue Length (EPM)

Based on the PRR, the cyclic order is redefined. At the beginning of the each cycle a dynamic cyclic order is defined and each pair is visited once before the cycle completes. In this scheme, instead of emptying the queues and then selecting the next slave in a round robin manner, the sequence of the slaves to select the next is decided based upon the queues at the master and slave. The master-slave pair having a larger queue length is kept on a higher level. i.e., they will be polled next.

Limited Round Robin (LRR)

In this scheme, the number of packets to be transmitted per cycle is limited to a fixed number. In the above schemes ERR and EPM, the queues at the master-slave pair are exhausted and then the master moves to the next slave. But, if the data flow is very much variable then it might happen that other slaves' queues get very large and this would be unfair to them. Therefore, in LRR, there is a limit parameter defined which works as the maximum allowed slots in a single cycle. This way can achieve fairness and good performance.

Limited and Weighted Round Robin Scheme (LWRR)

Based on the LRR, the scheme dynamically assigns a weight to each slave according to the observed queue status. The initial weight to each slave is Maximum Priority (MP), the lowest weigh is 1; when the slave has no packet to transmit at polling, its weight decreases 1. Only the slave with MP weight is allowed to transmit. The slave with weight 1 must wait for MP-1 cycles to get a permit to transmit.

Discussions

Capone et al. [8] compare the delay performance of these five schemes using the passive traffic model and active TCP connections. The results indicate that EPM based on the partial information of queue status' is not necessary comparing with ERR. PRR has a better performance that ERR when traffic load is high and worse performance when traffic load is lower. LRR can improve the performance of ERR at high traffic load. LWRR always does better that other schemes and close to the ERR but suffers the problem of channel capture [8].

Master-Slave Queue-State-Dependent Scheduling

Round Robin schemes result in slot wastage and un-fairness when there are reserved slots for voice traffic and variable sized data packets are used [16]. Bluetooth supports voice communication by SCO and data traffic by ACL. Voice traffic requires strictly timing to assure the voice quality, and voice traffic always uses the fixed slots with priority. In Bluetooth specification, data packet only can have one, three, and five slot length.

Kalia et al. [16] classify master-slave pairs into three classes based on the size of the Head-of-the-Line (HOL) packets at the master and slaves queues: 1) master-slave pair is 3-1, 1-3, 1-1 (wastage of 0%); 2) master-slave pair is 3-0, 0-3 (wastage of 25%); and 3) master-slave pair is 1-0, 0-1 (wastage of 50%), where master-slave pair 3-1 indicates that the pair has 3 HOL packets at the master queue and the one HOL packet at the slave queue. Based on the above classification, the following three scheduling algorithms are proposed.

- *HOL Priority Policy*: in this scheme, all the master-slave pairs with different priorities are visited in a weighted round robin manner. Class 1 is assigned the highest weight while class 3 is assigned the lowest weight.
- *HOL K-Fairness Policy (HOL KFP)*: This policy considers not only the fairness based on the HOL Priority Policy but also tries to ensure strict fairness. A fairness bound K is used to control the maximum allowed unfairness among any two master-slave pairs. Moreover, the policy maintains a counter for each pair of master-slave queue. The backlogged master-slave pairs are visited in Round Robin fashion and the pair belonging to class 1 is given high priority for the service. On the other hand, master-slave pair belonging to class 2 sacrifices its service for class 1. When a master-slave pair grasps its service from another pair, the counter of first pair will increment while the counter of sacrificed pair will decrement. When the difference between two pairs exceeds K, no sacrificed service happens to the pair which should get the service.
- *Wireless Adapted HOL-KFP*: HOL KFP-fairness policy doesn't count the channel errors. The policy extends HOL KFP by considering the wireless error factors which will hurt the fairness of HOL K-fairness policy. The scheduler will update the counter of master-slave pair which sacrifices its service due to the errors in the channel.

SAR and Scheduling-based on SAR

A data Segmentation and Reassembly (SAR) mechanism improves efficiency by supporting maximum transmission unit (MTU) size larger than the largest baseband packet. Overhead can be reduced by spreading the packets used by higher layer protocols over several baseband packets. Kalia et al. [16] propose two SAR policies based on the data traffic distribution pattern. The first policy is intelligent SAR which determines the size of data packet on the data arrival rate and categorizes the data traffic into three sets: high rates in both sides of the master-slave pair, high rate on one end and low rate on other end of the master-slave pair, and varied data rate at both ends of the master-slave pair. The data packet has a reserved bit to indicate the data rate. High rate data is segmented into large size packets while low rate data will be segmented into small size packets. Another policy is partial Reordering SAR (PRSAR) which reorders the second packet in both master and slave queues when it can't be transmit between two voice slots. The results in [16] show that the Master-Slave Queue-state-dependent Packet Scheduling Policy is better and the SAR and PRSAR can improve the performance with little overhead.

Das et al. [6] further investigate SAR scheduling algorithm based on the information of the size of the HOL packet at the master and slave queues. They study two policies for SAR:

- *SAR-BF (SAR –Best Fit)*: This algorithm tries to reduce the bandwidth wasted in the baseband packets. It uses a best-fit method to segment the higher layer packets. It tries segment the upper layer data packets into the baseband packet which as big as possible. For example, when the size of a coming upper layer packet is 556, the best fit 5-slot packet is 339; for best fit 3-slot packet is 183 and 1-slot is 27. According to this policy, the 556-byte packet will be segmented into one 5-slot packet, one 3-slot packet, and two 1-slot packets.

- *SAR-OSU (SAR Optimum Slot Utilization)*: This algorithm tries to decrease the transmission delay of baseband packets by reducing the queuing delay. This method segments the upper layer data packets into the minimum number of baseband packets. Thereby, data sent each time to a polled slave is maximized. For the same example of SAR-BF, the 556 byte packet will be segmented into two 5-slot packets.

The scheduling algorithms suggested by Das et al. [6] are based on the SAR policies as follows. The purpose of these scheduling algorithms is to address the problem of bandwidth wastage on polling the slave with low input rate. They propose several related scheduling algorithms as follows.

- *Queue Priority based on Flow Bit:* Baseband queues per-slave at the master and slave are maintained. They assign priorities to these queues based on the pending data in corresponding to L2CAP buffers. Flow bit present in the payload header field of the baseband packet is used to assign above mentioned priorities. Flow bit (*flow*) is set when the number of packets in the L2CAP buffer for a particular slave is larger than a specified *buf_thresh*.

- *Queue Stickiness:* To reduce the queue occupancy, it is proposed to transmit a number of baseband packets (*num_sticky*) successively for each queue having the *flow* parameter set.

- *Adaptive flow-based polling (AFP)*: Polling interval for each slave is dynamically adjusted based on their data arrival rate. The initial polling intervals during the master-slave setup are equal value. Each slave has one adaptive interval P which is changed with data rate indicated by the variable flow. If the slave replies with a null packet in response to the master's poll, its interval P will be doubled until pre-determined thresh hold is reached. If the flow value of the received packet by the master from a slave is 1, i.e., the slave's queue is longer than a pre-defined threshold, the slave adaptive interval P will be set to minimum value. Then the slave is polled more and thereby it gets more chance to send data.

- *Sticky*: In this policy, like the previous one it uses the flow bit which quantifies the traffic. If the slave queue size in terms of packets has more then a predefined threshold, the flow bit is set to 1; otherwise it is set 0. In the previous policy, the polling interval of the slave is increased if its queue has a queue size larger than the threshold. In Sticky, if the flow bit is 1 then the slave is allowed to send more than one packets at a time. The number of packets that can be transmitted at a time is quantified by the parameter *num_sticky*. If the flow bit is 0 then one packet is transmitted in Round-Robin fashion. The simulation results in [6] indicate that when *num_sticky* is 16, this policy gives best performance.

- *Sticky with AFP*: it is a combination of sticky algorithm and AFP. Here, when the *flow* bit is set, a maximum number of *num_sticky* packets in the queue is used for transmissions.

The results in [6] show that, with two-state Markov chain wireless channel model and TCP source, SAR-OSU has a better performance and the Sticky and AFP policies individually have the good performance when combining with SAR-OSU.

Pattern Matching Polling (PMP)

Bluetooth specification defines several different baseband packet types occupied in the channel of 1-slot, 3-slots, or 5-slots, respectively. Lin et al. [10] propose a PMP polling algorithm for the asymmetric traffic between masters and slaves. This scheme assumes that the ratio of traffic between the master and slave can be measured and estimated. A polling pattern is a sequence of Bluetooth packets of different type combinations (e.g., DH1/DH3/DH5/DM1/DM3/DM5) and they are exchanged by a master-slave pair that properly reflects the traffic ratio of pairs [10]. The asymmetric traffic is defined as the case that the average arrival rates in master-slave pairs are not same. Each side may have random busty traffic. The basic idea of PMP is to fill up the master-slave pair packets as more as possible, and the goal is to achieve the maximum bandwidth efficiency.

Power-Saving-Based Scheduling

Bluetooth specification defines four working modes for each device of Bluetooth piconet: active, sniff, hold and park. Keeping all slaves in a piconet awake wastes power because not all slaves have packets to transmit at all time. A slave in the active mode listens to the master all the time; if a packet transmitted from the master is not sent to the slave, the slave goes into the sleep state for the duration of the packet transmission. Only the slave receiving the packet needs to reply to the master.

In the sniff mode, the duty period of a slave can be changed. The master can only poll its slaves at specified time slots, and a slave only listens to the channel at the specified time slots but not all the time. The specified time is called sniff internal (T_{sniff}) and it can be $N_{Sniff\text{-}Attempt}$ number of time slots, called listening window. A slave is in the sleep state if it's not in the listening window to save energy. When the slave receives a packet during the $N_{Sniff\text{-}Attempt}$ slots, it keeps listening until $N_{Sniff\text{-}Timeout}$ slots occur or it uses up all $N_{Sniff\text{-}Attempt}$ slots.

In the hold mode, a slave sleeps during a predefined amount of hold mode time (holdTO) and then returns to the active mode. In the park mode, a slave stays in the sleep state until its master wakes it up. A slave in the park mode does not have an active address. One piconet has one master, up to seven slaves in the active mode, and up to 255 slaves in the park mode. The main difference between the hold mode and the park mode is that, in the hold mode, whenever the slave returns to the active state, it has to negotiate the next period of activity. On the other hand, the sniff intervals are negotiated by the master and a slave during the initial setup. Both the master and the salve know this pattern and may become active as the pattern. In the hold mode, a slave wastes time slots to decide the holdTO, and in the park mode, time slots are wasted during the procedure of parking and unparking. Therefore, the sniff mode at slaves is widely used in scheduling algorithms to optimize power consumption while increasing system throughput and reduce system delay. The hold and park modes are used when system's idle time is large.

Four Basic Power Saving Policies

Garg et al. [23] propose four basic power optimization policies by modifying two sniff mode parameters: T_{Sniff} and $N_{Sniff-Attempt}$ based on the buffers of Master-Slave Pairs (MSP).

- *Batched Round Robin (BRR)*: In BRR proposed in [23], each MSP is served for N_{brr} continuous slots in RR fashion. The main goal is to avoid the situation that occurs when buffers at the master and slaves become empty during an N_{brr} period. An average slot utilization parameter is maintained to monitor the buffer usage in each MSP. When the slot utilization of a slave is smaller than a threshold, T_{Sniff} interval for the slave is doubled and the MSP is served at a half polling rate; on the other hand, when the slot utilization of a slave is higher than the threshold, the MSP served the slots. This configuration is dynamically changed with the utilization of the monitored buffer usage. The policy limits at most of two possible sniff intervals, and it can decrease the power at slaves and increase throughput by minimizing the wastage of slots.

- *Variable Sniff Interval (VSI)*: The T_{Sniff} interval of different slaves is varied with the average slot utilization parameter in this policy proposed in [23]. The serving interval is never changed. When slot utilization is low, the MSP gets a higher T_{Sniff}, and vice-versa. The VSI policy defines the upper and lower bounds on the sniff intervals. The upper and lower bounds are dependent on the effective bandwidth available to an MSP. The T_{Sniff} of each slave is independent of others, and therefore, it is possible that some slots are empty or some slots are occupied with two or multiple slaves. In this policy, empty slots continue to serve the MSP. When one slot is used for more than one slave, these slaves run in RR.

- *Load-Based Service (LBS)*: In this policy, T_{Sniff} is kept as a constant and $N_{Siff-Attempt}$ is changed. All the MSPs are assigned continuous slots ($N_i \geq 1$, i is the i-th slave's address). Each MSP has an average slot utilization parameter which is initialized as 0.5. When the system finds that the slot utilization parameter of a MSP goes below a threshold, the system reduces its slot number by $N_k = N_k(1-\beta)$, where β is a constant. The policy adjusts βN_k slots among MSPs with high slot utilization. The system decreases the bandwidth to MSPs with lower slot utilization and increases the bandwidth to MSPs with high slot utilization because the number of slots allotted to a MSP is nearly in proportion to the utilization parameter.

- *Group Based Service (GBS)*: Slaves are divided into groups and both T_{Sniff} and $N_{Siff-Attempt1}$ are variable in this policy. The RR policy is used among the slave groups. Each group is allotted for a fixed number (N_{gbs}) of continuous slots. Therefore, $T_{Sniff} = N_{gbs} \times$ *(number of groups)*. In each group, active MSPs are served in RR. The policy maintains the slot utilization parameter for each MSP and keeps the each group only one MSP with high slot utilization. If a group has more than one MSP with high slot utilization, it is split into multiple groups and each new group only has one MSP with high slot utilization. If a group has all MSPs with low high slot utilization, these MSPs are distributed to other groups and the original group is removed. GBS dynamically changes the groups based on the slot utilization parameters of different MSPs to maximize the efficiency of bandwidth to keep the system on a low power state.

Adaptive Sniff Scheduling Scheme

Lin and Tseng [22] propose an adaptive approach to appropriately assign values to the sniff window size T_{Sniff} and the active window $N_{Siff-Attempt}$. The main goal is to dynamically adjust each slave's sniff parameters to the varying asymmetric traffic patterns among the master and slave so as to effectively schedule each slave's sniff period in the piconet and achieve power saving with the maximum utilization of the active windows.

In this approach, the master computes all parameters. For the salve k, let U_k be the utilization fraction of the assigned active window; let B_k be the backlog size; Assume that W_k is used to measure the current requirement: $W_k = \alpha U_k + (1-\alpha)B_k/B_{max}$, where B_{max} is the maximum buffer space and α is a constant ($0<\alpha<1$) to indicate the importance of U_k and B_k. The value of W_k is kept between a predefined lower bound and a predefined upper bound. If the value of W_k is beyond the bounds, the parameters of the slave k need to be changed. The expected slot occupancy S_k presents the expected ratio of the new $N_{Siff-Attempt1}/T_{Snif}$ and is determined by $S_k = (old\ N_{Siff-Attempt1}/\ old\ T_{Snif})\ W_k/\ \delta$, where δ is a positive constant between 0 and 1 to enlarge the expected ratio to tolerate certain level of inaccuracy. This scheduling approach can be used by multiple slaves simultaneously. Two scheduling policies are proposed in [23]: longest sniff interval first (LSIF) and shortest sniff interval first (SSIF). They suggest a two dimension matrix M as a research pool to present the time slots availability in a piconet under different scheduling schemes. These two policies are implemented by searching the resource pool matrix. Their simulation shows these scheduling policies are quite accurate and can dynamically adjust the scheduling decisions and also multiple slaves can work at same time.

Adaptive Probability-based Polling Interval (APPI)

Chakraborty et al. [24] present an idea to intelligently switch a piconet work mode between the active mode and the sniff mode by predicting inactivity based on the previous traffic arrival pattern using probability estimates. For a given piconet, the traffic distribution is estimated by recording a learning function H of observed inter-arrival times of data bursts. Only first data packet of a burst has been recorded and corresponded to the recorded and observed inter-arrival times of data bursts in the learning function, and other part of the burst are excluded. There are several independent functions such as the learning functionalities for the condition for sniffing, the method of deciding the polling interval, and the method of deciding the criterion of switching from the sniff mode to the active mode. A learning function H records the number of bursts and corresponding inter-arrival times. Switching system from the active mode to the sniff mode is dependent of inter-arrival time which is calculated when the system is in the active mode and a data burst ends. The parameter is determined by whether the probability of a coming data burst of sufficient length is greater or less than a threshold, which depends on QoS parameters.

In [24], two scheduling algorithms are proposed: Adaptive Probability based Polling Interval with Fixed Resolution (APPI-FR) and Adaptive Probability based Polling Interval with Adaptive Resolution (APPI-AR). In APPI-FR, when a slave is in the active mode, if the connection has no data to transmit and the condition of sniffing is met both on the master and the slave, the connection turns into the sniff mode; when the slave is in the sniff mode, if the criterion of switching from sniffing being checked by the master and slave is satisfied, the connection is switched into the active mode; otherwise, the slave is serviced and the master estimates the new poling interval and the connection is still put into the sniff mode.

In APPI-AR, the inter-arrival range has been divided into two zones by the expected probability of data arrival: data arrival zone with the higher probability and data arrival zone with the lower probability. The master or slave updates the learning algorithm function at the arrival of a data burst and also checks whether the expected probability of data arrival at a polling interval exceeds a prefixed threshold, which is a function of the total number of inter-arrival ranges. If this condition is satisfied, the inter-arrival ranges are divided by two intervals. To keep the number of inter-arrival constant, the system combines two adjacent inter-arrival ranges with the minimum sum of probability. The number of inter-arrivals is kept small and fixed, and when the data rate is high, higher resolution of the inter-arrival range is still achieved.

An Adaptive Energy-Efficient Polling Algorithm (ASP)

Perillo et al. [9] propose ASP for Bluetooth piconet in sensor networks, and it is designed to reduce power consumption when traffic patterns consist of short packets from constant bit rate applications such as sensor networks.

There are always a tradeoff between latency and energy-saving in a polling network. If the polling success rate is too high, there will be longer delays between polls; otherwise, if the polling success rate is too low, the slave will be polled too often, and then energy is wasted. In ASP, a pre-specified range of polling success rate is used to tradeoff the confliction. For the requirement of latency / power saving, the scheduler at the master learns the needed share of bandwidth for each slave based on observed polling success and failure. ASP need to change Bluetooth specification for an LMP (Link Message Protocol) message called the condition hold mode, which is similar to the hold mode except it contains three possible intervals for which the slave can enter the hold mode.

Unsuccessful poll and unwanted packet headers received by the slave that are not destined to them should be reduced. Unsuccessful poll refers to the situation when the master polls a salve and the slave replies back with the Null packet. Unwanted packet headers happen when the slaves are not being polled by the master but still the packets in the neighborhood are heard by the slaves which are not for them. Putting the slaves into temporary sleep or the hold mode can reduce unwanted packet headers.

ASP [9] puts the salves into the unconditional hold mode when they are not being polled. On the other hand, to avoid the unsuccessful polls, ASP uses an adaptive way to allocate bandwidth and poll slaves. The master maintains the target success range (ratio of the number of successful polls to the number of total polls) of each slave, and schedules the traffic in such a way that the success ratio always remains in this limit by increasing or decreasing the polling interval for the slave.

QoS-based Scheduling

Although Bluetooth specification defines a guaranteed service over SCO through fixed slots to provide real time voice traffic, there are still a lot of applications such as ftp, telnet, audio and video multimedia etc., with various QoS requirements which are not specified in the

Bluetooth Specification. This section discusses enhanced MAC scheduling algorithms to consider QoS.

A Priority-Based MAC Scheduling Scheme for QoS

Liu et al. [25] categorize the master-slave pairs into two classes: best-effort and real-time. The best effort service does not have QoS service, and the real-time service must meet the QoS requirements of the packets. The real-time class is assigned to a higher priority than the best-effort class. Each real-time connection assigns its own priority based on its delay requirement. The connections with same priorities get in the round-robin manner.

For the estimation of real-time traffic, denote each real time slave with S_i, its average bit rate with R_i, the maximum tolerable delay with D_i, the packet length with L_i, the token counter with C_i, and the token counter generation interval with $T_i = L_i/R_i$. The traffic of S_i increases C_i by 1 per T_i seconds. The priority of S_i is assigned according to D_i. The real time slaves are scheduled based on their priorities and tokens counters to meet the needs of delay and to avoid the frequent polling. For the best-effort slaves, the binary exponential backoff mechanism is used for best-effort slaves to control their polling times. Each best-off slave S_j has a poling window W_j and a polling interval I_j. W_j is initialized with 1 and increased by binary back-off mechanism while I_j is changed with W_j. The main aim is to process a real-time slave with a highest priority. If the master has any packet for S_i, it sends them to S_i and keeps polling S_i until it returns a NULL packet and then set $C_i=0$. Repeat the previous step for other real-time slaves from higher priority slaves to lower priority slaves. A slave without packets means its token counter is 0 and the master has no packet for it. After all the real-time slaves finish their packet transmissions, the best-effort slaves begin to be scheduled in a round robin manner. For best-effort slaves, if the master has no packets to S_j and S_j returns a NULL packet, W_j is doubled until reaching the maximum value W_{max}; otherwise W_j is set to 1. I_j is assigned the value of W_j. For each cycle, the each I_j of each slave is decreased by 1 until reaching 0. The slaves with $I_j = 0$ can get the service.

FEP: a Fair and Efficient Poling Algorithm with QoS Support

FEP [26] considers both the fairness and efficiency of the asymmetric traffic. The main goal of this scheme is to reduce too many POLL and NULL packets and giving more chances to packets waiting in queues. A packet from application layer is called an AP packet. The multiple AP packets come at same time will cause long transmission time. Therefore, the basic idea is to consequently handle AP packets, i.e., to complete an AP packet before another AP packet comes rather than queuing them up and sending at a time since it take more transmission time.

Inter-piconet Scheduling

In the previous sections, we describe various scheduling schemes within a single piconet. Bluetooth standard has left scheduling algorithms for scatternets open [1]. In this section, we describe various scheduling schemes proposed for two or more piconets forming a scatternet. We call it Inter-piconet scheduling. The bridge node connecting two or more piconets should be able to co-ordinate its presence in all of piconets. Scheduling of these bridge nodes is achieved by exploiting Bluetooth's power saving modes, e.g., the sniff and the hold mode.

Most of the schemes use the sniff mode to achieve this since the sniff mode gives better performance when the bridge mode is a member of multiple piconets. On the other hand, in the hold mode, whenever a bridge node changes piconet, it needs to schedule its next presence and it requires additional two cycles to negotiate this.

Inter-piconet Scheduling Using Sniff Mode

In this section we will present Inter-piconet scheduling algorithms that use Bluetooth's sniff mode.

Rendezvous Point Inter-piconet Scheduling Algorithms

Per Joansson et al. [4] present a family of algorithms referred to as rendezvous point algorithms. The slot at which the master and slave have decided to meet is referred to as a rendezvous point. In other words, the slot at which the bridge node has agreed to listen to the master and the master has agreed to address packet to this bridge node. Two major issues addressed by the rendezvous point inter-piconet algorithm are Rendezvous Point (RP) and the Rendezvous Window (RW).

For the RP, it is critical to determine the strictness of the commitment from the master and the bridge node. It may happen that either the master or the bridge node does not show up at the rendezvous point. Furthermore, the distribution of the RPs may be periodic, decided when they meet, or spread out in a pseudo-random fashion.

For the RW, the issue is to determine how much data will be exchanged given that the master and the bridge node are both present at the RP. In the case of a strict algorithm, both the master and the bridge node should be present and transfer data in each slot. Whereas, in a loose algorithm, the master and the bridge node may or may not be present and may not transfer any data. Therefore, the achieved throughput for the pair will depend on the duration of the RWs.

Based on the strictness of the above issues, following algorithms are proposed in [4].

- *Honoring-Periodic Static-Window (HPSW):* In this type, the master and the bridge node always honors the RPs, which occur periodically. The size of the RW is static and remains the same during the connection.

- *Honoring-Periodic Dynamic-Window (HPDW):* This algorithm is similar to the previous one such that the master and the bridge node always honor RPs, which are distributed periodically. However, the RW is dynamically changed based on traffic condition.

- *Honoring-Random Static-Window (HRSW):* In this scheme, the RPs are always honored by the master and the bridge node. Unlike the previous schemes, the RPs are spread in a pseudo-random sequence known to both the master and the bridge node. The size of RW is not fixed, and it may limit the number of piconets in which the bridge node can take part in.

- *Master-Honoring Dynamic-Window (MHDW):* The master always honors the RP, but the bridge node may not to give a priority to another piconet. The RPs may be periodic or in a pseudo-random manner known to both the master and the bridge node. The RW size is not fixed and may be changed in order to adapt to traffic/topology.

Results in [4] show that HPSW, HPDW, and HRSW usually can handle better traffic delay guarantees but are less adaptive to traffic changes. On the other hand, MHDW has less delay guarantees but can be adapted to traffic conditions easily.

Maximum Distance Rendezvous Scheduling

The basic idea of Johnsson et al. [27] is that the RPs should be as far from each other as possible. In the proposed Maximum Distance Rendezvous Point (MDRP), the master in a piconet considers the RPs of all the bridge nodes within its piconet. For a new rendezvous point with a bridge node, the master calculates the maximum allowable distance and then put it in the middle slot of the largest interval between successive rendezvous points. These rendezvous points are then periodically repeated in the next super-frame which is implemented by using the sniff mode of the bridge node. MDRP considers all bridge nodes simultaneously within a single piconet.

Randomized Rendezvous Scheduling for Scatternet

In [21], the connection of multiple piconets to form a scatternet is treated as a check-point rendezvous problem. The bridge node schedules the rendezvous for different piconets at different times. Racz et al. [21] propose a scheduling algorithm called pseudo random coordinated scatternet scheduling (PCSS) to schedule these rendezvous events. A rendezvous event is dependent on the master's clock and the slave's device address. The PCSS algorithm monitors the utilization of the piconet in a coarse-grain manner and adapts the inter-rendezvous time period according to the change of the utilization.

Locally Coordinated Scheduling in Scatternets

Tan and Guttag [26] propose an Locally Coordinated Scheduling algorithm (LCS), which schedules the rendezvous events in bridge nodes in a scatternet. The duration and the interval between communication events are dynamically adjusted based on the queue size and the past history of transmissions such that the duration is large enough to exchange all backlogged data. Furthermore, for responding to varying traffic quickly to save resources, LCS computes the start time of the next meeting based on whether the data rate observed is increasing, decreasing or stable. LCS groups these traffics with same characteristics together to reduce the wastage of bandwidth of nodes and end-to-end latency. In order to make as more as parallel communication as possible to increase system throughput, LCS aligns all rendezvous events at various parts of the scatternet in a hierarchical structure. For saving energy, LCS also can reduce the amount of time a node spends transmitting packets while the receiver is not ready.

Inter-piconet Scheduling Using Hold Mode

Liron Har-Shai et al. [17] present an Inter-Piconet Scheduling algorithm using the hold mode for small scatternets. The scheduling algorithm in large scale scatternets can be based on Bluetooth's sniff mode which provides recurring rendezvous points. In small scale scatternets, it is feasible that whenever a bridge node leaves a piconet, it can schedule its next rendezvous point instead of using periodic schedules. Load Adaptive Scheduling Algorithm (LAA) is proposed in [17], in which, when the bridge node switches to the other piconet, it enters the hold mode in the first piconet and sets the hold time-out to the value of the Time Commitment (TC). The master will poll the bridge every few slots based on its polling scheme after the TC expires. The bridge node will get higher priority after returns back to the piconet. To determine the time when the bridge node should switch the piconets, the algorithm uses the following few parameters. Maximum Queue Size (MQS) is used to decide when to switch piconets. If the queue size is bigger than the pre-determined MQS, the bridge node should switch the piconets. TC is a parameter used to inform the master of the current piconet before the bridge node leaves for another one indicating the minimum amount of time it will spend in the other piconet. Predictability factor (β) is used to calculate TC based on the queue size at other end. Max Time-Share (MTS) is used as a threshold of the maximum amount of time that can be spent by the bridge node in one piconet to ensure the fairness. If the time in piconet A > MTS or TC expired and the queue size to piconet B > MQS, we set TC = min (β * queue size to piconet B, MTS).

Conclusions

In this chapter, we introduced Bluetooth technology, classified scheduling algorithms in Bluetooth networks, and introduced some example algorithms. Scheduling algorithms are classified into intra-piconet scheduling and inter-piconet scheduling. In each of the above scheduling classes, scheduling algorithms are further classified into several categories based on considering different aspects, such as performance, power-saving, or QoS.

Another very-related aspect is routing in inter-connected piconets, which is not covered in this chapter.

References

[1] IEEE Standard 802.15.1 – Wireless Medium Access Control (MAC) and Physical Layer (PHY) Specifications for Wireless Personal Area Networks (WPANs), *IEEE*, 2002.

[2] R. Bruno, M. Conti, and E.Gregori, "Bluetooth Architecture, Protocols and Scheduling Algorithm," *Cluster Computing* 5, 2002, pp. 117-131.

[3] R. Bruno, M. Conti, and E.Gregori, "Wireless Access to Internet via Bluetooth: Performance Evaluation of the EDC Scheduling Algorithm," *Proc. of the First Workshop on Wireless Mobile Internet*, 2001.

[4] P. Johansson, M. Kazantzidis, R. Kapoor, and M. Gerla, "Bluetooth: An Enabler for Personal Area Networking," *IEEE Network*, pp. 28-37, September / October 2001.

[5] J. Lapeyrie and T. Turletti, "FPQ: a Fair and Efficient Polling Algorithm with QoS Support for Bluetooth Piconet," *Proc. of IEEE INFOCOM* 2003.

[6] Das, A. Ghose, A. Razdan, H. Saran and R. Shorey, "Enhancing Performance of Asynchronous Data Traffic over the Bluetooth Wireless Ad-hoc Network," *Proc. of IEEE INFOCOM*, 2001.

[7] Y. Kwok, "Time-Domain, Frequency-Domain, and Network Level Resource Management Schemes in Bluetooth Networks," *Resource Management in Wireless Network 2004*, Kluwer Academic Publishers.

[8] Capone, M. Gerla, and R. Kapoor, "Efficient Polling Schemes for Bluetooth Picocells," *Proc. of ICC 2001*, Vol. 7, pp. 1990-1994.

[9] M. Perillo and W. Heinzelman, "ASP: An Adaptive Energy-Efficient Poling Algorithm for Bluetooth Piconets," *Proc. of the 36th Hawaii International Conference on System Sciences (HICSS'03).*

[10] T. Lin, Y. Tseng and Y. Lu, "An Efficient Link Polling Policy by Pattern Matching for Bluetooth Piconets," *Proc. of the 36th International Conference on System Science (HICSS'03)*, 2003.

[11] R. A. Yaiz and G. Heijenk, "Polling Best Effort Traffic in Bluetooth," *Wireless Personal Communications* **23**, pp. 195-206, 2002.

[12] E. Callaway, P. Gorday, L. Hester, J. Gutierrez, M. Naeve, B. heile, and V. Bahl, "Home Networking with 802.15.4: A Developing Standard for Low-Rate Wireless Personal Area Networks," *IEEE Communication Magazine*, August 2002.

[13] J. Xue, and T. Todd, "Basestation Collaboration in Bluetooth voice networks," *Computer Networks* **41**, pp. 289-301, 2003.

[14] J. Misic and V. B. Misic, "Bridge of Bluetooth Country: Topologies, Scheduling, and Performance," *IEEE Journal on Selected Areas in Communications*, vol. 21, no. 2, pp. 240-258, Feb. 2003.

[15] J. Misic and V. B. Misic, "Modeling Bluetooth piconet performance," *IEEE Communication letter*, vol. 7, pp. 18-20, 2003.

[16] M. Kalia, D. Bansal, and R. Shorey, "MAC scheduling and SAR policies for Bluetooth: a master driven TDD poco-cellular wireless system," *IEEE International Workshop on Mobile Multimedia Communications*, 1999.

[17] L. Har-Shai, R. Kofman, G. Zussman, and A. Segall, "Inter-Piconet Scheduling in Bluetooth Scatternets," *Proc. of OPNTEWORK* 2002.

[18] Y. Liu, M. Lee, and T. Saadawi, "A Bluetooth Scatternet-Route Structure for Multihop Ad Hoc Networks," *IEEE Journal On Selected Areas in Communications*, vol. 21, No. 2, Feb. 2003.

[19] P. Johansson, R. Kapoor, M. Kazantzidis, and M. Gerla, "Rendezvous Scheduling in Bluetooth Scatternet," *Proc. of ICC 2002*, vol. 1, pp. 318-324, May 2002.

[20] S. Deb, M. Kapoor, and A. Sarkar, "Error Avoidance in Wireless Networks Using Link State History," *Proc. of INFOCOM 2001*, vol. 21, pp. 786-795, Apr. 2001.

[21] Racz, G. Miklos, F. Kubinszky, and A. Valko, "A Pseudo Random Coordinated Scheduling Algorithm for Bluetooth Scatternets," *Proc. of MobilHoc 2001*, pp. 193-203.

[22] T.-Y. Lin and Y.-C. Tseng, "An Adaptive Sniff Scheduling Scheme for Power Saving in Bluetooth", *IEEE Wireless Communications*, Vol. 9, No. 6, Dec. 2002, pp. 92-103.

[23] S. Garg, M. Kalia, and R. Shorey, "MAC scheduling Policies for Power Optimization in Bluetooth: A Master Driven TDD Wireless System," *IEEE Vehicular Technology Conference*, 2000.

[24] Chakrabory, A. Kashyap, A. Kumar, A. Rastogi, H. Saran, and R. Shorey, "MAC Scheduling Policies with Reduced Power Consumption and Bounded Packet Delays for Centrally Controlled TDD Wireless Networks," *IEEE international Conference on Communication*, 2001.

[25] Y. Liu, Q. Zhang, and W. Zhu, "A Priority-Based MAC Scheduling Algorithm for Enhancing QoS Support in Bluetooth Piconet", invited paper in *ICCCAS'02*, 2002.

[26] G. Tan and J. Guttag, "A Locally Coordinated Scatternet Scheduling Algorithm," *Proc. of IEEE LCN 2002*, pp. 293-303, Nov. 2002.

In: Wireless LANs and Bluetooth
Editors: Yang Xiao and Yi Pan, pp. 241-270

ISBN 1-59454-432-8
©2005 Nova Science Publishers, Inc.

Chapter 12

SCATTERNET FORMATION AND SELF-ROUTING IN BLUETOOTH NETWORKS

*Yu Wang**
Department of Computer Science,
University of North Carolina at Charlotte
Wen-Zhan Song[†] *and Xiang-Yang Li*
Department of Computer Science,
Illinois Institute of Technology

Abstract

In this chapter, we first summarize the criteria of scatternet design for Bluetooth networks, and review different scatternet formation algorithms for both single-hop and multi-hop networks. Then, we survey Bluetooth routing algorithms and review several scatternet topologies which have self-routing properties.

1 Introduction

Bluetooth [12] is a promising new wireless technology, which enables portable devices to form short-range wireless ad hoc networks based on a frequency hopping physical layer. Bluetooth ad-hoc networking presents some technical challenges, such as scheduling, network forming and routing. User mobility poses additional challenges for connection rerouting and QoS services. It has been widely predicted that Bluetooth will be a major technology for short range wireless networks and wireless personal area networks. This chapter deals with the problem of building ad hoc networks using Bluetooth technology.

According to the Bluetooth standard, when two Bluetooth devices come into each other's communication range, one of them assumes the role of *master* of the communication and the other becomes the *slave*. This simple one hop network is called a *piconet*,

---

*E-mail address: ywang32@uncc.edu
[†]E-mail address: songwen@iit.edu, xli@cs.iit.edu

and may include more slaves. The network topology resulted by the connection of several piconets is called a *scatternet* (as shown in Figure 1). There is no limit on the maximum number of slaves connected to one master, although the number of active slaves at one time cannot exceed seven. If a master node has more than seven slaves, some slaves must be parked. To communicate with a parked slave, a master has to *unpark* it, thus possibly parking another active slave instead. The standard also allows multiple roles for the same device. A node can be the master in one piconet and a slave in other piconets (as node a in Figure 1, which is the master of piconet I and a slave of piconet II) or be slaves in multiple piconets (as nodes b and c in Figure 1). A node with multiple roles acts as *bridge* or *gateway* between the piconets to which it belongs. However, one node can be active only in one piconet. To operate as a member of another piconet, a node has to switch to the hopping frequency sequence of the other piconet. Since each switch causes delay (e.g., scheduling and synchronization time), an efficient scatternet formation protocol can be the one that minimizes the roles assigned to the nodes, without losing network connectivity.

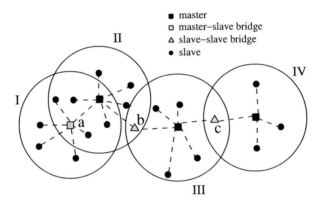

Figure 1: Scatternet formed by 4 piconets.

While several solutions and commercial products have been introduced for Bluetooth communication, the Bluetooth specification does not indicate any method for scatternet formation. The problem of scatternet formation has not been dealt with until very recently. The solutions proposed in the literature can be divided into single-hop and multi-hop solutions. Several criteria could be set as the objectives in forming scatternet. First of all, the formatted scatternets should keep the network connectivity, i.e., the scatternets are connected if the original communication graph is connected. Secondly, the protocol should create degree limited scatternets, to avoid parking any slave node. Thirdly, the number of piconets should be minimized to reduce the inter-piconet scheduling and communication cost. Fourthly, the formation and maintenance of scatternet should have small communication overhead. Fifthly, the diameter of the scatternet should be small, i.e., the maximum number of hops between any two devices must be small to provide faster routing. Sixthly, the scatternet formation may enable efficient self-routing algorithms in the scatternets. In this chapter, we survey the solutions for scatternet formation and self-routing for both single-hop and multi-hop ad hoc networks.

The rest of this chapter is organized as follows. Section 2 discusses a closely related problem of scatternet formation: *neighbor discovery* in Bluetooth networks. Section 3 surveys solutions that for generating scatternets for single-hop and multihop networks. Section 4 describes some self-routing methods for several proposed scatternets. Finally, we conclude our chapter in Section 5.

2   Neighbor Discovery

Previous literature on scatternet formation assumed that devices are not able to communicate unless they have previously discovered each other by synchronizing their frequency hopping patterns. Thus, even if all nodes are within direct communication range of each other, only those nodes, which are synchronized with the transmitter, can hear the transmission. Synchronizing the frequency hopping patterns is apparently a time consuming and pseudo-random process [59]. Most of the scatternet formation algorithms have *device discovery* procedure to learn about devices in its neighborhood. The device discovery procedure is also called *inquiry procedure* in Bluetooth specifications.

Bluetooth devices use the inquiry procedure to discover nearby devices, or to be discovered by devices in their locality. The inquiry procedure is asymmetrical. The inquiry procedure uses a special physical channel *inquiry scan channel* for the inquiry requests and responses. A Bluetooth device that tries to find other nearby devices is known as an *inquiring device* and actively sends inquiry requests. It iterates (hops) through all possible inquiry scan channel frequencies in a pseudo-random fashion, sending an inquiry request on each frequency and listening for any response. Bluetooth devices that are available to be found are known as *discoverable devices* and listen for these inquiry requests on their inquiry scan channel and send responses to those requests.

In previous methods [59, 9, 18, 60], the device discovery is performed as follows. Each device alternates between *inquiry* mode (as the inquiring device) and *inquiry scan* mode (as the discoverable device), remaining in each mode for a time selected randomly and uniformly in a predefined time range. Inquiry nodes select a repeated pattern of 32 frequencies in inquiry scan channel and send inquiry request on selected frequency. Inquiry scan nodes also select a frequency at random in each frequency of the the inquiry scan channel and listen to the requests. When two devices in opposite inquiry modes handshake (frequency-matching), they set up a temporary piconet that lasts only the time necessary to exchange their ID and other information necessary for the scatternet formation. Bohman *et al.* [13] conducted real-world measurements and simulations, derived the optimal parameters for symmetric ad hoc neighbor discovery.

Recently, several methods have been proposed to improve the Bluetooth device discovery procedure [28, 70, 16, 69, 34, 50, 61, 58]. Ferraguto *et al.* [28] let each device perform the device discovery protocol until it is connected with c neighbors, where c is a constant between 5 and 7. Their experiments show that the resulting graph is connected with high probability if the original communication graph is connected. Welsh *et al.* [69] suggested three possible changes to the Bluetooth specification: eliminating or decreasing the random backoff delay in INQUIRY SCAN, using a single frequency train instead of two in INQUIRY, and a combination of the two. Their experiments show that these methods can improve the connection setup time up to 75% without deteriorating the overall system performance. A hardware empirical testbed [50] is developed to verify these methods; the result suggests that a single train with no backoff has the best performance. Jiang *et al.* [34] also proposed three methods to speed up the device discovery: half inquiry interval (HII), dual inquiry scan (DIS), and combination of HII and DIS. The result shows a reduction of average frequency-matching time from 23.55 seconds to 11.38 seconds. Siegemund and Rohs [61] pointed out that the scalability of Bluetooth inquiry procedure is not sufficient if many devices are present. As a result of this observation, an adaptive protocol for cooperative device discovery is proposed to allow devices to exchange their knowledge of nearby devices, such as addresses and clocks, to reduce energy consumption and improve scalability for environments with many devices. Busboom *et al.* [70] and Woodings *et al.* [16] suggested to use auxiliary devices, such as IrDA interfaces or RFID transponders, to facilitate connection setup. Recently, Ronai and Kail [58] proposed a simple neighbor discovery (SND) procedure instead of Bluetooth inquiry procedure for Bluetooth, which is suited to systems where peer nodes are communicating.

3   Bluetooth Scatternet Formation

Given n nodes currently distributed in the network, Bluetooth scatternet formation algorithms group the nodes into piconets and join the piconets into a connected scatternet. After the neighbor discovery, the Bluetooth devices know the information of its neighbors in the communication graph. Here, the communication graph is a graph in which there is a link between any two devices who are in each other's transmission ranges. If we assume that all devices have the same transmission ranges, the communication graph is modelled by a *unit disk graph* in which there is a link between two nodes whose Euclidean distance is less than or equal to one. Then the problem of scatternet formation becomes to construct a connected subgraph of the unit disk graph and to select piconets (including assigning master and slave roles to nodes in each piconet) so that the resulting scatternet has some desirable properties.

3.1   Criteria of Scatternet Design

There are various desirable properties [64, 8, 52] for scatternets which have been used by different scatternet formation algorithms. We summarize the criteria of scatternet design as follows:

- **Guarantee of Connectivity.** If the communication graph from device discovery phase is connected, the scatternet formed by scatternet formation algorithm should also be connected. Connectivity is the most basic feature of the network topology, it guarantees that there exist at least one path from one device to any other devices.

- **Single Master Role.** Master node is belong to exactly one piconet, there is no master-master bridge. This is a requirement in the Bluetooth specifications.

- **Minimal Number of Roles.** The standard allows multiple roles for the same device, but one node can be active only in one piconet. To operate as a member of another piconet, a node has to switch its hopping frequency. The switch operation causes delays and big overheads. So an efficient scatternet formation algorithm may minimize the number of roles assigned to each node. Some algorithms even only allow bridges connect to at most two piconets.

- **Minimal Number of Piconets.** The number of piconets (i.e., the number of nodes with master role) should be minimized to provide faster routing and keep maintenance overhead small. Notice that the worse case we can have all nodes as masters of their neighbors.

- **Limited Piconet Size.** Though each piconet can have more than eight devices, only eight of them can be active as one master and seven slaves in the same time, other devices are forced to be parked. In order to communicate with all nodes, the master node need to park and unpark its slaves. This will significantly reduce the bandwidth and throughput of the network. Therefore, the size of piconet is expected to be limited by eight, so that the nodes can communicate with each other without parking and unparking operations. In other words, we hope the scatternet have node degree bounded by eight.

- **Minimal Number of Master-Slave Bridge.** When a device serves as a master-slave bridges (as node a in Figure 1) between two piconets, if it acts as the slave in one piconet, all the communication in the other piconet (where it serves as the master) will be "frozen". This reduces the throughput of the network. Therefore, comparing to master-slave bridges, slave-slave bridges (as nodes b and c in Figure 1) are to be preferred by scatternet formation.

- **Minimal Scatternet Diameter.** The diameter of the resulting scatternet is the number of hops of the longest path between any two devices in the networks. If the diameter is bounded by $f(n)$, then we can find a route with at most $f(n)$ hops for every pair of devices. For example, the diameter of dBBlue [62] is bounded by $O(\log n)$, which means the length of route is at most $O(\log n)$ for any pair of source and target.

- **Efficient Routing.** Several proposed scatternet formation algorithms [62, 65] also enable efficient self-routing in which device does not need to maintain routing table. Some routing protocols [14, 37] ask the topology be planar so that they can guarantee the delivery, then planar scatternets are constructed in some scatternet formation algorithms [67, 41]. In addition, the scatternet should have multiple routes between any pairs of devices to keep the routing robustness.

- **Easy To Formate, Update.** Due to the limited resources and high dynamics (e.g. node leaving, node joining or node moving) of the wireless nodes, it is preferred that the scatternet can be constructed and maintained in a distributed (or even localized) manner. Here, in localized scatternet formation, each node makes formation decisions solely based on the local information from its neighbors. When nodes move, appear or disappear from the network, the scatternet should be updated easily by scatternet maintenance (or self-healing) protocols.

- **Resource-based Master Selection.** Notice that a master need to handle and operate all the communication with its slaves in the piconet. So it will cost more resources in master node than in slave nodes. Therefore, scatternet formation algorithm may consider the available resources in each node when selecting the master node.

- **QoS: Delay, Throughput and Capacity.** Many algorithms [49, 48, 45, 2] also consider the QoS criteria during the scatternet formation. For example, given the traffic matrix of the network, find the scatternet that can minimize the average packet delay or maximize the network capacity.

Some of these properties are contradictive and hard to achieve together, but an efficient scatternet formation protocol can achieve most of them or at least several of them. The solutions proposed in literature can be divided into single-hop and multi-hop solutions.

3.2 Scatternet Formation Algorithms for Single-hop Networks

In a single-hop ad hoc network, all wireless devices are in the radio vicinity of each other, e.g., electronic devices in a house, or laptops in a conference room. A single-hop network can be modeled by a complete graph. In this subsection, we review several scatternet formation algorithms for single-hop networks.

3.2.1 Central Decision Methods

Salonidis *et al.* [59] proposed a topology construction algorithm based on leader election, called *Bluetooth Topology Construction Protocol* (BTCP). It first collects neighborhood information using an inquiry procedure, where senders search for receivers on randomly chosen frequencies, and the detected receivers reply after random backoff delay. Leader is elected in the first process, one for each connected component. In the second phase, leader then collects the information about the whole network, decides the roles for each node, and distributes back the roles to all nodes. In other words, basically, it is a centralized approach, and the decision is made by a central super node. Thus, the solution is not scalable (for dynamic environments where devices can join and leave after the scatternet is formed), and not localized, the time complexity is large. Moreover, how to assign the roles is not elaborated in their paper. They also assume up to 36 nodes in the network.

3.2.2 Tree Based Methods

Law, Mehta and Siu [39] described an randomized and distributed algorithm that creates connected degree bounded scatternet in single-hop networks. Every node starts out as a leader. Each leaser flips a coin to see whether it goes into *scan* or *seek* mode. When two leaders are connected, one must *retire* and the components will be merged. The authors gave five cases to handle the merge. The final structure is a tree like scatternet, which limits efficiency and robustness. They proved that the algorithm achieves O(log n) time complexity and O(n) message complexity. The scatternets formed by their protocol have the following properties: (1) any device is a member of at most two piconets, and (2) the number of piconets is close to be optimal. They validated the theoretical results by simulations, which also show that the scatternets formed have O(log n) diameter.

Tan *et al.* [66] proposed a distributed Tree Scatternet Formation (TSF) protocol for single-hop networks, which is similar with the multi-hop methods by Zaruba *et al.* [72]. TSF connects nodes in a tree structure that simplifies packet routing and scheduling. At any point in time, the TSF-generated scatternet is a forest consisting of connected tree components. Every root node in one component elects a single coordinator responsible for discovering other tree scatternets. The coordinator is preferred to be leaf nodes, since leaf nodes are not communication bottlenecks and have more spare capacity for discovering neighboring devices. TSF allows incrementally building a tree topology, nodes to arrive and leave at arbitrary times, and healing partitions when they occur. The extensive simulation results indicated relatively short scatternet formation latency. However, TSF is not designed to minimize the number of piconets. The simulation results suggested that each master usually has fewer than 3 slaves.

Sun, Chang and Lai [65] described a self-routing topology for single-hop Bluetooth networks where the routing overhead is kept to a minimum. Nodes are organized and maintained in a search tree structure, with Bluetooth ID's as keys (these keys are also used for routing). It requires only fix-sized message header and no routing table at each node regardless of the size of the scatternet. These properties make the solution scalable to deal with networks of large sizes. It relies on a sophisticated scatternet merge procedure with significant communication overhead for creation and maintenance.

Notice that the tree topology suffers from a major drawback: the root is a communication bottleneck as it will be overloaded by communications between the different parts of the tree. Figure 2(a) illustrates a BlueTree formed by four piconets, where the leaves are pure slaves, the root is a master, and other nodes are master-slave bridges.

3.2.3 Ring Based Methods

Bluerings as scatternets are proposed are proposed by Foo and Chua [29] and Lin *et al.* [43]. Ring structure for Bluetooth has simplicity, easy creation and easy routing as advantage, but it suffers large diameter (i.e., the maximum number of hops between any two devices can be as bad as $O(n/2)$) and large number of piconets. In the ring structure proposed by Foo and Chua [29], each device acts as a master-slave bridge to connect itself to the two neighbors

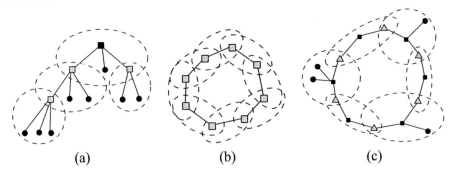

Figure 2: Different Scatternets: (a) BlueTree; (b) BlueRing with master-slave bridges; (c) BlueRing with slave-slave bridges.

in the ring. See Figure 2(b) for an illustration. However, Lin *et al.* [43] used slave-slave bridges and masters to form the ring, as in Figure 2(c). Lin *et al.* [43] also addressed in detail the formation, routing and topology maintenance for the ring structure. Due to the self-routing and easy to maintain, ring structure is good for small-size or median-size scatternets.

3.2.4 Other Well-known Structures Based Methods

Barriere, Fraigniaud, Narajanan, and Opatrny [3] described a connected degree limited and distributed scatternet formation solution based on projective geometry for single-hop networks. They assume that only slave nodes can act as bridges, in other words there are only slave-slave bridges. Figure 3(a) illustrates an example of the scatternet $SCT(54, 8, 1)$ based on projective geometry with 54 nodes. They described procedures for adding and deleting nodes from the networks and claimed that it uses $O(\log^4 n \log^4 \log n)$ messages and $O(\log^2 n \log^2 \log n)$ time in local computation, where n is the number of nodes in the network. The degree of the scatternet can be fixed to any $q + 1$, where q is a power of a prime number. The diameter of the scatternet is bounded by $O(\log^2 n \log^2 \log n)$. In addition, the connectivity of masters is high (i.e., for any pair of master, the number of edge-disjoint paths connecting them in the network is large than some constant). However, in their method, every node need hold information of the projective plane and the master node who has the "token" needs to know the information of the projective scatternet (which label should be used for the new coming master and which existing nodes need to be connected to it). The authors did not discuss in detail how to compute the labels for the new master and its slaves, and what will happen when the number of nodes reaches the number of nodes of a complete projective scatternets.

Song *et al.* [62] adopted the well-known structure *de Bruijn graph* to form the backbone of Bluetooth scatternet, called *dBBlue*, such that every master node has at most seven slaves, every slave node is in at most two piconets, and *no* node assumes both master and slave roles. Figure 3(b) illustrates an example of dbBlue based on the de Bruijn graph $B(2, 3)$. Their structure dBBlue also enjoys a nice routing property: the diameter of the

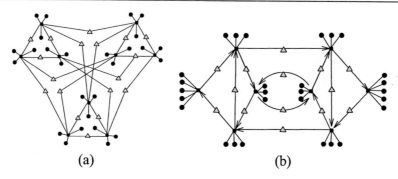

Figure 3: Different Scatternets: (a) Projective scatternet; (b) dBBlue based on de Bruijn graph.

graph is $O(\log n)$, s.t., it can find a path with at most $O(\log n)$ hops between every pair of nodes without any routing table. Moreover, the network congestion is at most $O(\log n / n)$, assuming that a unit total traffic demand is evenly distributed among all pair of nodes. They also proposed a vigorous method to *locally* update the structure dBBlue using at most $O(\log n)$ communications when a node joins or leaves the network. In most cases, the cost of updating the scatternet is actually $O(1)$ since a node can join or leave without affecting the remaining scatternet. The number of affected nodes is always bounded from above by a constant when a node joins or leaves the network. Their method can construct the structure dBBlue incrementally when the nodes join the network one by one. In addition, the structure formed by their method can sustain the faults of 2 nodes and the network is still guaranteed to be connected. If a node detects a fault of some neighboring master node or bridge slave node, it can dynamically re-route the packets and the path traveled by the packet is still at most $O(\log n)$ hops. By designing a novel method for assigning MAC addresses to nodes, dBBlue structure can enable the self-routing even during the updating procedures when node leaves or joins the network. Detailed discussion of the dBBlue and its self-routing method will be presented in Section 4.

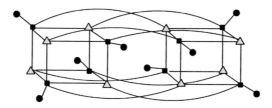

Figure 4: Scatternet: BlueCube.

Chang *et al.* [17] presented a three-stage distributed construction protocol to automatically construct a hypercube based scatternet, called *BlueCube*. Figure 4 illustrates an example of *BlueCube*. The proposed protocol tackles the link construction, role assignment, scatternet formation and network management problems, to construct efficiently a hypercube structure. The construction of the scatternet has three phases: first form a ring scatternet, then switch roles for some nodes to reduce the number of piconets and connect some unconnected devices, at last form the hypercube for all devices in the ring. The proposed protocol enables Bluetooth devices easily to construct a routing path, tolerate faults and create disjoint paths.

3.2.5 Cluster Based Methods

Ramachandran *et al.* [57] proposed a two-stage distributed $O(n)$ randomized cluster algorithm for a n node single-hop network, that always finds the minimum number of star-shaped clusters, which have maximum size 8. The first stage of the algorithm is randomized, at the end of which each node either becomes a master-designate or a slave-designate. The second stage corrects the effect of the randomness introduced in the previous stage by using a deterministic algorithm to decide on the final set of masters and slaves, and to efficiently assign slaves to masters. A super-master is elected, which counts the actual number of masters and collects information about all the nodes. The super-master can then run any centralized algorithm to form a network of desired topology (selecting the bridges). The election of the super-master is interleaved with the cluster formation, which speeds up the ad hoc network formation. The authors also proposed a deterministic distributed algorithm for the same model which achieves the same purpose. The basic idea of this algorithm is that nodes discovering each other form a tree of responses, the root of each tree being a master, all other nodes in the tree being its slaves. Each tree form a cluster. Then the second half of the algorithm involves the election of a super-master among the masters. They applied the same method (form a tree of responses) among all the masters. And again the super-master will decide the final scatternet.

3.2.6 QoS Based Methods

Baatz *et al.* [2] proposed a single-hop Bluetooth scatternet formation scheme based on 1-factors which allow a maximum aggregated throughput in the corresponding scatternet. They first elaborated on Bluetooth scatternet capacity with special respect to co-channel interference. Then they introduced a class of Bluetooth scatternet topologies (constructed from one-factorizations) with optimal aggregated throughput that are easy to schedule in a fair manner. In other words, the scatternet allows a maximum number of simultaneously active piconets. As a variable number k of 1-factors may be used to build a topology, one is able to find a tradeoff between scheduling overhead on the one hand and robustness and average path length on the other hand. Due to the chosen construction, the 1-factors can be computed easily for a given number of nodes and a given k (in time linear to the number of links). However, piconets are not degree limited in their scheme.

Miorandi and Zanella [49] investigated the impact of the master choice on the performance of a Bluetooth piconet. They assumed the end-to-end traffic matrix of the single-hop network is given. They proposed an optimal and a suboptimal criterion for the choice of the master unit to minimize the average packet delay. However, the optimization requires high computational capability. Miorandi, Trainito and Zanella [48] further studied the relationship between capacity and topology for Bluetooth scatternets. They discussed how Bluetooth nodes should be organized to build up a scatternet, where the efficiency of the resulting configuration is measured in terms of network capacity instead of packet delay. They presented a theoretical study of intrinsic capacity limits of a scatternet, where the maximum throughput may be achieved under local traffic. They first discussed some conditions to achieve efficient piconets interconnection. Then, they investigated the performance achieved by some specific scatternet topologies, both "planar" and "solid", in case of uniform traffic matrix, that is, assuming that every node in the network generates an equal amount of traffic towards any other node. Marsan *et al.* [45] also studied how to construct the optimal topology that provides full network connectivity, fulfills the traffic requirements and the constraints posed by the system specification, and minimizes the traffic load of the most congested node in the network, or equivalently its energy consumption. By using a min-max formulation, they provided a solution based on integer linear programming. Due to the problem complexity, the optimal solution is attained in a centralized manner, which is the limitation of their method.

3.2.7   Virtual Position Based Methods

Wang *et al.* [67] applied the position-based scheme proposed by Li *et al.* [41] for multi-hop networks. In case of multi-hop networks, these schemes require *exact position* information. Obtaining the precise positions currently poses challenging technological tasks [32] for short range Bluetooth devices, aimed primarily at home and office environments. However, when the same scheme is applied to single-hop network, *virtual positions* (random position selected by each node independently and without any hardware requirements) are sufficient. The problem with virtual positions being applied in multi-hop networks is that two nodes which select virtual positions that are close to each other may physically be outside of each other's transmission range. On the other hand, in single-hop ad hoc networks, every node can communicate with each other directly, and the problem in multi-hop networks does not occur. Another advantage of using virtual positions for single-hop network is that our scatternet formation can be used for wireless nodes in three-dimensional space (such as a building) by just generating 2-dimensional virtual positions in a virtual plane. In their method [67], nodes first randomly select their virtual positions, then based on these positions, a planar structure (minimum spanning tree, Gabriel graph, relative neighborhood graph or Delaunay triangulation) can be built. As in their multi-hop method [41], then they bound the degree by applying Yao graph [71] on the structure, and assign the roles for the scatternet. We will review the detailed multi-hop method [41] in Section 3.3.3.

3.2.8   Genetic Methods

Recently, Sreenivas and Ali [63] proposed an evolutionary approach to scatternet construction, wherein they used a genetic algorithm to find a global optimum: the best, or fittest, combination of masters, slaves and bridges in a given Bluetooth network. Their solution considered only slave-slave bridges. The algorithm executes in two phases, role determination and connection establishment. In the first phase, the genetic algorithm selects random groups of nodes: these groups constitute the initial population. Each group corresponds to a combination of masters, slaves and bridge nodes. The fitness of each group of nodes is evaluated based on the number of master nodes (or piconets), slave nodes and bridge nodes in the network. A desirable property of scatternets is to minimize the number of masters, maximize the number of slaves and ensure that the bridge nodes are not too few such that bottlenecks are created. Taking this property into consideration, a fitness value is derived for each group in the population. Then a new population will be generated repeatedly by the genetic algorithm, until the end condition based on the universal lower bound for the number of piconets is satisfied. They showed that their scatternet formation algorithm produces scatternets with certain desirable characteristics: minimal delay to the end-users during scatternet formation (i.e. the number of generations that the genetic algorithm in first phase iterates through), minimal number of piconets in order to reduce inter-piconet interference during communication and bounded number of slaves to minimize the overhead associated with slave parking and unparking operations.

3.3   Scatternet Formation Algorithms for Multi-hop Networks

In a single-hop topology, all devices are in the radio vicinity of each other, which is not always the case in realistic scenarios. Multi-hop network is a more general and attractive case, with flexible topologies it has a strong potential for various applications. In this section we review the solutions of scatternet formation for multi-hop networks.

3.3.1   Tree Based Methods

Zaruba, Basagni and Chlamtac [72] proposed two distributed tree-based methods for forming connected scatternet. In both methods, the resulting topology is termed as *BlueTree*. The first method is initiated by a single node, called the *blueroot*, which will be the root of the tree. A rooted spanning tree is built as follows. First, the root will be assigned as a master, and all of its one hop neighbors will be its children and its slaves. The children of the root will be then assigned an additional master role, and all their neighbors that are not assigned any roles yet will become children and slaves of these newly created masters. This procedure is repeated recursively till all nodes are assigned. Each node is slave for only one master, its parent that *paged* it first. Each internal node of the tree is a master of its children, and slave of its parent. See Figure 2(a) for an illustration. In order to limit the number of slaves, they [72] observed that if a node in unit disk graph has more than five neighbors, then at least two of them must be connected. This observation is used to re-configure the tree so that each master node has no more than five slaves. If a master node has more than five slaves, it selects its two slaves a and b that are connected, instructs a to be the master of b, and then disconnects a from itself. Such branch reorganization is carried throughout the network. However, whether this approach will terminate is not proved in the paper [72]. In the second method [72], several roots are initially selected. Each of them then creates its own scatternet as in the first method. After that, sub-tree scatternets are connected into one scatternet spanning the entire network. Remember that the tree topology suffers from a major drawback: the root is a communication bottleneck. In addition, dynamic updating that preserves correct routing is not discussed in these protocols. There are several modified versions of BlueTree, such as methods by Dong and Wu [27] and by Huang *et al.* [33], to improve the communication overhead or increase the connectivity. Cuomo *et al.* [22] also proposed a tree-based scatternet formation algorithm *SHAPER* for multi-hop network, which focuses on the self-healing behavior of the tree structure: i.e., it is able to dynamically reconfigure the scatternet after topological variations due to mobility or failure of nodes.

Guerin *et al.* [31] proposed depth/breath first search and MST-based scatternet formation schemes for unit disk graphs in two and three dimensions. They construct a tree where all nodes at one level are either masters or slaves (i.e., they construct bipartite graphs). Their construction does not guarantee maximum degree bound unless the structure itself provides the bound. For example, MST in two dimensions has a maximum degree of five, but in three dimensions, some nodes can have degrees up to 13. The schemes are also not localized.

3.3.2   Cluster Based Methods

Basagni, Petrioli and Chlamtac [54, 6] described a multihop scatternet formation scheme based on clustering scheme [42]. The constructed scatternet is called *BlueStars*. The protocol proceeds in three phases: device discovery, partitioning of the network into piconets (stars) by clustering, and interconnection of the piconets to connected scatternet. In the second phase, *BlueStars Formation*, clusterhead (master role) decisions are based on node weights (instead of node IDs, as used in the clustering scheme proposed by Lin and Gerla [42]), that express their suitability to become masters, following a variant of the clustering method described by Basagni [4]. All clusterhead nodes are declared master nodes in a piconet, with all nodes belonging to their clusters as their slaves. Then in the third phase, *BlueConstellation*, some of the slaves become masters of additional piconets, i.e. become master-slave bridges, to assure the connectivity of the scatternet. However, piconets in the scatternet may have more than seven slaves. This may result in performance degradation, as slaves need to be parked and unparked in order for them to communicate with their master. A performance evaluation of the clustering-based scatternet formation scheme [6] is given by Basagni *et al.* [5] and Petrioli *et. al* [54].

To fix the unbound slave number, Basagni, Petrioli and Chlamtac [55, 53] modified their protocol [54, 6] and proposed a new scatternet called *BlueMesh*. The idea of bounding the slave number in BlueMesh is again based on the observation (also used in the method by Zaruba *et al.* [72]) that if a node in unit disk graph has more than five neighbors then at least two of them must be connected. Same with *BlueStars*, the selection of the masters is based on the node weights. However, the selection of slaves is performed in such a way that if a master has more than seven neighbors, it only chooses seven slaves among them so that via them it can reach all the others. This phase proceeds in iterations. Initially all nodes are undecided. Nodes that participate in a given iteration perform the above modified clustering process (deciding the master and slave roles). In each iteration, the decided nodes and links will be removed from the next iteration. After the roles decided for all nodes, finally, the bridges are chosen to connect all piconets to the connected scatternet. The selection of bridges is same as in BlueStars, bridges are chosen so that there is an inter-piconet route between all masters that are at most three hops away.

Variants of clustering-based scatternet formation schemes [68, 30] were proposed. Wang, Thomas and Haas [68] proposed a scatternet formation shceme, called *Bluenet*. It is a 3-phase algorithm. In the first phase, nodes enter page state randomly, trying to invite less than seven neighbors to join its piconet. Once a node becomes a slave, it will stop paging or answering pages. When the first phase is finished, several separate piconets are formed, and there are also some isolated nodes. In the second phase, isolated nodes will page all of its neighbors and try to connect them to some initial piconets built in the first phase. In last phase, master of each piconet instructs their slaves to set up outgoing links, so that piconets are connected to form a scatternet. Guerin, Kim and Sarkar [30] also proposed a distributed cluster algorithm for scatternet formation. Initially all nodes have unassigned states, and nodes discover other nodes randomly. When two nodes meet for the first time and both are unassigned, the one with the highest ID becomes master, the other becomes its slave. When two nodes meet and one is unassigned while the other is master, the unassigned node become a slave of the master, if the master has less than seven slaves. When two nodes meet and one is unassigned while the other is slave, the unassigned node becomes master, and the slave becomes a bridge node. When two nodes meet and both are masters, nothing changes. When a master node meets a slave node, the slave will join the master's piconet, and becomes a bridge node. Both clustering processes [68, 30] follow a random fashion. Initial connections are made by nodes entering scan or inquiry scan phases at random. Already existing master nodes have priority in attracting more slaves, up to the limit. After each node is assigned master or slave role, or is unable to join any piconet or attract any neighbor as its slave to create its own piconet, some bridge piconets are added to connect the scatternet. However, both methods [68, 30] do not always lead to a connected structure.

3.3.3   Position Based Methods

Li, Stojmenovic and Wang [41, 40] proposed the first schemes that construct degree limited (a node has at most seven slaves) and connected piconets in multihop networks, without parking any node. Notice that the schemes by Petrioli and Basagni [55, 53] can also achieve bounded degree scatternet. Their neat scheme does not require position information, but instead the local information is extended to two hop information, with a two round device discovery phase for obtaining necessary information. In Li *et al.*'s solution (Algorithm 1), nodes know their positions and are able to establish connections with other nodes within their transmission radius in the neighbor discovery phase. The second phase of the proposed formation algorithm is optional, and can be applied to construct a sparse planar geometric structure, such as Gabriel graph (GG), relative neighborhood graph (RNG) or partial Delaunay triangulation (PDT). Note that each node can make local decisions about each of its edges in these graphs without any message being exchanged with any of its neighbors. Thus this construction has basically no cost involved. In the third mandatory phase, the degree of each node is limited to seven by applying Yao structure [1], and the master-slave relations are formed in created subgraphs. This phase follows clustering based approach, and consists of several iterations. In each iteration, undecided nodes with higher keys than any of their undecided neighbors apply Yao structure to bound the degree, decide master-slave relations on the remaining edges, and inform all neighbors about either deleting edge or master-slave decision. The authors considered two ways to decide master-slave relations: node with initially higher key is master, and cluster based (deciding node becomes master if and only if it has no previously assigned slave role). In cluster based approach, a dominating set of masters in the degree limited subgraph is implicitly constructed, and some gateway piconets are added to preserve connectivity. The creation and maintenance of the scatternets require small overhead in addition to maintaining accurate location information for one-hop neighbors. The experiments confirmed good functionality of created Bluetooth networks in addition to their fast creation and straightforward maintenance.

Algorithm 1 *Position-based Scatternet Formation Algorithm [41, 40]*

1. Neighbor discovery and information exchange (collecting the node degree information).

2. Planar subgraph construction (constructing RNG, GG, or PDT and degree information exchange), if desirable.

3. Bounding degree and assigning roles (consisting of several iterations).

   Initially all nodes are undecided. In each iteration, if a undecided node u has the highest degree among its all undecided neighbors, it runs the following steps:

   (a) Bound its degree (applying Yao structure).

   (b) Assign role to itself (based on the information on each link or using cluster based method).

   (c) Mark itself decided, and notice the deleted edges and its status to its undecided neighbors.

   Repeat the iterations, until all nodes are decided.

Recently, Basagni *et al.* [10, 7] described the results of an ns2-based comparative performance evaluation among four major solutions for forming multihop scatternet [41, 54, 72, 68]. They found that device discovery is the most time-consuming operation, independently of the particular protocol to which it is applied. The comparative performance

---

[1]The Yao graph [71] is proposed by Yao to construct MST of a set of points in high dimensions efficiently. At given node u, any k equal-separated rays originated at u define k cones. In each cone, choose the closest node v within the transmission range of u, if there is any, and add a directed link $\overrightarrow{uv}$. Ties are broken arbitrarily. The remaining edges are deleted from the graph.

evaluation showed that due to the simplicity of its operations BlueStars [54] is by far the fastest protocol for scatternet formation. However, BlueStars produces scatternets with an unbounded, possibly large number of slaves per piconet, which imposes the use of potentially inefficient Bluetooth operations. They proposed a combined solution by applying a Yao structure as described here on each piconet, to limit the degree of each master node to seven. This is a variant of the clustering-based scheme (Algorithm 1 [41, 40]), with degree limitation applied at the end instead of during the scatternet creation process.

3.3.4   On-demand Methods

Most above scatternet formation protocols tend to interconnect all Bluetooth devices at the initial network startup stage and maintain all Bluetooth links thereafter. The master or bridge nodes in the resulting scatternet may become the traffic bottleneck and reduce network throughput. To make the scatternet structure more suitable to serve in mobile ad hoc networks, recently several on-demand methods [44, 38, 51, 21] (to build scatternets only along the multihop routes with traffic demands and eliminate unnecessary link and route maintenances) are proposed.

Liu, Lee and Saadawi [44] proposed a scatternet-route structure to combine the scatternet formation with on-demand routing, thus build scatternets only along the multihop routes with traffic demands. This route-type scatternet is called scatternet route. As the scatternet routes survive along with the on-going traffic flows, no unnecessary Bluetooth link maintenance is needed. The scatternet route is designed to have a special master-slave alternate structure to enable the devices along the route to connect together via Bluetooth links. The formation of the scatternet route is similar to the common on-demand routing protocols. They introduced an extended ID (EID) connectionless broadcast scheme to expedite the route discovery and construction. To remove the piconet switch overhead suffered by the bridge devices inside the scatternet route, they proposed to align the time slot of all piconets along each scatternet route. The synchronized scatternet route is shown to reach higher network throughput and undergo shorter data transmission delays. Finally, in order to enable fair and efficient packet transmissions over scatternet routes, they also designed a route-based scatternet scheduling algorithm.

Kawamoto *et al.* [38] proposed a Two-Phase Scatternet Formation (TPSF) protocol with the aim of supporting dynamic topology changes while maintaining a high aggregate throughput. In the first phase, a control scatternet is constructed for control purposes (i.e., to support dynamic join/leave, route discovery, etc). After the control scatternet formation in the first phase, each master node maintains all the information of its slaves and bridges nodes within its piconet and adjacent piconets. This information is exploited during the second phase. The second phase is invoked whenever a node needs to initiate data communications with another node. A dedicated piconet/scatternet is constructed on-demand between the communicating nodes, using any on-demand source routing protocols proposed for wireless mobile ad hoc networks. Kawamoto *et al.* [38] use the dynamic source routing (DSR) protocol [35] for route selection. Since the on-demand scatternet can dedicate all the time slots to a single communication session, it has the capability to provide a high throughput and a small end-to-end data transfer delay. The on-demand scatternet is torn down when the data transmissions are finished. The simulation results showed that the proposed TPSF protocol achieves a higher average aggregate throughput when compared with BTCP [59].

Pagani *et al.* [51] also proposed an On-Demand Bluetooth scatternet formation algorithm (ODBT). ODBT characterizes an ad hoc infrastructure with a tree topology. It is able to cope with topology changes due to either leaving or moving Bluetooth devices, as well as with devices that dynamically join the scatternet. The authors described in detail how ODBT can be implemented in the Bluetooth protocol stack, and analyzed its performance by simulations.

3.3.5   QoS Based Methods

Marsan *et al.* [45] studied how to construct the optimal topology that provides full network connectivity, fulfills the traffic requirements and the constraints posed by the system specification, and minimizes the traffic load of the most congested node in the network, or equivalently its energy consumption. By using a min-max formulation, they provided a centralized solution based on integer linear programming.

Recently, Chiasserini *et al.* [19] extended the work of Marsan *et al.* [45] and enhanced the optimization problem by adding the constraints on the network capacity. They also gave a min-max formalization of the topology formation problem. They assume that just one route is used for each source destination pair. For each traffic source, they took the average traffic rate as an input parameter to the problem. The min-max problem is solved in a centralized manner due to its complexity and the large number of parameters involved. The solution provides topologies which minimize the traffic load of the most congested node in the network while meeting the constraints on the scatternet formation and network capacity. By varying the maximum number of piconets that can be created, they derived the performance of the attained solutions as the requirements on the throughput and on the role played by some of the network nodes change. The results can be used to find the optimal trade-off between system complexity and network efficiency. However, the optimization problem requires detailed system information and is not suited for a distributed implementation both for the algorithm characteristics and for its intrinsic complexity. It can only deal with a limited number of network nodes. Then, to overcome such a limitation, They discussed the key building blocks for a distributed solution approach to the scatternet formation problem. They outlined two procedures to handle the insertion and the removal of a node in/from the scatternet, in a distributed fashion. Both procedures aim at satisfying the Bluetooth technology constraints, while providing full network connectivity, high throughput, and reduced overhead due to control messages. Although these procedures may generate sub-optimal topologies, they can be easily implemented and are designed to deal with a large number of nodes.

Augel and Knoor [1] proposed an approach of scatternet formation in which the formation is dependent on the QoS requirements of the applications. In their solution, to avoid larger degree which may cause bad influence on throughput, nodes with high degree stop paging and instruct a neighbor with a low degree to start paging instead. Each device may try to influence the topology depending on the QoS requirements. They described a general scatternet formation design guidelines for QoS applications, but did not present any particular scatternet formation protocol.

Melodia and Cuomo [46, 24, 47] discussed the scatternet formation issue in Bluetooth by setting a framework for scatternet analysis based on a matrix representation, which allows developing and applying different metrics. They identified several metrics (capacity, average load, or path length) both in a traffic independent and in a traffic dependent context, and showed the relevant numerical results. In the traffic independent case, the scatternet is formed without knowledge of traffic relationships among involved devices. The scenario is described only by means of the adjacency matrix. If traffic relationships between nodes (e.g., flows at given data rates) have to be taken into account, they can be conveniently described by a traffic matrix. Then, a distributed algorithm for scatternet topology optimization, Distributed Scatternet Optimization Algorithm (DSOA), is introduced, that supports the formation of a locally optimal scatternet based on a selected metric. Numerical results obtained by adopting this distributed approach to optimize the network topology are shown to be close to the global optimum.

Cuomo, Melodia and Akyildiz [25, 23] extended their work [46, 24, 47] and provided an integrated approach for scatternet formation and quality-of-service support (called SHAPER-OPT) by combining the tree-based scatternet formation algorithm *SHAPER* [22] and the distributed scatternet optimization algorithm (DSOA) [46, 24, 47]. The approach produces a meshed topology by applying DSOA on the network built by SHAPER. Performance evaluation of the proposed algorithms, and of the accordingly created scatternets, is carried out by using ns2 simulation. Devices are shown to be able to join or leave the scatternet at any time, without compromising the long term connectivity. Delay for network setup and reconfiguration in dynamic environments is shown to be within acceptable bounds. DSOA is also shown to be easy to implement and to improve the overall network performance.

4   Self-Routing in Bluetooth Scatternet

Routing in Bluetooth network received little attention so far. Though considerable research has been done in the area of routing in ad hoc networks, the direct application of this may be inefficient to Bluetooth scatternets. Some routing schemes [11, 56, 20, 36] for scatternets have been proposed recently.

Bhagwat and Segall [11] proposed a routing method, Routing Vector Scheme (RVM), in Bluetooth based on a concept of route vector. In their scheme, the complete path is carried in the header (i.e., source routing) and Bluetooth addresses are expressed very efficiently. They described the protocols for on-demand route discovery and packet forwarding. Their design illustrates three design compromises, namely minimization of soft-state, protocol simplicity, and bandwidth conservation, all of which are crucial for efficient operation over small size Bluetooth scatternets. However, due to carrying the complete path in the source routing, their scheme will lead to a large packet overhead in large Bluetooth scatternets, particularly since Bluetooth packets are very small.

Prabhu and Chockalingam [56] proposed a routing protocol that employs flooding to obtain battery levels of nodes. The protocol uses the available battery power in the Bluetooth devices as a cost metric in choosing the routes. They proposed two techniques, namely a) battery power level based master-slave switch and b) distance based power control, to increase the network lifetime in scatternets. The master-slave switch technique is motivated by the fact that a piconet master has to handle the packet transmissions to/from all its slaves, and hence may drain its battery soon. By role switching, each device in a piconet may have to play the master role depending on its available battery power. In the second technique, devices choose their transmit powers based on their distances from their respective masters. Their performance results showed that a considerable gain in network lifetime can be achieved using these two power saving techniques.

There are also some Bluetooth routing protocols by applying ad hoc routing protocols with adjustments to fit Bluetooth own characteristics. Choon-sik Choi and Hae-Wook Choi [20] proposed a Bluetooth routing protocol based on DSR (Dynamic Source Routing) [35]. Kapoor and Gerla [36] presented a routing scheme for Bluetooth scatternets based on ZRP (Zone Routing Protocol) [73] by customizing the scheme for use in Bluetooth scatternets.

An important problem for scatternet formation algorithms is to choose the structure that also provides efficient routing on the designed scatternet, in terms of hop count, power consumption, and delay in message delivery (the delay depends on the amount of multiple roles performed by various nodes). Several scatternet formation algorithms consider routing issue in design. In the following, we will review those scatternet formation algorithms with self-routing properties.

4.1 Blue-tree Scatternet

Tree shaped scatternets are promising in terms of minimizing the number of piconets and allowing simpler routing protocols. BlueTree proposed by Sun *et al.* [65] is capable of self-routing for single-hop Bluetooth networks. Nodes are organized and maintained in a search tree structure, with Bluetooth ID's as keys (these keys are also used for routing).

Let $ADDR(x)$ be node x's Bluetooth MAC address as defined in the Bluetooth specification. Define $child(x)$ to be the set of children for a node x. Assuming the $ADDR$ has a total order, node x is before (after) node y if and only if $ADDR(x) < ADDR(y)$ $(ADDR(x) > ADDR(y))$. The $min(x)$ and $max(x)$ are defined to be the smallest and the largest $ADDR$ of the nodes in the subtree rooted at x. The $range(x) = (min(x), max(x))$ is defined as the address range of nodes in the subtree rooted at x. The Bluetree can be implemented by maintaining the following information at any node x: an array of range for all x's children and its own $range(x) = (min(x), max(x))$.

The concept of Bluetree is the extension of the binary search tree. Based on the limit imposed by Bluetooth piconet, the maximal number of children (the maximal number of branches at one node in the tree) is seven. Therefore, the Bluetree is a seven-way search tree. If we consider the destination address as the key, then routing is just like doing a search. In message routing, an unique $ADDR$ is given and one is required to find the device that has this address along the tree. If a scatternet is a Bluetree, as long as each node maintains the ranges of itself and its children, routing can be done easily using the following algorithm similar as binary search.

Algorithm 2 *Bluetree Routing Algorithm [65]*

when node x receives a packet m for destination address d.
  if $ADDR(x) = d$
    x is the destination and routing is terminated
  else
    if $\forall$ child c_i such that $d \notin range(c_i)$
      if x is not the root
        send m to x's parent
      else discard m since d cannot be found
    else
      if x is a leaf
        discard m since d cannot be found
      else
        if $\exists$ a child c_j such that $c_j \in range(c_j)$
          send m to c_j
        else discard m since d cannot be found

Worth to mention that, Bluetree scatternet relies on a sophisticated scatternet merge procedure with significant communication overhead for creation and maintenance.

4.2 BlueRing Scatternet

Bluerings as scatternets are proposed by Foo and Chua [29] and Lin *et al.* [43]. Ring structure for Bluetooth has simplicity, easy creation and easy routing as advantage. Routing on BlueRing is stateless in the sense that no routing information needs to be kept by any host once the ring is formed. This would be favorable for environments such as Smart Homes where computing capability is limited. Lin *et al.* [43] presented the detailed routing protocol, which supports both unicasting and broadcasting on BlueRing. In the protocol, data packets will be routed following the direction of the BlueRing. Since a packet flowing around the ring will eventually reach its destination piconet, no route discovery process is required. For detailed protocol, please refer to their paper [43]. Notice, due to large diameter (i.e., the packet may reach its destination after travelling the whole ring), ring structure is only good for small-size or median-size scatternets.

4.3 Projective Scatternet

Barriere *et al.* [3] also proposed a routing method for Bluetooth scatternets formatted by their method using their specific labels. The projective scatternet is constructed by using a basic procedure called Q-plication of scatternet S using a base scatternet N. The complete projective scatternet consists of many layers of scatternets. Each layer contains a finite number of scatternets, any one is obtained by a repeated Q-plication of the last element of the preceding level with a fixed base scatternet also taken from the preceding layer. The labeling rule of the scatternet is as follows. The master of a piconet is labeled 0, and the slaves are labeled arbitrarily from 1 to $p - 1$, where p is a integer larger than q (a power of a prime). Figure 5 shows the illustration of one piconet and a scatternet with 21 nodes, where $p = 8$ and $q = 1$. Given the labeling of the nodes in a scatternet S, a node x of the Q-plication of S receives as label $L(x)$ a pair (i, l) where i indicates the index of the copy of S where x is located, $0 \leq i \leq Q - 1$, and l is the label of x in this copy. A node resulting from the identification of $q+1$ free slaves receives a unique label (i, l) which is the smallest label among those $q + 1$ slaves, according to the standard lexicographic ordering of the labels. In Figure 5, the upper figure shows the labels for a piconet, which is the base scatternet. The lower figure shows the labels for projective scatternet formed by Q-plication of the base scatternet. For example, for the node with label 11, it is slave for both nodes 10 and 30. So its label is the smallest label between 11 (its label in the 10's piconet) and 31 (its label in the 30's piconet).

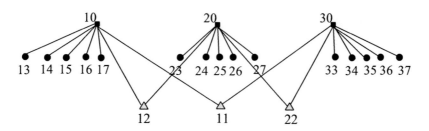

Figure 5: Node labeling for the projective scatternet.

Routing in the scatternet is based on following the path suggested by labels. Routing in a complete scatternet from a node x with label $a_k a_{k-1} \cdots a_1$ to a node y with label $b_k b_{k-1} \cdots b_1$ consists of routing from $a_k a_{k-1} \cdots a_1$ to a node $b_k c_{k-1} \cdots c_1$ to node $b_k b_{k-1} d_{k-2} \cdots d_1$, etc., each time matching one of the components in the label of the destination from the left until finally reaching the node $b_k b_{k-1} \cdots b_1$. Thus all we have to describe is how the routing proceeds from $a_k a_{k-1} \cdots a_1$ to a node $b_k c_{k-1} \cdots c_1$. Notice that the length of the label, k, is the level number in the construction of the scatternet. The routing algorithm works as follows. 1) Node x determines, using the block design information, the position of a slave z in its base scatternet of level k, that is shared by the two copies labeled by a_k and b_k. 2) x sends the message for y to z within the base scatternet shared by x and z. 3) z forwards the message to y within the subscatternet of level $k - 1$ recursively. For example, if we want to send a packet from 27 to 15. First, we find the slave 12 in its base scatternet that shared by piconets 2 and 1. Then 27 sends the message to 12 via 20 within the base scatternet piconet 2. At last, the 12 send the message to 15 via 10 within the subscatternet of level 0. For more detailed labeling rules and routing method, please refer to the paper [3].

4.4   dBBlue Scatternet

The dBBlue [62] scatternet first builds a backbone based on the well-known de Bruijn graph [26], then adds the remained nodes into the network with a flexible MAC assignment scheme to enable the self-routing in Bluetooth networks.

The de Bruijn graph, denoted by $B(d, k)$, is a directed graph with d^k nodes. Assume that each node is assigned a unique label of length k on the alphabet $\{0, \cdots, d - 1\}$. There is an edge in $B(d, k)$ from a node with label $x_1 x_2 \cdots x_k$ to any node with label $x_2 \cdots x_k y$, where $y \in \{0, \cdots, d - 1\}$. Figure 6 illustrates $B(2, 3)$. It is well-known that the de Bruijn graph enables self-routing intrinsically. The self-routing path from the source with label $x_1 x_2 \cdots x_k$ to the target with label $y_1 y_2 \cdots y_k$ is $x_1 x_2 \cdots x_k \rightarrow x_2 \cdots x_k y_1 \rightarrow x_3 \cdots x_k y_1 y_2 \rightarrow \cdots \rightarrow x_k y_1 \cdots y_{k-1} \rightarrow y_1 \cdots y_k$. Observe that, we could find a shorter route by looking for the longest sequence that is both a suffix of $x_1 x_2 \cdots x_k$ and a prefix of $y_1 y_2 \cdots y_k$. Suppose that $x_i \cdots x_k = y_1 \cdots y_{k-i+1}$ is such longest sequence. The shortest path between the source and the target is $x_1 \cdots x_k \rightarrow x_2 \cdots x_k y_{k-i+2} \rightarrow x_3 \cdots x_k y_{k-i+2} y_{k-i+3} \rightarrow \cdots \rightarrow x_{i-1} \cdots x_k y_{k-i+2} \cdots y_{k-1} \rightarrow y_1 \cdots y_k$. Clearly, the route between any two nodes is at most k hops, i.e., $B(d, k)$ has diameter $k = \log_d n$, where $n = d^k$ is the number of nodes of the graph.

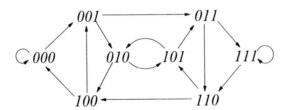

Figure 6: Node labeling of the de Bruijn graph $B(2, 3)$.

The classical de Bruijn graph is *balanced* in the sense that the labels of all nodes have the same length. A generalized de Bruijn graph is *pseudo-balanced* if the lengths of the labels are different by at most one. In dBBlue[62], they used a pseudo-balanced de Bruijn graph to be the backbone and handle the node leaving and joining. In a pseudo-balanced de Bruijn graph $B(2, k)$, each node has at most 4 out-neighbors and 2 in-neighbors. To route a packet from a node u with label $x_1 x_2 \cdots x_{s-1} x_s$ to another node v with label $y_1 y_2 \cdots y_{t-1} y_t$, where $s, t \in [k, k + 1]$. Node u will forward the packet to its neighbor node with label $x_2 \cdots x_{s-1} x_s$, or $x_2 \cdots x_{s-1} x_s y_1$, or $x_2 \cdots x_{s-1} x_s y_1 y_2$. Notice that since the labels of the nodes are a universal prefix set, we know that *exactly* one of these three labels does exist. The following nodes keep forwarding the packet similarly until it reaches node v. Consequently, the diameter of pseudo-balanced de Bruijn graph is still $O(\log n)$. dBBlue[62] proposes a scalable scatternet structure based on pseudo-balanced de Bruijn graph $B(2, k)$.

The authors presented a novel rule of assigning the MAC address in a piconet. In the dBBlue scatternet, when we route a packet to a destination node v, we only know the piconet ID of node v, say $y_1 y_2 \cdots y_k$, which is same as the label of its master node, and the MAC address, say $z_1 z_2 z_3$, of this node in that piconet. When some node joins or leaves the scatternet, we often have to reorganize some piconets and thus re-assign the MACs of some nodes. The method of assigning MAC addresses in a piconet and reorganizing the piconets guarantees that the new piconet (even the new MAC address) can be found by a simple appending or deleting the least significant bit, which keeps the label prefix of updating nodes unchanged so that even the delivery of the packets on the way to those updating nodes will not be interrupted. In a piconet, MAC 000 is always reserved by the master node. Remember that, in a pseudo-balanced de Bruijn graph, any node has 2 in-neighbors (except 0^m and 1^m) and at most 4 out-neighbors, so MAC addresses 011 and 111 are always reserved for the two bridge slaves to in-neighbors, MAC 010, 101, 001 and 110 are reserved for bridge slaves to out-neighbors if they exist, and 100 is reserved for the 7th slave (it must be a pure slave) if it exists. Table 1 summarizes the rule of assigning the MAC address to the bridge slave nodes in a piconet. Their MAC addresses can be decided uniquely according to the label bit difference between current piconet and neighbor piconet IDs. For example, if the master u is labeled $x_1 x_2 \cdots x_s$ and its out-neighbor v is labeled $x_2 \cdots x_s y_1 y_2$, then the MAC addresses of their bridge slave is $y_1 y_2 \overline{y_2}$ assigned by u, and $x_1 11$ assigned by v. Remember that every bridge slave has one MAC address in each of the two piconets it resides.

Table 1: The rule to assign MAC address to bridge slave nodes.

Node	In-Neighbor	Out-Neighbor		
	$y x_1 \cdots x_r$	$x_2 \cdots x_s$	$x_2 \cdots x_s y_1$	$x_2 \cdots x_s y_1 y_2$
$x_1 \cdots x_s$	$y11$	010	$y_1 \overline{y_1} y_1$	$y_1 y_2 \overline{y_2}$

Notice that, in bluetooth scatternet, the bridge slave nodes have two independent piconet IDs and MAC addresses in two piconets respectively. However, since the routing mechanism in de Bruijn is directional, only their piconet ID and MAC address assigned by their in-master is public and meaningful for routing, saying *label* in the remaining paper, and the other one is only used for inter-communication in a piconet.

The updating of scatternet due to node joining or leaving is to maintain the pseudo-balanced de Bruijn based backbone, conforming the labelling rule as described before. More details, please refer to the paper [62].

5   Conclusion

In this chapter, we reviewed different scatternet formation algorithms for both single-hop and multi-hop networks, and surveyed some Bluetooth routing algorithms and several scatternet topologies which have self-routing properties. Due to the space limit, we did not present technical details and theoretical proofs for most of these algorithms. Reader can check the references for details.

References

[1] Markus Augel and Rudi Knorr. Bluetooth scatternet formation - state of the art and a new approach. In *Proc. of the 17th International Conference on Architecture of Computing Systems (ARCS), LNCS 2981*, Augsburg, Germany, 2004.

[2] Simon Baatz, Christoph Bieschke, Matthias Frank, Carmen Kuhl, Peter Martini, and Christoph Scholz. Building efficient Bluetooth scatternet topologies from 1-factors. In *Proceedings of the IASTED International Conference on Wireless and Optical Communications, WOC 2002*, Banff, Alberta, Canada, July 2002.

[3] Lali Barriere, Pierre Fraigniaud, Lata Narayanan, and Jaroslav Opatrny. Dynamic construction of Bluetooth scatternets of fixed degree and low diameter. In *Proceedings of the fourteenth annual ACM-SIAM symposium on Discrete algorithms*, pages 781–790. Society for Industrial and Applied Mathematics, 2003.

[4] S. Basagni. Distributed clustering for ad hoc networks. In A. Y. Zomaya, D. F. Hsu, O. Ibarra, S. Origuchi, D. Nassimi, and M. Palis, editors, *Proceedings of the 1999 International Symposium on Parallel Architectures, Algorithms, and Networks (I-SPAN'99)*, pages 310–315, Perth/Fremantle, Australia, June 23–25 1999. IEEE Computer Society.

[5] S. Basagni, R. Bruno, and C. Petrioli. Performance evaluation of a new scatternet formation protocol for multi-hop Bluetooth networks. In *Proceedings of the 5th International Symposium on Personal Wireless Multimedia Communications, WPMC 2002*, pages 208–212, Honolulu, Hawaii, October 27–30 2002.

[6] S. Basagni and C. Petrioli. A scatternet formation protocol for ad hoc networks of Bluetooth devices. In *Proceedings of the IEEE Semiannual Vehicular Technology Conference, VTC Spring 2002*, Birmingham, AL, May 6–9 2002.

[7] Stefano Basagni, Raffaele Bruno, Gabriele Mambrini, and Chiara Petrioli. Comparative performance evaluation of scatternet formation protocols for networks of Bluetooth devices. *Wirel. Netw.*, **10**(2):197–213, 2004.

[8] Stefano Basagni, Raffaele Bruno, and Chiara Petrioli. Scatternet formation in Bluetooth networks. in: *Mobile Ad Hoc Networking*, S. Basagni, M. Conti, S. Giordano and I. Stojmenovic (eds.), IEEE Press, Wiley Interscience.

[9] Stefano Basagni, Raffaele Bruno, and Chiara Petrioli. Device discovery in Bluetooth networks: A scatternet perspective. In *Proceedings of the Second International IFIP-TC6 Networking Conference on Networking Technologies, Services, and Protocols; Performance of Computer and Communication Networks; and Mobile and Wireless Communications*, pages 1087–1092. Springer-Verlag, 2002.

[10] Stefano Basagni, Raffaele Bruno, and Chiara Petrioli. A performance comparison of scatternet formation protocols for networks of Bluetooth devices. In *Proc. IEEE International Conference on Pervasive Computing and Communications (PerCom)*, 2003.

[11] P. Bhagwat and A. Segall. A routing vector (RVM) for routing in Bluetooth scatternets. In *Proc. IEEE Int. Workshop on Mobile Multimedia Communications MoMuC*, 1999.

[12] Bluetooth SIG. Specification of the Bluetooth system. http://www.bluetooth.com/.

[13] Diego Bohman, Matthias Frank, Peter Martini, and Christoph Scholz. Performace of symmetric neighbor discovery in Bluetooth ad hoc networks. In *2nd German Workshop on Mobile Ad-hoc Networking (WMAN 2004)*, Ulm, Germany.

[14] P. Bose, P. Morin, I. Stojmenovic, and J. Urrutia. Routing with guaranteed delivery in ad hoc wireless networks. In *3rd int. Workshop on Discrete Algorithms and methods for mobile computing and communications*, 1999.

[15] P. Bose, P. Morin, I. Stojmenovic, and J. Urrutia. Routing with guaranteed delivery in ad hoc wireless networks. *ACM/Kluwer Wireless Networks*, 7(6), 2001.

[16] A. Busboom, Ian Herwono, M. Schuba, and G. Zavagli. Unambiguous device identification and fast connection setup in Bluetooth. In *Proceedings of the European Wireless 2002*, Florence, Italy, 2002.

[17] Chao-Tsun Chang, Chih-Yung Chang, and Jang-Ping Sheu. Bluecube: Constructing a hypercube parallel computing and communication environment over Bluetooth radio system. In *Proc. 2003 International Conference on Parallel Processing*, Kaohsiung, Taiwan, 2003.

[18] K. Cheolgi, M. Joongsoo, and L. Joonwon. A random inquiry procedure using Bluetooth. *IEICE Trans. Communications*, **E-82**(1), 1999.

[19] Carla-Fabiana Chiasserini, Marco Ajmone Marsan, Elena Baralis, and Paolo Garza. Towards feasible distributed topology formation algorithms for Bluetooth-based wpans. In *Proc. of 36th Hawaii International Conference on System Science (HICSS-36)*, Big Island, Hawaii, 2003.

[20] C.S. Choi and C.W. Choi. DSR Based Bluetooth Scatternet. In *ITC-CSCC 2002*, 2002.

[21] Ming-Te Chou and Ruay-Shiung Chang. Blueline: A distributed Bluetooth scatternet formation and routing algorithm. 2004.

[22] F. Cuomo, G. di Bacco, and T. Melodia. Shaper: a self-healing algorithm producing multi-hop Bluetooth scatternets. In *Proceedings of IEEE Globecom 2003*, San Francisco, CA, USA, December 2003.

[23] F. Cuomo, G. di Bacco, and T. Melodia. Optimized scatternet topologies for personal area networking in dynamic environments. In *Proceedings of IEEE IEEE International Conference on Communications (ICC 2004)*, Paris, France, June 2004.

[24] F. Cuomo and T. Melodia. A general methodology and key metrics for scatternet formation in Bluetooth. In *Proceedings of IEEE Globecom 2002*, Taipei, Taiwan, November 2002.

[25] F. Cuomo, T. Melodia, and I. F. Akyildiz. Distributed self-healing and variable topology optimization algorithms for qos provisioning in scatternets. *IEEE Journal on Selected Areas in Communications*, **22**(7):1220–1236, 2004.

[26] N.G. de Bruijn. A combinatorial problem. In *Koninklijke Nederlandsche Akademie van Wetenschappen*, July 1946.

[27] Yuhong Dong and Jie Wu. Three Bluetree formations for constructing efficient scatternets in Bluetooth. In *Proc. of the 7th Joint Conference on Information Sciences*, 2003.

[28] Fabrizio Ferraguto, Gabriele Mambrini, Alessandro Panconesi, and Chiara Petrioli. A new approach to device discovery and scatternet formation in Bluetooth networks. In *Proc. IEEE 18th International Parallel and Distributed Processing Symposium (IPDPS04)*, 2004.

[29] Cgun-Choong Foo and Kee-Chaing Chua. Bluerings - Bluetooth scatternets with ring structure. In *Proceedings of the IASTED International Conference on Wireless and Optical Communications, WOC 2002*, Banff, Alberta, Canada, July 2002.

[30] R. Guerin, E. Kim, and S. Sarkar. Bluetooth technology: Key challenges and initial research. In *Conference on Network and Distributed Simulations*, 2002.

[31] R. Guerin, J. Rank, S. Sarkar, and E. Vergetis. Forming connected topologies in Bluetooth adhoc networks. In *Proceedings of ITC'18*, Berlin, 2003.

[32] Jeffrey Hightower and Gaetano Borriello. Location systems for ubiquitous computing. *Computer*, **34**(8):57–66, 2001.

[33] Tsung-Chuan Huang, Chu-Sing Yang, Chao-Chieh Huang, and Shen-Wen Bai. Hierarchical grown Bluetrees (HGB) - an effective topology for Bluetooth scatternets. In *Proc. of International Symposium on Parallel and Distributed Processing and Applications (ISPA 2003), LNCS 2745*, Aizu, Japan, 2003.

[34] J.-R. Jiang, B.-R. Lin, and Y.-C. Tseng. Analysis of Bluetooth device discovery and some speedup mechanisms. *Int'l J. of Electrical Engineering*, 2004.

[35] David B Johnson and David A Maltz. Dynamic source routing in ad hoc wireless networks. In Imielinski and Korth, editors, *Mobile Computing*, volume 353. Kluwer Academic Publishers, 1996.

[36] Rohit Kapoor and Mario Gerla. A Zone Routing Protocol for Bluetooth scatternets. In *Proc. of IEEE Wireless Communications and Networking Conference (WCNC03)*, New Orleans, LA, 2003.

[37] Brad Karp and H.T. Kung. GPSR: Greedy perimeter stateless routing for wireless networks. In *Proc. of the ACM/IEEE International Conference on Mobile Computing and Networking (MobiCom)*, 2000.

[38] Yoji Kawamoto, Vincent W.S. Wong, and Victor C.M. Leung. A two-phase scatternet formation protocol for Bluetooth wireless personal area networks. In *Proc. of IEEE Wireless Communications and Networking Conference (WCNC03)*, New Orleans, LA, 2003.

[39] C. Law, A.K. Mehta, and K.Y. Siu. Performance of a new Bluetooth scatternet formation protocol. In *Proc. ACM Symposium on Mobile Ad Hoc Networking and Computing MobiHoc*, pages 183–192, 2001.

[40] Xiang-Yang Li and Ivan Stojmenovic. Partial delaunay triangulation and degree limited localized Bluetooth scatternet formation. In *AdHocNow*, 2002.

[41] Xiang-Yang Li, Ivan Stojmenovic, and Yu Wang. Partial delaunay triangulation and degree limited localized Bluetooth multihop scatternet formation. *IEEE Transaction on Parallel and Distributed Systems*, 15(4):350–361, 2004. The short version appeared at AdHocNow 2002.

[42] Chunhung Richard Lin and Mario Gerla. Adaptive clustering for mobile wireless networks. *IEEE Journal of Selected Areas in Communications*, 15(7):1265–1275, 1997.

[43] T. Y. Lin, Y. C. Tseng, and K. M. Chang. A new Bluering scatternet topology for Bluetooth with its formation, routing, and maintenance protocols. *Wireless Communications and Mobile Computing*, 3(4):517–537, June 2003.

[44] Yong Liu, M.J. Lee, and T.N. Saadawi. A Bluetooth scatternet-route structure for multihop ad hoc networks. *IEEE Journal on Selected Areas in Communications*, **21**(2):229–239, 2003.

[45] M.A. Marsan, C.F. Chiasserini, A. Nucci, G. Carello, and L. de Giovanni. Optimizing the topology of Bluetooth wireless personal area networks. In *INFOCOM*, 2002.

[46] T. Melodia and F. Cuomo. Ad hoc networking with Bluetooth: Key metrics and distributed protocols for scatternet formation. *Ad Hoc Networks (Elsevier)*, **2**(2):185–202, April 2004.

[47] T. Melodia and F. Cuomo. Locally optimal scatternet topologies for Bluetooth ad hoc networks. In *Proceedings of First Working Conference on Wireless On-demand Network Systems (WONS 2004)*, Madonna di Campiglio, Italy, January 2004.

[48] D. Miorandi, Arianna Trainito, and A. Zanella. On efficient topologies for Bluetooth scatternets. In *Proc. IFIP-TC6 8th International Conference, PWC 2003, LNCS 2775*, Venice, Italy, 2003.

[49] D. Miorandi and A. Zanella. On the optimal topology of Bluetooth piconets: Roles swapping algorithms. In *Proc. Mediterranean Conference on Ad Hoc Networks (Med-Hoc)*, Sardinia, Italy, 2002.

[50] P. Murphy, E. Welsh, and P. Frantz. Using Bluetooth for Short-Term Ad-Hoc Connections Between Moving Vehicles: A Feasibility Study. In *IEEE Vehicular Technology Conference (VTC)*, volume 1, Birmingham, AL, May 2002.

[51] Elena Pagani, Gian Paolo Rossi, and Stefano Tebaldi. An on-demand Bluetooth scatternet formation algorithm. In *Proceedings of First Working Conference on Wireless On-demand Network Systems (WONS 2004)*, Madonna di Campiglio, Italy, January 2004.

[52] K. Persson, D. Manivannan, and M. Singhal. Bluetooth scatternet formation: Criteria, models, and classification. In *IEEE Consumer Communications and Networking Conference 2004 (CCNC'04)*, Las Vegas, NV, 2004.

[53] C. Petrioli and S. Basagni. Degree-constrained multihop scatternet formation for Bluetooth networks. In *Proceedings of IEEE Globecom 2002*, pages 222–226, Taipei, Taiwan, R.O.C., November 17–21 2002.

[54] C. Petrioli, S. Basagni, and I. Chlamtac. Configuring Bluestars: Multihop scatternet formation for Bluetooth networks. *IEEE Transactions on Computers*, **52**(6):779–790, 2003.

[55] C. Petrioli, S. Basagni, and I. Chlamtac. Bluemesh: degree-constrained multi-hop scatternet formation for Bluetooth networks. *Mobile Networks and Aplications*, **9**(1):33–47, 2004.

[56] Balakrishna J. Prabhu and A. Chockalingam. A Routing Protocol and Energy Efficient Techniques in Bluetooth Scatternets. In *IEEE International Conference on Communications (ICC 2002)*, New York, NY, April 2002.

[57] Lakshmi Ramachandran, Manika Kapoor, Abhinanda Sarkar, and Alok Aggarwal. Clustering algorithms for wireless ad hoc networks. In *Proceedings of the 4th international workshop on Discrete algorithms and methods for mobile computing and communications*, pages 54–63. ACM Press, 2000.

[58] Miklos Aurel Ronai and Eszter Kail. A simple neighbour discovery procedure for Bluetooth ad hoc networks. In *proceedings of IEEE GlobeCom 2003*, San Francisco, CA, USA.

[59] T. Salonidis, P. Bhagwat, L. Tassiulas, and R. LaMaire. Distributed topology construction of Bluetooth personal area networks. In *Proc. IEEE INFOCOM*, 2001.

[60] Theodoros Salonidis, Pravin Bhagwat, and Leandros Tassiulas. Proximity awareness and fast connection establishment in Bluetooth. In *Proceedings of the 1st ACM international symposium on Mobile ad hoc networking & computing*, pages 141–142. IEEE Press, 2000.

[61] Frank Siegemund and Michael Rohs. Rendezvous layer protocols for Bluetooth-enabled smart devices. *Personal Ubiquitous Comput.*, 7(2):91–101, 2003.

[62] Wen-Zhan Song, Xiang-Yang Li, Yu Wang, and Weizhao Wang. dBBlue: Low diameter and self-routing Bluetooth scatternet. *Elsevier Journal of Parallel and Distributed Computing (JPDC)*, 65(2):178-190, Feb. 2005. The short version appeared at ACM DIALM-POMC 2003.

[63] Hiranmayi Sreenivas and Hesham Ali. An evolutionary Bluetooth scatternet formation protocol. In *Proceedings of the Proceedings of the 37th Annual Hawaii International Conference on System Sciences (HICSS'04) - Track 9*, page 90306.3. IEEE Computer Society, 2004.

[64] I. Stojmenovic and N. Zaguia. Bluetooth scatternet formation in ad hoc wireless networks. in: *Performance Modeling and Analysis of Bluetooth Networks: Network Formation, Polling, Scheduling, and Traffic Control*, J. Misic and V. Misic (eds.), CRC Press.

[65] M.T. Sun, C.K. Chang, and T.H. Lai. A self-routing topology for Bluetooth scatternets. In *Proc. IEEE International Symposium on Parallel Architectures, Algorithms and Networks (ISPAN '02)*, Philipini, 2002.

[66] G. Tan, A. Miu, J. Guttag, and H. Balakrishnan. Forming scatternets from Bluetooth personal area networks. Technical Report MIT-LCS-TR-826, MIT, 2001. Also in First Annual Student Oxygen Workshop, Gloucester, MA, July 2001.

[67] Yu Wang, Ivan Stojmenovic, and Xiang-Yang Li. Bluetooth scatternet formation for single-hop ad hoc networks based on virtual positions. *Journal of Internet Technology (JIT)*, **6**(1):43-52, Jan. 2005. The short version appeared at IEEE ISCC 2004.

[68] Z. Wang, R.J. Thomas, and Z. Haas. Bluenet – a new scatternet formation scheme. In *Proceedings of the 35th Hawaii International Conference on System Science (HICSS-35)*, Big Island, Hawaii, 2002.

[69] E. Welsh, P. Murphy, and P. Frantz. Improving Connection Times for Bluetooth Devices in Mobile Environments. In *International Conference on Fundamentals of Electronics Communications and Computer Sciences (ICFS)*, March 2002.

[70] Ryan Woodings, Derek Joos, Trevor Clifton, and Charles D. Knutson. Rapid heterogeneous connection establishment: Accelerating Bluetooth inquiry using IrDA. In *Proceedings of the Third Annual IEEE Wireless Communications and Networking Conference (WCNC '02)*, 2002.

[71] A. C.-C. Yao. On constructing minimum spanning trees in k-dimensional spaces and related problems. *SIAM J. Computing*, **11**:721–736, 1982.

[72] G.V. Zaruba, S. Basagni, and I. Chlamtac. Bluetrees - scatternet formation to enable Bluetooth based ad hoc networks. In *Proc. IEEE International Conference on Communications(ICC)*, 2001.

[73] Haas Z.J. and Pearlman M.R. The zone routing protocol(zrp) for ad hoc networks. In *Internet draft - Mobile Ad hoc NETworking (MANET), Working Group of the Internet Engineering Task Force (IETF)*, Novermber 1997.

In: Wireless LANs and Bluetooth
Editors: Yang Xiao and Yi Pan, pp. 271-294

ISBN: 1-59454-432-8
© 2005 Nova Science Publishers, Inc.

Chapter 13

HIGH CAPACITY BLUETOOTH ACCESS POINT DESIGN FOR INTERFERENCE ELIMINATION[1]

Zhifeng Jiang[2], Qixiang Pang[3], Victor C.M. Leung[4] and Vincent Wong[5]

Department of Electrical and Computer Engineering, the University of British Columbia, Vancouver, BC, Canada

Abstract

One attractive scenario of large scale deployment of Bluetooth involves the use of Bluetooth access points (BAPs) to provide Bluetooth devices with Internet access capability. A BAP equipped with one radio transceiver can only support a maximum of 1 Mbps raw data rate and at most 7 active terminals. To increase the capacity, the use of multiple radio transceivers in a BAP can be an effective option. Each radio transceiver of the BAP may act as the master of its own piconet providing 1 Mbps access rate. However, when multiple radio transceivers coexist, frequency hop collisions among these piconets may severely reduce the total throughput. In this chapter, novel non-collaborative and collaborative methods are presented to address the collision issue in high capacity BAP design. The non-collaborative approach employs an orthogonal hop set partitioning (OHSP) scheme that partitions the hop frequencies into up to 5 orthogonal subsets. When different piconets select different subsets, collisions can be avoided. In the collaborative approach, a centralized collision avoidance scheduling (CAS) scheme is deployed in the BAP to schedule the transmissions without collisions. Both approaches are designed under the constraints of FCC rules. Simulation results show that the collaborative approach using CAS can significantly improve the throughput. The non-collaborative approach using OHSP also shows performance improvement in various cases.

---

[1] This work was supported by the Canadian Natural Sciences and Engineering Research Council under grant STPGP 257684-02, and the OPNET University Program.
[2] E-mail-address: zhifengj@ece.ubc.ca
[3] E-mail-address: qixiangp @ece.ubc.ca
[4] E-mail-address: vleung @ece.ubc.ca
[5] E-mail-address: vincentw @ece.ubc.ca

Keywords: WPAN, Bluetooth access point, Piconet, Frequency hopping, Interference, Collision avoidance, Scheduling, Orthogonal hop set

Introduction

Bluetooth [1][2] is a widely-deployed technology for low cost short-range wireless communications using frequency hopping spread spectrum (FHSS) transmissions over the 2.4 GHz unlicensed Industrial, Scientific, Medical (ISM) band. Two types of links can be established in a Bluetooth wireless personal area network (WPAN): synchronous connection oriented (SCO) links to support realtime traffic such as voice, and asynchronous connectionless (ACL) links to support non-realtime data traffic. In total, 13 different types of application profiles are supported by Bluetooth, including serial port, file transfer, LAN access, headset, and cordless telephony. Bluetooth devices can communicate with each other by forming a piconet, in which one device functions as the master unit that controls the hop sequence and time synchronization of up to 7 active slave devices. Several piconets may be inter-connected via bridge nodes to form a scatternet. All piconets share the same set of hop frequencies with 79 channels that span the 2.4 GHz ISM band.

Although Bluetooth was initially designed for wire replacement, the technology can also be used for wireless Internet access as more people are equipped with Bluetooth-enabled devices such as personal digital assistants and cell phones [3][4]. As extensions of wired networks, Bluetooth access points (BAPs) can be installed at hot spots to provide cost effective means for these devices to access the Internet.

A BAP equipped with one radio transceiver can only provide a maximum of 1 Mbps access data rate and support up to 7 active slaves. To increase the access rate and user capacity, use of multiple radio transceivers in a high capacity BAP can be an effective option, where each radio transceiver constructs an independent piconet providing 1 Mbps access rate. However, when multiple piconets co-exist within radio range of each other, their hop sequences may collide over some channels resulting in mutual interference that reduces the overall system throughput. The interference between collocated WLAN and Bluetooth devices has been discussed in [5]-[11], although few effective solutions have been offered to address the coexistence issue of multiple Bluetooth piconets.

In this chapter, we present two methods to solve the collision problem in high capacity BAPs employing multiple transceivers and thereby improving the system throughput. The first one is a non-collaborative approach using the orthogonal hop set partitioning (OHSP) scheme [12]. The OHSP scheme partitions the 79 hop frequencies in the 2.4 GHz ISM band into up to 5 orthogonal subsets. When each piconet selects a different subset, frequency hop collisions can be avoided. The second one is a collaborative approach using a novel collision avoidance scheduling (CAS) scheme [13]. In the CAS scheme, multiple Bluetooth masters in the BAP are time synchronized and a common baseband processor schedules the transmissions of the piconets to avoid collisions. Both approaches are designed to satisfy FCC Parts 15 regulations for unlicensed ISM band usage [14]. We present the performance of these two approaches, which has been evaluated using the OPNET simulator [15]. This chapter expands on the original presentations in [12] and [13].

The remainder of this chapter is organized as follows. The next section discusses the issue in high capacity BAP design. The third section reviews the related work. The fourth section presents the non-collaborative collision avoidance approach using the OHSP scheme. The fifth section presents the collaborative approach using the CAS scheme. The sixth section concludes this chapter.

Coexistence Issues in High Capacity Bluetooth AP Design

High Capacity Bluetooth Access Point

According to the Bluetooth specifications [1][2], each piconet supports a raw data rate of 1 Mbps. When multiple Bluetooth terminals connect to a BAP equipped with one radio transceiver, the maximum capacity of the BAP is limited by its ability to connect only 7 active slaves at a channel data rate of 1 Mbps. Use of multiple radio transceivers in a BAP can be an effective way to overcome such a limitation. An example of a BAP supporting five piconets is shown in Fig. 1, where "pn-i" represents the i-th piconet. However, the throughput of the BAP in Fig. 1 is less than five times that of an isolated piconet, due to collisions of transmissions between piconets that hop onto the same frequency channel. This problem becomes progressively worse when the number of collocated piconets and traffic load increase.

Collision Issues

As the current Bluetooth specification has neither provisions for orthogonal hop sequences nor intelligent scheduling of hop sequences among piconets, multiple piconets within radio range of each other may interfere with each other to cause collisions and data losses when they happen to occupy the same hop frequency.

A simplified Bluetooth system model has been proposed in [16][17][18] to analyze the collision probability when multiple piconets coexist. The main analysis in [16][17][18] is summarized below.

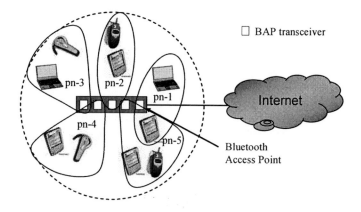

Fig. 1. A high capacity Bluetooth access point with five transceivers

Assume N collocated piconets are sufficiently close to one another such that a collision between 2 or more packets over the same hop channel will destroy all packets. For simplicity, we assume that only 1 bit of overlap is enough to destroy all packets involved. Forward error correction and capture effect are neglected. Because of the strong adjacent channel rejection requirement imposed by the standard, adjacent channel interference is not considered. Assume that all packets occupy a single slot and the probability to have a packet in a slot is G.

First we assume that all piconets are synchronized so that the start of each time slot is aligned. For a 1-slot packet in piconet A, the probability of an unsuccessful transmission in the presence of another synchronized piconet B is equal to GP_0, where $P_0 = 1/79$ is the probability that piconet B chooses the same hop frequency as piconet A. With N collocated piconets, piconet A has $N - 1$ adversary piconets. The probability of an unsuccessful transmission is

$$P_S(N,G) = 1 - (1 - GP_0)^{(N-1)} \qquad (1)$$

Next, we consider the case where different piconets are not synchronized and the actual duration of a packet is smaller than the duration of a slot. A single slot packet is 366 bits long (duration $t_d = 366$ µs at 1 Mbps) and the duration of the slot is $t_s = 625$ µs. Consider the situation with two piconets. Depending on the relative time phase, one or two slots from the adversary piconet B can interfere with the packet of interest in piconet A. We assume that the time shift between A and B is a random variable uniformly distributed between 0 and t_s. The time shift is random, but it is constant for any given pair of piconets assuming that the slow clock drifts are neglected. The probability that the time shift is such that a packet in piconet B is a potential threat to 2 packets in piconet A can be expressed by $d = 2t_d / t_s - 1$. The probability that the time shift is such that a packet in piconet B is a potential threat to 1 packet in piconet A is the complement, $s = 1 - d = 2(1 - t_d / t_s)$.

If the adversary piconet B is shifted such that one of its packets is threatening two slots in piconet A, the probability of an unsuccessful transmission in piconet A is given by $1 - (1 - GP_0)^2$, as both the preceding and following slots must have chosen different frequencies. If all $N-1$ adversary piconets are shifted such that each of the packets sent by them is threatening packets sent in two adjacent slots in piconet A, the probability of unsuccessfully transmission becomes

$$P_D(N,G) = 1 - (1 - GP_0)^{2(N-1)} \qquad (2)$$

In a practical situation, from the $N-1$ adversary piconets, there will be a number, N_S, of piconets threatening a single slot in piconet A and a number, $N_D = N - 1 - N_S$, of piconets threatening 2 slots in piconet A. These numbers are random but remain constant over time for any given set of active piconets. The random variable N_S follows the binomial distribution,

$$P(N_S = n_S) = \binom{N-1}{n_S} \cdot s^{n_S} \cdot (1-s)^{N-1-n_S}.$$

For any given N and N_S, the probability of a transmission encountering a collision can be expressed as

$$P_c(N, N_S, G) = 1 - (1 - GP_0)^{N_S} (1 - GP_0)^{2(N-1-N_S)} \tag{3}$$

From eqns. (1)-(3), we can see that the collision probability is related to the number of piconets and the traffic load in each piconet. Fig. 2 shows the collision probabilities given by eqns. (1) and (2) when $G = 1$. When the number of piconets is large, the collision probability can be quite high. From Fig. 2 we can also deduce that by avoiding collisions, throughput can be substantially increased.

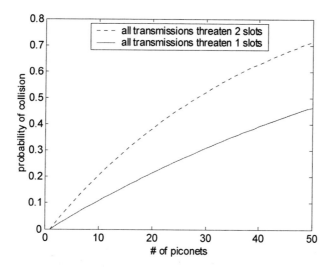

Fig. 2. Collision probability due to frequency hop collisions

More detailed analyses of Bluetooth system considering the propagation aspects and the possibility of multi-slot packet transmissions are given in [19]-[21]. The simple analysis given above, however, is sufficient to motivate the need to reduce interference between collocated piconets.

FCC Constraints on Bluetooth System Design

Before we discuss the solutions to the collision problem in BAP design, the applicable FCC regulations need to be reviewed first. FCC Section 15.247 specifies the regulations that a FHSS system operating in the 2.4 GHz ISM band must comply with [14]. Two of the regulations are directly related to the discussions in this chapter and are specifically cited as follows:

(1)   Frequency hopping systems in the 2400-2483.5 MHz band may utilize hopping channels whose 20 dB bandwidth is greater than 1 MHz provided the systems use at least 15 non-overlapping channels. The total span of hopping channels shall be at least 75 MHz.

(2)   The incorporation of intelligence within a FHSS system that permits the system to recognize other users within the spectrum band so that it individually and independently chooses and adapts its hop sets to avoid hopping on occupied channels is permitted. The coordination of frequency hopping systems in any other manner for the express purpose

of avoiding the simultaneous occupancy of individual hopping frequencies by multiple transmitters is not permitted.

The design of high capacity BAPs supporting multiple piconets is constrained by these regulations.

Related Work

Interference with other ISM Band Users

Since the 2.4 GHz ISM band is unlicensed, a variety of communication devices may coexist and the mutual interference among them may lead to degraded performance for all. Besides Bluetooth WPANs, one of the most popular types of ISM band devices is 802.11 WLANs [22]. Many research activities have been devoted to the coexistence of Bluetooth WPANs with 802.11 WLANs [6]-[11], leading to the IEEE 802.15.2 standard [5] published in August 2003.

In IEEE 802.15.2, eight coexistence mechanisms classified into two categories: collaborative and non-collaborative, are described. Three collaborative mechanisms, namely, alternating wireless medium access, packet traffic arbitration, and deterministic interference suppression, enable coexistence of an 802.11 WLAN and a Bluetooth WPAN by sharing information between collocated 802.11 and Bluetooth radios to facilitate control of their transmissions to avoid interference. Five non-collaborative mechanisms, namely, adaptive interference suppression, adaptive packet selection, packet scheduling for ACL links, packet scheduling for SCO links, and adaptive frequency-hopping, employ techniques such as measuring the packet error rate, the signal strength or the signal to interference ratio to detect the presence of other types of devices in the band. The non-collaborative mechanisms are useful when it is not possible, or necessary, to collocate a WLAN and WPAN radios within the same physical unit.

As described above, interference issues between 802.11 WLANs and Bluetooth WPANs have been intensively studied; however, collision issues among Bluetooth piconets accessing a high capacity BAP employing multiple Bluetooth radios as presented above have not attracted the same level of attention. Addressing these issues is the main focus of this chapter.

Existing High Capacity BAP Design

The design of a Bluetooth system with mobile LAN access capability presented in [23] has not considered the use of multiple transceivers in high capacity BAPs. The performance of a Bluetooth system with multiple radio transceivers has been evaluated in [18] and multi-AP strategies to support more SCO links has been discussed in [24]. However, neither [18] nor [24] offer solutions to eliminate interference and collisions. The scheme in [25] uses directional antennas to reduce interference, but it needs a complicated control system. The implementation difficulty of directional antennas increases cost and reduces its usefulness.

Bluetooth Research Activities at the University of British Columbia

The work presented in this chapter has resulted from an ongoing project titled "Enabling technologies for ubiquitous personal area networking" funded by the Canadian Natural Sciences and Engineering Research Council under the Strategic Project Grant program and in collaboration with several companies in the Canadian wireless industry. A group of researchers at the University of British Columbia spanning several research areas including radio propagation, digital transmissions, networking and chip design are collaborating in this project. One of the major tasks in the project is the research on Bluetooth network architecture and protocols. In addition to the study of collision avoidance approaches in high capacity BAP design reported in this chapter, substantial research has also been done in scatternet formation and scheduling algorithms for ad hoc Bluetooth WPANs. These include the proposal of the original two-phase scatternet formation (TPSF) algorithm [26] as well as its improvement [27], development of the BlueScout scatternet formation method that employs mobile agents to optimize the scatternet after a Bluetooth device initially connects itself to the scatternet [28][29][30], and development of an adaptive scheduling method [31] for bridging piconets to form scatternets. Other major tasks of the project include: propagation measurement and channel modeling for Bluetooth radio transmissions, design of advanced receivers and next generation Bluetooth signaling techniques, and the development of a systems on chip (SoC) implementation platform. A particular highlight is the development of new noncoherent sequence estimation schemes [32][33] and a new decoding scheme [34] that allow various performance-complexity trade-offs and yield a significantly better performance (up to 4 dB gain) than the current limiter-discriminator-integrator Bluetooth receivers. In our investigation of programmable baseband architectures for Bluetooth amenable to flexible SoC implementation, it has been determined that the level of flexibility is best achieved using a synthesizable embedded programmable logic core [35]; both software [36] and firmware based programmability for the logic core is being studied.

Non-collaborative Solution – Orthogonal Hop Set Partitioning

The first approach to solve the collision problem of high capacity BAPs supporting multiple piconets is a non-collaborative solution. It attempts to reduce the intrinsic collisions among Bluetooth piconets employing a common hop set, by means of an orthogonal hop set partitioning (OHSP) scheme [12]. In this approach, no centralized controller is needed. A high capacity BAP is a simple and straightforward combination of several single-transceiver BAPs. There is no explicit control information exchanged among these single-transceiver BAPs. Therefore this scheme can also be applied to any multi-piconet collocation system besides the infrastructure mode Bluetooth access network.

Description of OHSP Scheme

Construction of Orthogonal Hop Subsets
We introduce a hop subset construction method that partitions the 79 channels in the original Bluetooth hop set into several orthogonal hop subsets that do not share any common

channels. To comply with FCC 15.247 regulations for FHSS systems in the 2.4 GHz ISM band [14], which require at least 15 channels in a hop set (see "FCC Constraints ..." section above), the original 79 channels hop set can be partitioned into up to 5 orthogonal hop subsets for selection by Bluetooth piconets. This is similar to IEEE 802.11 FHSS, which provides three orthogonal hop sets for selection by each basic service set [22].

Each hop subset should approximately cover the entire frequency band according to FCC [14]. We denote $b_{ij} \in \{0, 1, 2, ..., 78\}$ as the channel number of the j-th channel in the i-th orthogonal hop subset. The five orthogonal hop subsets are defined as follows:

$$\text{Set } i = \{ b_{ij} \} = \{ i + 5j \}, i = 0, 1, 2, 3, 4; j = 0, 1, 2, ... 15; \qquad (4)$$

except that channel $b_{4,15} = 79$ is not part of subset 4 since there are only 79 channels available in total. Thus, subsets 0, 1, 2, 3 have $M_1 = 16$ channels each, but subset 4 has only $M_2 = 15$ channels.

Each piconet independently selects one of these orthogonal hop subsets. The piconet then hops through the frequency channels in the hop subset in a pseudo-random manner, based on the master's identity and clock phase as in the original Bluetooth FHSS algorithm. The proposed method minimizes collisions in that two piconets will never collide if their choices of orthogonal hop subsets are different. Even if they choose the same hop subset, the pseudo-random hop pattern ensures that collisions only occur at some channels. However, in this case the collision probability is expected to be higher than that with the original single hop set, as the number of channels in each hop subset is smaller.

Implementation of OHSP Scheme

To implement OHSP, the frequency synthesizer module in the transceiver needs to be modified. The additional logic needed is shown in

Fig. 3. Two synchronized switches shown as A and B are used to select between the original single hop set scheme and the proposed orthogonal sub-hop band. The "mod" module determines the modulo value (M_1 or M_2) of the shifted index depending on the size of the selected hop subset. This results in a new pseudorandom hop sequence for addressing the channels in the selected hop subset.

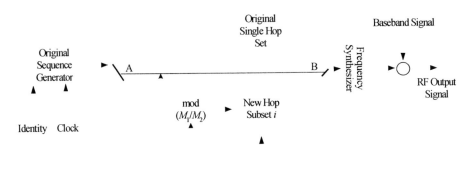

Fig. 3. Frequency synthesizer logic to implement OHSP

Selection of Orthogonal Subsets

Assuming all Bluetooth devices are equipped with the ability to generate the five orthogonal subsets as described above, it will be the responsibility of the master in each piconet to select one of the five orthogonal hop subsets and broadcast the selection to its corresponding slaves using the link management protocol command. Since no coordination for hop subset selection is allowed by FCC Parts 15 rules, the hop subset must be independently selected by each piconet.

Depending on whether or not the piconet has the ability to change the selected piconet dynamically, two methods can be defined: static selection and adaptive selection. Static selection is the simplest selection method, in which the subset once selected remains unchanged. In order to minimize the selection possibilities of hop subsets that are already heavily used by other piconets, more sophisticated hop subset selection methods using adaptive techniques can be developed. In this chapter, we consider the performance of static OHSP only. Research work is ongoing to develop adaptive OHSP schemes and investigate their performance.

Performance Evaluation of the Static OHSP Scheme

In the static OHSP scheme, once a piconet has selected a hop subnet at random, the subset will not be changed thereafter. In this section, its performance under different numbers of piconets is studied via simulations.

Simulation Model

We built an OPNET simulation model to evaluate the OHSP collision reduction effects by comparing its throughput with the original Bluetooth FHSS mechanism employing a single hop set. We consider piconets operating in synchronized mode and unsynchronized mode. In synchronized mode, time slots in all piconets within radio range are aligned with each other. Time slot alignment is not enforced in the unsynchronized mode. The simulation results compare OHSP throughput improvements over the baseline system employing the original single hop set FHSS scheme, under different hop subset selection scenarios.

ACL links are modeled in the simulations. The master and slaves take turn to communicate over an ACL link in each piconet, with the master starting transmissions in even slots and slaves starting transmissions in odd slots. Three types of ACL packets, DH1, DH3, and DH5, which span 1, 3, or 5 slots, respectively, are considered. We consider corruption of packet transmissions due only to collisions with another piconet in this system. The channel is otherwise assumed free of noise or interference. A successful packet transmission is confirmed at the sender when it receives an ACK from the receiver, either piggybacked on a return data packet, or explicitly in a control packet. A data packet transmission is unsuccessful if any part of the packet collides with another packet transmitted over the same frequency channel in another piconet. However, a piggybacked ACK is correctly received even if the data packet carrying the ACK has suffered a collision, if the header of the data packet is not involved in the collision.

The hop sequence in each piconet, regardless of whether the original FHSS scheme or OHSP is used, is generated by a pseudorandom sequence that is determined by the address and clock of its master, according to the Bluetooth specification [1][2]. A Poisson traffic arrival model is employed. In each piconet, 500-bit source packets arrive at the master at rate $\lambda = 640$ packets/s. The same arrival rate applies to all the slaves in each piconet collectively. The actual number of slaves does not affect the performance. DHk packets are serviced at the rate of one DHk packet/$2k$ slots/piconet starting at an even slot for master and at an odd slot for slave, where $k = 1, 3, 5$. All piconets are assumed to service the same type of packets. The length of each time slot, including guard time, is 625 bits (i.e., 625 μs) and the channel data rate is 1 Mbps. For performance evaluation, each generated packet is stamped by its start time, expiry time, hop frequency number, and piconet number in the simulations. Based on this information, the simulation tool checks whether the packet is involved in a collision. The statistics on successful packet transmissions are collected to determine system throughput at the baseband layer. The simulation parameters and their values are listed in Table 1.

Table 1. Values of parameters in BAP simulation model.

Parameters	Values
Service rate	1 DHk packet/$2k$ slots, $k = 1, 3, 5$
Standard time slot	625 μs
Frame access code and header duration	126 μs
Frame settling time	259 μs
DH1 packet duration	366 μs
DH3 packet duration	1616 μs
DH5 packet duration	2866 μs

Simulation Results and Discussions

In total, 10000 random scenarios have been simulated for each specified number of piconets. In each scenario, each piconet employs a hop subset selected independently and at random by the master, and then the throughput is calculated after a 7 seconds simulation run.

We represent the hop subsets selected by the piconets in each scenario by the combination $\{y_1, y_2, y_3, y_4, y_5\}$, where $y_1 \geq y_2 \geq y_3 \geq y_4 \geq y_5$ indicate the numbers of piconets selecting the same hop subsets arranged in decreasing order, and $y_1 + y_2 + y_3 + y_4 + y_5$ is the total number of piconets. Zero elements (for hop subsets not selected by any piconets) are not included in the combination. Since only five hop subsets are available, there are at most five elements in the combination. Table 2 gives an example of the possible combinations of hop subset selection for 8 piconets and their corresponding probabilities.

In Table 2, the worst case is $\{8\}$, which corresponds to the case that all piconets select the same hop subset and hence the highest collision probability. Fortunately, the probability of this combination being selected by the piconets has a very small value of 0.000013. The best case combination that minimizes collisions is $\{2, 2, 2, 1, 1\}$, which has a probability of 0.129024. The most likely case is the combination $\{3, 2, 2, 1\}$, which has the highest probability of being selected, 0.258048.

Table 2. Probabilities of different hop subset combinations for 8 piconets.

Hop subset combinations	Probability of each combination
{8}, {7, 1}, {6, 2}	0.000013, 0.00041, 0.001434
{6, 1, 1}, {5, 3}, {5, 2, 1}	0.004301, 0.002867, 0.025805
{5,1,1,1}, {4, 4}, {4, 3,1}	0.017203, 0.001792, 0.043008
{4, 2, 1, 1}, {4, 1, 1, 1, 1}	0.129024, 0.021504
{3, 3, 2}, {3, 3, 1, 1}	0.043008, 0.086016
{3, 2, 1, 1, 1}, {2, 2, 2, 2}	0.172032, 0.032256
{2, 2, 2, 1, 1}, {3, 2, 2, 1}	0.129024, 0.258048
{4, 2, 2}	0.032256

Given the number of piconets (from 2 to 10), the most likely and the best case combinations of hop subset selections are listed in Table 3 with their corresponding probabilities. In contrast, the worst case combination $\{y_i\}$, where $y_i = 2, 3, ..., 10$, i.e., the number of piconets, has a selection probability of $(0.2)^{(y_i-1)}$ that decreases rapidly with the number of piconets.

Table 3. Probabilities of the most likely and the best case hop subset combinations.

Number of piconets	Most likely	Probability	Best case	Probability
2	{1, 1}	0.80	{1, 1}	0.80
3	{1, 1, 1}	0.48	{1, 1, 1}	0.48
4	{2, 1, 1}	0.58	{1, 1, 1, 1}	0.19
5	{2, 1, 1, 1}	0.38	{1, 1, 1, 1, 1}	0.04
6	{2, 2, 1, 1}	0.35	{2, 1, 1, 1, 1}	0.12
7	{3, 2, 1, 1}	0.32	{2, 2, 1, 1, 1}	0.16
8	{3, 2, 2, 1}	0.26	{2, 2, 2, 1, 1}	0.13
9	{3, 2, 2, 1, 1}	0.23	{2, 2, 2, 2, 1}	0.06
10	{3, 2, 2, 2, 1}	0.16	{2, 2, 2, 2, 2}	0.01

Fig. 4 presents the system throughput versus the number of piconets for the original single hop set FHSS, which serves as baseline for comparison with our proposed OHSP. It can be seen from Fig. 4 that higher system throughput can be achieved by using a larger packet size, which reduces the fraction of overhead, and by synchronizing the piconets, which eliminates partial collisions.

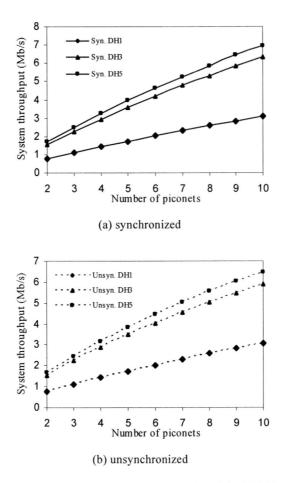

(a) synchronized

(b) unsynchronized

Fig. 4. System throughput baseline in the original FHSS

The simulation results for OHSP are presented in Fig. 5 and Fig. 6 in terms of the throughput improvements (the difference between the total throughput using OHSP and the total throughput using the original scheme) of different hop subset combination cases: Best, Most likely and Average. The "Best" case is based on the hop subset selection combination that minimizes collisions. The "Most likely" case is based on the hop subset selection combination that has the highest probability of being selected by the piconets. The throughput averaged over the 10000 simulated scenarios with random hop subset selection by each piconet is denoted "Average" in the graphs.

Fig. 5 shows that, in synchronized mode, the best case combination achieves a maximum throughput improvement of better than 10% in some cases. However, the improvement of throughput on average is marginal, and negative for some number of piconets. The most likely combinations achieve varying throughput improvements between the best case and the average. Some combinations in the most likely case yield good throughput improvements while others do not. For example, the most likely combination {2, 1, 1, 1} for 5 piconets performs close to the best combination {1, 1, 1, 1, 1} and gives a good throughput improvement. However, the most likely combination {3, 2, 1, 1} for 7 piconets under-performs the best case combination {2, 2, 1, 1, 1} significantly. In all cases, a higher throughput improvement is achieved using a bigger packet size to reduce the transmission overhead. Similar results are shown in Fig. 6 for unsynchronized mode.

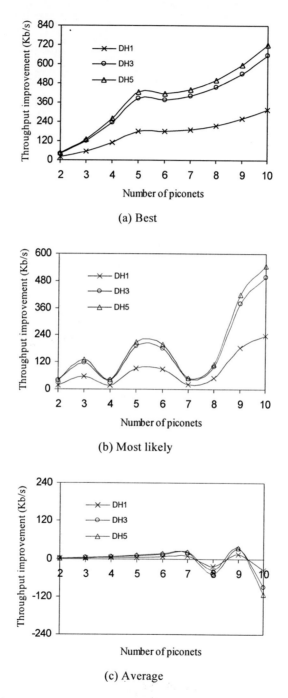

(a) Best

(b) Most likely

(c) Average

Fig. 5. Throughput improvements in synchronized mode

Although not shown in the graphs in Figs. 5 and 6, under the worst case hop subset combinations, the throughput is in fact degraded by using OHSP scheme for both synchronized and unsynchronized modes compared with the original scheme. This is because when all the piconets use the same hop subset, the smaller size of each hop subset in OHSP with 15-16 channels results in a higher collision probability than the original hop set with 79 channels.

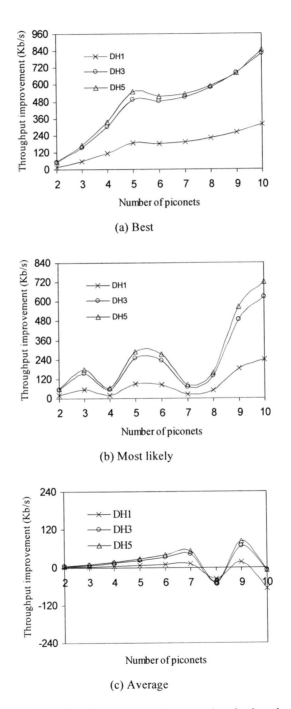

(a) Best

(b) Most likely

(c) Average

Fig. 6. Throughput improvements in unsynchronized mode

Results in Fig. 5 and Fig. 6 show large variations in the overall trend depending on the packet length and number of piconets. Variations with packet lengths are attributed to the complex collision mechanism as illustrated by the three collision scenarios in Fig. 7. Case (a) shows that in the unsynchronized mode a collision can corrupt only the payload but not the ACK piggybacked in the header. Case (b), which corresponds to the synchronized mode, shows that collisions always corrupt both the header and payload. This case can also occur in unsynchronized mode but with a low probability. Case (c) shows that in the unsynchronized mode a packet can collide with and corrupt two adjacent packets. These scenarios occur with different probabilities for different packet types and transmission modes.

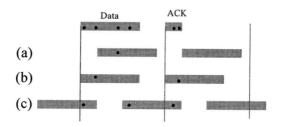

Fig. 7. Three collision scenarios

The simulation results show that a trade-off exists in static OHSP scheme in that two piconets can reduce their collision probability by choosing different hop subsets, but if they happen to choose the same hop subset, then the collision probability is increased due to the reduced number of frequencies in the hop subsets. Nevertheless, the potential throughput improvement under ideal hop set selection scenarios motivates further ongoing research on adaptive hop set selection.

Collaborative Solution – Collision Avoidance Scheduling

The marginal throughput improvement in the static OHSP scheme motivates the need for either an adaptive OHSP scheme or a collaborative interference avoidance scheme in which more intelligence is employed. This section presents a collaborative approach using a collision avoidance scheduling (CAS) scheme in high capacity BAP design. The CAS scheme is used to minimize the detrimental effects of interference among piconets [13]. Different from the non-collaborative OHSP scheme, in the collaborative scheme a centralized controller is implemented in the BAP.

Design of Bluetooth Access Point with Collaborative Control

Requirements for Collaborative BAP Design

To increase the throughput capacity of a BAP, as discussed above, multiple Bluetooth transceivers are installed each belonging to a different piconet. While each transceiver may function as either a slave or a master in the piconet to which it belongs, efficiency considerations require that it functions as a master. Should the BAP transceiver function as a slave, other active slaves in the piconet can only access the BAP through double hopping via the master of the piconet, thus severely limiting the throughput of the BAP.

The hopping sequences employed by all Bluetooth nodes in a piconet are synchronized to that of the master, generated by a pseudo-random sequence kernel based on the master's Bluetooth device ID and native clock. The slaves add time offsets to their respective native clocks to synchronize their frequency hopping sequences to that of the master. Bluetooth devices employ time division duplex (TDD) to transmit and receive data in 625 µs time slots at different hop frequencies, and the slaves' transmissions are always scheduled by their respective masters. When multiple Bluetooth transceivers share a common antenna at a BAP, it has been found that if one transmits while others are receiving, the receivers tend to be saturated even though the receive frequencies are different from the transmit frequency, due to insufficient attenuations between transmitters and receivers. If the time slots between different piconets are not aligned, a transmission in one time slot can corrupt receptions in two consecutive time slots overlapping with it. Fortunately, as we have determined that all Bluetooth transceivers in the BAP should be masters, it is possible for all the masters collocated in a BAP to be synchronized so that their time slots are aligned to each other. This is the second requirement in our collaborative high capacity BAP design.

Architecture of Collaborative BAP

The BAP architecture consists of five parts as shown in Fig. 8. The shared antenna is used to transmit and receive Bluetooth radio signals. "TR" represents an independent Bluetooth transceiver that may be implemented as part of an array of transceivers, and all transceivers use the same system clock to facilitate time slot synchronization. The core baseband scheduler/processor is the key element in the proposed architecture, responsible for special functions such as maintaining master's role for each TR, synchronization between piconets, collision avoidance algorithm, data exchange between piconets, etc. The "glue" function may be implemented as a bridge or router between the core baseband scheduler and the high-speed Internet interface. The high-speed interface provides various interfaces for accessing the Internet via Ethernet, ATM, wireless LAN, etc.

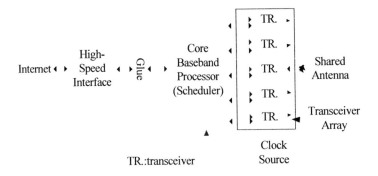

Fig. 8. Architecture of novel Bluetooth access point

The functional architecture of the core baseband processor/scheduler is shown in Fig. 9. The frequency occupation table (FOT) is used to record the frequency occupation of each piconet, which includes the frequency occupied, and the start and end time. These parameters are read and modified by the collision avoidance algorithm to determine whether collision will occur and how to avoid it. The packet switch supports local switching based on the Bluetooth device's address, which allows piconets to exchange data through the access point without going through higher layer processing. The hop selection array implements the pseudo-random hop sequence kernels for the transceivers, taking the master addresses as input and employing a common clock to ensure time slot synchronization between the piconets. Its outputs through the RF interface control the frequency synthesizers of the array of transceivers. The timing management module derives different clocks from the reference system clock for internal modules managed by the core scheduler. Detailed descriptions of core scheduler functions are given below.

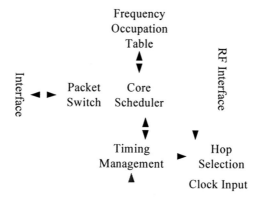

Fig. 9. Functional architecture of core processor

Maintenance of Master's Role

According to the Bluetooth specifications, any Bluetooth device may assume a master or slave role when a link is initially established between two devices, through the inquiry-page process. To maximize throughput of the BAP, as discussed above, the core processor needs to maintain a master's role for each Bluetooth transceiver all the time. This can be accomplished by ensuring that all Bluetooth transceivers start in the inquiry mode but never respond to inquiries. Furthermore, each Bluetooth transceiver periodically goes to the inquiry mode to facilitate connection establishment with any newly active Bluetooth device. How often a master goes to inquiry mode can depend on the current traffic load of the specific master compared with the others, so that some degree of load balancing can be achieved.

Collision Avoidance Scheduling Algorithm

As the core processor has full information regarding the hop sequence and traffic demand of each piconet, it can take advantage of this information in the novel CAS algorithm described in detail below.

Since Bluetooth devices may employ 1, 3, or 5 slots at each hop frequency to transmit data depending on the type of data being transmitted, the piconets controlled by the masters at the BAP may not change hop frequencies at the same time even though their time slots are synchronized. Thus, there are two possible scenarios regarding collisions that the CAS algorithm tries to avoid.

When multiple piconets attempt to hop to the same frequency to transmit new data, the resulting collision is referred as a synchronous collision. The "competition" mechanism in the CAS is designed to randomly choose one of the piconets that will be involved in a synchronous collision as a candidate to transmit data while delaying data transmissions from the other piconets until the next hop. However, before the chosen piconet can access the frequency slot and update the FOT accordingly, it must go through a second checking mechanism to ensure that there is no ongoing transmission present in the frequency slot. Since the core processor knows the next hops of all the piconets at least one time slot in advance, the competition mechanism can operate in a predictive manner.

When one piconet is already occupying a hop frequency to transmit a multi-slot packet, and another piconet attempts to hop onto that frequency to transmit a new packet, the resulting collision is referred as an asynchronous collision. The processes described below are designed to avoid asynchronous collisions, by requiring the new packet to yield to the ongoing packet transmission.

When a piconet is selected to transmit data by "winning" the competition process described above, and the data transfer is from master to slaves, the CAS looks up the FOT to ensure that the intended frequency slot is not already occupied by an ongoing transmission from the master or a slave in another piconet. If the frequency slot is available, the master is allowed to transmit its data and the FOT is updated with the transmission's frequency slot information, i.e., frequency, start time and end time. Otherwise, the transmission is not allowed to proceed and is deferred until the next hop.

Alternately, to enable a slave in the piconet winning the competition process to transferring data to the master, the slave must be scheduled via the master's transmission in the previous slot. Using the FOT, the CAS can predict whether the slot to be used by the slave has an ongoing transmission, and if so, the master will defer its permission for the slave to transmit. Otherwise, the master polls the slave as normal and the FOT is updated with the frequency slot information pertaining to the slave's transmission.

Note that the CAS algorithm first goes through a synchronous collision check using the competition mechanism, then goes through the asynchronous collision detection. In order to reduce or avoid possible collision detection delay, the CAS operates in a predictive and cyclic manner, at time T ahead of each time slot boundary. T is determined by the processing time, and can range from a few tens ns to a few ms depending on the implementation. During T, both synchronous and asynchronous collision checks should be completed so that the core scheduler can schedule the next master transmission on time. In addition, slaves' transmissions are scheduled at the same time that the master transmission is scheduled.

Performance Evaluation of CAS

In this section, we present simulation results to compare our proposed CAS scheme with the original scheme in which piconets operate without scheduling.

Simulation Model

As we have identified at the beginning of this section, a requirement of collaborative high capacity BAP design is that constituent piconets are synchronized. A Poisson traffic arrival model is employed in the simulation. In each piconet, 500-bit source packets arrive at the master at rate $\lambda = 320$ packets/s. The same arrival rate applies to all the slaves in each piconet collectively. Again the number of slaves in each piconet does not matter. DHk packets are serviced at the rate of one DHk packet/$2k$ slots/piconet starting at an even slot for master and at an odd slot for slave, where $k = 1, 3, 5$. All piconets are assumed to service the same type of packets. The length of each time slot, including guard time, is 625 bits (i.e., $625\ \mu s$) and the channel data rate is 1 Mbps. Other parameters for BAP simulation are the same as those listed in Table 1. Besides the three scenarios of fixed types of packets, DH1, DH3 and DH5, we also investigate a mixed case where each piconet randomly chooses its packet type.

Simulation Results

Fig. 10 shows that CAS always achieves better system throughput than the original scheme for each specified packet type over an ACL link. The performance advantage of CAS increases with longer packets since the longer packets can transfer more data with proportionally smaller packet overheads, which saves the transmission time and promotes efficiency.

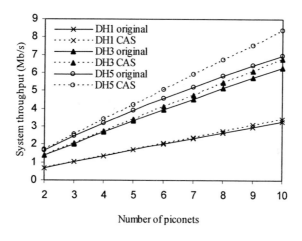

Fig. 10. Throughput vs. number of piconets

Fig. 11 shows that source average delays (to successfully transmit the source packets) with CAS are shorter in comparison with the original scheme as CAS avoids collision and thus saves on retransmission time. For any given number of piconets, shorter packets have smaller source average delays because of their correspondingly shorter transmission time, However, longer packets have less overhead and thus the source average delays are proportionally shorter. While average delays under both schemes increase with the number of piconets due to increased collisions, the increases under CAS are much smaller than the corresponding increases under the original scheme.

In practice, a more common situation is that different packet types are used over different piconets (referred as the mixed case here). In the simulations of the mixed case, each piconet selects its packet type at random, using the same Poisson arrival model described above. In Fig. 12, we see that the system throughput of CAS is approximately 20% greater than that of the original scheme in the mixed case when the number of piconets is large. Fig. 13 shows that the source average delays with CAS are less than those in the original scheme.

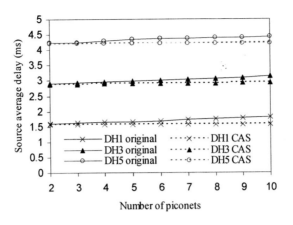

Fig. 11. Average delay vs. number of piconets

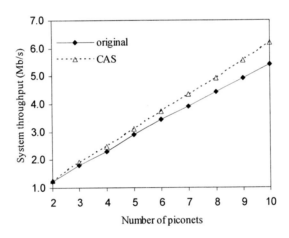

Fig. 12. Throughput vs. number of piconets (mixed case)

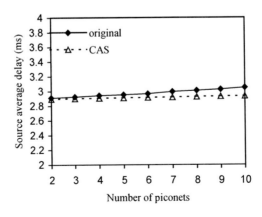

Fig. 13. Average delay vs. number of piconets (mixed case)

Conclusions

This chapter considers the interference and collision issues in high capacity BAP design employing multiple Bluetooth transceivers. Although interference between Bluetooth and 802.11 WLANs has been intensively studied, relatively few results have appeared in the literature that address the Bluetooth FHSS hop collision issue. We have addressed this issue by presenting in this chapter two novel schemes, OHSP and CAS, aimed at reducing hop collisions among multiple piconets/transceivers collocated in a BAP.

In the OHSP scheme, the original 79 Bluetooth hop frequencies are partitioned into 5 orthogonal hop subsets. When different piconets select different subsets, collision is avoided. It is a simple method based on an easy modification of the frequency synthesizer module in the Bluetooth transceiver. No collaborative control is needed in OHSP. Therefore it can be applied not only in BAPs but also in more general cases where multiple piconets are collocated within the same radio range. The OHSP scheme can be either static or adaptive depending on whether the selected hop subset is adjustable or not. We have presented simulation results for non-adaptive OHSP, which show that while significant performance improvement is possible under the best case subset selection, on average the performance improvement is marginal. These results motivate further work to develop adaptive OHSP aimed at approaching the best case performance.

In the CAS scheme, collaborative control is required. A central scheduler in the BAP employs the CAS algorithm with the aid of a frequency occupation table to avoid collisions. The baseband layer in the BAP is common to all the transceivers, which are configured as masters and synchronized in their transmission time slots. We have presented simulation results, which show that the BAP design using CAS achieves 20% improvement in system throughput when the number of transceivers collocated at the access point is large.

A comparison of the characteristics of the two collision avoidance schemes presented in this chapter are given in Table 4.

Table 4. Comparison of collision avoidance schemes in BAP.

Scheme	Static OHSP	CAS
Type	Non-collaborative	Collaborative
Centralized controller	No	Yes
Baseband layer implementation	Separate, independent	Common
Online measurement and adjustment	No	No
Performance improvement	Marginal	Significant

Research is ongoing to develop an adaptive OHSP scheme motivated by the discussions above. In the adaptive OHSP scheme, each piconet dynamically monitors the channel conditions to determine the collision rate, and selects a different hop subset when the subset current used results in a high collision rate (which implies that this subset is very likely being used by other piconets). This method can potentially reduce mutual interference between collocated piconets. A detailed performance investigation of the adaptive OHSP scheme is in progress and results will be presented in a future paper.

In this chapter we have addressed the collision problem due to overlap of FHSS hop frequencies in a pure Bluetooth environment. As we have described above, IEEE 802.15.2 recommends 8 coexistence schemes to reduce interference between Bluetooth WPANs and 802.11b/g WLANs. When multiple Bluetooth and WLAN devices coexist in a site and all require Internet access through either a common or separate access point(s), three types of collisions: between Bluetooth devices, between WLAN devices, and between Bluetooth and WLAN devices may occur. How to integrate the two novel schemes studied in this chapter with the 8 schemes recommended by IEEE 802.15.2 to minimize all three possible types of collisions is an interesting problem we intend to address in the future.

References

[1]   Bluetooth SIG, Bluetooth Specification, http://www.bluetooth.com.

[2]   IEEE Std 802.15.1, Wireless Medium Access Control (MAC) and Physical Layer (PHY) Specifications for Wireless Personal Area Networks (WPANs), June 2002.

[3]   A. S. Tanenbaum, *Computer Networks*, Fourth edition, Prentice Hall PTR, Upper Saddle River, NJ, 2003.

[4]   K. V. S. Sairam, N. Gunasekaran, and S. R. Redd, "Bluetooth in Wireless Communication," *IEEE Communications Magazine*, vol. 40, no. 6, pp. 90-96, June 2002.

[5]   IEEE Std 802.15.2, Coexistence of Wireless Personal Area Networks with Other Wireless Devices Operating in Unlicensed Frequency Bands, August 2003.

[6]   N. Golmie, N. Chevrollier, and O. Rebala, "Bluetooth and WLAN Coexistence: Challenges and Solutions," *IEEE Wireless Communications Magazine*, vol. 10, no. 6, pp. 22-29, December 2003.

[7]   C.F. Chiasserini and R.R. Rao, "Coexistence Mechanisms for Interference Mitigation in the 2.4-GHz ISM Band," *IEEE Transactions on Wireless Communications*, vol. 2, no. 5, pp. 964-975, September 2003.

[8]   K. Kim and G.L. Stuber, "Interference Mitigation in Asynchronous Slow Frequency Hopping Bluetooth Networks," *Proceedings of the 5th International Symposium on Wireless Personal Multimedia Communications*, pp. 198-202, October 2002.

[9]   C.D.M. Cordeiro and D.P. Agrawal, "Employing Dynamic Segmentation for Effective Co-located Coexistence between Bluetooth and IEEE 802.11 WLANs," *Proceedings of IEEE GLOBECOM*, Taipei, Taiwan, pp. 17-21, November 2002.

[10] N. Golmie, "Bluetooth Dynamic Scheduling and Interference Migration," *Mobile Networks and Applications*, vol. 9, no. 1, pp. 21-31, September 2004.

[11] N. Golmie, R.E.V. Dyck, A. Soltanian, A. Tonnerre, and O. Rebala, "Interference Evaluation of Bluetooth and IEEE 802.11b systems," *Wireless Networks*, vol. 9, no. 3, pp. 201-211, September 2003.

[12] Z. Jiang, V.C.M. Leung, and V.W.S. Wong, "Reducing Collisions between Bluetooth Piconets by Orthogonal Hop Set Partitioning," *Proceedings of IEEE RAWCON*, Boston, MA, pp. 229-232, August 2003.

[13] Z. Jiang and V.C.M. Leung, "Novel Design of High Capacity Bluetooth Access Point with Collision Avoidance Scheduling", *Proceedings of IEEE PIMRC*, Barcelona, Spain, September 2004.

[14] FCC Parts 15 Regulations, http://www.fcc.gov/oet/info/rules/part15.

[15] OPNET, http://www.opnet.com.

[16] A. El-Hoiydi, "Interference between Bluetooth Networks - Upper Bound on the Packet Error Rate," *IEEE Communications Letters*, vol. 5, pp. 245-247, June 2001.

[17] A. El-Hoiydi and J.D. Decotignie, "Soft Deadline Bounds for Two-way Transactions in Bluetooth Piconets under Co-channel Interference," *Proceedings of the 8th IEEE International Conference on Emerging Technologies and Factory Automation*, pp. 143-150, October 2001.

[18] Y. Lim, J. Kim, S.L. Min, and J.S. Ma, "Performance Evaluation of the Bluetooth-based Public Internet Access Point," *Proceedings of International Conference on Information Networking*, Beppu, Japan, pp. 643-648, February 2001.

[19] T.Y. Lin, Y.C. Tseng, "Collision Analysis for a Multi-Bluetooth Picocells Environment," *IEEE Communications Letters*, vol. 7, no. 10, pp. 475-477, October 2003.

[20] T.Y. Lin, Y.K. Liu, and Y.C. Tseng, "An Improved Packet Collision Analysis for Multi-Bluetooth Piconets Considering Frequency-hopping Guard Time Effect," *IEEE Journal on Selected Areas in Communications*, vol. 22, no. 10, pp. 2087-2094, December 2004.

[21] G. Pasolini, "Analytical Investigation on the Coexistence of Bluetooth Piconets," *IEEE Communications Letters*, vol. 8, no. 3, pp. 144-146, March 2004.

[22] IEEE Std 802.11, Wireless LAN Medium Access Control (MAC) And Physical Layer (PHY) Specifications, November 1997.

[23] S. Chiu, H. Chang, and R. Chang, "Providing Mobile LAN Access Capability for Bluetooth Devices," *Proceedings of the Ninth International Conference on Parallel and Distributed Systems*, pp. 631-636, December 2002.

[24] A. Dahlberg, H.-J. Zepernick, G. Mercankosk, and M. Fiedler, "Multi AP Strategies for SCO Traffic in a Bluetooth Based Wireless LAN," *Proceedings of the 57th IEEE Semiannual Vehicular Technology Conference*, pp. 970-974, April 2003.

[25] P. Salonen, L. Sydänheimo, M. Keskilammi, and M. Kivikoski, "A Novel Antenna Solution for Bluetooth Access Point," *Proceedings of IEEE WCNC*, Chicago, IL, pp. 431-436, September 2000.

[26] Y. Kawamoto, V.W.S. Wong, and V.C.M. Leung, "A Two-Phase Scatternet Formation Protocol for Bluetooth Wireless Personal Area Networks," *Proceedings of IEEE WCNC*, New Orleans, LA, pp. 1453-1458, March 2003.

[27] C. Zhang, V.W.S. Wong and V.C.M. Leung, "TPSF+: A New Two-Phase Scatternet Formation Algorithm for Bluetooth Ad Hoc Networks," *Proceedings of IEEE GLOBECOM*, Dallas, TX, pp. 3599-3603, November 2004.

[28] S. Gonzalez-Valenzuela, S.T. Vuong, and V.C.M. Leung, "Efficient Formation of Dynamic Bluetooth Scatternet via Mobile Agent Processing," *Proceedings of International Workshop on Mobile Agents for Telecommunication Applications*, Marrakech, Morocco, October 2003.

[29] S. Gonzalez-Valenzuela, S.T. Vuong, and V.C.M. Leung, "BlueScouts - A Scatternet Formation Protocol Based on Mobile Agents," *Proceedings of IEEE ASWN*, Boston, MA, August 2004.

[30] S. Gonzalez-Valenzuela, S.T. Vuong, and V.C.M. Leung, "Programmable Agents for Efficient Topology Formation of Bluetooth Scatternets," *International Journal of Wireless and Mobile Computing* (in press).

[31] R. Lee and V.W.S. Wong, "An Adaptive Scheduling Algorithm for Bluetooth Ad-hoc Networks," *Proceedings of IEEE ICC*, Seoul, Korea, May 2005.

[32] M. Jain, L. Lampe, and R. Schober, "Sequence Detection for Bluetooth Systems", *Proceedings of IEEE GLOBECOM*, Dallas, TX, November 2004.

[33] L. Lampe, R. Schober, and M. Jain, "Noncoherent Sequence Detection Receiver for Bluetooth Systems," *IEEE Journal on Selected Areas in Communications* (in press).

[34] L. Lampe, M. Jain, and R. Schober, "Improved Decoding for Bluetooth Systems," *IEEE Transactions on Communications*, vol. 53, no. 1, pp. 1-4, January 2005.

[35] J.C.H. Wu, V. Aken'Ova, S.J.E. Wilton, and R. Saleh, "SoC Implementation Issues for Synthesizable Embedded Programmable Logic Cores," *Proceedings of IEEE Custom Integrated Circuits Conference*, Santa Clara, CA, pp. 45-48, September 2003.

[36] S.J.E Wilton, N. Kafafi, J.C.H. Wu, K. Bozman, V. Aken'Ova, and R. Saleh, "Design Considerations for Soft Embedded Programmable Logic Cores," *Solid State Circuits Journal*, vol. 40, pp. 485-497, February 2005.

INDEX

Q

R

S

T